ACT

& College Preparation Course for the Christian Student

» 50 Easy & Comprehensive Lessons

» Includes English, Math, Reading & Science

» Strategies to Increase Vocabulary & Writing Skills

JAMES P. STOBAUGH

First printing: January 2012

ISBN: 978-0-89051-639-3
Library of Congress: 2011944158

Scripture quotations taken from the New International Version of the Holy Bible, copyright 1973, 1978, 1984 by the International Bible Society.

Quotes from *Greek Morphemes Lessons* and *Latin Morphemes Lessons*, by Alene Harris, PhD, are used by permission.

Select portions of the Introduction and Lessons 13, 14, 19, 20, 21, 22, 24, 26, 28, 35, 41, and 48 are used courtesy of the Enhanced Edition of the *SAT & College Preparation Course for the Christian Student* by James P. Stobaugh (Green Forest, AR: Master Books, 2011).

Images are from Shutterstock, Clipart, Dreamstine, Library of Congress, and J.P. Stobaugh.

Please consider requesting that a copy of this volume be purchased
by your local library system.

Printed in the United States of America

Please visit our website for other great titles:
www.masterbooks.net

For information regarding author interviews,
please contact the publicity department at (870) 438-5288

Master Books®
A Division of New Leaf Publishing Group
www.masterbooks.net

This book is gratefully dedicated to my wife,

Karen Elizabeth Stobaugh

"North? North is there, my love.

The brook runs west."

"West-running Brook then call it."

(West-Running Brook men call it to this day.)

"What does it think k's doing running west

When all the other country brooks flow east

To reach the ocean? It must be the brook

Can trust itself to go by contraries

The way I can with you — and you with me —

Because we're — we're — I don't know what we are.

What are we?"

From "West-Running Brook," Robert Frost

The author wishes to thank Mr. Daniel Greenridge and John Braswell for their help in the math and science sections. Likewise, the author wishes to thank the editorial staff at New Leaf Publishing Group, especially Mr. Craig Froman and Ms. Judy Lewis.

Contents

Introduction: Come to

MT. MORIAH

Come to Mt. Moriah, young people, where God demands everything and nothing must be taken for granted. The ACT is a great opportunity, but first, join me on Mt. Moriah!

Hebrews 11:17 (the first commentary on Geneis 22) says, "By faith Abraham, when God tested him, offered Isaac as a sacrifice. He who had received the promises was about to sacrifice his one and only son." This man Abraham was called by God into the Promised Land. And he went. He was promised many descendants. And he waited — even into his nineties. And God gave him a son . . . but now he must go to Mt. Moriah.

Dr. William Willimon tells of a congregant who said to him one day, "I am looking for another church because when I look at that God, the God of Abraham, I feel I'm near a real God, not the sort of dignified business-like . . . God we chatter about here on Sunday mornings. Abraham's God could blow a man to bits, give and then take a child, ask for everything from a person and then want more. I want to know that God."[1]

Do you know that God? A God who means business? Not some existential reality grounded in warm fuzzy feelings, but a God who brings chills up your spine. Not the God whom we meet on the silver screen, full of maudlin aphorisms, who can barely manage happy endings.

No, the God on Mt. Moriah is the God Abraham meets in Genesis 22, the God Moses meets in Exodus 3 in the bush that is on fire but does not burn, the God who does not make polite conversation. This is the God who struck Annais and Shappirah dead for their lying and intrigue. This is the God who Abraham meets this day. This is the God who is leading you in this new century, in this post-Christian world. He means business, young people.

This is the God you will meet in this ACT preparation book.

How much does your God demand of you? Come to Mt. Moriah, where God demands everything. I am not kidding around, young people. God demands everything from you. This course demands everything from you.

This is even a different God from the one Abraham thought he knew. God had called him into the wilderness and he had gone. And God took care of him. He had come through with a child when none seemed available. But this was something new, this command of God to go to Mt. Moriah. Perhaps we, too, have known God to be our savior, our friend, our companion — and He is all these — but I wonder if we have known a God who demands everything from us.

God is not to be trifled with. You are asked, now, in this course, to devote everything you have — and more — to prepare to be the next generation of godly leaders. This is serious business — your "work" for the next 50 lessons.

Abraham knew that God is not safe, not to be controlled, not to be mocked or tampered with. He knew that God was God. And Abraham intended to treat Him that way.

This faith to which Abraham is called and for which he is celebrated — particularly in the New Testament — means the acknowledgment of a particular God. A God who means business. Who calls us to Mt. Moriah. Abraham trusts in a God who can violate religious conventions, shatter normal definitions of reality, and bring about newness. Isaac — long anticipated, finally given — is suddenly demanded back, and he is the embodiment of the newness God can bring to us. To us. To a people who know only three cars and two color TVs and affluence. To a people who really know only barrenness. This God who calls us to Mt. Moriah has no parallel, no analogy. This God we serve is not predictable, not safe, and not controllable. He loves whom He wants to love — even those whom we cannot forgive. He saves those whom He chooses. He is a God who cannot be controlled by our minds, our political situations, or our religions.

On Mt. Moriah God brings something new — a young ram. He does not merely patch up what is old. He makes something entirely new. And on Mt. Moriah we find that all that we once believed, all that once demanded our allegiance, has come in question.

The theologian Walter Brueggemann, in his exposition of this passage, challenges us to embrace the God on Mt. Moriah. The modern world that so celebrates freedom also believes that present life is closed and self-contained in known natural laws, just waiting to be uncovered. In this world there can be no real change, no newness. But our world is not after all a human artifact; it is created by God. And He shall not be thwarted by our puny efforts to control Him. Abraham knew that our world needs more than a faith whose only claim is that its God can be served without cost. No! The God on Mt. Moriah wants everything we have. This God we serve is determined to have His own way with us, no matter what the cost.

When Abraham comes down from Mt. Moriah he is a new man. God has demanded all and Abraham has delivered. God provides a substitute, but that is incidental. This faith of Abraham is replicated throughout history. Moses foolishly stands before Pharaoh and demands that he let God's people go. Moses has been to his Moriah. Shadrach, Meshak, and Abednego have been to Moriah, too. During the Babylonian captivity they are told to worship the Persian king. They refuse. They might be burned alive in the fire. "The God we serve is able to save us from it, and he will rescue us from your hand, O king. But even if he does not, we want you to know, O king, that we

will not serve your gods or worship the image of gold you have set up," they defiantly tell the king (Daniel 3:17–18). They have met a God who demands everything and then more. They have been to Moriah.

My prayer is that these 50 review lessons will take you to Mt. Moriah, so that when you do well on the ACT — and I believe you will — that you will do well in college, also. Then you will get an important job, or you will raise your children at home. Or both. I pray that you remember that you serve a mighty, an awesome, a loving God. The God who calls us to Mt. Moriah.

The ACT Test: General Overview

The ACT test assesses high school students' general educational development and their ability to complete college-level work. It does this by assessing students' performance in high school and, therefore, it is more a measure of college readiness than it is a prediction of college performance. The converse is true for the SAT. The ACT is an achievement verses aptitude test. An achievement test is based upon a corpus of information. The multiple-choice tests cover four skill areas: English, mathematics, reading, and science. If students are competent in these areas, if they know enough information related to these disciplines, and can apply this information to cognitive challenges, then they will receive a high score. In that sense, the ACT is of the same genre as an Iowa Basic or Stanford Achievement test.

The SAT, on the other hand, is an IQ-type test. It is not based upon epistemology; it is based upon critical thinking. In other words, the SAT measures students' ability to problem solve. The ACT measures students' knowledge acquisition. Therefore, the SAT preparation ideally needs a commitment of one to three years. Students cannot raise their IQ scores nor improve critical thinking skills overnight, or even in two months. But students can raise ACT scores in 50 days.

The writing test, which is an optional test on the ACT (but not on the SAT) measures skill in planning and writing a short essay.

For a long time, the SAT was by far the most popular college entrance exam in the United States. Even though a high percentage of high school students who hope to go on to a university still rely on the SAT to show their academic prowess, the ACT has gained a lot of ground over the years.

The ACT is divided into four individual subject examinations, each one covering a separate subject area. The material includes:

English — Students are tested on grammar rules and rhetorical skills. Rhetoric requires students to discern the writing strategy of a passage. The exam consists of several literary passages, which are followed by several questions on the passage or selected parts. The test is designed to check understanding of English usage, not spelling and vocabulary. Indirectly,

though, vocabulary is important because the student will need a robust vocabulary to understand the subtleties in the reading passages. Spelling is important in the writing section. The single best preparation event for the ACT is active reading of challenging literary works. Students should read about one book per week.

Mathematics — Students are tested on mathematical concepts and practices endemic to 11th grade goals. The test is designed to check for mathematical reasoning and basic computational skills, so no complex formulas or elaborate computations will be included in the exam. Calculators are allowed, although there are restrictions.

Reading — Students are tested on direct reading comprehension and inference based on the material presented. Similar to the English exam, the test consists of several different literary genre passages from multiple disciplines, which are followed by several questions on the passage. Since reading skills such as determining the main idea and understanding causal relationships are being tested, rote fact checking is not included in the exam.

> *The single best preparation event for the ACT is active reading of challenging literary works. Students should read about one book per week.*

Writing — The writing test, which is an optional portion of the ACT, is a short written exercise that is given at the end of the regular exam. It is my firm belief, based upon decades of coaching the SAT and ACT, that the writing section is literally a gift horse the students are looking in the mouth. It is a great opportunity! The bar is so low, the grading criteria so easy, that it would be a poor writer indeed who received a poor score on this section of the ACT. The writing section itself consists of a writing prompt, generally about a social issue that a high school student would be expected to encounter, and two opposing points of view on the subject discussed in the prompt. The student is expected to then write a short essay defining the student's position on the issue and explaining the reasons behind it. There is no guideline on the essay structure, and the student may write as long or short an essay as he or she is capable of in the time allotted. Remember: longer is always better! Scoring of the writing essay is different than that of the regular exam. Two essay readers will read the student's essay and score it on a scale of 0 to 6, 0 being assigned if the essay is illegible, not in English, blank, completely off-topic, or fails to meet the stated guidelines for the exam in some other fashion. The scores are then summed to create the composite score for the exam. If the graders disagree by a margin greater than one point, then a third grader evaluates the essay and provides a final scoring.

Science — Students are tested on critical thinking and problem-solving skills. Students should have had courses in biology, earth sciences, and the physical sciences by the 11th grade. The test consists of several data sets presented as data representation (graphs, charts, etc.) and research expressions of conflicting hypotheses, which are followed by several questions after each set. Calculators are not allowed during the science exam.

What Is It?

Like the SAT, the ACT is a standardized test. With the exception of the optional writing section, all of the questions are multiple choice. There are 215 questions in all, and the exam takes about three hours to complete. The questions focus on four core academic subject areas: math, English, reading, and science, and scores range between 1 and 36.

What does the ACT Measure?

ACT questions focus upon academic knowledge that high school seniors should already have acquired. Since the four sections of the ACT correspond with introductory courses most students will be required to complete during their freshman year of college, the ACT is a good indication of whether or not students are adequately prepared for the academic challenges of the university. In my opinion, the SAT is a better predictor of college performance; the ACT is a better evaluation of high school performance. If then, the SAT is like an IQ test, the ACT is like a national achievement test.

When Was the ACT First Administered?

The first group of students were tested on the ACT in 1959. From the very beginning, the ACT was intended to be a competitor to the SAT. Today, the test is administered and overseen by ACT, Inc. It is more popular than ever before and, in 2007, a little over 40 percent of U.S. high school graduates opted to take the ACT in lieu of the SAT. Part of the reason for this preference is the belief among many educators that the SAT is culturally biased and therefore an unfair assessment tool.

How Are ACT Scores Used by Colleges?

Exactly how a student's ACT scores will be used by a college varies from school to school. In some schools, a student's ACT score, along with his or her GPA, is the chief criteria upon which acceptance decisions are made. At other schools, ACT scores play only a minor role in determining acceptance, and applicants' GPA, class rank, and cultural backgrounds may be viewed as more important. In the case of home-schoolers, for obvious reasons, a standardized test — in this case the ACT — is significantly more important than grades, recommendations, or any other admission criteria.

In any case, a strong ACT score will boost students' chances of being accepted to the college of their choice and, concurrently, will greatly increase the chances of generous financial aid and scholarships. Along with using ACT scores to make acceptance decisions, colleges can use a student's test results in other ways as well. Some colleges offer different course sections — there may be a regular and an advanced course in English literature, for example. Looking at a student's scores on the English and reading sections of the ACT can help college officials choose which course selections would be more suitable to student skill level (adapted from the official ACT website).

Finally, the writing section of the ACT (and SAT) is extremely important. Many colleges purchase copies of the ACT writing section from the ACT. These colleges compare the ACT essay with student college admission essays. If there are marked differences, the ACT essay can hurt student admission chances. On the other hand, if the ACT essay is better than the college admission essay, then students have a much better chance to be admitted and receive a scholarship at aforementioned colleges.

The ACT and College Preparation Course for the Christian Student

This book includes the following components:

- ☐ Scripture Memory Verse (in the lesson and in the appendices)
- ☐ Devotion
- ☐ Test-taking Insights
- ☐ Test Practice
- ☐ Math
- ☐ Vocabulary
- ☐ Reading
- ☐ English
- ☐ Writing
- ☐ Science

It is critical that ACT students develop two habits:

- ☐ Reading (vocabulary and reading skills)
- ☐ Prayer (stress reduction)

Both a prayer devotion guide and a college preparation reading list are found in the appendices.

Ideally, students will go through this book about 50 days before the exam. It can be repeated several times.

Implementation Suggestion

Since the ACT is an achievement test, it does not require a long, arduous preparation experience — as opposed to the SAT, which is more of an "IQ" type test. Therefore, students can complete this book 50 days before the exam (and complete one lesson per day) or complete this book 50 weeks before the exam — one lesson per week. I recommend that you spend about a year preparing for this exam. This course is also perfect as a one-semester private or public school course. If you would like a 17-week suggested implementation schedule, write me at jpstobaugh@forsuchatimeasthis.com.

Special Circumstances

The ACT has several contingencies in place to help students overcome issues of disability, economic hardship, and other limitations. Students who meet certain qualifications as listed on the official ACT fee waiver form are eligible to receive a total of two fee waivers, but only a certain number are granted each testing year. Students at any grade level with a documented disability are eligible for special arrangements for the ACT. For further information, visit http://act.org. Students who have religious beliefs that prevent them from Saturday testing may apply for non-Saturday testing. Students who are too ill to leave their residence or are confined may use the ACT Request for Arranged Testing application to arrange testing. Whatever special challenges students face, they should begin the application process at least a year before their scheduled ACT.

Students should note that the ACT does not make accommodations for limited English proficiency; the ACT is not offered in any other language than English, and limited proficiency is not at present an eligible reason to request extended time periods for testing. Likewise, at the present time, the student will have to take a handwritten exam — there are no ACT computer exams.

Stress Reduction

My 35 years of coaching remind me how important stress reduction is to high ACT scores. In fact, in my opinion, it is the most important preparation variable. Much research supports my argument. For Christians, at least, stress reduction is best accomplished by a frequent and thorough devotional and Bible memorization program. The *ACT and College Preparation Course for the Christian Student* amply discusses this point and provides preparation exercises that will equip the student to be ready for the ACT. If you need Bible verses to memorize and to meditate upon, see the appendices.

An example of a "living in Scripture" meditation exercise is provided in Appendix D.

Important Note to Parents

You and your family are encouraged to join your student in this time of preparation. For example, everyone can join in learning new vocabulary words.

Also, consider having your child learn Latin and/or Greek instead of a modern language. Modern languages can be picked up fairly easily in college. Greek and Latin will help in vocabulary preparation and grammar skills. At the same time, consider purchasing Alene Harris, PhD's Greek and Latin root book. Contact http://forsuchatimeasthis.com if you have any questions.

A vital part of ACT preparation is taking an actual ACT exam. I recommend your student take a mock ACT after every five lessons. SATs can be obtained from http://forsuchatimeasthis.com.

Finally, you are asked to spend time with your child in prayer and review of his or her vocabulary cards. Do not take this lightly. Encourage your student to work hard. Make sure your child memorizes Scriptures. Keep him or her reading. And, most importantly, pray for him or her! To that end, I have included prayer pointers in each lesson.

The ACT Day

Here is one example of a typical test-day schedule. Times will vary depending on the actual time of the test, how far away the test site is, etc.

6:00 a.m.

Wake up and eat a healthy breakfast. You should have been arising at this time for at a week or two before the exam to prepare your body. The whole family should gather and pray for the student.

6:30 a.m.

Last minute checkup: six sharpened #2 pencils, calculator with fresh battery, snack (no candy), ticket, picture ID, watch

7:00 a.m.

Parents should take the student to the test site, and then stay and pray for the student through the morning. It is a good idea to scout out the location the week before. Pray over the building. Relax in the car and meditate on Scriptures.

7:30 a.m.

As soon as the test site opens, go get a seat. Then return to the car. Do not hang around in the test site. Save a seat on the end of the row fairly distant from high traffic areas (doorways and bathrooms). By this time you should leave the car and go back into the test site. Parents should pray for the student one last time.

8:00 a.m.–12:15 p.m.

Take the exam. Be sure to use the exam to work the problems, not the answer sheet. I do not recommend sending your scores to a college until you get the score you want.

12:30 p.m.

Celebrate! Celebrate God's faithfulness! Meditate on what God has done in your life through this preparation process. Consider Joshua 4. You will receive your scores in six weeks.

Ten Week Plan
Normally in the 11th Grade

Monday	Tuesday	Wednesday	Thursday	Friday
Devotion	Devotion	Devotion	Devotion	Devotion
Memorize a Scripture	Memorize a Scripture	Memorize a Scripture	Memorize a Scripture	Memorize a Scripture
ACT Practice Test	ACT Practice Test	ACT Practice Test	ACT Practice Test	ACT Practice Test
Read 50 Pages	Read 50 Pages	Read 50 Pages	Read 50 Pages	Read 50 Pages
Math Practice	Vocabulary Practice	Reading Practice	English and Writing Practice	Science Practice

50 Day Plan
Normally in the 11th Grade

Day 1	Day 2	Day 3	Day 4	Day 5
Devotion	Devotion	Devotion	Devotion	Devotion
Memorize a Scripture	Memorize a Scripture	Memorize a Scripture	Memorize a Scripture	Memorize a Scripture
ACT Practice Test	ACT Practice Test	ACT Practice Test	ACT Practice Test	ACT Practice Test
Read 50 Pages	Read 50 Pages	Read 50 Pages	Read 50 Pages	Read 50 Pages
Math Practice	Vocabulary Practice	Reading Practice	English and Writing Practice	Science Practice

Repeat this schedule, Lessons 1–50, for 50 days

College Admission Averages

These are only averages and you should not be discouraged if you have a lower score. Colleges have admission criteria: race, gender, nationality, and income. The ACT is only one criterion.

Carnegie Mellon	29
Cedarville	26
Duke	29
Grove City	28
Harvard	33
John Brown University	25
Liberty	21
MIT	33
Stanford	30
West Point	28
Vanderbilt	30
U.S. average	21.1

The Loss of
TRANSCENDENCE

"You are to be holy to me because I, the LORD, am holy, and I have set you apart from the nations to be my own."
~ Leviticus 20:26

There is a moment in the life of Henry Fleming, protagonist in Stephen Crane's *Red Badge of Courage*, when he has to plumb the depths of his worldview and decide, once and for all, if he believes in a personal, caring God. As you remember, Fleming is a Union soldier fighting at the Battle of Chancellorsville, May 1863. His unit is under attack. At first he holds firm. While he is hardly brave, he draws strength from the crowd. But the crowd thins. And as a second attack occurs, he runs. He runs from his friends, from his enemy, from his duty, and from his God. From that moment forward he rejects the transcendent, omniscient, "friendly" Judeo-God. He replaces this God with a naturalistic, uncaring, utilitarian deity who cares nothing about Fleming or the world in general. Fleming ultimately returns to duty a new man. While this new revelation causes Fleming to be "courageous," the reader knows that Fleming is more "cynical" than courageous.

In Henry Fleming's world there is no courage because there is no transcendence. Everything is instinctive. People make decisions out of what is best for them, not out of anything noble.

From the beginning of this ACT preparation it is important that you decide if this is a frantic rush to a high score or is it a measured, intentional time to prepare for the ACT, for college, and most importantly, to be a faithful follower of Jesus Christ. Think and pray about it.

Are you doing a devotion everyday?

PRAYER POINTS
GENTLENESS

"Make sure that nobody pays back wrong for wrong, but always try to be kind to each other and to everyone else."
~ 1 Thessalonians 5:15

> *"I never made a mistake in grammar but one in my life and as soon as I done it I seen it."*[1]
>
> — Carl Sandburg

TEST-TAKING INSIGHT

Unlike the SAT, where you will be penalized 1.25 for every question you miss, there is no penalty for a wrong answer on the ACT. Since you are not penalized for incorrect answers, it is to your advantage to answer every question, even if you have to guess.

However, you should make every effort to eliminate any incorrect answers before making your selection. If you can narrow your choice to two, you have a 50-50 chance. In your test booklet, cross off answers you know are definitely wrong. This will help you to your goal. When you remove all the wrong answers, which I will call "detractors," make a guess. Remember: never leave an ACT problem blank.

VOCABULARY

In the English language, big words are often made up of small word parts, called morphemes, that come from other languages — especially Greek and Latin. These morphemes are building blocks for thousands of words.[2]

THEO = God

PHIL = love

(O)US = full of

Therefore, Theophilus means "Full of the Love of God."

Memorize the Latin and Greek roots found in Appendix E and F.

"The longer I live, the more I realize the impact of attitude on life. Attitude, to me, is more important than facts. It is more important than the past, the education, the money, than circumstances, than failure, than successes, than what other people think or say or do. It is more important than appearance, giftedness or skill. It will make or break a company . . . a church . . . a home. The remarkable thing is we have a choice everyday regarding the attitude we will embrace for that day. We cannot change our past . . . we cannot change the fact that people will act in a certain way. We cannot change the inevitable. The only thing we can do is play on the one string we have, and that is our attitude. I am convinced that life is 10% what happens to me and 90% of how I react to it. And so it is with you . . . we are in charge of our Attitudes."[3]

— Pastor Charles R. Swindoll

MATH

The following are the different mathematical operations that exist on the ACT. Review them and make sure that you know how to perform these operations.

- ☐ Averages
- ☐ Factoring
- ☐ Percentages
- ☐ Probability
- ☐ Tables
- ☐ Perpendicular Line
- ☐ Ratios
- ☐ Roots
- ☐ Quadratic Equations
- ☐ Graphs
- ☐ Area
- ☐ Coordinate Plane
- ☐ Variables
- ☐ Linear Equations
- ☐ Exponents
- ☐ Trigonometry
- ☐ Charts
- ☐ Polygons
- ☐ Complex Numbers
- ☐ Functions
- ☐ Matrices
- ☐ Quadratic Inequalities
- ☐ Number Line
- ☐ Sequences
- ☐ Distance and Midpoint
- ☐ Conic Sections
- ☐ Parallel Lines
- ☐ Polynomials
- ☐ Quadratic Formula
- ☐ Systems of Equations
- ☐ Inequalities
- ☐ Proportions
- ☐ Perimeter
- ☐ Volume
- ☐ Right Triangles
- ☐ Series

READING

The following components will be tested in the reading section:

- Vocabulary
- Main Idea
- Idea Stated
- Infer from Text
- Text Development

■ ■ ■

What can be inferred from the following passage:

> The degree to which Christians deal with the problem of pluralism will determine the Church's relevancy as a viable American institution. Indeed, the very survival of American civilization will be determined by how well the American Church deals with racial issues. If there is no peace among races in the Church, there will be no peace in America. The American Church must overcome many obstacles for widespread racial reconciliation to occur.

A. The author is a Christian.
B. The Church is a very important institution in American society.
C. Racial reconciliation is an important goal in American society.
D. A only
E. All

> *"Every act of will is an act of self-limitation. To desire action is to desire limitation. In that sense, every act is an act of self-sacrifice. When you choose anything, you reject everything else."[4]*
>
> — G.K. Chesterton

ENGLISH

The following components will be tested in the English section:

Usage/Mechanics

- Punctuation
- Grammar, Usage, and Mechanics
- Sentence Structure
- Diction

■ ■ ■

What is wrong with this sentence?

Everyone should work hard in their studies.

Rhetorical Skills

Which sentence does not belong in this paragraph?

Everyone celebrates our diversity, but no one knows how to live with it. One hundred and sixty years after the Emancipation Proclamation, forty years after the civil rights victories of the 1960s, there is as much anger, misunderstanding, and disagreement among the races as there ever was. Nothing has been as enduring and damaging to the American nation as racial anger. Racial anger is as strong today as it was when the first black slave stepped into Jamestown in 1619. Martin Luther King is the earliest leader in the Civil Rights movement. There exists in America a "paradox of pluralism": the American people, a nation of diversity, remains ambivalent about the value of pluralism. From this tension flows the essence of the American character. Pluralism is both our greatest strength and our greatest weakness.

WRITING

The following content will be tested in the essay section:

- ☐ Essay Overview
- ☐ Point of View
- ☐ Organization and Focus
- ☐ Use of Language
- ☐ Sentence Structure Variety
- ☐ Essay Grammar Usage and Mechanics

■ ■ ■

What is the point of view of this essay?

I hate my computer. Just as soon as I halfway understand a Windows platform they change it. Where is Windows 98 when you need it! I mean peanut butter is the same forever; why can't computers stay the same? And to make matters worse, my son persuaded me to buy a Mac. A what??? A Mac! The darn thing has a delete key that moves to the left instead of to the right. Never trust a computer that has a delete key that moves to the left instead of the right!

I share the misgivings of one of my least favorite philosophers, existentialist Martin Heidegger. What Heidegger called "the essence of technology" infiltrates human existence more intimately than anything humans could create. The danger of technology lies in the transformation of the human being, by which human actions and aspirations are fundamentally distorted. Not that machines can run amok, or even that we might misunderstand ourselves through a faulty comparison with machines. Instead, technology enters the inmost recesses of human existence, transforming the way we know and think and will. Technology is, in essence, a dehumanizing influence by humanizing us!?!

Heidegger died in 1976, long before the personal computer and computer networks, such as the web, much less iPods, iPads, etc., became a reality. However, as early as 1957 Heidegger foresaw the computer, what he called the "language machine." But it is no such thing — the computer creates no language at all. It creates symbols that are meaningless. FYI KWIM (For your information, know what I mean? DUMMY!)

Man is the master of the language machine. But the truth of the matter is that the language machine may be mastering the essence of what it means to be a human being.

" *The broad masses of a population are more amenable to the appeal of rhetoric than to any other force.*"[5]

— Adolf Hitler

SCIENCE

The following skills will be tested in the science section:

- ☐ Experimental design
- ☐ Predicting outcomes
- ☐ Inducing principles
- ☐ Comparing theories and experiments
- ☐ Performing calculations
- ☐ Representing data

■ ■ ■

Which of the following experiments will prove the following conclusion: 14 inches of rain in 24 hours will inevitably cause flooding in lowland areas.

A. Measure the width of the Mississippi River.
B. Measure the depth of the Mississippi River.
C. Measure rainfall in the mountains and in the lowlands during the same amount of time in the same time of season.
D. Count the times that flooding occurs in the lowlands during ordinary rainfall periods and compare this to flooding during times when there is 14 inches of rain in 24 hours.

■ ■ ■

On the ACT you will both evaluate persuasive arguments and write persuasive arguments (in the writing section). When evaluating an argument look for three major elements:

- ☐ The purpose
- ☐ The development of the argument — usually pro and con on an issue.
- ☐ The conclusion: often a restatement of the purpose

The Way, the Truth, and

THE LIFE

The British author G.K. Chesterton writes, "The madman's explanation of a thing is always complete, and often in a purely rational sense satisfactory."[1] While this author agrees that absolute objectivity has yet to be attained, it is not the same for absolute truth. In any event, the idea of objectivity as a guiding principle is too valuable to be abandoned. Without it, the pursuit of knowledge is indeed hopelessly lost. As Aristotle argues in his seminal work *Nicomachean Ethics*, ". . . the great majority of mankind are agreed about this; for both the multitude and persons of refinement speak of it as Happiness, and conceive 'the good life' or 'doing well' to be the same thing as 'being happy.' But what constitutes happiness is a matter of dispute; and the popular account of it is not the same as that given by the philosophers."[2] Objectivity is as elusive as happiness, but truth is real. Are people better at making observations, discoveries, and decisions if they remain neutral and impartial? Only if they pursue truth.

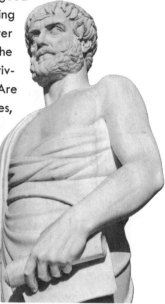

Lewis Carroll's Alice in *Alice in Wonderland* falls into the rabbit hole and knows that she is lost. "Read the directions and directly you will be directed in the right direction,"[3] the doorknob tells Alice. She has lost all objectivity. She is in trouble. She knows it. But she still has truth — the doorknob has given her truth. Read the directions! Alice is not neutral and, in her crisis, is making observations and decisions galore. She has lost her objectivity, though. She wants to go home. The truth will lead her home. Impartiality, then, is immaterial. She has a need, a stated objective, and she can have the truth. The truth will lead her home.

Young people, this ACT preparation course is not on a search for the truth. Most assuredly, we know the Truth. Jesus Christ is the Way, the Truth, and the Life.

" *If Christians want us to believe in a Redeemer, let them act redeemed."[4]*

— Voltaire

Work as fast as you effectively are able. Don't waste time on questions that are too difficult for you. If you're not sure about an answer, take your best guess and put a symbol next to the question so that you can come back and answer it if you have time. Unlike in the SAT, in the ACT the questions do not follow a specific order of difficulty. The first ten and the last ten in each section are equal in difficulty. If you cannot answer a difficult question, quickly move to the next question. Occasionally you will find a question that you could answer if you have/had time, but for now you will skip. You may return to answer it later. In any event, do not leave any answers blank on the ACT. Unlike the SAT, where there is a .25 penalty for guessing, there is no penalty for guessing on the ACT.

Use this marking system:

√ Answer if I have time.

X Never answer. I can't figure this out.

+ Be certain to find time to answer this.

Remember, you get the same number of points for an easy question as for a hard one, so try to answer as many questions as you can.

R E A D I N G

Main Idea

"In the period between the landing of the English at Jamestown, Virginia, in 1607, and the close of the French and Indian war in 1763 — a period of a century and a half — a new nation was being prepared on this continent to take its place among the powers of the earth. It was an epoch of migration. Western Europe contributed emigrants of many races and nationalities. The English led the way. Next to them in numerical importance were the Scotch-Irish and the Germans. Into the melting pot were also cast Dutch, Swedes, French, Jews, Welsh, and Irish. Thousands of slaves were brought from Africa to till Southern fields or labor as domestic servants in the North. Why did they come? The reasons are various. Some of them, the Pilgrims and Puritans of New England, the French Huguenots, Scotch-Irish and Irish, and the Catholics of Maryland, fled from intolerant governments that denied them the right to worship God according to the dictates of their consciences. Thousands came to escape the bondage of poverty in the Old World and to find free homes in America. Thousands, like the captives from Africa, were dragged here against their will. The lure of adventure appealed to the restless and the lure of profits to the enterprising merchants."[5] — Charles & Mary Beard

The main idea of this passage is:

A. The origin of slavery in the New World.
B. Immigration occurred for many different reasons but all, except for African slaves, came with the expectation that their lives would be improved.
C. The two main purposes for immigration were the allure of adventure and profits.
D. The English were the most important group to immigrate to America.

M A T H

Basic Algebra

A. Solve for x, if $x + 14 = 34$.
B. For what value of x is $3(x + 3) - 4x = 14$?

V O C A B U L A R Y

☐ anthrop = man, mankind
☐ bibl; biblio = book
☐ graph; gram = write, draw, record
☐ miso = hate
☐ phil = love
☐ phon = sound
☐ scop; skept = look at, examine

What do these words mean?

☐ anthropophobiac
☐ philanthropy
☐ misanthrope

The remainder of important suffixes and roots can be found in the Appendix.

"Grasp the subject, the words will follow."[6]

— Cato

Grammar

As a father of three adopted children; it grieves me that some mothers choose to abort their children.

A. No change
B. As a father of three adopted children
C. As a father of three adopted children,
D. As a father of three adopted children —
E. As a father of three adopted children.

■ ■ ■

(A comma follows an introductory clause.)

Correct any wrong sentences.

A. He likes to boast of Mary cooking.
B. It is an error and which can't be corrected.
C. He said he should come if he could.
D. Can I use your pencil?
E. If you were I, what would you do?
F. We would like to go.
G. Neither the members of the committee nor the chairman is present.
H. He only spoke of history, not of art.
I. Socialists don't have no use for trusts.
J. This is John's book.[7]

"*Words ought to be a little wild for they are the assaults of thought on the unthinking.*"[8]

— John Maynard Keyes

The Essay Overview

The ACT Assessment Writing Test was added to the ACT Assessment in February 2005. It is a 30-minute student-produced essay written to a specific prompt. The prompts are based on topics concerning young people — this is different from the SAT. I advise you to take the writing portion of the ACT. It is a great opportunity to show colleges that you are a competent writer. It is also the easiest portion of the ACT for which to prepare.

You will receive a prompt. You will first write a thesis statement — a one-sentence purpose statement. You will then write an outline based on the thesis statement.

You will have 30 minutes to write your essay. Therefore, you will be tempted to skip the outline step. Don't do that. The less time you have, the more concise you have to be, and the more important an outline becomes.

Why create an outline?

• Helps you organize your ideas
• Shows the relationships among ideas in your writing
• Defines the limit and purpose of your essay
• How do I create an outline?
• Determine the purpose (thesis) of your paper.
• Determine the audience you are writing for.

Then:

• Organize: Group related ideas together. I give you two ways to do that in the following exercises.
• Sequence: Arrange material in subsections from general to specific or from abstract to concrete.

An outline is a kind of graphic scheme of the organization of your paper. It indicates the main arguments for your thesis as well as the subtopics under each main point.

Remember: An outline is a critical, necessary step!

■ ■ ■

The following is an essay prompt similar to one provided by ACT. Before you write an essay on this topic, create an outline. The first outline should be an orthodox outline (i.e., I, A, B, etc.). The second outline should be a schematic/graphic organization of your essay. Of course you will only choose one option when taking your exam.

"*Do not accustom yourself to use big words for little matters.*"[9]

— Samuel Johnson

WRITING

ACT Prompt

Over the past several years many schools have gone from a nine-month school year to year-round schooling. Although students attend school the same number of days, they have several shorter breaks throughout the year instead of one long summer break. Advocates of year-round schooling claim that students are able to retain more of what they have learned, while opponents feel that it disrupts summer vacation. In your opinion, is year-round school better than a traditional nine-month school year?

Write an essay in which you take a position on this question. You may choose either argument presented above or introduce a different point of view. Develop your essay with specific details that support your opinion (ACT).

The ACT essay prompt generally concerns a social issue relevant to high school students. For example: should dress codes be required in public schools? Your response must be a well-structured argument supporting a definite point of view.

Create an outline for this ACT essay.

SCIENCE

Here are things you will need to do on the science portion of the ACT:

- analysis
- make value judgments
- reason
- solve problems

A popular problem on the ACT is related to designing experiments to prove a scientific thesis. Questions of this kind describe an experiment, including the pro forma conditions under which it is performed and the outcome of the experiment. You will be asked to deduce the purpose of the experiment.

■ ■ ■

The following is an example taken from the TCA website:

A lima bean is planted under similar conditions in each of three containers The containers are placed in a dark room, and the soil in each one is moistened with an equal amount of water each day. A week later it is observed that a young plant, with bean still attached, has emerged through the soil in each container. The seed coat and the bean are carefully removed from the first plant. The seed coat and half the bean are carefully removed from the second plant. The third plant is not altered in any way. Two weeks later it is observed that the first plant has grown very little and that the third plant has grown higher than the second plant.

One of the purposes of this experiment is to determine

A. the effect of darkness on the growth of seedlings
B. whether bean plants can be grown from seed
C. the function of the seed in plant development
D. if lima beans will sprout only in dark locations

> "The science part of the ACT was the easiest. I knew that the answer was always found in the problem description. The math was not hard. The hard part was the thinking."
>
> — A home school student who scored 32 on the ACT

> "Science is nothing but developed perception, interpreted intent, common sense rounded out and minutely articulated."[10]
>
> — George Santayana

What is TRUTH?

SCRIPTURE

" 'What is truth?' Pilate asked. With this he went out again to the Jews and said, 'I find no basis for a charge against him.' "

~ John 18:38

"What is truth?" Pilate asked (John 18:38). Jesus Christ was concerned about the truth: "I tell you the truth, until heaven and earth disappear, not the smallest letter, not the least stroke of a pen, will by any means disappear from the Law until everything is accomplished" (Matt. 5:18). "And if anyone gives even a cup of cold water to one of these little ones because he is my disciple, I tell you the truth, he will certainly not lose his reward" (Matthew 10:42). And so forth. For over a hundred times Jesus punctuated his aphorisms with this phrase, "I tell you the truth."

You should be concerned about the truth.

The pursuit of truth is older even than our Lord's bodily presence on this earth. Besides the Old Testament dialogues about truth (e.g., Proverbs), secular philosophers were also discussing truth thousands of years before Christ the man walked the earth. For example, the Greek philosopher Plato (a contemporary of Daniel) was discussing truth 500 years before Christ was born. A long, long, time ago, in a place far, far away, Plato was discussing things like truth, politics, justice, and beauty. To Plato, the pursuit of truth was the beginning and ending of all things. Plato was convinced, for instance, that if people knew the truth they would obey the truth. Plato argued that if people knew the right thing to do they would do it. In other words, immorality was nothing more than ignorance. Were it so, students! Were it so!

Of course, we who live on the backside of Auschwitz, the Great Leap Forward, and September 11, 2001, know that that is absurd. People are quite capable of knowing the truth and acting immorally. In fact they do it all the time. Sometimes really smart people can make very bad choices.

We all know that "There is no one righteous, not even one; there is no one who understands, no one who seeks God. All have turned away, they have together become worthless; there is no one who does good, not even one" (Romans 3:10–12). Everyone sins. Smart people also make bad choices. Indeed. We have to be more than smart. We have to be redeemed! And redemption is not dependent upon what we know; it is dependent upon whom we know.

While I was a graduate student at Harvard I lived outside Harvard Yard. New to the area, while I was traveling to class one day, I found myself hopelessly lost. Seeing some august, famous professors traveling at deliberate speed toward their destination I was sure that they knew the way to the Promised Land (i.e., Danforth Hall gate at the Yard). The truth was, I doubted for a few moments. In fact, as I followed these capable, sagacious professors I remembered a better way. But, no, what did I know! These were the world's smartest men! But I was very late to my history class! They were more lost than I!

Young people, let me make myself very clear. We are not on a search for the truth. This is not an inquiry into the cosmos. No, there is only one Truth and His name is Jesus Christ. And we know His name and we know Him personally. Hallelujah!

PRAYER POINTS

FELICITY

"Create in me a pure heart, O God, and renew a steadfast spirit within me."

~ Psalm 51:10

Today, or this week, I want you to take an ACT test. You can contact me at jpstobaugh@aol.com if you need a sample test, or you can purchase one from another source, but take a practice test now.

You need to obtain a baseline score. A simple and effective way to become familiar with the format and content of the ACT is to take a practice test and it will allow you to build on your results. Besides, results of recent research indicate an association between taking practice tests and increased ACT scores.

In a group of about 69,000 students, those who reported spending two or more hours taking practice tests prior to taking the test the first time earned ACT composite scores that averaged almost 1/2 scale score point higher than the scores of those who did not take practice tests (ACT website). This occurred irrespective of students' grade levels, gender, race/ethnicity, and family income groups.

The achievement/knowledge–based ACT score can more easily be increased by practice tests than the more coaching unfriendly, coaching-resistant SAT. In fact, the ACT is actually very coaching friendly. If you follow the suggestions and complete the practice examples in this book you can easily raise your scores.

One final thought: ultimately high scores on the ACT will result from building on strengths — not from mitigating weaknesses. Use your practice test scores to identify and enlarge strengths.

M A T H

Ratio

A ratio analyzes the relative number of parts of a problem or dilemma. If the ratio of two quantities is x : y, then x and y represent the relative number of parts of the two quantities. For instance, if there are 3 cookies in a jar — 2 chocolate cookies and 1 vanilla cookie — and if another jar with 12 cookies has the same ratio, then this jar would have 8 chocolate cookies and 4 vanilla cookies (TCA website).

■ ■ ■

A basket contains 10 balls, some white and some red.

Which of the following is NOT a possible ratio of white to red balls?

A. 1:1
B. 4:1
C. 1:4
D. 2:1
E. All of the above are possible ratios.

"*If people do not believe that mathematics is simple, it is only because they do not realize how complicated life is.*"[2]
— John Louis Von Neumann

"*If you look for truth, you may find comfort in the end; if you look for comfort you will not get either comfort or truth only soft soap and wishful thinking to begin, and in the end, despair.*"[1]

— C.S. Lewis

WRITING

Beginning

Having a well-organized essay is crucial in order to get a high score on the ACT Writing Assessment. An effective essay requires good planning. You will only have 30 minutes to write a clear, effective essay. In Lesson 2 you created an outline. Now you will begin your essay. Remember the prompt.

ACT Prompt

Over the past several years many schools have gone from a nine-month school year to year-round schooling. Although students attend school the same number of days, they have several shorter breaks throughout the year instead of one long summer break. Advocates of year-round schooling claim that students are able to retain more of what they have learned, while opponents feel that it disrupts summer vacation. In your opinion, is year-round school better than a traditional nine-month school year?

Write an essay in which you take a position on this question. You may choose either argument presented above or introduce a different point of view. Develop your essay with specific details that support your opinion (ACT).

The introduction is the broad beginning of the essay that asks three important questions:

- What is this?
- Why am I reading it?
- What argument/position do you want me to accept?

You should ask these questions by doing the following:

- Establish the background — provide general information about the main idea, explaining the situation so the grader can make sense of the topic and the claims you make and support. Restate the question and ask it.
- State why the main idea is important — tell the grader why s/he should care and keep reading. Your goal is to create a compelling, clear, and convincing essay the grader will want to read and act upon. The grader needs to see how this essay will change his/her world.
- State your thesis/purpose — compose a sentence or two stating the position you will support with logos (sound reasoning: induction, deduction), pathos (balanced emotional appeal), and ethos (author credibility).

In summary, all information discussed in the essay is presented in the introduction. No new arguments may be added after the introduction is created. Don't surprise your reader! Presume nothing. Explain everything.

One final word: Avoid format writing. What is format writing? The following are indicators of format writing:

- Inevitably, format writing emphasizes form over content. Normally, format writers use some sort of contrived checklist.
- Format writing is full of broad, predictable generalizations where the writer purports to be a specialist in everything. But, in fact, the format writer is substantially unable to develop, and much less to defend, any serious rhetorical point. One rarely finds a credible thesis (i.e., purpose statement) in a format writing piece.
- All essays begin and end exactly the same way. Predictability is a sign of inferior writing and endemic to format writing.
- Format writing does not consider audience, content, or purpose.

Your ACT essay graders are trained, certified, professionals — usually English teachers. They know inferior writing when they see it.

■ ■ ■

Complete the following introduction for your essay based on the prompt.

I. Introduction

A. Opening comment — set the context (you need to take control of the topic right here!):

_____

_____

B. Restatement of the question and why it is a compelling question:

_____

_____

C. Thesis — the purpose, claim, and position of this essay — the grader should know exactly what you are arguing and have a hint at how you will argue it:

_____

_____

R E A D I N G

Reading for Detail

- ☐ Set aside a designated reading time each day.
- ☐ Have parents read the book. Discuss the book with your parents.
- ☐ Have "book talks" with friends who are also reading the book.
- ☐ Become an active reader by applying reading strategies:

    predict what will happen next;

    visualize characters, events, and setting;

    connect with what you are reading;

    clarify — stop occasionally to review what you understand;

    evaluate — form opinions about what you read.

■ ■ ■

Reading for detail, analyze the following essay and answer accompanying questions.

For thousands of years before men had any accurate and exact knowledge of the changes of material things, they had thought about these changes, regarded them as revelations of spiritual truths, built on them theories of things in heaven and earth (and a good many things in neither), and used them in manufactures, arts, and handicrafts, especially in one very curious manufacture wherein not the thousandth fragment of a grain of the finished article was ever produced.

The accurate and systematic study of the changes which material things undergo is called chemistry; we may, perhaps, describe alchemy as the superficial, and what may be called subjective, examination of these changes, and the speculative systems, and imaginary arts and manufactures, founded on that examination.

We are assured by many old writers that Adam was the first alchemist, and we are told by one of the initiated that Adam was created on the sixth day, being the 15th of March, of the first year of the world; certainly alchemy had a long life, for chemistry did not begin until about the middle of the 18th century.

No branch of science has had so long a period of incubation as chemistry. There must be some extraordinary difficulty in the way of disentangling the steps of those changes wherein substances of one kind are produced from substances totally unlike them. To inquire how those of acute intellects and much learning regarded such occurrences in the times when man's outlook on the world was very different from what it is now, ought to be interesting, and the results of that inquiry must surely be instructive.[3] (Muir, *The Story of Alchemy and the Beginnings of Chemistry*)

Answer the following questions based on detail in the essay.

Which of the following statement(s) is (are) true:

A. Chemistry in its early stages was a form of religion.
B. Chemistry was opposed to alchemy.
C. Adam was the first chemist.

Another question often asked on the ACT is an inference question. This kind of question is difficult to answer because you are looking for something that is not directly stated in the reading passage. You must read carefully and critically. Sometimes you will be asked to draw conclusions based upon what you have read.

■ ■ ■

From the above passage one can infer:

I. The author feels that chemistry is an important subject to study.

II. The author would agree with Carl Sagan (who is an atheist).

    A. I
    B. II
    C. Both
    D. Neither

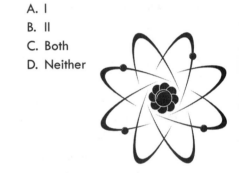

SCIENCE

Predicting Outcomes

Predict what you might find and why in the following incident.

Returning from the grocery story you inadvertently place a glass jar of spaghetti sauce in the freezer. What will you find when you retrieve it in three days?

A. Water expands when it is frozen and since spaghetti sauce is mostly water, the glass jar broke.

B. Nothing happened. The liquid did not freeze.

C. Since water contracts when frozen, the spaghetti sauce had shrunk to half its size.

D. Water expands when it is frozen, and spaghetti sauce is mostly water, but because it has a lot of salt it did not freeze and everything was fine.

"Science without religion is lame, religion without science is blind."[4]

— Albert Einstein.

VOCABULARY

Arguably, the best way to obtain vocabulary words is to keep vocabulary cards. On one side of 3 by 5 cards write the word. On the back define the word and give the context from a book or other source. In a real sense, then, the single best thing you can do to improve your English/reading score is to read good books and keep vocabulary cards.

And Then There Were None[5]
Agatha Christie

First, there were ten — a strange collection of strangers invited as weekend guests to an island off the coast of England. Their host, an odd millionaire unknown to all of them, is nowhere to be found. All the guests have a deplorable past that they are unwilling to reveal. One by one they die. Before the weekend is gone, there will be none (Stobaugh, *Companion to 50 Classics*[6]).

Suggested Vocabulary Words

A. "There was a silence — a comfortable <u>replete</u> silence. Into that silence came The Voice. Without warning, inhuman, <u>penetrating</u>. . . . 'Ladies and gentlemen! Silence, please! . . . You are charged with the following <u>indictments</u>.' " (chapter 3)

B. "But — <u>incongruous</u> as it may seem to some — I was <u>restrained</u> and <u>hampered</u> by my <u>innate</u> sense of justice. The innocent must not suffer." (epilogue)

"Truth, however bitter, can be accepted, and woven into a design for living."[7]

—Agatha Christie

ENGLISH

Sentence Structure

Throughout the ACT English test you will be expected to select the best of four possible ways to express the same idea. To do this, not only must you have mastered the rules that govern such matters as subject-verb agreement; you must also be able to determine whether or not the parts of a sentence work logically and clearly together.

Choose the best sentence:

A. In highly developed commercial communities banks cannot afford space in their vaults for valuables. Especially, they cannot afford it merely to accommodate their patrons. Hence, in such communities the furnishing of places for safe deposit has become a separate business.

B. In highly developed commercial communities banks cannot afford space in their vaults for valuables so they form separate businesses that specialize in providing safe deposit boxes.

Finish the
RACE

SCRIPTURE

"I have fought the good fight, I have finished the race, I have kept the faith."

~ 2 Timothy 4:7

I want to fight the good fight, finish the race, keep the faith.

I belong to a weight reduction, health accountability group at my YMCA called Guts and Butts (G&B). (I am not making this up!) I am the youngest member (58). Our group is the main competitor of the YMCA perennial favorites, Silver Sneakers (SSs) who are fortunate enough to have Medicare and Blue Cross and Blue Shield Insurance with no deductible. We G&B have hybrid high deductible insurance plans of dubious quality.

We have periodic contests with the Silver Sneakers. So far they have beat us every time. Last Christmas we had a contest to see how many pounds each group could lose between Thanksgiving and Christmas. The SS champs lost 150 pounds. We gained a net 9 pounds. They received gift certificates for Subway. We gave ourselves a party.

Last Easter we competed in the swim-the-most miles contest. Each person was on an honor code and wrote his daily mileage on a poster board behind the life guard, who very carefully scrutinized both pool performance and log in totals. Once I logged a mile. The life guard scowled at me.

"Well, if you consider the back strokes, it was a mile," I sheepishly offered. Of course it took me about half the life span of the teenage life guard sitting on his exalted lifeguard throne to accomplish it, but I did it. Really.

The G&Bs logged 150 miles. The SSs soared at 350. They got free coupons to the local Subway. We had a party.

Well, another contest is in the works this year. We are led by a fairly aggressive 75-year-old Amazon, Margaret. "This is our year," she prophesies.

The SSs all have little red roses embroidered on their swimming suits. Wheezing B&G High Pockets — we call him that because that is how he breathes after even the most moderate exercise and he wears his pants up too high above his ample stomach — has a USMC symbol on his left forearm. That is the best swimming motif we can sport.

The SSs have the newest rental lockers sporting top-of-the-line master combination locks. The G&Bs can't be sure we can remember or combinations, so we try another approach. We put our stuff in the broken lockers hoping that potential brigands will ignore our depositories.

I am an inveterate G&B. I like to swim my laps and pray and take my time. I have no destination, no pressure to perform. I love my swimming and I love my God. And in that pool, with other G&Bs, I find my way again to the sublime perpendicular line that tells me again, for one more Christmas, good and faithful servant, you have reached the end and need to turn around. I don't know how to flip over like the SSs, but I know how to turn around and go back in the other direction when I meet the wall. And that is enough.

Not that I will win any coupons to Wendy's this Christmas. But this I know — I will enjoy my time with brothers and sisters, old and infirm, faithful and unpretentious, who, if we can't win a contest, still have fun along the way.

And sometimes, when I am in that surreal pool lap "life," I just enjoy my God so much. I can feel His presence. I can feel His pleasure. And that is enough winning for me.

And I know, no matter what happens, at the end of the great swim I am going to party with my brothers and sisters — and no doubt a few SSs too — at the end of the long swim. The God of history is faithful and true.

PRAYER POINTS
COURAGE

"Be strong and courageous. Do not be afraid or terrified because of them, for the LORD your God goes with you; he will never leave you nor forsake you."

~ Deuteronomy 31:6

"We are half-hearted creatures, fooling about with drink and lust and ambition when infinite joy is offered to us, like an ignorant child who wants to keep on making mud-pie in the slums because he cannot imagine what is meant by the offer of a vacation at the beach. If I really wanted to be happy, I would seek God. Oh, but God is abstract! It takes effort to reach God. So I settle. I settle for weak amusements that require no effort. What a lazy fool I am!"[1]

— C.S. Lewis

Reading for Detail

These questions ask about details stated in the passage-information. For example, you may be asked to identify:

- facts included in the passage,
- the author's thesis,
- the setting,
- the order in which a series of events occurred.

■ ■ ■

The closing years of the eighteenth century and the opening years of the nineteenth represent the most splendid period in the annals of the British Navy. Howe destroyed the French fleet in the Atlantic on "the glorious First of June, 1794," Nelson died in the midst of his greatest victory off Cape Trafalgar on 21 October, 1805. Little more than eleven years separated the two dates, and this brief period was crowded with triumphs for Britain on the sea. The "First of June," St. Vincent, Camperdown, the Nile, Copenhagen, and Trafalgar are the great names in the roll of victory; but "the meteor flag of England" flew victorious in a hundred fights on all the seas of the world.

Men who were officers young in the service on the day when Rodney broke at once the formal traditions of a century and the battle-line of the Comte de Grasse lived through and shared in the glories of this decade of victory. A new spirit had come into the navy. An English admiral would no longer think he had done his duty in merely bringing his well-ordered line into cannon-shot of an enemy's array and exchanging broadsides with him at half-cannon range. Nor was the occupation of a port or an island recognized as an adequate result for a naval campaign. The enemy's fighting-fleet was now the object aimed at. It was not merely to be brought to action, and more or less damaged by distant cannonading. The ideal battle was the close fight amid the enemy's broken line, and victory meant his destruction.

The spirit of the time was personified in its greatest sailor. Nelson's battles were fought in grim earnest, taking risks boldly in order to secure great results. Trafalgar — the last of his battles, and the last great battle of the days of the sail — was also the final episode in the long struggle of Republican and Imperial France to snatch from England even for a while the command of the sea.[2] (John Richard Hale, *Famous Sea Fights*)

This passage occurs during:

A. The American Revolution
B. The English Civil War
C. The French and Indian War
D. The Napoleonic Wars

A new sort of naval warfare is emerging. What is it?

A. A new battle line approach with close fighting
B. New cannon allowed ships to fight from great distance
C. Steam power transformed the line of battle
D. Naval warfare was essentially unchanged

V O C A B U L A R Y

Animal Farm[3]
George Orwell

Animal Farm is a great fable turned into a novel. Its simple plot camouflages a much deeper, darker message. The story is about a farm run by a mean farmer, who is later run out of the farm by the animals. The animals take control of the farm and find that it isn't as easy to run as they thought.

Suggested Vocabulary Words

A. The pigs had an even harder struggle to <u>counteract</u> the lies put about by Moses, the tame raven. Moses, who was Mr. Jones's special pet, was a spy and a tale-bearer, but he was also a clever talker. He claimed to know of the existence of a mysterious country called Sugarcandy Mountain, to which all animals went when they died. It was situated somewhere up in the sky, a little distance beyond the clouds, Moses said. In Sugarcandy Mountain it was Sunday seven days a week, clover was in season all the year round, and lump sugar and linseed cake grew on the hedges. The animals hated Moses because he told tales and did no work, but some of them believed in Sugarcandy Mountain, and the pigs had to argue very hard to <u>persuade</u> them that there was no such place. (chapter 2)

B. The animals were not badly off throughout that summer. . . . The <u>advantage</u> of only having to feed themselves, and not having to support five <u>extravagant</u> human beings as well, was so great that it would have taken a lot of failures to outweigh it. And in many ways the animal method of doing things was more <u>efficient</u> and saved labor. Such jobs as weeding, for instance, could be done with a thoroughness impossible to human beings. And again, since no animal now stole, it was unnecessary to fence off pasture from <u>arable</u> land. (chapter 6)

C. As yet no animal had actually retired on pension, but of late the subject had been discussed more and more. Now that the small field beyond the orchard had been set aside for barley, it was rumored that a corner of the large pasture was to be fenced off and turned into a grazing-ground for <u>superannuated</u> animals. (chapter 9)

D. There was the same hearty cheering as before, and the mugs were emptied to the dregs. But as the animals outside gazed at the scene, it seemed to them that some strange thing was happening. What was it that had <u>altered</u> in the faces of the pigs? Clover's old dim eyes flitted from one face to another. Some of them had five chins, some had four, some had three. But what was it that seemed to be melting and changing? (chapter 10)

M A T H

Percentages

The term *percent* means "hundredths" or "per 100." Changing a decimal to a percent or a percent to a decimal involves the movement of the decimal point two places to the right.

■ ■ ■

Mary was able to win a math competition 7 times out of 28 attempts. To the nearest percent, what percentage of the time did Mary win the math competition?

A. 15
B. 40
C. 25
D. 68
E. 83

110% of 116 equals

A. 0
B. 1
C. 12.76
D. 127.60
E. 116.5

> "*Read, every day, something no one else is reading. Think, every day, something no one else is thinking. Do, every day, something no one else would be silly enough to do. It is bad for the mind to be always part of unanimity.*"[4]
>
> — Christopher Morley

SCIENCE

Principles

This particular question type evaluates your ability to discern a scientific principle illustrated by a scientific experiment.

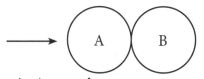

What scientific principle is illustrated by the following illustration.

→ A B

I. A mass of matter moves because energy has been spent upon it, and has acquired energy equal to the work done on it, and this is believed to hold true, no matter what the kind of energy was that moved it. If a body moves, it moves because another body has exerted pressure upon it.

II. There is no need to assume anything more mysterious than mechanical action. Whether body B moves this way or that depends upon the direction of the push, the point of its application. Whether the body be a mass as large as the earth or as small as a molecule, makes no difference in that particular.

A. I only
B. II only
C. both

> "The height of your accomplishments will equal the depth of your convictions."[5]
> — William F. Scholavino

ENGLISH

Grammar, Usage, and Mechanics

In the following passage certain words and phrases are underlined. The answer choices present alternatives for each underlined part. Choose the alternative that is best according to the rules of standard written English and to the context of the passage. If you think the original version is best, choose No Change.

His own galleys were prepared for service under the orders of Prince Colonna, and a subsidy was sent to Venice from the papal treasury to aid in the equipment of the Venetian fleet. The papal envoys appealed to the Genoese Republic, the Knights of Malta, and the Kings of France and Spain to reinforce the fleets of Rome and Venice. But France and Spain were more interested in their own local ambitions and jealousies, and even Philip II gave at first very limited help. With endless difficulty a fleet of galleys was at last assembled, Maltese, Genoese, Roman, Venetian, united under the command of Colonna. By the time the Christian armament was ready a larger Turkish fleet had appeared in the waters of Cyprus and landed an army, which, under their protection, began the siege of Nicosia. After long delays Colonna's fleet reached Suda Bay in Crete, and joined a squadron of Venetian galleys kept for guardship duties in Cretan waters.[6] (John Richard Hale, *Famous Sea Fights*)

His own galleys were prepared for service under the orders of Prince Colonna, and a subsidy was sent to Venice from the papal treasury to aid in the equipment of the Venetian fleet.

A. Prince Colonna ordered the preparation of his galleys and the papal treasury aided in the equipping of the Venetian fleet.
B. Prince Colonna orders the preparation of his galleys and the papal treasury aids in the equipping of the Venetian fleet.
C. Prince Colonna ordered the preparation of his galleys and aided in the equipping of the Venetian fleet.
D. No Change
E. their
F. his
G. its
H. no change

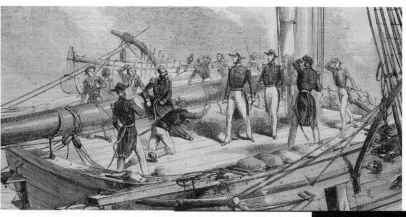

WRITING

The body of an essay is the core of the essay. It is where the argument is developed and the evidence provided.

The three elements of a good body include paragraphs that have:

1. a topic sentence that tells the grader what you will be arguing in the paragraph;
2. specific evidence and analysis that supports your thesis and that provides a deeper level of detail than your topic sentence;
3. a brief wrap-up sentence that tells the reader how and why this information supports the paper's thesis. The brief wrap-up is also known as the warrant. The warrant is important to your argument because it connects your reasoning and supports your thesis. It shows that the information in the paragraph is related to your thesis and helps defend it.

ACT Prompt

Over the past several years many schools have gone from a nine-month school year to year-round schooling. Although students attend school the same number of days, they have several shorter breaks throughout the year instead of one long summer break. Advocates of year-round schooling claim that students are able to retain more of what they have learned, while opponents feel that it disrupts summer vacation. In your opinion, is year-round school better than a traditional nine-month school year?

Write an essay in which you take a position on this question. You may choose either argument presented above or introduce a different point of view. Develop your essay with specific details that support your opinion.

Write the body of an essay where you extend your argument introduced in Lesson 3.

To those who are Christian believers I must warn you that consistently the ACT chooses prompts that are controversial and, in my opinion, prejudiced against our Judeo-Christian morality. We believers will be offended, no doubt, and may be tempted to use this portion of the ACT as a forum to share our beliefs. Don't do that. It might hurt your score, and, in defense of the ACT Board, you are being asked to discuss what an issue means, or what a quote means, or what an authority means — you are rarely asked to offer your opinion. So, if you need some wriggle room, I would state what the quote means, communicate a scholarly opinion, and quietly pray for the ACT essay creators and the ACT Board! I would not use this venue as a forum to parade my own beliefs, however laudable and accurate they might be!

Write the first argument for your essay body.

Argument 1

_____

_____

Evidence 1

_____

_____

Build Your Writing Skills

Here are some ways you can strengthen your writing skills:

- Read and write frequently. Read as much as you can from a variety of sources, including plays, essays, fiction, poetry, news stories, business writing, and magazine features.

- Become familiar with current issues in society and develop your own opinions on the issues. Think of arguments you would use to convince someone of your opinion. Taking speech and debate classes can help you think through issues and communicate them to others.

- Practice writing in different formats and in as many real situations as possible. Write letters to the editor, or letters to a company requesting information.

- Share your writing with others and get feedback. Feedback helps you anticipate how readers might interpret your writing and what types of questions they might have. This can help you anticipate what a reader might want to know.

- Learn to see writing as a process — brainstorming, planning, writing, and then editing. This applies to all writing activities. Avoid format writing.

- Strive for your writing to be well developed and well organized, using precise, clear, and concise language.

I Can't
THINK

SCRIPTURE

"For the word of God is living and active. Sharper than any double-edged sword, it penetrates even to dividing soul and spirit, joints and marrow; it judges the thoughts and attitudes of the heart."

~ Hebrews 4:12

In *Newsweek* recently there was an article called "I Can't Think." It is about the fact that we are overloaded by information. "The Twitterization of our culture has revolutionized our lives, but with an unintended consequence — our overloaded brains freeze when we make decisions," journalist Sharon Begley writes. Begley warns us that we are overloaded with information, choices, and alternatives. When we have so many choices, we are unable to make any choice at all. As a result, when we finally do respond "the ceaseless influx trains us to respond instantly, sacrificing accuracy and thoughtfulness to the false god of immediacy."[1]

In other words, we respond out of exigency and expediency and not out of thoughtfulness and care. We choose the quick not the right, the convenient not the just.

George Loewen of Carnegie Mellon University warns that "getting 30 texts per hour up to the moment when you make a decision means that the first 28 or 29 have virtually no meaning."[2] Immediacy dooms thoughtful deliberation.

Another casualty is creativity. Creative decisions are more likely to bubble up from a brain that applies unconscious thought to a problem, rather than going at it in a full-frontal, analytical assault. So much for making decisions in the shower or on a quiet walk. We swamp ourselves with text messages and twitter and IMs. We don't need to reflect on a problem — we can google our crisis away with hundreds of hits.

Oh, that it were so! No one, my friend, can put humpty together again but the Maker. Yes, God. Unless we can Twitter our way to the Holy Spirit or text God we might be in trouble. We will not be able to send an SOS out on Facebook to solve our sorry lives — we need a direct, old-fashioned touch of God. In the midst of so much information the thing that really matters, we discover, is WHO we know and not WHAT we know. Well, all this information is only information, after all. Aha! Our epistemology will take us no further than our metaphysics.

How can you protect yourself from having your decisions warped by excess information? Ms. Begley suggests we take our e-mails in limited fashion, like a glass of wine before bedtime. She wants us to control our access to Facebook — only twice a day.

Silly me. May I suggest an alternative? Why not turn off the computer. And pick up your Bible. And read it.

PRAYER POINTS
LOVE

"Since we live by the Spirit, let us keep in step with the Spirit."

~ Galatians 5:25

R E A D I N G

Author's Tone

The term "tone" refer to the author's slant on a subject, emotions, or feelings. To determine tone in a literary piece, you have to consider diction and syntax, the grammatical structure of the sentence. You also have to consider which details are included and which are left out.

What is the tone of the following passage?

"What soul in the land but has felt and witnessed this grief — this unavailing sorrow for the brave and untimely dead? I thought of the letter from the sorrowing one in Iowa, whose son, a prisoner, I had nursed, receiving with the last breath words for the distant, unconscious mother; of her sorrow in writing of him in his distant grave; of her pride in him, her only son. How many in the land could take her hand and weep over a mutual sorrow! And in the hospital wards, men, who still hold the name of Americans, together were talking of battles, prisoners, and captors, when each told the other of acts of bravery performed on hostile fields, and took out pictures of innocent babes, little children, and wives, to show each other, all feeling a sympathy and interest in the unknown faces. Verily, war is a species of passionate insanity."[3] (Mary Ann Loughborough, *My Cave Life in Vicksburg*)

The author's tone is:

A. Somber
B. Flippant
C. Critical
D. Neutral

The author's tone is established by:

A. The setting
B. Language
C. Plot
D. All of the above

M A T H

General Problems

The sum of two numbers is 60, and the greater is four times the lesser. What are the numbers?

If the difference between two numbers is 48, and one number is five times the other, what are the numbers?

There are three numbers whose sum is 96; the second is three times the first, and the third is four times the first. What are the numbers?

Divide the number 126 into two parts such that one part is 8 more than the other.

The Autobiography of Benjamin Franklin[4]
Benjamin Franklin

Speaking to his "Dear Son," Benjamin Franklin began what is one of the most famous autobiographies in world history. At the age of 62, Franklin wrote his reminiscences for the benefit of his son, William Franklin (1731–1813). The book was composed in sections, the first part dealing with Franklin's first 24 years. He finished this in 1771. Then, with the end of the American Revolution, he resumed his writing in 1783 and finished it in 1789. Ironically, though, the autobiography covers his life only until 1757. There is no mention even of the American Revolution. Full of anecdotes and wisdom, *The Autobiography of Benjamin Franklin* remains a timeless classic.

" *Most people won't realize that writing is a craft. You have to take your apprenticeship in it like anything else.*"[5]
— Katherine Anne Porter

Suggested Vocabulary Words

A. Having emerged from the poverty and <u>obscurity</u> in which I was born and bred, to a state of <u>affluence</u> and some degree of reputation in the world, and having gone so far through life with a considerable share of <u>felicity</u>, the conducing means I made use of, which with the blessing of God so well succeeded, my <u>posterity</u> may like to know, as they may find some of them suitable to their own situations, and therefore fit to be imitated. (part 1)

B. It was written in 1675, in the home-spun verse of that time and people, and addressed to those then concerned in the government there. It was in favor of liberty of conscience, and in behalf of the Baptists, Quakers, and other sectaries that had been under persecution, ascribing the Indian wars, and other distresses that had befallen the country, to that persecution, as so many judgments of God to punish so <u>heinous</u> an offense, and <u>exhorting</u> a repeal of those <u>uncharitable</u> laws. (part I)

C. At his table he liked to have, as often as he could, some sensible friend or neighbor to converse with, and always took care to start some <u>ingenious</u> or useful topic for <u>discourse</u>, which might tend to improve the minds of his children. (part 1)

D. I continu'd this method some few years, but gradually left it, retaining only the habit of expressing myself in terms of modest <u>diffidence</u>. (part 2)

E. In his house I lay that night, and the next morning reach'd Burlington, but had the <u>mortification</u> to find that the regular boats were gone a little before my coming, and no other expected to go before Tuesday, this being Saturday; wherefore I returned to an old woman in the town, of whom I had bought gingerbread to eat on the water, and ask'd her advice. (part 2)

F. My ideas at that time were, that the sect should be begun and spread at first among young and single men only; that each person to be initiated should not only declare his assent to such creed, but should have exercised himself with the thirteen weeks' examination and practice of the virtues as in the before-mention'd model; that the existence of such a society should be kept a secret, till it was become considerable, to prevent <u>solicitations</u> for the admission of improper persons, but that the members should each of them search among his acquaintance for <u>ingenuous</u>, well-disposed youths, to whom, with <u>prudent</u> caution, the scheme should be gradually communicated these proverbs, which contained the wisdom of many ages and nations, I assembled and form'd into a connected <u>discourse</u> prefix'd to the Almanack of 1757, as the <u>harangue</u> of a wise old man to the people attending an auction. (part 3)

G. In 1751, Dr. Thomas Bond, a particular friend of mine, conceived the idea of establishing a hospital in Philadelphia (a very <u>beneficent</u> design, which has been ascrib'd to me, but was originally his), for the reception and cure of poor sick persons, whether inhabitants of the province or strangers. He was <u>zealous</u> and active in endeavoring to <u>procure</u> subscriptions for it, but the proposal being a <u>novelty</u> in America, and at first not well understood, he met with but small success. (part 4)

E N G L I S H

Diction

Diction involves word choice. Some of the questions on the ACT English Test require that you identify the words that are unacceptable.

■ ■ ■

Identify the usage problems in the following sentences:

I. I effected the outcome by my choices.
II. It was alright for me to borrow my mother's car.
III. Please lay next to the water fountain.
IV. I cannot choose between the three food dishes.

???

Are you reading

50 to 100 pages

a day

???

W R I T I N G

The Conclusion

In a general way, your conclusion will:

- restate your topic and why it is important
- restate your thesis/claim

Remember that once you accomplish these tasks you are finished. Done. Don't try to bring in new points or end with a sermon or polemic. Stay focused! Stay on task! Finish with confident humility.

The conclusion:

_____

_____

_____

S C I E N C E

Comparing Theories

One type question in the Science Reasoning portion may present two opposing viewpoints. These may be different interpretations of experimental results or different theories to explain some phenomena.

You will be presented with questions about the two viewpoints. You will have to delineate the different assumptions behind each viewpoint.

The Evolution of Man
Theory A

The modern theory concerning the evolution of man proposes that humans and apes derive from an ape-like ancestor that lived on earth a few million years ago. The theory states that man, through a combination of environmental and genetic factors, emerged as a species to produce the variety of ethnicities seen today, while modern apes evolved on a separate evolutionary pathway.

The following are assumptions of this theory:

A. Mankind evolved into its present species by trial and error.
B. The earth is millions of years old.
C. There is no God.
D. A and B
E. A, B, & C

Theory B

Creation occurred in six normal-length days about 6,000 years ago, just the way it is described in the Bible, and that God destroyed the earth with a global Flood about 1,600 years later.

A. The Bible is authoritative and should be accepted literally.
B. The earth is no more than 6,000 years old.
C. A
D. B
E. A & B

Masters of
DISGUISE

SCRIPTURE

"Jesus answered, 'I am the way and the truth and the life. No one comes to the Father except through me.' "

~ John 14:6

Last week I was reading the *New York Times* and, being somewhat bored, I visited the "dining" section. I love to compare the culinary offerings in Johnstown, Pennsylvania, to New York City, New York. Of course, we don't have the Red Rooster Harlem, serving gourmet Southern cuisine — what an oxymoron! — but we do have Hong Kong Buffet that lovingly serves amuse-bouche fried cheese sticks, a Johnstown favorite.

I remember attending my son's wedding reception, so wonderfully hosted by his Indianapolis in-laws. There was a nice man with white gloves standing next to me. Not sure why he was there, I tried to shake his hand, which he politely did but kept standing there. I was handed a warm cloth by a man wearing white gloves. I wasn't sure what he wanted me to do with it — I am embarrassed to tell you what I do with small white clothes—but I saw that most folks were wiping their hands, and some pioneering souls were even wiping their faces. I, being a real trailblazer, went further. I wiped my hands, my face, nose, and when I was moving on to my ears my wife Karen stopped me with a glaring frown. I guess those things are not for ears.

Next, the nice man with a towel on his arm offered me one little bread roll that he parsimoniously placed on a plate that swallowed the pathetic thing. The nice man, no doubt discerning my disappointment, asked me if I wanted a couple more rolls, but my sweet wife, who occasionally helps me out this way, with somewhat too much enthusiasm replied, "No."

Next the waiter — what was he really? — gave me something that looked a lot like a salad except that it had all kinds of red stuff, allegedly lettuce. It looked nothing like my personal favorite — an iceberg wedge smothered in real blue cheese dressing. I graciously gave my salad to my wife, hoping she would reciprocate by giving me her pigs in a blanket and rigatoni that every Johnstown wedding sports — but do you know what? Apparently these poor Indiana people have not yet discovered these foods of the gods. There were no pigs in a blanket and rigatoni at this Indianapolis wedding. I suppose nobody told these poor folks that wedding cuisine always includes these two items. In fact, if food has two motifs, if life is full of motifs, in Johnstown, Pennsylvania, one fills one's wedding reception and life with simple, tasty metaphors.

I am an inveterate Johnstown cuisine lover. My love affair, my wife Karen would say, has put 80 pounds on me in the last 21 years, but she is being ungenerous since I mostly eat her wonderful cooking. And what fine cooking it is! I remember the first meal Karen cooked for me in 1977. It was broiled chicken seasoned with salad dressing and boiled broccoli seasoned with lemon pepper. Until then, I had never eaten broiled chicken — my chicken was always fried — unless Big Momma served her famous chicken and dumplings. After that inaugural advent, I never had fried chicken again! Broccoli, southern style, was cooked longer than it took General Grant to capture Vicksburg, and I had heard of pepper (and used it liberally after I coated everything

PRAYER POINTS
LOYALTY

"Let love and faithfulness never leave you; bind them around your neck, write them on the tablet of your heart."

~ Proverbs 3:3

with salt) and lemons (which I put in my sweetened ice tea) — but never both together. Actually, my first meal was pretty good as were the next 33,000 or so she has cooked for me — my expanding waistline is a testament to my thorough conversion to Nouveau Yankee cuisine. Yummy good!

Well, anyway, the *New York Times* article argues that finally — finally — there is a vegetarian burger that rivals the most delicious Whopper or Quarter Pounder. Apparently, while the rest of us languish in the throes of the new Angus Quarter Pounder, inventive New York chefs have been working tirelessly to create the penultimate veggie burger. Food reviewer Jeff Gordinier is veritably overcome with joy when he writes "Veggie burgers . . . have explored into countless variations of good, and in doing so they've begun to look like a bellwether for the American appetite."[1]

Bellwether for the American appetite? Excuse me, but I doubt it. Can you imagine cruising through the MacDonald's drive through and asking for a veggie burger with fries and milk shake? Hmm. . . .

But excuse me. I respect vegetarians. More power to you. But why do you want to copy my food? Do I try to copy yours? Respectfully, I doubt, even in NYC, that one can find broccoli and asparagus that will match the effervescence of a Quarter Pounder with cheese. Nonetheless, "There is something very satisfying about holding one's dinner in one's hand." Indeed. But it can't be done. Not really. A meatless burger is an oxymoron and it can never be a dinner.

And here is another oxymoron — and this is where I am taking this — our society is desperate to emulate the Christian life. The Christian life, like the hamburger, is genuine, real, juicy, and full of protein. Lived in the right way, it can bring great life to a person and to his world. And it cannot be replaced by good feelings, good intentions, or other existential offerings. As Tolstoy writes in *War and Peace*, "Let us be persuaded that the less we let our feeble human minds roam, the better we shall please God, who rejects all knowledge that does not come from Him; and the less we seek to fathom what He has been pleased to conceal from us, the sooner will he vouchsafe its revelation to us through His divine Spirit."[2]

M A T H

General Math

Divide the number 126 into two parts so that one part is 8 more than the other.

The sum of two numbers is 25, and the larger is 3 less than three times the smaller. What are the numbers?

Mr. Y gave $6 to his three boys. To the second he gave 25 cents more than to the third, and to the first three times as much as to the second. How much did each receive?

Arthur bought some apples and twice as many oranges for 78 cents. The apples cost 3 cents apiece, and the oranges 5 cents apiece. How many of each did he buy?

"*The light was frozen, dead, a ghost. Only from the yellow barrels of the microscopes did it borrow a certain rich and living substance, lying along the polished tubes like butter, streak after luscious streak in long recession down the work tables.*"

— Aldous Huxley, *Brave New World*

Mathematic Calculations

Light has a velocity of 186,000 miles in a second. It takes about eight minutes to reach us from the sun. How far away is the sun?

    A. 8 X 186,000

    B. 600 X 186,000

    C. 8 X 60 X 186,000

    D. None of the Above

Assume a straight bar electromagnet in circuit, so that a current can be made intermittent, say, once a second. When the circuit is closed and the magnet is made, the field at once is formed and travels outward at the rate of 186,000 miles per second. When the current stops, the field adjacent is destroyed. Another closure develops the field again, which, like the other, travels outward; and so there may be formed a series of waves in the ether, each 186,000 miles long, with an electro-magnetic antecedent. If the circuit was closed 186,000 times a second, they would be but one mile long.

If the circuit were closed ten times a second, how long would the waves be?

    A. 18,600 miles long

    B. 186,000 miles long

    C. 350,000 miles long

    D. The answer cannot be determined by the information given.

> "Science is facts; just as houses are made of stone, so is science made of facts; but a pile of stones is not a house, and a collection of facts is not necessarily science."[3]
>
> — Jules Henri Poincaré

Brave New World[4]
Aldous Huxley

Huxley's vision of the future in his astonishing 1931 novel *Brave New World* continues to intrigue readers into the 21st century. Huxley's world is one in which Western civilization has been maintained through the most efficient scientific and psychological engineering, where people are genetically designed to be useful to the ruling class.

Suggested Vocabulary Words

A. The Director opened a door. They were in a large bare room, very bright and sunny; for the whole of the southern wall was a single window. Half a dozen nurses, <u>trousered</u> and jacketed in the regulation white <u>viscose-linen</u> uniform, their hair <u>aseptically</u> hidden under white caps, were engaged in setting out bowls of roses in a long row across the floor. Big bowls, packed tight with blossom. Thousands of petals, ripe-blown and silkily smooth, like the cheeks of <u>innumerable</u> little <u>cherubs</u>, but of cherubs, in that bright light, not exclusively pink and Aryan, but also <u>luminously</u> Chinese, also Mexican, also <u>apoplectic</u> with too much blowing of <u>celestial</u> trumpets, also pale as death, pale with the <u>posthumous</u> whiteness of marble. (chapter 2)

B. An almost naked Indian was very slowly climbing down the ladder from the first-floor terrace of a neighboring house — rung after rung, with the <u>tremulous</u> caution of extreme old age. His face was <u>profoundly</u> wrinkled and black, like a mask of <u>obsidian</u>. The toothless mouth had fallen in. At the corners of the lips, and on each side of the chin, a few long bristles gleamed almost white against the dark skin. The long unbraided hair hung down in grey <u>wisps</u> round his face. His body was bent and <u>emaciated</u> to the bone, almost fleshless. Very slowly he came down, pausing at each rung before he ventured another step. (chapter 7)

C. Lenina alone said nothing. Pale, her blue eyes clouded with an <u>unwonted</u> <u>melancholy</u>, she sat in a corner, cut off from those who surrounded her by an emotion which they did not share. She had come to the party filled with a strange feeling of anxious <u>exultation</u>. (chapter 12)

D. But who was he to be <u>pampered</u> with the daily and hourly sight of loveliness? Who was he to be living in the visible presence of God? . , . Seeing them, the Savage made a <u>grimace</u>; but he was to become <u>reconciled</u> to them in course of time; for at night they twinkled gaily with geometrical constellations, or else, flood-lighted, pointed their <u>luminous</u> fingers (with a gesture whose significance nobody in England but the Savage now understood) solemnly towards the plumbless mysteries of heaven. (chapter 18)

Sentence Structure

German letter to America at beginning of World War I:

I do not know what is thought of this war in America. <u>I assume there have been published in America the telegrams exchanged between the German Emperor, the Emperor of Russia, and the King of England,</u> containing the history of the events that preceded the outbreak of the war, and which bears irrefutable testimony of how the Emperor, until the last moment, strove hard to preserve the peace.

These efforts had to be futile, as Russia, under all circumstances, had resolved upon war, and as England, which for decades had encouraged the anti-German nationalism in Russia and France, did not avail herself of the splendid opportunity offered her to prove her often-emphasized love of peace. . . .

<u>When once the archives are opened the world will learn how often Germany extended to England her friendly hand, but England did not desire the friendship of Germany.</u> Jealous of the development of Germany, and feeling that by German efficiency and German industry she has been surpassed in some fields, she had the desire to crush Germany by brute force, as she in former times subdued Spain, Holland, and France. She believed the moment had arrived, and therefore the entry of German troops into Belgium gave her a welcome pretext to take part in the war.

Germany, however, was forced to enter Belgium because she had to forestall the planned French advance, and Belgium only awaited this advance to join France. That only a pretext was involved as far as England is concerned is proved by the fact that already on the afternoon of Aug. 2, that is, prior to the violation of Belgium neutrality by Germany, Sir Edward Grey assured the French Ambassador unconditionally of the help of England in case the German fleet attacked the French coast.

Moral scruple, however, the English policy does not know. And thus the English people, who always posed as the protagonist of freedom and right, has allied itself with Russia, the representative of the most terrible barbarism, a country that knows no spiritual or no religious freedom, that tramples upon the freedom of peoples as well as of individuals. Already England is beginning to recognize that she has made a mistake in her calculations. . . .

Having strangled <u>the news service of Germany to the whole world, and having opened the campaign against us with a falsehood, England will tell your countrymen that the German troops burned down Belgian villages and cities, but will pass over in silence the fact that Belgian girls gouged out the eyes of defenseless wounded.</u> Officials of Belgian cities have invited our officers to dinner and shot and killed them across the table. Contrary to all international law, the whole civilian population of Belgium was called out, and after having at first shown friendliness, carried on in the rear of our troops a terrible warfare with concealed weapons.[5]

I assume there have been published in America the telegrams exchanged between the German Emperor, the Emperor of Russia, and the King of England.

A. I assume there have been published in America the telegrams exchanged among the German Emperor, the Emperor of Russia, and the King of England.

B. There have been published in America the telegrams exchanged between the German Emperor, the Emperor of Russia, and the King of England.

C. Exchanged between the German Emperor, the Emperor of Russia, and the King of England I assume there have been published in America the telegrams.

D. No change is necessary.

When once the archives are opened the world will learn how often Germany extended to England her friendly hand, but England did not desire the friendship of Germany.

A. When once the archives are opened the world will learn how often Germany extended to England her friendly hand; however, England did not desire the friendship of Germany.

B. When once the archives are opened the world will learn how often Germany extended to England their friendly hand, but England did not desire the friendship of Germany.

C. When once the archives are opened the world will learn how often Germany extended to England her friendly hand, but England did not desire the friendship of Germany.

D. No change is necessary.

Strangling the news service of Germany to the whole world, and having opened the campaign against us with a falsehood, England will tell your countrymen that the German troops burned down Belgian villages and cities, but will pass over in silence the fact that Belgian girls gouged out the eyes of defenseless wounded.

A. Having strangled the news service of Germany to the whole world, and having opened the campaign against us with a falsehood, England will tell your countrymen that the German troops burned down Belgian villages and cities, but will pass over in silence the fact that Belgian girls gouged out the eyes of defenseless wounded.

B. Having strangled the news service of Germany to the whole world, and having opened the campaign against us with a falsehood, England will tell your countrymen that the German troops burned down Belgian villages and cities, but will pass over in silence the fact that Belgian girls gouged out the eyes of defenseless wounded.

C. Having strangled the news service of Germany to the whole world, and having opened the campaign against us with a falsehood, furthermore England will tell your countrymen that the German troops burned down Belgian villages and cities, but will pass over in silence the fact that Belgian girls gouged out the eyes of defenseless wounded.

D. No change is necessary.

Infer from the Text

I was reading an essay by Neil Postman, author of *Amusing Ourselves to Death*. He reminds us that 1984 came and went and Orwell's nightmare did not occur. The roots of liberal democracy had held.

But we had forgotten that alongside Orwell's dark vision, there was another equally chilling apocalyptic vision: Aldous Huxley's *Brave New World*. Contrary to common belief, Huxley and Orwell did not prophesy the same thing. Orwell warns that we will be overcome by an externally imposed oppression — Big Brother. But in Huxley's vision, no Big Brother is required to deprive people of their autonomy, volition, and history. As he saw it, people will come to love their oppression, to cherish the technologies that undo their capacities to think.

What Orwell feared were those who would ban books. "What Huxley feared was that there would be no reason to ban a book, for there would be no one who wanted to read one. Orwell feared those who would deprive us of information. Huxley feared those who would give us so much that we would be reduced to passivity and egoism. Orwell feared that the truth would be concealed from us. Huxley feared the truth would be drowned in a sea of neglect. Orwell feared we would become a captive to ubiquitous culture. Huxley feared we would become a trivial culture. As Huxley remarked in his sequel *Brave New World Revisited*, the civil libertarians who are ever on the alert to oppose tyranny 'failed to take into account man's almost infinite appetite for distractions.' In Orwell's *1984*, Huxley added, people are controlled by inflicting pain. In *Brave New World*, they are controlled by inflicting pleasure. In short, Orwell feared that what we hate will ruin us. Huxley feared that what we love will ruin us."[6] (Based on Neil Postman's foreword).

■ ■ ■

From the text the reader may infer that:

A. The author believes that Aldous Huxley is the best British author of the 19th century.
B. The author is opposed to banning books.
C. The author is concerned because culture has been trialized.
D. The author is probably an ecologically minded liberal.

The reader may infer:

A. The author is concerned about the future of the world.
B. The author likes science fiction.
C. The author thinks Huxley and Orwell say the same thing.
D. None of the above.

Top Ten Most Frequent Essay Problems

1. Agreement between the subject and verb: Use singular forms of verbs with singular subjects and use plural forms of verbs with plural subjects.

   WRONG: Everyone who comes to class are bringing the assignment.
   RIGHT: Everyone who comes to class is bringing the assignment.

2. Using the second person pronoun — "you" and "your" should rarely, if ever, be used in a formal essay.

   WRONG: You know what I mean (too informal).

3. Redundancy: Never use "I think" or "It seems to me."

   WRONG: I think that is true.
   RIGHT: That is true. (We know you think it, or you would not write it!)

4. Tense consistency: Use the same tense (usually present) throughout the paper.

   WRONG: I *was* ready to go, but my friend *is* tired.
   RIGHT: I *am* ready to go but my friend *is* tired.

5 Misplaced Modifiers: Place the phrase or clause close to its modifier.

   WRONG: The man drove the car with a bright smile into the garage.
   RIGHT: The man with a bright smile drove the car into the garage.

6. Antecedent Pronoun Problems: Make sure pronouns match (agree) in number and gender with their antecedents.

   WRONG: Mary and Susan both enjoyed her dinner.
   RIGHT: Mary and Susan both enjoyed their dinners.

7. Parallelism: Make certain that your list/sentence includes similar phrase types.

   WRONG: I like to take a walk and swimming.
   RIGHT: I like walking and swimming

8. Affect vs. effect: *affect* is a verb; *effect* is a noun unless it means to achieve.

   WRONG: His mood effects me negatively.
   RIGHT: His mood affects me negatively.
   RIGHT: The effects of his mood are devastating.

9. Dangling Prepositions: Rarely end a sentence with an unmodified preposition.

   WRONG: Who were you speaking to?
   RIGHT: To whom were you speaking?

10. Transitions: Make certain that paragraphs are connected with transitions (e.g., furthermore, therefore, in spite of).

   RIGHT: Furthermore, Jack London loves to describe animal behavior.

> *You can find your way across this country using burger joints the way a navigator uses stars. . . . We have munched Bridge burgers in the shadow of the Brooklyn Bridge and Cable burgers hard by the Golden Gate, Dixie burgers in the sunny South and Yankee Doodle burgers in the North. . . . We had a Capitol Burger — guess where. And so help us, in the inner courtyard of the Pentagon, a Penta burger."*[7]
> — Charles Kuralt

Problem Sentence	Problem Number	Correct Sentence
I believe that Nazi Germany started World War II.		
Hitler attacked Stalin in 1941; he destroyed most of Russia's military.		
The German army attacked on July 22, 1941, but the Russian army is not ready		
The German aoldier attacked the train station with a black SS uniform.		
The surprise attack completely affected the outcome of the first year of fighting.		
The German Army loved to fight and overwhelming its enemies.		
You should know that Germany almost captured Moscow in 1941.		
Every soldier finished their tour of duty.		
Hitler and his generals enjoyed his victories.		
Ultimately the German army won the Kiev campaign because they tried to.		

"There is a great deal of difference between an eager man who wants to read a book and a tired man who wants a book to read."[8]

— G.K. Chesterton

Crossing the CREEPY LINE

Google CEO Eric Schmidt made the now infamous remark about Google's practice of getting very close to the "creepy line" but not going over. With the decision to release an update to Google Goggles that will allow cell phone owners to identify human faces, Google has arguably crossed "the creepy line."

What this would effectively permit is the identification of people on the street or in a public place by simply pointing your phone camera at them.

Now that is creepy.

The need to control one's privacy is basic. We like to remain unknown in a crowd, or at least we deserve the privilege to reveal ourselves to whomever we please. If we commit a crime, perhaps that right is abrogated. We may be, even should be, identified and apprehended. But the notion than an innocent bystander be identified by perfect strangers, gratuitously, randomly, is creepy.

Human beings are created in the image of God and do not deserved to be mishandled by Mr. Schmidt. Only God deserves to peer into our souls, or metaphorically, to focus his cell phone on us and identify us. Joseph Conrad, in *Lord Jim* warns, "There is something haunting in the light of the moon; it has all the dispassionateness of a disembodied soul, and something of its inconceivable mystery."[1] Zip! With the focus of an iPhone the mystery disappears.

Many people "are rightfully scared of it," one journalist said. You think? "In particular, women say, 'Oh, my God. Imagine this guy takes a picture of me, and then he knows my address just because somewhere on the web there is an association of my address with my photo.' That's a scary thought. So I think there is merit in finding a good route that makes the power of this technology available in a good way."

In a good way. Use this technology in a good way. Interesting thought. We dare not STOP using the creepy thing — we have to find a laudable reason to use it. I am sure Eichmann appreciated that irony when he realized that the technology was there to murder six million Jews so he might as well do it. Surely, if the technology is there, we have to use it.

I like Google's response — a typical post-modern response: "I think we are taking a sort of cautious route with this," Google said. "It's a sensitive area, and it's kind of a subjective call on how you would do it."

Another signature mark of the times: Each person decides for himself if he uses a certain thing.

No, not this time. I don't want perverts to identify and to visit my grandchildren whenever they like! I don't care if the technology is there or not. Get rid of it.

Now that is a novel idea — get rid of it. What ya say? Get rid of it? That is exactly what I am saying. Get rid of the technology.

SCRIPTURE

"O LORD, you have searched me and you know me. You know when I sit and when I rise; you perceive my thoughts from afar. You discern my going out and my lying down; you are familiar with all my ways. Before a word is on my tongue you know it completely, O LORD. You hem me in — behind and before; you have laid your hand upon me. Such knowledge is too wonderful for me, too lofty for me to attain."

~ Psalm 139:1–6

PRAYER POINTS
POSITIVE IDENTITY

"For we are God's workmanship, created in Christ Jesus to do good works, which God prepared in advance for us to do."

~ Ephesians 2:10

Not only do we want never to use it, we need to erase our footsteps and get rid of our ability to do the thing. There is no good, no possible good, in a perfect stranger being able to identify another private human being without his knowledge or consent.

Can we deal with that? Giving up bad technology? I doubt it.

It is coming, folks. Apparently Google got over its concerns and has decided to roll facial recognition out in a mobile context. Science and technology have their own logic and momentum. Because something is possible there's an impulse to see it realized or implemented in the world. Perhaps there's such identification at Google with "innovation" that it was "culturally" impossible for Google not to roll this out.

Creepy, I tell you, creepy.

Okay. I can and do turn off the television. I show discipline in what Internet sites I visit. I try to put boundaries on myself and help others do the same. But this is different. This is another person, perhaps a stranger, focusing his cell phone camera on me and revealing my private affairs. This stranger presumes to know me intimately without my consent. It is a form of abuse.

Don't get me wrong, there are those whose cameras are welcome to focus on me. There is one power, one power who does know me. Always has, always will. Knows my next thought, predestined my next action. Someone who is in absolute control of everything — Almighty God. But He alone deserves this sort of power. He loves me, He cares for me, His Son died on the Cross at Calvary for me.

I do not fear His perusal, but my friend, if you swing your Motorola toward my grandchildren and I think you are identifying them, not merely taking a picture, I am going to smack you.

Not really. But I am going to think you and Google are creepy. Take that.

MATH

Probability

- If you roll a die, what are the chances of rolling a two?

- If you roll a die, what is the probability that you will roll an even number?

- A bag contains 3 red marbles, 3 blue marbles, and 1 green marble. If a marble is drawn from the bag at random, what is the probability that the marble will be blue?

- A bag contains 6 numbered tiles. The numbers in the bag are 3, 7, 8, 9, 13, and 15. If you randomly draw one tile from the bag, what is the probability of picking an odd number?

- Mr. Jones has a hot air balloon. Because the basket is so small, he can take only one child for a ride with him. Mary, Carla, John, Lynda, Peter, and Janessa all want to go. They each write their name on a piece of paper and place them in a hat. Mr. Jones randomly selects one child to go with him. What is the probability that he will select a boy? What is the probability that he will select a girl?[2]

" *Part of the American myth is that people who are handed the skin of a dead sheep at graduating time think that it will keep their minds alive forever.*"[3]

— John Mason Brown

Test Day Procedures

- Arrive at your assigned test center 30 minutes prior to the reporting time (8:00 a.m.) listed on your admission ticket. You will not be admitted to the test if you are late.

- Bring acceptable identification. You will not be admitted to the test without it. Homeschoolers should be very careful to have picture IDs and multiple IDs (driver's license, social security card, passport).

- ACT staff will check your ID and admission ticket, admit you to your test room, direct you to a seat, and provide test materials. You normally cannot choose your seat, but if you can, try to sit away from gabby friends and away from the bathrooms (that might have overflow crowds during the break)

- You may use a permitted calculator on the mathematics test only. Some models and features are prohibited. You are responsible for knowing if your calculator is permitted and bringing it to the test center. Do not use your cell phone as a calculator and do not have a calculator that also has a thesaurus or dictionary.

- A short break is scheduled after the first two tests. You will not be allowed to use cell phones or any electronic devices during the break, and you may not bring food or drinks back to the test room. You should, however, walk around during the break. Do not merely sit. Eat your snack (ham sandwich or something substantial). If you take the ACT Plus Writing, you will have time before the writing test to relax and sharpen your pencils.

- Students taking the ACT (No Writing) with standard time are normally dismissed at about 12:15 p.m.; students taking the ACT Plus Writing are normally dismissed about 1:00 p.m.

- If you do not complete all your tests for any reason, tell a member of the testing staff whether or not you want your answer document scored before you leave the test center. If you do not, all tests attempted will be scored (adapted from the ACT site).

VOCABULARY

The Brothers Karamazov[4]
Fyodor Dostoyevsky

Dostoyevsky's last and greatest novel, *The Brothers Karamazov*, is both a crime drama and a pedantic debate over truth. In fact, no novel — since Plato's *Republic* — so fervently addresses the issue. The worthless landowner Fyodor Pavlovich Karamazov is murdered. His sons — the atheist intellectual Ivan, the hot-blooded Dmitry, and the saintly novice Alyosha — are all at some level involved. As one critic explains, "Bound up with this intense family drama is Dostoyevsky's exploration of many deeply felt ideas about the existence of God, the question of human freedom, the collective nature of guilt, the disastrous consequences of rationalism."[5]

The novel is also richly comic: the Russian Orthodox Church, the legal system, and even the author's most cherished causes and beliefs are presented with a note of irreverence, so that orthodoxy and radicalism, sanity and madness, love and hatred, right and wrong — all are no longer mutually exclusive. Rebecca West considered it "the allegory for the world's maturity, but with children to the fore. The new translations do full justice to Dostoyevsky's genius, especially in the use of the spoken word, ranging over every mode of human expression."[6]

Suggested Vocabulary Words

A. At the time of Yefim Petrovitch's death, Alyosha had two more years to complete at the <u>provincial</u> gymnasium. The <u>inconsolable</u> widow went almost immediately after his death for a long visit to Italy with her whole family, which consisted only of women and girls. (part 1, book 1, chapter 4)

B. As he hastened out of the hermitage <u>precincts</u> to reach the monastery in time to serve at the Father Superior's dinner, he felt a sudden <u>pang</u> at his heart, and stopped short. He seemed to hear again Father Zossima's words, foretelling his approaching end. What he had foretold so exactly must <u>infallibly</u> come to pass. Alyosha believed that <u>implicitly</u>. But how could he go? (part 1, book 2, chapter 7)

C. "Quite so, quite so," cried Ivan, with <u>peculiar</u> eagerness, obviously <u>annoyed</u> at being interrupted, "in anyone else this moment would be only due to yesterday's impression and would be only a moment. But with Katerina Ivanovna's character, that moment will last all her life. What for anyone else would be only a promise is for her an everlasting burdensome, grim perhaps, but <u>unflagging</u> duty. And she will be <u>sustained</u> by the feeling of this duty being fulfilled. Your life, Katerina Ivanovna, will henceforth be spent in painful <u>brooding</u> over your own feelings, your own heroism, and your own suffering; but in the end that suffering will be softened and will pass into sweet <u>contemplation</u> of the fulfillment of a bold and proud design. Yes, proud it certainly is, and desperate in any case, but a triumph for you. And the consciousness of it will at last be a source of complete satisfaction and will make you resigned to everything else." (part 2, book 4, chapter 5)

D. "After a month of hopeless love and moral <u>degradation</u>, during which he betrayed his <u>betrothed</u> and <u>appropriated</u> money entrusted to his honour, the prisoner was driven almost to frenzy, almost to madness by continual jealousy — and of whom? His father! And the worst of it was that the crazy old man was alluring and <u>enticing</u> the object of his affection by means of that very three thousand roubles, which the son looked upon as his own property, part of his inheritance from his mother, of which his father was cheating him. Yes, I admit it was hard to bear! It might well drive a man to madness. It was not the money, but the fact that this money was used with such revolting cynicism to ruin his happiness!" (part 3, book 12, chapter 7)

Organization and Writing Strategy

What sentence(s) should be removed from the following paragraph?

Since the end of the civil war in the United States, whoever has occasion to name the three most distinguished representatives of our national greatness is apt to name Washington, Lincoln, and Grant. Not that General Rosecran shouldn't be in the mix. He was a pretty good general. General Grant is now our national military hero. Of Washington it has often been said that he was "first in war, first in peace, and first in the hearts of his countrymen." George Washington, of course, lived in Virginia anyway. When this eulogy was wholly just the nation had been engaged in no war on a grander scale than the war for independence. That war, in the numbers engaged, in the multitude and renown of its battles, in the territory over which its campaigns were extended, in its destruction of life and waste of property, in the magnitude of the interests at stake (but not in the vital importance of the issue), was far inferior to the Civil War. And you should think about World War II — now that was a great war. It happens quite naturally, as in so many other affairs in this world, that the comparative physical magnitude of the conflicts has much influence in moulding the popular estimate of the rank of the victorious commanders.[7] — William Allen, *Ulysses S. Grant*

S C I E N C E

What is the purpose of this scientific instrument?

I. To measure temperature.
II. To measure atmospheric pressure
III. To measure salt content in liquid
IV. To measure snowfall totals

A. I
B. II
C. I & II
D. I & III
E. IV
F. None
G. All

" *Science can only ascertain what is, but not what should be, and outside of its domain value judgments of all kinds remain necessary.*"[8]
— Albert Einstein

Top Ten Most Frequent Essay Problems

You should organize your sentences into groups of related ideas, or paragraphs. Each paragraph should have a main idea or topic sentence. Next, the body of the paragraph develops the main idea with supporting facts. Finally, a new paragraph begins when the scene or topic changes.

In the following essay on George Herbert's poem "The Collar,"[9] indent where each new paragraph begins.

> The struggle is daily. There are choices we make, people we talk to, and sights that we see. This all is unavoidable, and goes on outside of us but mostly inside. This struggle forces us to choose between the hard way of the cross, or the easy broad path leading to destruction. For example, George Herbert (1593–1633), one of the 17th century poets, wrote a beautiful poem titled, "The Collar." This poem is written in the first person about himself, and not only identifies the struggle between good and evil, but in it he also faces the struggle, and in the end, he wins. The poem begins with the words, "I struck the board, and cried, 'No more! I will abroad.' " Here Herbert is fearfully running away from God and telling Him "no more," and to leave him alone. He knows that he has been given free will, "My lines and life are free; free as the road, loose as the wind, as large as store." But he is not sure he wants to use it, "Shall I still be in suit?" Next, he begins to struggle with what he has lost, "Have I no harvest but a thorn to let me blood, and not restore what I have lost with cordial fruit? Is the year only lost to me? Have I no bays to crown it? No flowers no garlands gay? All blasted? All wasted?" But telling himself that that cannot be all, "Not so, my heart; but there is fruit, and thou hast hands," he begins to calm down, and see what he has really been given. Then the struggle changes, from being a struggle between running away or staying and becoming having to let go. "Leave thy cold dispute of what is fit and not; forsake thy cage, thy rope of sands, which petty thoughts have made." Here Herbert writes beautiful examples of how we are often tied up in things that we think are important. But in reality if we shake them off, we find that they are of no use to us at all. He goes on to say, "Tie up thy fears," which is another example of leaving behind something that we do not need and cannot enter the Kingdom with. The poem ends very simply in submission, "Me thoughts I heard one calling, 'Child'; and I replied, 'My Lord.' " At that point there is no struggle, he is at complete peace. Leaving behind the struggle to immerse oneself in complete submission is an idea at which some people would laugh. But not George Herbert. When he wrote this poem, he knew that it was a beautiful action. And so it has been captured onto paper, for all of us (Anna).

Identifying Topic Sentences

A topic sentence expresses the main idea or purpose of a paragraph. All the other sentences in the paragraph support that main idea. Underline the topic sentences in the follow essay.

"The Lost Tools of Learning"
Dorothy Sayers

That I, whose experience of teaching is extremely limited, should presume to discuss education is a matter, surely, that calls for no apology. It is a kind of behavior to which the present climate of opinion is wholly favorable. Bishops air their opinions about economics; biologists, about metaphysics; inorganic chemists, about theology; the most irrelevant people are appointed to highly technical ministries; and plain, blunt men write to the papers to say that Epstein and Picasso do not know how to draw. Up to a certain point, and provided that the criticisms are made with a reasonable modesty, these activities are commendable. Too much specialization is not a good thing. There is also one excellent reason why the veriest amateur may feel entitled to have an opinion about education. For if we are not all professional teachers, we have all, at some time or another, been taught. Even if we learnt nothing — perhaps in particular if we learnt nothing — our contribution to the discussion may have a potential value.

However, it is in the highest degree improbable that the reforms I propose will ever be carried into effect. Neither the parents, nor the training colleges, nor the examination boards, nor the boards of governors, nor the ministries of education, would countenance them for a moment. For they amount to this: that if we are to produce a society of educated people, fitted to preserve their intellectual freedom amid the complex pressures of our modern society, we must turn back the wheel of progress some four or five hundred years, to the point at which education began to lose sight of its true object. . . .

When we think about the remarkably early age at which the young men went up to university in, let us say, Tudor times, and thereafter were held fit to assume responsibility for the conduct of their own affairs, are we altogether comfortable about that artificial prolongation of intellectual childhood and adolescence into the years of physical maturity which is so marked in our own day? To postpone the acceptance of responsibility to a late date brings with it a number of psychological complications which, while they may interest the psychiatrist, are scarcely beneficial either to the individual or to society. The stock argument in favor of postponing the school-leaving age and prolonging the period of education generally is there is now so much more to learn than there was in the Middle Ages. This is partly true, but not wholly. The modern boy and girl are certainly taught more subjects — but does that always mean that they actually know more?[10]

R E A D I N G
Infer from the Text

Many years ago, before railroads were thought of, a company of Connecticut farmers, who had heard marvelous stories of the richness of the land in the West, sold their farms, packed up their goods, bade adieu to their friends, and with their families started for Ohio.

After weeks of travel over dusty roads, they came to a beautiful valley, watered by a winding river. The hills around were fair and sunny. There were groves of oaks, and maples, and lindens. The air was fragrant with honeysuckle and jasmine. There was plenty of game. The swift-footed deer browsed the tender grass upon the hills. Squirrels chattered in the trees and the ringdoves cooed in the depths of the forest. The place was so fertile and fair, so pleasant and peaceful, that the emigrants made it their home, and called it New Hope.

They built a mill upon the river. They laid out a wide, level street, and a public square, erected a school-house, and then a church. One of their number opened a store. Other settlers came, and, as the years passed by, the village rang with the shouts of children pouring from the school-house for a frolic upon the square. Glorious times they had beneath the oaks and maples.

One of the jolliest of the boys was Paul Parker, only son of Widow Parker, who lived in a little old house, shaded by a great maple, on the outskirts of the village. Her husband died when Paul was in his cradle. Paul's grandfather was still living. The people called him "Old Pensioner Parker," for he fought at Bunker Hill, and received a pension from government. He was hale and hearty, though more than eighty years of age.

The pension was the main support of the family. They kept a cow, a pig, turkeys, and chickens, and, by selling milk and eggs, which Paul carried to their customers, they brought the years round without running in debt. Paul's pantaloons had a patch on each knee, but he laughed just as loud and whistled just as cheerily for all that.

In summer he went barefoot. He did not have to turn out at every mud-puddle, and he could plash into the mill-pond and give the frogs a crack over the head without stopping to take off stockings and shoes. Paul did not often have a dinner of roast beef, but he had an abundance of bean porridge, brown bread, and milk.[11] (Charles Coffin, *Winning His Way*)

■ ■ ■

Why does the author have the farmers leaving Connecticut (a known geographical location) and moving to a place named New Hope (an unknown geographical location)?

A. The author does not think this information is important.
B. The setting is unimportant.
C. The author had no particular reason in mind.
D. The author wished to use New Hope as a type of place, a place representing any place that was generous and bountiful.

What sort of person was Paul Parker?

A. A selfish, unhappy boy.
B. A generous, unselfish, happy boy.
C. A veteran of the Revolutionary War.
D. A physically challenged boy who received a government pension.

Based upon the information provided in this passage, the setting is most likely:

A. Early 20th century rural America
B. Late 18th century rural America
C. Early 19th century rural America
D. Late 19th century rural America

Captain America:

A DIFFERENT KIND OF HERO

SCRIPTURE

"And I tell you that you are Peter, and on this rock I will build my church, and the gates of Hades will not overcome it."

~ Matthew 16:18

For years, the American notion of a hero has been accosted, compromised, and generally diluted. Gone are the days when John Wayne rode into town and took care of business. We knew he was good — really good — and we were comforted by the fact that he would kill no one who did not deserve to die. "A man's got to do what a man's got to do," is a quote attributed to Wayne. "Women have the right to work wherever they want, as long as they have the dinner ready when you get home."[1] Oops! I guess he said that, too, but never mind. . . .

Not so today. Heroes exude empathy not goodness. Witness Robert Downey's flawed, self-centered Ironman. Or Hugh Jackson's moody Wolverine. And who can forget the poor, pathetic Hulk? Everyone wants to forget the shady, morally dubious Christian Bale's Batman! But my personal favorite for sissy of the year is Spiderman. One Freudian self-identity crisis after another. He whines all the time. Can you imagine John Wayne whining?

One sidebar — I am arguably a candidate for sissy of the year myself. Last week I had to have a tetanus booster. Don't you hate doctor waiting rooms? And I emphasize WAITING rooms — sometimes for hours. As I waited for my tetanus shot I imagined myself waiting for the guillotine with Sydney Carton at the end of *A Tale of Two Cities*.

Finally my executioner appeared. "Roll up your sleeve," the perfunctory and sturdy 8´3" Nurse Roxanne quipped.

"Hello," I replied.

"Do you mind shots?" the Nurse Roxanne asked as she ignored my greeting.

"Yes, I do," I quivered, almost in tears.

"Too bad," Nurse Roxanne replied with the first hint of enthusiasm.

I muttered, "It is a far better thing I have done than I have ever done before. . . ."

Nurse Roxanne, who obviously had not read Dickens, attacked me with the needle as if she were going after a dart board.

I whimpered a little and Nurse Roxanne frowned and pointed her index finger at me, "No wimps allowed."

PRAYER POINTS
RESPECT

"Show proper respect to everyone: love the brotherhood of believers, fear God, honor the king."

~ 1 Peter 2:17

No wimps allowed. Yes, fellow Americans, we have dumbed down, glamorized, and wimped down our heroes to the point where they hardly seem to be heroes at all.

But now, suddenly, on the silver screen, appears Captain America. Captain America is a different kind of hero. In 1940s America, ordinary, unspectacular, five-feet-something, Steve Rogers inadvertently receives an injection that turns him into a superhero. But not a run-of-the-mill hero, he is actually a genuine hero. As one reviewer explains, "He's got a lot of ailments, but it hasn't made him bitter or jaded in anything. Even after he has been given his great gift, he still continues to do the right thing."[2] No that is a novel idea — doing the right thing. Take that, Will Smith and your character Hancock!

Yes, a new hero has arrived — a hero who does the right thing without equivocation or self-interest. Captain America. Or is he that new after all?

Sounds to me like Moses who left the courts of Egypt to obey God. Or Joshua who conquered the Promised Land. Or Peter, even after much failure, found that even hell itself could not prevail against the Church he founded.

Yes, and again perhaps we meet a man who even John Wayne would like. Wayne was fond of saying, "Courage is being scared to death — but saddling up anyway."[3] Roll up your sleeves, America — Nurse Roxanne and Captain America are finally here. And there is no room for wimps.

M A T H

Algebra Word Problems

- What number added to twice itself and 40 more will make a sum equal to eight times the number?

- Divide the number 72 into two parts such that one part shall be one-eighth of the other.

W R I T I N G

In persuasive writing, an argument can be developed these three ways:

1. Dialectic: The writer presents two positions and concludes with a compromise between both.
2. Inductive: The writer presents all the facts and then forms a conclusion.
3. Deductive: The writer presents his argument(s) and then applies it (them) to several situations/incidences.

"To read is to fly: it is to soar to a point of vantage which gives a view over wide terrains of history, human variety, ideas, shared experience and the fruits of many inquiries."[4]

— A.C. Grayling

The cold passed reluctantly from the earth, and the retiring fogs revealed an army stretched out on the hills, resting. As the landscape changed from brown to green, the army awakened, and began to tremble with eagerness at the noise of rumors. It cast its eyes upon the roads, which were growing from long troughs of liquid mud to proper thoroughfares. A river, amber-tinted in the shadow of its banks, purled at the army's feet; and at night, when the stream had become of a sorrowful blackness, one could see across it the red, eyelike gleam of hostile camp-fires set in the low brows of distant hills.

Once a certain tall soldier developed virtues and went resolutely to wash a shirt. He came flying back from a brook waving his garment bannerlike. He was swelled with a tale he had heard from a reliable friend, who had heard it from a truthful cavalryman, who had heard it from his trustworthy brother, one of the orderlies at division headquarters. He adopted the important air of a herald in red and gold.

"We're goin' t' move t'morrah — sure," he said pompously to a group in the company street. "We're goin' 'way up the river, cut across, an' come around in behint 'em."

To his attentive audience he drew a loud and elaborate plan of a very brilliant campaign. When he had finished, the blue-clothed men scattered into small arguing groups between the rows of squat brown huts. A negro teamster who had been dancing upon a cracker box with the hilarious encouragement of twoscore soldiers was deserted. He sat mournfully down. Smoke drifted lazily from a multitude of quaint chimneys.

"It's a lie! that's all it is — a thunderin' lie!" said another private loudly. His smooth face was flushed, and his hands were thrust sulkily into his trouser's pockets. He took the matter as an affront to him. "I don't believe the derned old army's ever going to move. We're set. I've got ready to move eight times in the last two weeks, and we ain't moved yet."

The tall soldier felt called upon to defend the truth of a rumor he himself had introduced. He and the loud one came near to fighting over it.

A corporal began to swear before the assemblage. He had just put a costly board floor in his house, he said. During the early spring he had refrained from adding extensively to the comfort of his environment because he had felt that the army might start on the march at any moment. Of late, however, he had been impressed that they were in a sort of eternal camp.

Many of the men engaged in a spirited debate. One outlined in a peculiarly lucid manner all the plans of the commanding general. He was opposed by men who advocated that there were other plans of campaign. They clamored at each other, numbers making futile bids for the popular attention. Meanwhile, the soldier who had fetched the rumor bustled about with much importance. He was continually assailed by questions.[5]
(Stephen Crane, *Red Badge of Courage*)

Why does the author begin this passage with a picture of the setting?

- A. No particular reason
- B. The author wishes to establish that God is absent.
- C. The setting foreshadows ominous events.
- D. The comparison of the camp to a snake implies a naturalist theme.

What metaphor is used in the first paragraph?

- A. A sleeping snake
- B. A winding road
- C. A tight rope
- D. None of the above

Why do the characters have no names?

- A. No particular reason
- B. The characters are unimportant.
- C. The characters represent a type-character.
- D. Their names will appear as needed.

Why does the author use colloquial language?

A. Colloquial language is humorous

B. Colloquial language draws the reader to the protagonist

C. Colloquial language creates needed realism

D. Colloquial language reinforces character fears of the unknown

What is the tone of this piece?

A. Serious

B. Humorous

C. Cynical

D. Sarcastic

SCIENCE

A mushroom consists of a stem and a cap, or pileus. The cap is the most conspicuous part. The color varies from white and the lightest hues of brown up to the brightest yellow and scarlet. Its size is from an eighth of an inch to sixteen inches and more in diameter. The surface is smooth or covered with little grains (granular) or with minute scales (squamulose) shining like satin, or kid-like in its texture. It may be rounded and depressed (concave), elevated (convex), level (plane), or with a little mound in the centre (umbonate). It may be covered with warts, marked with lines (striate), or zoned with circles. The margin may be acute or obtuse, rolled backward or upward (revolute), or rolled inward (involute); it may be thick or thin.

It is interesting to observe where different mushrooms love to dwell. Some are always found on roadsides, as if seeking the notice of passers-by. These are the Clitocybes and Stropharia, and many of the cup-fungi, while the Boleti take shelter in clay banks and hide in every cranny and nook that they can find. Russulas are seen in open woods, rising out of the earth, also the Lactarius, which seems to like the shade of trees. The Cortinarius also prefers their shelter. The Coprinus loves the pastures and fields, near houses and barns, and dwells in groups upon the lawns. The Hypholoma grows in clusters on the stumps of trees. Marasmius is found among dead twigs and leaves. The white Amanitas flourish in woods and open ground. There are some, like Pleurotus, that grow in trunks of trees, and make their way through openings in the bark. Every dead tree or branch in the forest is crowded with all species of Polyporus, while carpets, damp cellars, plaster walls and sawdust are favorite abodes of many fungi.[6] (Ellen Dallas and Caroline Burgin, *Among the Mushrooms*)

Based on this passage what statements are true:

I. Mushrooms generally thrive in cool, moist areas.

II. Marasmius mostly grows among dead twigs and leaves.

III. Mushrooms would be found in the same genus as Abies concolor, white fir trees

    A. I

    B. II

    C. I, II, III

    D. I and III

    E. I and II

    F. All

ENGLISH

Punctuation

Rewrite the following material. All punctuation has been removed.

indian history begins 4,000 years ago india is a success story india's population recently exceeded 1 billion people yet a noted indian historian said that " although it is difficult to accept, the indians totally lacked the historical sense" the ancient indians made great inroads into astronomy, physics, mathematics, all kinds of literature and arts but never seriously took to documenting their history and their indifference has cost their posterity very dearly civilization, when an agricultural economy gave rise to extensive urbanization and trade the second stage occurred around 1000 bc, when the ganga-yamuna river basin and several southern river deltas experienced extensive agricultural expansion and population growth

■ ■ ■

When you write, choose words that are appropriate to the setting and audience. In this case, the ACT, write in the most precise, informed style that you have. Do not "hang out" on the ACT! Write with as much energy and talent as you have. At the same time, don't use pretentious, fancy words if a simpler, more precise word will do.

VOCABULARY

The Chosen[7]
Chaim Potok

The Chosen is basically the story of two cultures colliding. On one level it is the story of Orthodox Judaism versus Hasidic Judaism. On the other hand, it embraces life at many different levels. In fact, it also celebrates human virtues like respect and loyalty.

> "*Shall I refuse my dinner because I do not fully understand the process of digestion?*"[8]
> ~ Oliver Heaviside

Suggested Vocabulary Words

A. I had spent five days in a hospital and the world around seemed <u>sharpened</u> now and <u>pulsing</u> with life. (chapter 5)

B. A span of life is nothing. But the man who lives that <u>span</u>, he is something. (chapter 13)

C. It makes us aware of how <u>frail</u> and tiny we are and of how much we must depend upon the Master of the Universe. (chapter 18)

D. We shook hands and I watched him walk quickly away, tall, lean, bent <u>forward</u> with eagerness and hungry for the future, his metal capped shoes tapping against the sidewalk. (last chapter)

WRITING

Supporting Details

As we saw in the previous exercise, writers often place the topic sentence in the beginning of the paragraph. Then they provide supporting details. Analyze the following paragraph by completing the chart below.

Paragraph	When we think about the remarkably early age at which the young men went up to university in, let us say, Tudor times, and thereafter were held fit to assume responsibility for the conduct of their own affairs, are we altogether comfortable about that artificial prolongation of intellectual childhood and adolescence into the years of physical maturity which is so marked in our own day? To postpone the acceptance of responsibility to a late date brings with it a number of psychological complications which, while they may interest the psychiatrist, are scarcely beneficial either to the individual or to society. The stock argument in favor of postponing the school-leaving age and prolonging the period of education generally is there is now so much more to learn than there was in the Middle Ages. This is partly true, but not wholly. The modern boy and girl are certainly taught more subjects — but does that always mean that they actually know more?[9]
Main Idea	
Detail	
Detail	
Detail	

PRETENDING

SCRIPTURE

"There the angel of the LORD appeared to him in flames of fire from within a bush. Moses saw that though the bush was on fire it did not burn up."

~ Exodus 3:2

I like to pretend.

Every trip to the post office, every trip across country — it doesn't matter where I go — I like to pretend I am on a mission.

My wife Karen doesn't like to join my team, or army, or panzer group — even when I offer her a lieutenancy. Of course I am always the captain, but that is incidental.

Karen just frowns at me.

"Look to the south, good buddy," I warn. "The Nazis are coming fast. . . ."

"Keep your eyes on the road, Jim," she scolds.

"10-4," I respond as I pull the Tiger Tank (aka Toyota Prius) back to the center of the road.

How about you?

Why not make a mundane trip to the grocery store into a mission behind enemy lines? Why not make a trip to church into a scouting mission across the Sahara?

Life is interesting enough, I suppose, without all the pretending, but it is never as much fun.

My seven-year-old grandson Zion will pretend with me.

Last Christmas high command gave us a mission to take important orders to Second Army (i.e., Karen told me to take a letter to our mail box at the end of our 150-yard driveway). Brave Master Sergeant Zion volunteered to join me.

"General Granna (i.e., Karen)," I warned. "Do not be surprised if we don't make it back alive. My will is in the safe deposit box. If we don't make it, honey, know that I died with your gentle face in my mind. "

"Don't miss the mail run, Jim," Karen responded.

"Yes ma'am," I deferentially responded. "10-4."

After establishing our password, Zion and I grabbed our browning automatics (broken broom handles), grenades (plastic donuts from Zion's sister Emily's pretend kitchen set), and bowie knives (Karen's carrots) and quietly, with great alacrity, approached the dangerous German bunker (mail box).

"Sergeant, you cover my back. I am going in, Good Buddy!"

PRAYER POINTS
MERCY

"Be merciful, just as your Father is merciful."

~ Luke 6:36

Along the way, of course, we were attacked by banzai warriors (our four barn cats), a German Stuka (our Black Lab), and an enemy patrol (our neighbors on a walk). Against all odds, we made it.

But not without casualties. I sustained a serious leg injury and Zion was nicked in the left arm. In fact, we lost several good pretend companions.

Sly Zion, halfway, as we hid behind the chicken coop, insisted on a field promotion to lieutenant or he would desert. I reluctantly agreed. In the midst of such carnage, what was I to do?

After such an arduous and dangerous mission, newly promoted Lieutenant Zion and I celebrated at Granna's kitchen table. She unceremoniously served us A-rations (Christmas cookies) and mess coffee (hot chocolate with marshmallows).

It doesn't get much better than this, 10-4?

V O C A B U L A R Y

The Civil War[1]
Shelby Foote

Newsweek magazine described Foote's three-volume masterpiece this way: "Foote is a novelist who temporarily abandoned fiction to apply the novelist's shaping hand to history: his model is not Thucydides but the Iliad, and his story, innocent of notes and formal biography, has a literary design."[2] This great historical work has the distinction of being the best single work on the American Civil War. It is well worth the effort to read all three volumes.

Suggested Vocabulary Words
A. Perhaps by now McClellan had learned to abide the <u>tantrums</u> and <u>exasperations</u> of his former friend and sympathizer. (vol. 1)
B. McClellan was quite aware of the danger of <u>straddling</u> what he called "the <u>confounded</u> Chickahominy." (vol. 1)
C. In addition to <u>retaining</u> the services of Seward and Chase, both excellent men at their respective posts, he had managed to turn aside the <u>wrath</u> of the <u>Jacobins</u> without increasing their bitterness toward himself or <u>incurring</u> their open hatred. . . . <u>Paradoxically</u>, because of the way he had done it. . . . (vol. 2)
D. Stuart had accepted the <u>gambit</u>. . . . (volume 3)
E. Poor as the plan was in the first place, mainly because of its necessary surrender of the <u>initiative</u> to the enemy, it was rendered even poorer — in fact <u>inoperative</u> — by the speed in which Sherman moved through the supposedly <u>impenetrable</u> swamps. (vol. 3)

M A T H

Algebra Review
• The half and fourth of a certain number are together equal to 75. What is the number?

• What number is that which being increased by one-third and one-half of itself equals 22?

W R I T I N G

Style (Writing and Speaking): Paragraph Main Body

If the introduction is the bait, so to speak, to attract the attention of the readers, the main body is the hook that actually catches readers. It is the meal provided for the readers. Every paragraph has a topic sentence and several supporting sentences; they make up the body of the paper. Every essay has an introductory paragraph that always presents the purpose statement (or thesis) of the essay, and every essay has several supporting paragraphs (the main body).

How many sentences or paragraphs should be in the main body of this prose unit? Enough to develop thoroughly the thesis statement. That may be 3 paragraphs or it may be 300 paragraphs. However, use as few paragraphs as possible to accomplish your purpose. Writing more to just fill up the page is not indicative of good writing. Every sentence that is included in a paragraph should have a reason for being there. Which paragraphs belong in the body of this essay? Check the ones that belong. Here is the introduction:

> Japan is a study of contrasts. On the one hand, it is Asia's first industrialized nation. On the other hand, it is still a very conservative nation.

A. The Japanese could be the most cosmopolitan people in Asia, if not the world. They are so dependent on world markets that it imports virtually all of its iron ore, bauxite, oil, copper, and nickel. Japan relies on foreign supplies for over 90 percent of its coal, natural gas, and lead. Over 85 percent of its total energy is imported from abroad. It is perhaps the greatest importer of agricultural goods. Japan is second only to the United States in terms of the total value of its industrial exports. It is the world's greatest exporter of automobiles; it has the greatest number of merchant ships in the world.

B. Yamato emperors expanded their rule over all of the main islands of Japan except Hokkaido. This ultimately brought great upheaval in Japanese society. Likewise a great smallpox epidemic of 735–737 indelibly changed early Japan. Perhaps one-third of the population perished in those two years.

C. Yet the Japanese people are more intimately tied to their ancient ancestral roots than they are to events in the rest of the world. Third and fourth-generation Japanese, when asked where they are "from," still name the "old home" of their ancestors. Their lives are tied more closely to the ancient rural agricultural rhythms than to the modern industrial cities where they reside.[3]

■ ■ ■

Avoid loaded words. Loaded words are words that will evoke a response — usually a bad one — from your audience. Your audience probably will be secular, mostly progressive (a euphemism for liberal) with attitude! So don't say things like, "If you disagree with me, well, you are going to hell."

ENGLISH

Audience

Different audiences require different writing styles. It matters to whom you are writing a piece! Choose the audience of each passage and circle words that tell why you chose a particular audience. Hint: clues regarding audience lie in word choice and content.

A. Teachers   B. Doctors   C. Magazine for women   D. Teenagers
E. Football fans   F. Computer nerd

_____We conducted a single-center, randomized, controlled trial of arthroscopic surgery in patients with moderate-to-severe osteo-arthritis of the knee.

_____Colston tried to continue playing with the injury during the Saints' 24-20 victory over the Bucs, but finished with only three catches for 26 yards.

_____What is editing? Ruth Culham of the Northwest Regional Education Laboratory separates revision (last month's column topic) from editing (spelling, grammar, capitalization, and punctuation).

_____My guy loves music, and he had just bought himself a new iPod. He's obsessed with the painting *The Great Wave*, and I found an iPod skin with the exact painting on it. He loved it, and now he thinks of me every time he listens to his music!

_____You want: to look bright-eyed. Hide dark circles around the eye area with an apricot-tinted color, or if you have darker skin, one that's one shade lighter than your skin tone.

_____Making the user interface for one device easy, slick, fun, and fast is a challenge. If you have multiple devices and they need to cooperate, the challenge increases dramatically. As wired and wireless communications hardware gets cheaper, the design opportunities for communicating devices become more common.

Active Reading

Call of the Wild[4]

By Jack London

As you read, use these marks to help you understand the text.

✓ This is important.

? This is not clear to me.

☆ Interesting point!

Buck did not read the newspapers, or he would have known that trouble was brewing, not alone for himself, but for every tide-water dog, strong of muscle and with warm, long hair, from Puget Sound to San Diego. Because men, groping in the Arctic darkness, had found a yellow metal, and because steamship and transportation companies were booming the find, thousands of men were rushing into the Northland. These men wanted dogs, and the dogs they wanted were heavy dogs, with strong muscles by which to toil, and furry coats to protect them from the frost.

Buck lived at a big house in the sun-kissed Santa Clara Valley. Judge Miller's place, it was called. It stood back from the road, half hidden among the trees, through which glimpses could be caught of the wide cool veranda that ran around its four sides. The house was approached by graveled driveways which wound about through wide-spreading lawns and under the interlacing boughs of tall poplars. At the rear things were on even a more spacious scale than at the front. There were great stables, where a dozen grooms and boys held forth, rows of vine-clad servants' cottages, an endless and orderly array of outhouses, long grape arbors, green pastures, orchards, and berry patches. Then there was the pumping plant for the artesian well, and the big cement tank where Judge Miller's boys took their morning plunge and kept cool in the hot afternoon.

And over this great demesne Buck ruled. Here he was born, and here he had lived the four years of his life. It was true, there were other dogs, There could not but be other dogs on so vast a place, but they did not count. They came and went, resided in the populous kennels, or lived obscurely in the recesses of the house after the fashion of Toots, the Japanese pug, or Ysabel, the Mexican hairless — strange creatures that rarely put nose out of doors or set foot to ground. On the other hand, there were the fox terriers, a score of them at least, who yelped fearful promises at Toots and Ysabel looking out of the windows at them and protected by a legion of housemaids armed with brooms and mops.

But Buck was neither house-dog nor kennel-dog. The whole realm was his. He plunged into the swimming tank or went hunting with the Judge's sons; he escorted Mollie and Alice, the Judge's daughters, on long twilight or early morning rambles; on wintry nights he lay at the Judge's feet before the roaring library fire; he carried the Judge's grandsons on his back, or rolled them in the grass, and guarded their footsteps through wild adventures down to the fountain in the stable yard, and even beyond, where the paddocks were, and the berry patches. Among the terriers he stalked imperiously, and Toots and Ysabel he utterly ignored, for he was king — king over all creeping, crawling, flying things of Judge Miller's place, humans included.

His father, Elmo, a huge St. Bernard, had been the Judge's inseparable companion, and Buck bid fair to follow in the way of his father. He was not so large — he weighed only one hundred and forty pounds — for his mother, Shep, had been a Scotch shepherd dog. Nevertheless, one hundred and forty pounds, to which was added the dignity that comes of good living and universal respect, enabled him to carry himself in right royal fashion. During the four years since his puppyhood he had lived the life of a sated aristocrat; he had a fine pride

in himself, was even a trifle egotistical, as country gentlemen sometimes become because of their insular situation. But he had saved himself by not becoming a mere pampered house-dog. Hunting and kindred outdoor delights had kept down the fat and hardened his muscles; and to him, as to the cold-tubbing races, the love of water had been a tonic and a health preserver.

And this was the manner of dog Buck in the fall of 1897, when the Klondike strike dragged men from all the world into the frozen North. But Buck did not read the newspapers, and he did not know that Manuel, one of the gardener's helpers, was an undesirable acquaintance. Manuel had one besetting sin. He loved to play Chinese lottery. Also, in his gambling, he had one besetting weakness — faith in a system; and this made his damnation certain. For to play a system requires money, while the wages of a gardener's helper do not lap over the needs of a wife and numerous progeny. (chapter 1)

■ ■ ■

Setting is a critical component of this book. What is the setting in chapter 1?

Which setting is most friendly?

SCIENCE

Conclusions From Data

With the Apache, as with other tribes, the clan organization has an important bearing on property right. Regardless of what property either spouse may hold or own at the time of marriage, the other immediately becomes possessed of his or her moiety. Should the wife die, her husband retains possession of the property held in common so long as he does not remarry, but what might be termed the legal ownership of the wife's half interest becomes vested in her clan. Should he attempt to dissipate the property the members of the deceased wife's clan would at once interfere. If the widower wishes to marry again and the woman of his choice belongs to the clan of his former wife, then he and the new wife become owners in common of all personal property held by him; but if the second wife belongs to a different clan from that of the former wife, then the husband must make actual transfer of half of the common property to the clans people of the deceased woman, who inherited the legal interest in it at their relative's death. The same tribal law applies in the case of a widow.

Much internal strife naturally results whenever an actual distribution of property is made. In the first place, the surviving spouse unwillingly relinquishes the moiety of the property to the relatives of the deceased, and the immediate relatives often disagree with the remainder of the clan. In former times, death of one or more members of contending clans often resulted when the division of much property was made. Having no tribunal for making an equitable division, the matter was left to mutual agreement, resulting in disputes and frequently murder.

With the breaking up of the clans, together with the rapid disintegration of ancient customs and laws, this property law is fast becoming forgotten; but as recently as 1906 such disputes as those mentioned occurred under both the Fort Apache and San Carlos agencies, creating no little ill-feeling. In one instance a man refused to deliver possession of half of his little herd of horses to his deceased wife's clans people when contemplating marriage with another woman, and appealed to the missionaries for aid. He was compelled to make the division, however, before he could remarry.[6]

■ ■ ■

The above anthropological data is evidence that:

A. Apache men are often married to many women.

B. Property rights are very intimately tied to clan connections created in marriage.

C. Polygomy creates several society problems.

D. A only

E. A and C

F. All

BOKONONISM

"I am with you and will watch over you wherever you go, and I will bring you back to this land. I will not leave you until I have done what I have promised you."

~ Genesis 28:15

The late Kurt Vonnegut Jr.'s *Cat's Cradle* creates a new religion, Bokononism. The bible of Bokononism is the "Books of Bokonon," written by Bokonon — a British Episcopalian black from the Carribean island of San Lorenzo whose real name was Lionel Boyd Johnson — as a way to distract the people of the island from their unhappy lives.

What is important to Bokononists? Not God; just one thing: man. Bokononism is a strange, post-modern subjective faith that combines nihilistic, and cynical observations about life and God's will. The supreme act of worship is an intimate act consisting of prolonged physical contact between the naked soles of the feet of two persons, supposed to result in peace and joy between the two communicants. Hmmmm.

I know a lot of Bokononists these days. Post-modern, post-Christian Bokononist American leadership are asking us to suspend belief. Pastor Clinton C. Gardner, in his book *Beyond Belief: Discovering Christianity's New Paradigm* says, "Raised on Christian fundamentalism, he felt liberated by the grand picture of evolution and the empirical science of the Enlightenment."[1] Okay, Brother Clinton! Imagine, there are people who believe that God really loved us enough that He sent His only begotten Son to die for our sins! How uncool! And, get this, some of those remnant fundamentalist Christians — who have not yet bowed down and worshiped at the altar of Bokononism — actually believe that Jesus Christ is the only way, the only truth, the only life. How old-fashioned can you get!

The last line of *Cat's Cradle* includes a warning that I offer here: Pow Tee Weet. At one time song birds were lowered into coal mines to ascertain if methane gas was of dangerous high density. Everything was fine as along as the miners heard "Pow Tee Weet." However, quite literally, if the bird stopped singing, everyone was in trouble.

I wonder how much longer the old song bird will sing.

Pastor Gardner quotes Edward O. Wilson's *Consilience: The Unity of Knowledge*. Wilson's grand conclusion is that "all tangible phenomena, from the birth of stars to the workings of social institutions, are based on material processes that are ultimately reducible, however long and tortuous the sequences, to the laws of physics." He envisions the unification

PRAYER POINTS

"He has showed you, O man, what is good. And what does the LORD require of you? To act justly and to love mercy and to walk humbly with your God."

~ Micah 6:8

of the natural sciences with the social sciences and humanities. As he puts it, "The human condition is the most important frontier of the natural sciences," and "the material world exposed by the natural sciences is the most important frontier of the social sciences and humanities. The consilience argument can be distilled as follows: the two frontiers are the same."[2]

The bird is being lowered into the mines. . . .

Can you imagine how much fun it must be to sit through a sermon with Brother Clinton? Wow — consilience — nice word. What biblical text would he use? Existentialism and nascent naturalism can be pretty cold bedfellows. Won't find it in the lectionary. Ain't gonna mend many broken hearts either!

Seriously, though, these peckerwoods are arguing quite eloquently that (1) my fundamentalism is not only irrelevant, it is uncool and rude (what a low blow!); (2) my belief that that the Bible is the inerrant, infallible Word of God is, well, old fashioned (true); and (3) finally, my belief in a creation that took seven 24-hour days is likewise dumb.

What can I say? I believe all these things and more. The God I serve is amazing, far more amazing than the God of Brothers Clinton and Edward.

Pow tee weet.

WRITING

Eyewitness Account

Most of the ACT prompts will invite you to share an eyewitness account of an actual event of your life. An eyewitness account is an essay that attempts to recreate an event as it actually happened. Using powerful imagery and precise language, the eyewitness account recreates an event in precise language. The reader vicariously experiences the described event. Record an eyewitness account using the following guidelines.

What happened?_____

_____

_____

Who participated?_____

_____

_____

When did it happen?_____

_____

Where did it happen?_____

_____

_____

Why did it happen?_____

_____

_____

How did it happen?_____

_____

_____

What is the significance of the event?_____

_____

_____

MATH

Geometric Word Problems

In order to solve geometric word problems, you will need to have memorized some geometric formulas for at least the basic shapes (circles, squares, right triangles, etc.). Or you can refer to them on the ACT — they are provided — but that takes time. You will usually need to figure out from the word problem which formula to use, and many times you will need more than one formula for one exercise.

A water tank in the shape of a right circular cylinder is thirty feet long and eight feet in diameter. How much material was used in its construction?

A piece of wire 42 cm long is bent into the shape of a rectangle whose width is twice its length. Find the dimensions of the rectangle.[3]

VOCABULARY

The Count of Monte Cristo[4]
Alexandre Dumas

Like so many of Dumas's novels, *Count of Monte Cristo* is set at the end of the Napoleonic era, which the French regard as one of the most exciting and tumultuous eras of modern times. It is a story of Edmond Dantès, a charismatic young seaman falsely accused of treason. The story of his cruel imprisonment, miraculous escape, and carefully engineered revenge keeps the reader spellbound.

Suggested Vocabulary Words

A. Now, in spite of the <u>mobility</u> of his <u>countenance</u>, the command of which, like a finished actor, he had carefully studied before the glass, it was by no means easy for him to assume an air of <u>judicial</u> <u>severity</u>. Except the recollection of the line of politics his father had adopted, and which might <u>interfere</u>, unless he acted with the greatest <u>prudence</u>, with his own career, Gerard de Villefort was as happy as a man could be. (chapter 7)

B. "Then," answered the elder prisoner, "the will of God be done!" and as the old man slowly <u>pronounced</u> those words, an air of <u>profound</u> <u>resignatio</u>n spread itself over his <u>careworn</u> <u>countenance</u>. Dantès gazed on the man who could thus philosophically resign hopes so long and <u>ardently</u> <u>nourish</u>ed with an <u>astonishment</u> <u>mingled</u> with <u>admiration</u>. (chapter 16)

C. He had a very clear idea of the men with whom his lot had been cast. . . . It spared him <u>interpreters</u>, persons always troublesome and frequently indiscreet, gave him great facilities of communication, either with the vessels he met at sea, with the small boats sailing along the coast, or with the people without name, country, or occupation, who are always seen on the quays of seaports, and who live by hidden and mysterious means which we must suppose to be a direct gift of providence, as they have no visible means of support. It is fair to assume that Dantès was on board a smuggler. (chapter 22)

D. It would be difficult to describe the state of <u>stupor</u> in which Villefort left the Palais. Every <u>pulse</u> beat with feverish excitement, every nerve was <u>strained</u>, every vein swollen, and every part of his body seemed to suffer distinctly from the rest, thus multiplying his agony a thousand-fold. He made his way along the <u>corridors</u> through force of habit; he threw <u>aside</u> his magisterial robe, not out of deference to etiquette, but because it was an <u>unbearable</u> burden, a <u>veritable</u> garb of Nessus, <u>insatiate</u> in torture. Having <u>staggered</u> as far as the Rue Dauphine, he perceived his carriage, awoke his sleeping coachman by opening the door himself, threw himself on the cushions, and pointed towards the Faubourg Saint-Honoré; the carriage drove on. The weight of his fallen fortunes seemed suddenly to crush him; he could not foresee the <u>consequences</u>; he could not contemplate the future with the <u>indifference</u> of the hardened criminal who merely faces a <u>contingency</u> already familiar. God was still in his heart. "God," he <u>murmured</u>, not knowing what he said — "God — God!" Behind the event that had <u>overwhelmed</u> him he saw the hand of God. The carriage rolled rapidly onward. Villefort, while turning restlessly on the cushions, felt

something press against him. He put out his hand to remove the object; it was a fan which Madame de Villefort had left in the carriage; this fan awakened a <u>recollection</u> which darted through his mind like lightning. He thought of his wife. (chapter 111)

READING

Infer from Text

Monday, May 17, 1915

One of my cooks has a revolver, and early this morning she was unloading it when it went off and hit me on the arm; fortunately it was not serious. The shot went through her box, then a thick pocket book, and thence into a tea caddy, where it remained. It was really very terrifying. A Russian and French Military Attaché came in this afternoon.

We have ten hospital tents and each one holds ten patients, and as they are all full more tents have to be put up. At 9 o'clock this evening a very bad case of typhus arrived in an ox cart — a poor soldier who was just on leave. His old mother and father came with him; they were to sleep under the cart, and as the ground was inches thick with mud, we got them bundles of straw; we also gave them hot coffee and bread. One sees some sad sights.

I went again to the market; it is very picturesque. Some of the gipsy women are very handsome and their costumes charming. Most of the materials for their dresses and aprons are homespun. The different shades of reds, blues, yellow and green are lovely, they all tone so well. We are just on 200 at the camp now, but the numbers never worry me. We bought cheese and great rolls of sausages in the market. My store tent is almost under water. I have had to put

down bricks and planks and have a trench dug through the centre. We are told we shall have it wet for three weeks. The rain comes down in torrents, much heavier than in England. The patients are all looking so much better and much fatter. I have bought two large copper boilers for soup; one cost 123 dinas and the other 77 dinas, but I should think they would last for ever. I have had a brick wall set round them and a flue at the back and a grate underneath. We only cook with wood; it is really very excellent as it retains the heat so long, and really I like it better than coal. But at first the smoke made us all cry until I got the stoves properly set.

Thursday, July 29, 1915

This has been a dull day. The doctor would not allow me to go out as my temperature is inclined to go up and I have a bad pulse. The Austrians are splendid men, and it seems so terrible to see these nice refined men doing all kinds of dirty work; it makes me think of our poor English prisoners in Germany.[5] (Monica Stanley, *My Diary in Serbia*)

■ ■ ■

Which facts are stated or can be inferred in the diary entries?

I. This was the author's first visit to Serbia.
II. The author despised Austria and German prisoners.
III. IThe author was a stalwart, uncomplaining woman.

A. I, II, and III
B. I
C. II
D. III
E. I and III
F. II and III
G. None

The author is sympathetic to enemy prisoners because:

A. She recognizes that her own countrymen are prisoners and she hopes that they are treated well.
B. She needs them to help her.
C. Secretly she is supportive of the enemy's cause.
D. She is homesick.

" *We are what we repeatedly do. Excellence, then, is not an act, but a habit.*"[6]

— Aristotle

SCIENCE

Organizing Data

The Ozone Layer

What is the best way to ascertain if the ozone layer is decreasing:

I. Take satelite pictures of the ozone layer and compare similar pictures from 50 years ago.

II. Measure the air temperature in Greenland and Antarctica over a ten-year spread of time.

III. Check the temperature of the Arctic Ocean over a ten-year spread of time.

IV. Measure the size of glaciers in Greenland and the ice cap in Antarctica in a ten-year spread of time.

A. I

B. II

C. III

D. IV

E. All

F. None

G. I and III

H. II and IV

ENGLISH

Rules of Capitalization

Rule 1: Capitalize a proper noun. Example: the Empire State Building

Rule 2: Capitalize the titles of high-ranking government officials when used with or before their names. Do not capitalize the title if it is used instead of the name. Example: The president addressed the nation. President Smith addressed the nation.

Rule 3: Capitalize the first word of all sentences, including quoted sentences.

Examples: He said, "Make a right choice." The man made a right choice.

Rule 4: Capitalize points of the compass only when they refer to specific regions. Example: We have had three relatives visit from the South. Go south three blocks and then turn left.

Rule 5: Always capitalize the first and last words of titles of publications regardless of their parts of speech. Capitalize other words within titles, including the short verb forms Is, Are, and Be. Exception: Do not capitalize little words within titles such as a, an, the, but, as, if, and, or, nor, or prepositions, regardless of their length. Example: A Tale of Two Cities

Rule 6: Do not capitalize names of seasons. Example: I love spring rain and fall colors.

Correct the following sentences:

1. The President recently finished reading the bible.

2. Our Company is called For Such A Time As This.

3. "open the door now!" exclaimed the soldier!

4. I visited the washington monument.

5. The north defeated the south in the american civil war.

The Eradication of Smallpox

In 1967, when the World Health Organization started international eradication efforts, smallpox, was estimated to have afflicted up to 15 million people annually, of whom some two million died, with millions more left disfigured and sometimes blind. By 1980 smallpox was eradicated.

If smallpox were not eradicated, there would have been 350 million new victims in the past 20 years — roughly the combined population of the USA and Mexico — and an estimated 40 million deaths — a figure equal to the entire population of Spain or South Africa.[7]

How many victims would have died between 1980 and 1995?

A. 40 million

B. 35 million

C. 30 million

D. 1.75 million

"Grace is represented as the Church's inexhaustible treasury, from which she showers blessings with generous hands, without asking questions or fixing limits. Grace without price; grace without cost! The essence of grace, we suppose, is that the account has been paid in advance; and, because it has been paid, everything can be had for nothing."[8]

— Bonhoeffer

Moral Man and
IMMORAL SOCIETY

SCRIPTURE

"And now, O Israel, what does the LORD your God ask of you but to fear the LORD your God, to walk in all his ways, to love him, to serve the LORD your God with all your heart and with all your soul, and to observe the LORD's commands and decrees that I am giving you today for your own good?"

~ Deuteronomy 10:12–13

PRAYER POINTS
KNOWLEDGE

"They are more precious than gold, than much pure gold; they are sweeter than honey, than honey from the comb."

~ Psalm 19:10

Moral Man and Immoral Society, by Reinhold Niebuhr, was written during the period of the Great Depression (1929–1940). In *Moral Man*, Niebuhr insists on the necessity of politics in the struggle for social justice because of the sinfulness of human nature, that is, the self-centeredness of individuals and groups. He fervently hopes that a person can experience redemption and redeem his society by a Hegelian, reductionist struggle with sinfulness. Niebuhr advanced the thesis that what the individual is able to achieve singly cannot be simply regarded as a possibility for social groups. He marked a clear distinction between the individual and the group, lowering significantly the moral capacity of the group in relation to that of the individual.

He sees the limitations of reason to solve social injustice by moral and rational means, "since reason is always the servant of interest in a social situation."[1] This is his critique of liberal Christian theology, which strongly believes in the rational capacity of humans to make themselves be moral, and he accepts the tentativeness of this view. In other words, Neibhur correctly saw the immorality of systems in society (e.g., social welfare) and its futile attempts to ameliorate individuals and their needs through systemic interventions. In other words, Niebuhr was not naïve — he knew that systems and cultures change and individual hearts change.

Niebuhr cautions us about embracing "herd mentalities." According to him, individuals are morally capable of considering the interests of others and acting. That is, individuals can be unselfish. Societies, however, cannot. "In every human group there is less reason to guide and to check impulse, less capacity for self-transcendence, less ability to comprehend the needs of others, therefore more unrestrained egoism than the individuals, who compose the group, reveal in their personal relationships."[2]

My point is, individuals may be sincere in their understanding about several issues. In fact, they may be right about some issues. But they are wrong, too. But when that group gains political hegemony, it can lose focus and direction.

Individuals can be moral in purpose and in actions. But combining a bunch of individuals into a coercive group can cause the group to become immoral. For example, Adolf Hitler's rise to power was initially a good thing for Germany. He brought jobs and prosperity to his nation. However, as he gained power, the good was replaced by the bad. This may not be inevitable, but it happens so often that we should be cautious in giving so much power to groups. As an interesting sidebar, Niebuhr is directly contradicting the liberal Dewey who applauded the notion that the community, or larger society, created the greater good.

The answer to this apparent contradiction is, of course the gospel. Niebuhr stresses the role of the Holy Spirit (what he calls the "religious imagination"). In a sense the group remains moral because the individuals in that society answer to a "higher power," not to the coercion of the group or to the agenda of the group. Dietrich Bonhoeffer, a German World War II martyr, for example, was perhaps the most patriotic of Germans because he loved his God and his country enough to obey God and His Word above all persons. This was the only way, Bonhoeffer understood, that his nation could be moral and right before the God he served. Unfortunately, he was a lone voice in the wilderness!

Today, young people, as you look ahead of you, do the right thing. All the time. Every time. Do not seek to overcome evil with evil, even if your society tells you it is all right. Make the Word of God central to your life and, as you do, and as thousands do, society will change, too.

R E A D I N G

Text Development

When, on the 22d day of April, 1898, Michael Mallia, gun-captain of the United States cruiser *Nashville*, sent a shell across the bow of the Spanish ship *Buena Ventura*, he gave the signal shot that ushered in a war for liberty for the slaves of Spain.

The world has never seen a contest like it. Nations have fought for territory and for gold, but they have not fought for the happiness of others. Nations have resisted the encroachments of barbarism, but until the nineteenth century they have not fought to uproot barbarism and cast it out of its established place.

Nations have fought to preserve the integrity of their own empire, but they have not fought a foreign foe to set others free. Men have gone on crusades to fight for holy tombs and symbols, but armies have not been put in motion to overthrow vicious political systems and regenerate iniquitous governments for other peoples.

For more than four centuries Spain has held the island of Cuba as her chattel, and there she has revelled in corruption, and wantoned in luxury wrung from slaves with the cruel hand of unchecked power. She has been the unjust and merciless court of last resort. From her malignant verdict there has been no possible appeal, no power to which her victims could turn for help.

But the end has come at last. The woe, the grief, the humiliation, the agony, the despair that Spain has heaped upon the helpless, and multiplied in the world until the world is sickened with it, will be piled in one avalanche on her own head.

Liberty has grown slowly. Civilization has been on the defensive. Now liberty fights for liberty, and civilization takes the aggressive in the holiest war the world has even known.[4] (Trumbull White , *Our War with Spain for Cuba's Freedom*)

What language does the author use to persuade his audience?

TEST-TAKING INSIGHT

English Test-taking Tips

- Be aware of the writing style used in each passage. Rarely are you asked to ascertain writing style, but it affects most everything: theme, tone, and plot.

- Consider the elements of writing that are included in each underlined portion of the passage. Passages should be read holistically, but remember that underlined portions are the crux of the matter for these particular questions.

- Be aware of questions with no underlined portions — that means you will be asked about the passage as a whole.

- Examine each answer choice and determine how it differs from the others. Many of the questions in the test will involve more than one aspect of writing.

- Read and consider all of the answer choices before you choose the one that best responds to the question.

- Determine the best answer, not the perfect answer.

- Reread the sentence, using your selected answer. (Informed by the ACT test site.)

Achieving Unity

Every paragraph and every essay will have unity if all its sentences support the main idea. Remove the sentences that do not belong in this essay.

Samurai Warriors

As the effective influence of the imperial court gradually waned from the 9th century through the 12th century, power moved away from the emperor to local warriors (bushi or samurai). The warriors were typically landholders, many minor landholders, yeoman farmers really. They were not necessarily rich noblemen. They lived in small, fortified compounds, and they offered the surrounding peasant communities succor and protection. Often warriors served as local district officials, judges, even priests. They were, however, quintessential warriors. Much of their time was devoted to the cultivation of warfare. As a result they were very effective administrators and warriors. With their land holdings, military skills, and administrative skills, the warriors were a powerful presence in Japanese society.

At times, samurai families joined together for protection into larger groups based on kinship ties. The emperor, with no standing army, relied on samurai families to maintain local law and order.

By the middle of the 13th century, samurai had become so valuable to the emperor that he appointed a "head samurai" called a shogun. A shogun was a military governor, so to speak, who answered directly to the emperor. He was responsible for maintaining peace in the provinces. He arbitrated differences between rival samurai and other divergent groups.

In the 1870s Japanese leadership sent a group on a diplomatic mission around the world. Under the leadership of Iwakura Tomomi, they were to learn about technologically advanced countries of the West. The Iwakura mission's direct observation of the West left them feeling challenged but hopeful and it seemed possible that Japan could catch up with the Western nations.

In 1232 the shogun promulgated the Joei Code. It clarified the duties of samurai and other officials. The code also restrained unruly samurai by requiring them to respect the rights of the religious temples and shrines.

This era, called the Hojo era, saw the spread of Buddhism. Buddhism stressed personal salvation for ordinary believers. This was in direct contrast to much Japanese thinking that emphasized the needs of the community above the needs of the individual.

There were a series of civil wars that resulted in great turmoil from 1300–1400. Real unity did not occur until a new religious movement emerged, Shintoism.

Japan lost World War II but emerged as one of the premier economic powers of the post-World War II world.

MATH

What is the value of Y if X is 80 degrees?

$$X$$

$$X + 10 = Y$$

"The secret of success is constancy of purpose."[5]
—Benjamin Disraeli

ENGLISH

Identifying Independent and Dependent Clauses

When you want to use commas and semicolons in sentences and when you are concerned about whether a sentence is or is not a fragment, a good way to start is to be able to recognize dependent and independent clauses.

Independent Clause

An independent clause is a group of words that contains a subject and verb and expresses a complete thought. An independent clause is a sentence.

Dependent Clause

A dependent clause is a group of words that contains a subject and verb but does not express a complete thought. A dependent clause cannot be a sentence. Often a dependent clause is marked by a dependent marker word.

Coordinating Conjunction

The seven coordinating conjunctions used as connecting words at the beginning of an independent clause are *and, but, for, or, nor, so,* and *yet.* When the second independent clause in a sentence begins with a coordinating conjunction, a comma is needed before the coordinating conjunction.

Independent Marker Words

An independent marker word is a connecting word used at the beginning of an independent clause. These words can always begin a sentence that can stand alone. When the second independent clause in a sentence has an independent marker word, a semicolon is needed before the independent marker word. Some common independent markers are *also, consequently, furthermore, however, moreover, nevertheless,* and *therefore.*

■ ■ ■

Combine two sentences into one.[6]

1. Mark is ready. Mary is not.

2. When I speak . . . I know who is listening.

3. Nothing matters more to a mom. She loves to see her daughters safe.

4. Hitting a ball. When I step up to the plate.

5. I love eating berries. They do not love me!

VOCABULARY

The Crucible[7]
Arthur Miller

The Crucible is set in a time in which the church and the state are one, and the religion is a strict, austere form of Puritanism. Sin and the status of an individual's soul are matters of public concern. Within this setting a tragedy unfolds.

Suggested Vocabulary Words

A. I look for John Proctor that took me from my sleep and put knowledge in my heart! I never knew what <u>pretense</u> Salem was, I never knew the lying lessons I was taught by all these Christian women and their <u>covenanted</u> men! And now you bid me tear the light out of my eyes? I will not, I cannot! You loved me, John Proctor, and whatever sin it is, you love me yet!

B. This is a sharp time, now, a <u>precise</u> time — we live no longer in the dusky afternoon when evil mixed itself with good and <u>befuddled</u> the world.

SCIENCE

Inducing Principles

What principles can you deduce from pictures of this vegetation:

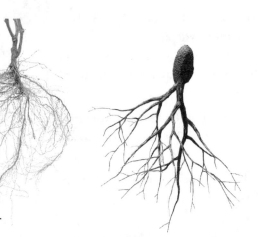

A. The vegetation exhibits characteristics of seeds.

B. The examples are leafs.

C. The examples are roots.

D. None of the above.

Under
MY BED

S C R I P T U R E

" 'I am the Alpha and the Omega,' says the Lord God, 'who is, and who was, and who is to come, the Almighty.' "

~ Revelation 1:8

You should see what is under our queen-size, cherry-stained bed with bent metal stays that are quiet testimony to the fact that this old boy weighed 148 in 1977 but — well, anyway, don't tell my wife I shared this.

Stashed in disheveled piles are my World War II history books and other treasures.

Inevitably, Karen (my wife) will spend eons of time preparing for bed. While she is brushing her teeth, washing her face, and performing other necessary hygienic penultimate mysteries, I grab a book from my under-the-bed library and I read about the German U-boat campaign in the North Atlantic.

I have several libraries in other places in the house. There is the academic library — full of Bible commentaries and useless graduate school books I never read but I cannot do without. That one is stashed in the basement next to my desktop computer — the one with Windows 98, the last Microsoft software program I fully comprehended. Next, there is the classical library in the family room. This is the library that is full of "pretty books." No one touches that library; it is there for show. But across the room is the "grandchildren library," full of children's classics that Karen reads to our cherubic grandchildren, ample evidence that we were exemplary parents if our children could produce such offspring.

But my favorite library is the library under my bed.

Under my bed, safe and clear, are my treasured reading books. Their diverse title names are appropriate metaphors for my anachronistic, never-ending education.

I have perennial classics — *Run Silent, Run Deep*. Occasionally other favorites sneak in. Milton's *Paradise Lost* — which I re-read bi-annually — is propped up next to *Operation Barbarossa*. John Keegan's *World War II* is a great read and can keep me awake through Karen's most extensive diurnal, twilight, pre-sleep preparations.

I hope you have things you treasure and that you keep them close at hand.

I keep one special book under the bed: my dad's Bible. It is an old leather black Bible, expensive leather, worn now, with the edges exhibiting light brown cow leather intruding out of the faded black. The cover has "Holy Bible" and "Billy Stobaugh" written in fractured gold letters.

Inside the Bible in my Mammaw's handwriting is "1939. To Billy from Mother and Daddy, 8 years." My dad was born in 1932 and apparently this was his 8th birthday present. When my dad died on Father's Day in 1982, when he was only 49, my mom gave me this Bible.

I imagine Dad got other things for his birthday. Toy soldiers? A pop gun? I will never know. But I know he got this Bible. If you found your deceased dad's Bible, what would you do? I immediately

PRAYER POINTS
S ELF-CONTROL

"So then, let us not be like others, who are asleep, but let us be alert and self-controlled."

~ 1 Thessalonians 5:6

looked for evidence that he read it. I looked for a mark, any mark, that would evidence that he read it, studied it, applied it to his life. Nothing.

Nothing. Nothing in the family register. Nothing next to John 3:16. I know my dad knew God loved him. I heard him say it a few hours before he died. But there were no marks in his Bible.

I know I have lots of marks in my Bible. I can't keep up with Karen though. She is the "master marker." Her Bible is full of underlines. Her Bible underlines are straight and neat. I can't do it. My lines inevitably invade other verses. I gave up drawing straight lines under verses — I now put squiggly lines. I once asked Karen to show me how she made straight lines under her Bible verses — sometimes without even a straight edge. She ignored my question.

I don't have my dad anymore but I have his Bible. And there is nothing written in it.

I wish my dad wrote in his Bible, the Bible I keep under my bed. I would like something — anything — that reminds me of him. I am 58 now and it is 30 years since he died. I can hardly remember what he looks like now.

Paul says in 2 Corinthians 3:1–3, "Are we beginning to commend ourselves again? Or do we need, like some people, letters of recommendation to you or from you? You yourselves are our letter, written on our hearts, known and read by everybody. You show that you are a letter from Christ, the result of our ministry, written not with ink but with the Spirit of the living God, not on tablets of stone but on tablets of human hearts." My dad's life is written on my heart. It gives me pleasure still to read his Bible.

Parents, write in your Bible! Even if you use squiggly lines. Your kids will thank you someday! But more important, write your lives on their hearts, that someday, perhaps one cold night, as they wait to go to sleep, they will read your Bible, see your marks, and, more importantly, remember that day, long ago, when you wrote your life on their lives.

And who knows, they might stash it under their beds.

- Read each question carefully to make sure you understand the type of answer required. Answer the question — not the question you think is asked.

- If you choose to use a calculator, be sure it is permitted, is working on test day, and has reliable batteries. Do not use a calculator if you can figure out the answer without one. It saves time.

- Solve the problem. Leave no question blank.

- Remove detractors and then answer the question.

- Check your work.

WRITING

Conciseness

Write concisely. Avoid sentences that have unnecessary words.

Mark the sentence that is the most concise sentence.

1. ____ I believe that the Germans caused World War II.
   ____ The Germans caused World War II.

2. ____ Mary, who was young, published her first novel at age 12.
   ____ Mary published her first novel at age 12.

3. ____ Although, I never visited Hong Kong, my wife tells me it is beautiful.
   ____ I never visited Hong Kong. My wife tells me it is beautiful.

VOCABULARY

Little Women[1]
Louisa Alcott

Little Women has delighted readers for generations. It combines superb characterization with an inspiring story to make this a timeless classic. Meet the March sisters: the inimical Jo, the beautiful Meg, the frail Beth, and the spoiled younger daughter Amy. Watch as they mature into young women.

Suggested Vocabulary Words

A. Amy rebelled <u>outright,</u> and <u>passionately</u> declared that she had rather have the fever than go to Aunt March. Meg reasoned, pleaded, and commanded, all in vain. Amy protested that she would not go, and Meg left her in despair to ask Hannah what should be done. Before she came back, Laurie walked into the parlor to find Amy sobbing, with her head in the sofa cushions. She told her story, expecting to be <u>consoled,</u> but Laurie only put his hands in his pockets and walked about the room, whistling softly, as he knit his brows in deep thought. Presently he sat down beside her, and said, in his most <u>wheedlesome</u> tone, "Now be a sensible little woman, and do as they say. No, don't cry, but hear what a jolly plan I've got. You go to Aunt March's, and I'll come and take you out every day, driving or walking, and we'll have capital times. Won't that be better than <u>moping</u> here?" (chapter 17)

B. Jo's face was a study next day, for the secret rather weighed upon her, and she found it hard not to look mysterious and important. Meg observed it, but did not trouble herself to make inquiries, for she had learned that the best way to manage Jo was by the law of <u>contraries,</u> so she felt sure of being told everything if she did not ask. She was rather surprised, therefore, when the silence remained unbroken, and Jo assumed a <u>patronizing</u> air, which decidedly aggravated Meg, who in turn assumed an air of dignified reserve and devoted herself to her mother. This left Jo to her own devices, for Mrs. March had taken her place as nurse, and bade her rest, exercise, and amuse herself after her long confinement. Amy being gone, Laurie was her only <u>refuge,</u> and much as she enjoyed his society, she rather dreaded him just then, for he was an <u>incorrigible</u> tease, and she feared he would coax the secret from her. (chapter 21)

C. There were to be no ceremonious performances, everything was to be as natural and homelike as possible, so when Aunt March arrived, she was <u>scandalized</u> to see the bride come running to welcome and lead her in, to find the bridegroom fastening up a garland that had fallen down, and to catch a glimpse of the <u>paternal</u> minister marching upstairs with a grave <u>countenance</u> and a wine bottle under each arm. (chapter 25)

D. "You look like the <u>effigy</u> of a young knight asleep on his tomb," she said, carefully tracing the well-cut profile defined against the dark stone. (chapter 39)

E. Yes, Jo was a very happy woman there, in spite of hard work, much anxiety, and a <u>perpetual</u> racket. She enjoyed it heartily and found the applause of her boys more satisfying than any praise of the world, for now she told no stories except to her flock of enthusiastic believers and admirers. As the years went on, two little lads of her own came to increase her happiness — Rob, named for Grandpa, and Teddy, a happy-go-lucky baby, who seemed to have inherited his papa's sunshiny temper as well as his mother's lively spirit. How they ever grew up alive in that whirlpool of boys was a mystery to their grandma and aunts, but they flourished like dandelions in spring, and their rough nurses loved and served them well. (chapter 47)

ENGLISH

Combining Sentences with Conjunctions

Your writing will be better and will express your thoughts better if you combine sentences with appropriate conjunctions. This type of transition improves paragraph coherence.

■ ■ ■

Rewrite the following sentences:

1. The mayor is not a mean man. He has limits. (join with but)

2. He was sure there would be an end to the war. The enemy surrendered. (join with when)

3. I really want to go to Dallas, Texas. I want to watch the Steelers beat the Cowboys. (join with and)

Reading for Detail

In confining himself exclusively to the Piano, Chopin has, in our opinion, given proof of one of the most essential qualities of a composer — a just appreciation of the form in which he possessed the power to excel; yet this very fact, to which we attach so much importance, has been injurious to the extent of his fame. It would have been most difficult for any other writer, gifted with such high harmonic and melodic powers, to have resisted the temptation of the singing of the bow, the liquid sweetness of the flute, or the deafening swells of the trumpet, which we still persist in believing the only fore-runner of the antique goddess from whom we woo the sudden favors. What strong conviction, based upon reflection, must have been requisite to have induced him to restrict himself to a circle apparently so much more barren; what warmth of creative genius must have been necessary to have forced from its apparent aridity a fresh growth of luxuriant bloom, unhoped for in such a soil! What intuitive penetration is repealed by this exclusive choice, which, wresting the different effects of the various instruments from their habitual domain, where the whole foam of sound would have broken at their feet, transported them into a sphere, more limited, indeed, but far more idealized! What confident perception of the future powers of his instrument must have presided over his voluntary renunciation of an empiricism, so widely spread, that another would have thought it a mistake, a folly, to have wrested such great thoughts from their ordinary interpreters! How sincerely should we revere him for this devotion to the Beautiful for its own sake, which induced him not to yield to the general propensity to scatter each light spray of melody over a hundred orchestral desks, and enabled him to augment the resources of art, in teaching how they may be concentrated in a more limited space, elaborated at less expense of means, and condensed in time!

Far from being ambitious of the uproar of an orchestra, Chopin was satisfied to see his thought integrally produced upon the ivory of the key-board; succeeding in his aim of losing nothing in power, without pretending to orchestral effects, or to the brush of the scene-painter. Oh! we have not yet studied with sufficient earnestness and attention the designs of his delicate pencil, habituated as we are, in these days, to consider only those composers worthy of a great name, who have written at least half-a-dozen Operas, as many Oratorios, and various Symphonies: vainly requiring

every musician to do every thing, nay, a little more than every thing. However widely diffused this idea may be, its justice is, to say the least, highly problematical. We are far from contesting the glory more difficult of attainment, or the real superiority of the Epic poets, who display their splendid creations upon so large a plan; but we desire that material proportion in music should be estimated by the same measure which is applied to dimension in other branches of the fine arts; as, for example, in painting, where a canvas of twenty inches square, as the *Vision of Ezekiel*, or *Le Cimetiere* by Ruysdael, is placed among the chefs d'oeuvre, and is more highly valued than pictures of a far larger size, even though they might be from the hands of a Rubens or a Tintoret. In literature, is Beranger less a great poet, because he has condensed his thoughts within the narrow limits of his songs? Does not Petrarch owe his fame to his Sonnets? and among those who most frequently repeat their soothing rhymes, how many know any thing of the existence of his long poem on Africa?

We cannot doubt that the prejudice which would deny the superiority of an artist — though he should have produced nothing but such Sonatas as Franz Schubert has given us — over one who has portioned out the insipid melodies of many Operas, which it were useless to cite, will disappear; and that in music, also, we will yet take into account the eloquence and ability with which the thoughts and feelings are expressed, whatever may be the size of the composition in which they are developed, or the means employed to interpret them.[2] (Franz Litszt, *Life of Chopin*)

■ ■ ■

The main concept of this passage is:

A. The genius of Chopin.
B. Chopin, against all convention, ignoring all other instruments in the orchestra, chose to compose exclusively for the piano.
C. Chopin, while admiring the piano most of all, chose, instead, to write compositions for other music instruments.
D. Chopin loved writing intricate, complicated piano pieces.

" *Before God we are all equally wise — and equally foolish.*"[3]

— Albert Einstein

M A T H

What does this graph illustrate?

A. Probability
B. Averages
C. Ratios
D. Derivatives

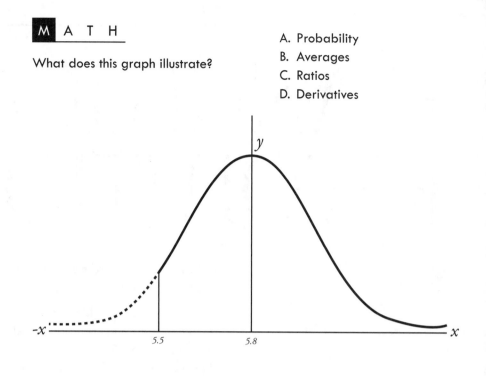

S C I E N C E

Calculations/Data

In the early to mid 1950s, DDT became one of the most widely used pesticides. It had an immediate laudable effect on human life. Malaria, for instance, nearly disappeared from the planet. Eventually, we realized that some DDT was staying in our bodies. DDT was being used in the environment, on agricultural products, and on livestock. In the 1960s, concern arose about the widespread use of DDT and its effects on humans. A study in 1968 showed that Americans were consuming an average of 0.025 milligrams of DDT per day! At concentration above 236 mg DDT per kg of body weight, people will die. One kilogram equals approximately 2 pounds. How much DDT will kill a hundred pound boy?[4]

■ ■ ■

Some words sound like what they mean — such as "buzz." These words are called onomatopoeia. Other words also, though, feel like they sound. "Alone," for instance feels like "lonely" would feel. How do these made-up words feel?

Manicottalopa
Silliapagos
Lambicottacy
UpaUpaUpa

Write words that have feelings! Aristotle called it "pathos."

The EVANGELICAL REVOLUTION

PART I

"In days to come, when your son asks you, 'What does this mean?' say to him, 'With a mighty hand the LORD brought us out of Egypt, out of the land of slavery. . . . And it will be like a sign on your hand and a symbol on your forehead that the LORD brought us out of Egypt with his mighty hand."
~ Exodus 13:14–16

PRAYER POINTS
INTEGRITY

"May integrity and uprightness protect me, because my hope is in you."
~ Psalm 25:21

Who could imagine that a movement — evangelical home-schooling — that began so quietly in the 1970s and 1980s would someday generate such a vital and anointed generation that is emerging at the beginning of this century? It is a time to celebrate and to reflect.

The new ACT is an ideal milieu for evangelical Christians to score highly. When I was growing up, eons ago, elite prep schools dominated the college admission classes. Today, the new "elite" are evangelicals, especially home-schooled evangelical graduates. They are the most highly recruited, most highly valued freshmen at secular and Christian schools alike.

I spoke to a Yale recruiter and she told me that, while Yale wants home-schoolers, homeschoolers do not seem to want Yale. They are not applying to Yale. Likewise, I have two distance-learning students who were heavily recruited by Ivy League schools. They both chose local alternatives (a state school and a Christian school).

It is not my purpose to lobby for any particular post-graduate choice, although I found my wife at Harvard — and Intervarsity Fellowship Cambridge is larger than the entire student body at Gordon College (a Christian College) in South Hamilton. Mostly for fiscal reasons, the majority of evangelicals go to secular colleges.

To most evangelical Christians, the modern secular university is a hostile place. It was not always so.

In fact, the American university was built solidly on evangelical principles. There were no so-called "official" "secular" colleges until the rise of the land grant colleges in the middle of the 19th century. An early brochure, published in 1643, stated that the purpose of Harvard University (the oldest American university) was "To advance Learning and perpetuate it to Posterity; dreading to leave an illiterate Ministry to the Churches."

Harvard's motto for 300 years was "Christo et Ecclesiae." In fact, most of the U.S. universities founded before the 20th century had a strongly religious, usually Protestant evangelical Christian character. Yale, Princeton, Chicago, Stanford, Duke, William and Mary, Boston University, Michigan, and the University of California had a decidedly evangelical Christian character in the early years of their existence but abandoned it by the 20th century. By the 1920s, the American university had stepped completely back from its evangelical roots. This was true of almost every American university founded in the first 200 years of our existence.

Readers would be surprised to see how evangelical, Christ-centered early universities were. They had pastors as presidents. These men closely tied the identity of their university to a strong Christian worldview. The core curriculum included Bible courses and Christian theology. These were mandatory Bible courses. All American universities insisted on a doctrinally sound content for sensitive courses and often required that faculty be born-again Christians! Imagine this: the famous historian Frederick Jackson Turner was refused a professorship at Princeton because he was a Unitarian! Chapel attendance was required at Harvard and Yale! It is more than coincidental that the architects who designed early universities designed them to look like churches. At the University of Pittsburgh, for instance, the most prominent building on campus is the Cathedral of Learning.

Universities were founded because early Americans earnestly believed that American society should be governed by evangelical Christian people. They believed that American industry should be run by evangelical Christian entrepreneurs. They believed that American culture should be created by evangelical artists. The early American university was committed to making sure that that happened.

The marriage of spiritual maturity and elite education is a potent combination and to a large degree assured the success of the American experiment. Its divorce may presage its demise.

W R I T I N G

Drawing Conclusions

What can you infer from this poem by Robert Frost?

Fire and Ice

Some say the world will end in fire,
Some say in ice.
From what I've tasted of desire
I hold with those who favor fire.
But if it had to perish twice,
I think I know enough of hate
To know that for destruction ice
Is also great
And would suffice.

■ ■ ■

Answer these questions true or false.

True or False. Robert Frost likes to play in the snow.

True or False. Someone must have hurt Frost.

True or False. Frost seems to be unhappy as he writes this poem.

True or False. Frost is writing a poem about fire and ice.

True or False. Frost is writing a poem about love and hatred.

M A T H

Word Problems

Your church youth group is hosting a fundraising event this weekend. Youth have been pre-selling tickets to the event; adult tickets are $5.00, and child tickets (for kids six years old and under) are $2.50. From past experience, you expect about 10,000 people to attend the event. However, you cannot be sure.

You consult with your ticket-sellers, and discover that they have not been keeping track of how many child tickets they have sold. The tickets are identical, until the ticket-seller punches a hole in the ticket, indicating that it is a child ticket. But they don't remember how many holes they've punched. They only know that they've sold 448 tickets for $2460. How much revenue from each of child and adult tickets can you expect?[1]

???

Are you reading

50 to 100 pages

a day

???

Reading Test Insights

The Reading Test is a 40-question, 35-minute test that measures your ability to read and to comprehend reading material. You're asked to read four passages and answer questions that show your understanding of:

- what is directly stated
- statements with implied meanings
- tone
- literary elements
- logic
- vocabulary words

Specifically, questions will ask you to use critical thinking skills to:

- discern main ideas
- analyze significant details
- understand sequences of events
- make comparisons
- comprehend cause-effect relationships
- determine the meaning of context-dependent words, phrases, and statements
- draw generalizations
- analyze the author's or narrator's tone and mood

The test comprises four prose passages that are representative of the level and kind of reading required in first-year college courses; passages on topics in social sciences, natural sciences, prose fiction, and the humanities are included.

As ACT explains, "Each passage is accompanied by a set of multiple-choice test questions. These questions do not test the rote recall of facts from outside the passage, isolated vocabulary items, or rules of formal logic. Instead, the test focuses on the complementary and supportive skills that readers must use in studying written materials across a range of subject areas."[3]

VOCABULARY

Don Quixote[4]
Miguel de Cervantes

Don Quixote is a worn-out, older Spanish gentleman who sets off on a great imagined quest to win honor and glory in the name of his imaginary damsel-in-distress, Dulcinea. Don Quixote is much more; he is larger than life. He represents Cervantes's satire of the 16th-century Spanish aristocracy. Don Quixote longs for a world that does not exist — a world of beauty and achievement. He naively seeks to bring order into this Renaissance world by Middle Age chivalry. But Don Quixote, nearly blind figuratively and literarily, with the best of intentions, harms everyone around him.

As the novel progresses, Don Quixote, with the help of his modern, loyal squire, Sancho, who is able to see things as they are, slowly distinguishes between reality and the pictures in his head. Even though he ceases to attack windmills, he never loses his conviction that fair Dulcinea is his salvation from all heartache.

Suggested Vocabulary Words

A. You must know, then, that the above-named gentleman whenever he was at leisure (which was mostly all the year round) gave himself up to reading books of <u>chivalry</u> with such ardor and <u>avidity</u> that he almost entirely neglected the pursuit of his field-sports, and even the management of his property; and to such a pitch did his eagerness and <u>infatuation</u> go that he sold many an acre of land to buy books of chivalry to read, and brought home as many of them as he could get. (part 1, chapter 1)

B. He approved highly of the giant Morgante, because, although of the giant breed which is always <u>arrogant</u> and ill-conditioned, he alone was <u>affable</u> and well-bred. (part 1, chapter 1)

C. Thus setting out, our new-fledged adventurer paced along, talking to himself and saying, "Who knows but that in time to come, when the

veracious history of my famous deeds is made known, the sage who writes it, when he has to set forth my first sally in the early morning, will do it after this fashion? 'Scarce had the <u>rubicund</u> Apollo spread o'er the face of the broad spacious earth the golden threads of his bright hair, scarce had the little birds of painted plumage attuned their notes to hail with <u>dulcet</u> and <u>mellifluous</u> harmony the coming of the rosy Dawn, that, deserting the soft couch of her jealous spouse, was appearing to mortals at the gates and balconies of the Manchegan horizon, when the renowned knight Don Quixote of La Mancha, quitting the lazy down, mounted his celebrated steed Rocinante and began to traverse the ancient and famous Campo de Montiel' "; which in fact he was actually traversing. "Happy the age, happy the time," he continued, "in which shall be made known my deeds of fame, worthy to be moulded in brass, carved in marble, limned in pictures, for a memorial for ever. And thou, O <u>sage</u> magician, whoever thou art, to whom it shall fall to be the chronicler of this wondrous history, forget not, I <u>entreat</u> thee, my good Rocinante, the constant companion of my ways and wanderings." Presently he broke out again, as if he were love-stricken in earnest, "O Princess Dulcinea, lady of this captive heart, a grievous wrong hast thou done me to drive me forth with scorn, and with <u>inexorable</u> <u>obduracy</u> banish me from the presence of thy beauty. O lady, deign to hold in remembrance this heart, thy vassal, that thus in anguish pines for love of thee." (part 1, chapter 2)

D. Seeing what was going on, Don Quixote said in an angry voice, "<u>Discourteous</u> knight, it ill becomes you to <u>assail</u> one who cannot defend himself; mount your steed and take your lance" (for there was a lance leaning against the oak to which the mare was tied), "and I will make you know that you are behaving as a coward." The farmer, seeing before him this figure in full armor brandishing a lance over his head, gave himself up for dead, and made answer meekly, "Sir Knight, this youth that I am <u>chastising</u> is my servant, employed by me to watch a flock of sheep that I have hard by, and he is so careless that I lose one every day, and when I punish him for his carelessness and <u>knavery</u> he says I do it out of niggardliness, to escape paying him the wages I owe him, and before God, and on my soul, he lies." (part 1, chapter 4)

E. Such was the end of the Gentleman of La Mancha, whose village Cide Hamete would not indicate precisely, in order to leave all the towns and villages of La Mancha to contend among themselves for the right to adopt him and claim him as a son, as the seven cities of Greece contended for Homer. The <u>lamentations</u> of Sancho and the niece and housekeeper are omitted here, as well as the new <u>epitaphs</u> upon his tomb. (part 2, chapter 74)

CIENCE

Reading Architectural Designs

What obvious advantages does this house design offer rural, northern Wisconsin homeowners?

At what locations would you predict that roof leaks will occur in the future?

Active/Passive Voice

In active voice sentences the subject does the action. Therefore, there is normally a direct object.

Example: Mary hit the ball.

In passive voice sentences the subject receives the action.

Example: The ball was hit by Mary

The sentence that uses the active voice is stronger, uses fewer words, and clearly shows who performs the action. The sentence that uses the passive voice is weaker and less direct. In writing, especially on the ACT, try to use active voice.

■ ■ ■

Directions: Rewrite the passive voice sentences as active voice sentences.

Passive: The deer was hit by the car.

Active: _____

Passive: The football stadium was built by workers in five months.

Active: _____

■ ■ ■

Directions: Rewrite the active voice sentences as passive voice sentences.

Active: Rosco finished his homework.

Passive: _____

Active: My dog practices his tricks.

Passive: _____

> ❝And so sepulchered in such pomp dost lie,
> that kings for such a tomb would wish to die."[5]
> — John Milton

Reading for Details

Before the building of regular playhouses the itinerant troupes of actors were accustomed, except when received into private homes, to give their performances in any place that chance provided, such as open street-squares, barns, town-halls, moot-courts, schoolhouses, churches, and — most frequently of all, perhaps — the yards of inns. These yards, especially those of carriers' inns, were admirably suited to dramatic representations, consisting as they did of a large open court surrounded by two or more galleries. Many examples of such inn-yards are still to be seen in various parts of England. In the yard a temporary platform — a few boards, it may be, set on barrel-heads — could be erected for a stage; in the adjacent stables a dressing-room could be provided for the actors; the rabble — always the larger and more enthusiastic part of the audience — could be accommodated with standing-room about the stage; while the more aristocratic members of the audience could be comfortably seated in the galleries overhead. Thus a ready-made and very serviceable theatre was always at the command of the players; and it seems to have been frequently made use of from the very beginning of professionalism in acting.[6] (Joseph Quincy Adams, *Shakespearean Playhouses*)

■ ■ ■

What is the main idea of this passage?

A. Drama developed slowly in Britain.
B. The first plays were held in open courtyards.
C. The open courtyard was the ideal location for a play.
D. Shakespeare took his plays from open courtyards to the Globe Theatre.

Which of the following paragraphs most likely would follow the above paragraph?

A. In the smaller towns the itinerant players might, through a letter of recommendation from their noble patron, or through the good will of some local dignitary, secure the use of the town hall, or the schoolhouse, or even of the village church. In such buildings, of course, they could give their performances more advantageously, for they could place money-takers at the doors, and exact adequate payment from all who entered. In the great city of London, however, the players were necessarily forced to make use almost entirely of public inn-yards — an arrangement which, we may well believe, they found far from satisfactory. Not being masters of the inns, they were merely tolerated; they had to content themselves with hastily provided and inadequate stage facilities; and, worst of all, for their recompense they had to trust to a hat collection, at best a poor means of securing money. Often too, no doubt, they could not get the use of a given inn-yard when they most needed it, as on holidays and festive occasions; and at all times they had to leave the public in uncertainty as to where or when plays were to be seen. Their street parade, with the noise of trumpets and drums, might gather a motley crowd for the yard, but in so large a place as London it was inadequate for advertisement among the better classes. And as the troupes of the city increased in wealth and dignity, and as the playgoing public grew in size and importance, the old makeshift arrangement became more and more unsatisfactory.

B. The hostility of the city to the drama was unquestionably the main cause of the erection of the first playhouse; yet combined with this were two other important causes, usually overlooked. The first was the need of a building specially designed to meet the requirements of the players and of the public, a need yearly growing more urgent as plays became more complex, acting developed into a finer art, and audiences increased in dignity as well as in size. The second and the more immediate cause was the appearance of a man with business insight enough to see that such a building would pay. The first playhouse, we should remember, was not erected by a troupe of actors, but by a money-seeking individual. Although he was himself an actor, and the manager of a troupe, he did not, it seems, take the troupe into his confidence. In complete independence of any theatrical organization he proceeded with the erection of his building as a private speculation; and, we are told, he dreamed of the "continual great profit and commodity through plays that should be used there every week."

The EVANGELICAL REVOLUTION PART II

SCRIPTURE

"[Saul] sent men to capture [Samuel]. But when they saw a group of prophets prophesying, with Samuel standing there as their leader, the Spirit of God came on Saul's men and they also prophesied."

~ 1 Samuel 19:20

PRAYER POINTS
GENEROUS HEART

"Command them to do good, to be rich in good deeds, and to be generous and willing to share. In this way they will lay up treasure for themselves. . . ."

~ 1 Timothy 6:18–19

Today most universities are not even loosely a Christian institution. Religion in the university and in public life is relegated to the private experience. So-called "academic freedom" has become a sacrosanct concept and precludes anything that smacks of religiosity — especially orthodoxy that evangelicals so enthusiastically embrace. Religion is represented on campus in sanitary denominational ministries and token chapel ministries (that are hardly more than counseling centers).

To a large degree, then, the American university abandoned the evangelical and the evangelical abandoned the American university.

This created a crisis in the American university, in the evangelical community, and in American society at large. The secular American university compromised its "soul" for the naturalistic; evangelicalism compromised its epistemological hegemony for ontological supremacy. In other words, the secular university became a sort of an academic hothouse for pompous rationalism. Evangelicals abandoned the secular university, and, until recently, more or less compromised their academic base. Evangelicals even founded their own universities, but they were poor academic substitutes for secular offerings. American society no longer had spirit-filled, evangelical leaders in its leadership cadre.

Even as I write this book, this is changing.

The university, if it has any value, must be involved in the communication of immutable, metaphysical truth. The American secular university is not about to accept such limits. It recognizes no citadel of orthodoxy, no limits to its knowledge. But, like Jesus reminds Thomas in John 14, our hope lies not in what we know, but most assuredly in whom we know.

Most secular universities have concluded that abstract concepts like grace, hope, and especially faith are indefinable, immeasurable, and above all unreasonable. Not that God or the uniqueness of Jesus Christ can be proved, or disproved. There are certain issues which the order of the intellect simply cannot address, so we must rise above that to the order of the heart. Faith is our consent to receive the good that God would have for us. Evangelicals believe that God can and does act in our world and in our lives. Human needs are greater than this world can satisfy and therefore it is reasonable to look elsewhere. The university has forgotten or ignores this fact.

That is all changing — and partly due to the popularity of the American homeschooling movement. In massive numbers, the American homeschool movement — initially and presently primarily an evangelical Christian movement — is depositing some of the brightest, capable students in our country into old, august institutions like Harvard. And what is more exciting, the flashpoint of cultural change is changing from Harvard, Princeton, Darmouth, and Stanford to Wheaton, Grove City, Calvin, and Liberty (all evangelical universities). Before long the new wave of elite culture creators will be graduating from American secular universities and Christian universities and they shall be a great deal different from the elite of which I was a part in the middle 1970s. I am not saying the secular university will change quickly — intellectual naturalistic reductionism makes that extremely difficult. However, I do see the whole complexion of university graduates changing significantly in the next 20 years. Never in the history of the world has such a thing happened.

Young people, make sure that you know who you are and who your God is. "By faith, Moses, when he had grown up, refused to be known as the son of Pharaoh's daughter" (Hebrews 11:24). Theologian Walter Brueggemann calls American believers to "nurture, nourish, and evoke a consciousness and perception alternative to the consciousness and perception of the dominant culture around us."[1]

Refuse to be absorbed into the world but choose to be a part of God's kingdom. There is no moderate position anymore in American society — either we are taking a stand for Christ in this inhospitable culture or we are not.

You are a special and peculiar generation. Much loved. But you live among a people who do not know who they are. A people without hope. You need to know who you are — children of the Living God — and then you must live a hopeful life. Quoting C.S. Lewis, we "are half-hearted creatures, fooling about with drink and sex and ambition when infinite joy is offered us, like an ignorant child who wants to go on making mud pies in a slum because he cannot imagine what is meant by the offer of a holiday at the sea."[2]

Take responsibility for your life. Moses accepted responsibility for his life. "He chose to be mistreated along with the people of God

rather than to enjoy the pleasures of sin for a short time" (Hebrews 11:25). If you don't make decisions for your life, someone else will.

Get a cause worth dying for. Moses accepted necessary suffering even unto death. You need a cause worth dying for (as well as living for). "He [Moses] regarded disgrace for the sake of Christ as of greater value than the treasures of Egypt, because he was looking ahead to his reward" (Hebrews 11:26). We are crucified with Christ, yet it is not we who live but Christ who lives in us (Galatians 2:20).

Finally, never take your eyes off the goal. "By faith he left Egypt, not fearing the king's anger; he persevered because he saw him who is invisible" (Hebrews 11:27). What is your threshold of obedience?

Young people, if you are part of this new evangelical elite, you have immense opportunities ahead of you. A new godly generation is arising. You will be called to guide this nation into another unprecedented revival. We shall see.

The Persuasive Essay

The goal of persuasion is to convince someone to adopt a position or an opinion. Read the following sermon and complete the chart.

> The really good news of Isaiah 35, and of the gospel, is that as we — the chosen community, today the Church — rejoice, grow healthy, and find ourselves living in Zion, so also will the land and those who live in it find hope, health, and wholeness. Health to the Jew, as it was to the Greek, means far more than physical health. It means healing, wholeness. Indeed, the Greek word salvation has at its root the word health. We are the light of the world, and we can change our world as we share the good news. The Christ whom we represent is the only real hope the world has for wholeness. And we should be outspoken and unequivocal with this message. As we sing, with our words and our lives, the land will be saved, made whole. "Say to those with fearful hearts, 'Be strong; do not fear.' . . . Then the eyes of the blind be opened and the ears of the deaf unstopped" (Is. 35:4–5).

> Again, this was awfully good news to a community that faced the awful King Sennacherib. King Hezekiah, Uzziah's successor, was sorely tempted to trust in Egypt, but frankly, Isaiah in chapter 35 is making an offer that Hezekiah cannot refuse. Likewise, today, when we live a holy life, when we trust in God with faith and hope, the land in which we work and live becomes holy. In this God, of whom we bear witness with our words and lives, we, like the faithful Israelites, find wholeness, health, and life. This news is good news!

Problem_____

_____

Solution _____

_____

End result _____

_____

Summary Steps to Writing the ACT Essay

1. Make an outline

2. Use specific, not vague, abstract ideas

3. State your case

4. Achieve emphasis through position, statement, and proportion

5. Use transitions to link your paragraphs

6. Offer at least four examples

7. Restate your thesis at least three times

8. Summarize your argument in the conclusion

Emma[3]

Jane Austen

In this reader's opinion, *Emma* is the best of Jane Austen. Emma, the person, defies archetypal categories. She transcends her time and place and will remain one of the most remarkable protagonists in Western literature.

Suggested Vocabulary Words

A. Harriet Smith's intimacy at Hartfield was soon a settled thing. Quick and decided in her ways, Emma lost no time in inviting, encouraging, and telling her to come very often . . . Her father never went beyond the shrubbery, where two divisions of the ground suffised him for his long walk, or his short, as the year varied; and since Mrs. Weston's marriage her exercise had been too much confined. (volume 1, chapter 4)

B. In short, she sat, during the first visit, looking at Jane Fairfax with twofold complacency . . . that case, nothing could be more pitiable or more honourable than the sacrifices she had resolved on. Emma was very willing now to acquit her of having seduced Mr. Dixon's actions from his wife, or of anything mischievous which her imagination had suggested at first . . . and from the best, the purest of motives, might now be denying herself this visit to Ireland, and resolving to divide herself effectually from him and his connections by soon beginning her career of laborious duty. (volume 2, chapter 2)

C. As long as Mr. Knightley remained with them, Emma's fever continued; but when he was gone, she began to be a little tranquillized and subdued — and in the course of the sleepless night . . . but she flattered herself, that if <u>divested</u> of the danger of drawing her away, it might become an increase of comfort to him. . . . At any rate, it would be a proof of attention and kindness in herself, from whom every thing was due; a separation for the present; an averting of the evil day, when they must all be together again. (book 3, chapter 14)

R E A D I N G

The Use of Dialogue

"I would ask you a favour," said the German captain, as we sat in the cabin of a U-boat which had just been added to the long line of bedraggled captives which stretched themselves for a mile or more in Harwich Harbour, in November, 1918.

I made no reply; I had just granted him a favour by allowing him to leave the upper deck of the submarine, in order that he might await the motor launch in some sort of privacy; why should he ask for more?

Undeterred by my silence, he continued: "I have a great friend, Lieutenant-zu-See Von Schenk, who brought U.122 over last week; he has lost a diary, quite private, he left it in error; can he have it?"

I deliberated, felt a certain pity, then remembered the Belgian Prince and other things, and so, looking the German in the face, I said: "I can do nothing."

"Please."

I shook my head, then, to my astonishment, the German placed his head in his hands and wept, his massive frame (for he was a very big man) shook in irregular spasms; it was a most extraordinary spectacle.

It seemed to me absurd that a man who had suffered, without visible emotion, the monstrous humiliation of handing over his command intact, should break down over a trivial incident concerning a diary, and not even his own diary, and yet there was this man crying openly before me.

It rather impressed me, and I felt a curious shyness at being present, as if I had stumbled accidentally into some private recess of his mind. I closed the cabin door, for I heard the voices of my crew approaching.

He wept for some time, perhaps ten minutes, and I wished very much to know of what he was thinking, but I couldn't imagine how it would be possible to find out.

I think that my behaviour in connection with his friend's diary added the last necessary drop of water to the floods of emotion which he had striven, and striven successfully, to hold in check during the agony of handing over the boat, and now the dam had crumbled and broken away.

It struck me that, down in the brilliantly-lit, stuffy little cabin, the result of the war was epitomized. On the table were some instruments I had forbidden him to remove, but which my first lieutenant had discovered in the engineer officer's bag.

On the settee lay a cheap, imitation leather suit-case, containing his spare clothes and a few books. At the table sat Germany in defeat, weeping, but not the tears of repentance, rather the tears of bitter regret for humiliations undergone and ambitions unrealized.

We did not speak again, for I heard the launch come alongside, and, as she bumped against the U-boat, the noise echoed through the hull into the cabin, and aroused him from his sorrows. He wiped his eyes, and, with an attempt at his former hardiness, he followed me on deck and boarded the motor launch.

Next day I visited U.122, and these papers are presented to the public, with such additional remarks as seemed desirable; for some curious reason the author seems to have omitted nearly all dates. This may have been due to the fear that the book, if captured, would be of great value to the British Intelligence Department if the entries were dated. The papers are in the form of two volumes in black leather binding, with a long letter inside the cover of the second volume.[4] (Unknown, *A Diary of a U-Boat Commander*)

How does the narrator develop his character?

Data Analysis

Disease is the general term for any deviation from the normal or healthy condition of the body. The morbid processes that result in either slight or marked modifications of the normal condition are recognized by the injurious changes in the structure or function of the organ, or group of body organs involved. The increase in the secretion of urine noticeable in horses in the late fall and winter is caused by the cool weather and the decrease in the perspiration. If, however, the increase in the quantity of urine secreted occurs independently of any normal cause and is accompanied by an unthrifty and weakened condition of the animal, it would then characterize disease. Tissues may undergo changes in order to adapt themselves to different environments, or as a means of protecting themselves against injuries. The coat of a horse becomes heavy and appears rough if the animal is exposed to severe cold. A rough, staring coat is very common in horses affected by disease. The outer layer of the skin becomes thickened when subject to pressure or friction from the harness. This change in structure is purely protective and normal. In disease, the deviation from normal must be more permanent in character than it is in the examples mentioned above, and in some way prove injurious to the body functions.

Non-specific diseases have no constant cause. A variety of causes may produce the same disease. For example, acute indigestion may be caused by a change of diet, watering the animal after feeding grain, by exhaustion, and intestinal worms. Usually, but one of the animals in the stable or herd is affected. If several are affected, it is because all have been subject to the same condition, and not because the disease has spread from one animal to another.

Specific Diseases — The terms *infectious* and *contagious* are used in speaking of specific diseases. Much confusion exists in the popular use of these terms. A contagious disease is one that may be transmitted by personal contact, as, for example, influenza, glanders and hog cholera. As these diseases may be produced by indirect contact with the diseased animal as well as by direct, they are also infectious. There are a few germ diseases that are not spread by the healthy animals coming in direct contact with the diseased animal, as, for example, black leg and southern cattle fever. These are purely infectious diseases. *Infection* is a more comprehensive term than *contagion*, as it may be used in alluding to all germ diseases, while

the use of the term *contagion* is rightly limited to such diseases as are produced principally through individual contact.

Parasitic diseases are very common among domestic animals. This class of disease is caused by insects and worms, as for example, lice, mites, ticks, flies, and round and flat worms that live at the expense of their hosts. They may invade any of the organs of the body, but most commonly inhabit the digestive tract and skin. Some of the parasitic insects, mosquitoes, flies and ticks, act as secondary hosts for certain animal microorganisms that they transmit to healthy individuals through the punctures or the bites that they are capable of producing in the skin.

Causes — For convenience we may divide the causes of disease into the predisposing or indirect, and the exciting or direct.

The predisposing causes are such factors as tend to render the body more susceptible to disease or favor the presence of the exciting cause. For example, an animal that is narrow chested and lacking in the development of the vital organs lodged in the thoracic cavity, when exposed to the same condition as the other members of the herd, may contract disease while the animals having better conformation do not . Hogs confined in well-drained yards and pastures that are free from filth, and fed in pens and on feeding floors that are clean, do not become hosts for large numbers of parasites. Hogs confined in filthy pens are frequently so badly infested with lice and intestinal worms that their health and thriftiness are seriously interfered with. In the first case mentioned the predisposition to disease is in the individual, and in the second case it is in the surroundings.

The exciting causes are the immediate causes of the particular disease. Exciting causes usually operate through the environment. With the exception of the special disease-producing germs, the most common exciting causes are faulty food and faulty methods of feeding. The following predisposing causes of disease may be mentioned:

Age is an important factor in the production of disease. Young and immature animals are more prone to attacks of infectious diseases than are old and mature animals. Hog-cholera usually affects the young hogs in the herd first, while scours, suppurative joint disease and infectious sore mouth are diseases that occur during the first few days or few weeks of the animal's life. Lung and intestinal parasites are more commonly found in the young, growing animals. Old animals are prone to fractures of bones and degenerative changes of the body tissues. As a general rule, the young are more subject to acute diseases and the old to chronic diseases.

The surroundings or environments are important predisposing factors. A dark, crowded, poorly ventilated stable lowers the animal's vitality, and renders it more susceptible to the disease. A few rods difference in the location of stables and yards may make a marked difference in the health of the herd. A dry, protected site is always preferable to one in the open or on low, poorly drained soil. The majority of domestic animals need but little shelter, but they do need dry, comfortable quarters during wet, cold weather.

Faulty feed and faulty methods of feeding are very common causes of diseases of the digestive tract and the nervous system. A change from dry feed to a green, succulent ration is a common cause of acute indigestion in both horses and cattle. The feeding of a heavy ration of grain to horses that are accustomed to exercise, during enforced rest may cause liver and kidney disorders. The feeding of spoiled, decomposed feeds may cause serious nervous and intestinal disorders.

One attack of a certain disease may influence the development of subsequent attacks of the same, or a different disease. An individual may suffer from an attack of pneumonia that so weakens the disease-resisting powers of the lungs as to result in a tubercular infection of these organs.

In the horse, one attack of azoturia predisposes it to a second attack. One attack of an infectious disease usually confers immunity against that particular disease. Heredity does not play as important a part in the development of diseases in domestic animals as in the human race. A certain family may inherit a predisposition to disease through the faulty or insufficient development of an organ or group of organs. The different species of animals are affected by diseases peculiar to that particular species. The horse is the only species that is affected with azoturia. Glanders affects solipeds, while black leg is a disease peculiar to cattle.[5]

1. What is disease?

2. What is a predisposing cause? Exciting cause?

The Writing Test

The writing test is a 30-minute essay test that measures your writing skills. The test consists of one writing prompt that will define an issue and describe two points of view on that issue. You are asked to respond to a question about your position on the issue described in the writing prompt. In doing so, you may adopt one or the other of the perspectives described in the prompt, or you may present a different point of view on the issue. Your score will not be affected by the point of view you take on the issue. One word of caution: in my opinion, it would be injudicious to tell your grader that you are a homeschooler or that you are a born-again Christian. My impressions are that such appellations inevitably evoke negative responses.

• Carefully read the instructions on the cover of the test booklet.

• Mark up the prompt and write an outline.

• Do not skip lines and do not write in the margins. Write your essay legibly, in English. Remember: longer is always better.

• If possible, discuss the issue in a broader context or evaluate the implications or complications of the issue.

• Address what others might say to refute your point of view and present a counterargument. This is critical and different from the SAT.

• Use specific examples. Do not write in generalities.

• Vary the structure of your sentences, and use varied and precise word choices. Make logical relationships clear by using transitional words and phrases.

• Stay focused on the topic. Mention your thesis multiple times.

• End with a strong conclusion that summarizes or reinforces your position. Correct any mistakes in grammar, usage, punctuation, and spelling. Write legibly.

> "The person, be it gentleman or lady, who has not pleasure in a good novel, must be intolerably stupid."[6]
>
> — Jane Austen

M A T H

Word Problem

What is the total square footage of this house?

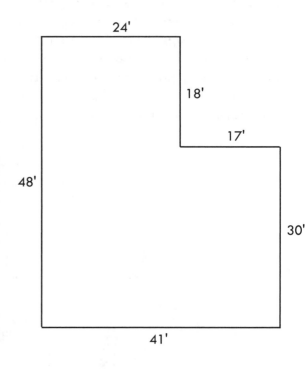

E N G L I S H

Writing with Sensory Words

Write with words that appeal to the senses.

Write a short essay describing a time when you ate an ice cream cone. Use at least 5 words from the list below.

Sight Words	Audible Words	Sensory/Touch Words	Taste/Smell Words
ample	smash	chilly	fruity
drab	yelp	oily	rancid
disheveled	jarring	slippery	flowery
hilarious	hiss	frigid	musty
scrawny	clanging	clammy	zesty

HO HO HO

SCRIPTURE

"Simeon took him in his arms and praised God, saying: 'Sovereign Lord, as you have promised, you now dismiss your servant in peace. For my eyes have seen your salvation, which you have prepared in the sight of all people, a light for revelation to the Gentiles, and for glory to your people Israel.' "

~ Luke 2:28–32

PRAYER POINTS
PEACE

"Let us therefore make every effort to do what leads to peace and to mutual edification."

~ Romans 14:19

'Twas the night before Christmas, when all through the house
not a creature was stirring, not even a mouse.
The stockings were hung by the chimney with care,
in hopes that St. Nicholas soon would be there.[1]

'Twas the day before the opening of Santa Claus season, and on the way to his first holiday gig, Santa's helper Walter Roach made a very important stop — to say goodbye to his reindeer — No! — to see his hair colorist. After all, if Santa's beard isn't as white as the snow, then he can't be the real Santa. And Roach is about as real as a Santa Claus can be.

No, he isn't the jolly fellow who lives at the North Pole. He's a sixth grade teacher at Norwood Creek Elementary School, where the little kids reverentially believe that he's the real deal.

The children were nestled all snug in their beds,
while visions of sugar plums danced in their heads.
And Mama in her 'kerchief, and I in my cap,
had just settled our brains for a long winter's nap.

For Roach, 63, the Santa persona isn't just something he puts on seasonally for parties and festive yuletide functions. No, his red suit, beard, morbid obesity, and jingle bells are for real. Since entering the Santa Claus business eight years ago, Roach has embraced the look and character of the Claus year round. Scorning the role of a nifty elf, Roach morphed into the Big Guy himself.

It wasn't that difficult. At 6 foot 3 and 287 pounds, with his ample teacher voice and snow white hair, he doesn't exactly blend into the crowd. Add the twinkly grin and striking white beard, and it's no wonder wide-eyed postmodern munchkins stare at him wherever he goes.

He was dressed all in fur, from his head to his foot,
and his clothes were all tarnished with ashes and soot.
A bundle of toys he had flung on his back,
and he looked like a peddler just opening his pack.

His eyes — how they twinkled! His dimples, how merry!
His cheeks were like roses, his nose like a cherry!
His droll little mouth was drawn up like a bow,
and the beard on his chin was as white as the snow.

The stump of a pipe he held tight in his teeth,
and the smoke it encircled his head like a wreath.
He had a broad face and a little round belly,
that shook when he laughed, like a bowl full of jelly.
He was chubby and plump, a right jolly old elf,
and I laughed when I saw him, in spite of myself.
A wink of his eye and a twist of his head
soon gave me to know I had nothing to dread.

And he goes a lot of places. Roach is quite the entrepreneur. This year Roach has 64 gigs lined up between Thanksgiving and Christmas Eve, ranging from corporate galas and parades to school visits and small private parties. He also books jobs from $125 for a 20-minute "fly-by" to $225 an hour if he brings along an elf and Mrs. Claus. Mrs. Claus isn't Mrs. Roach. There is no way Mrs. Roach is going to look like Mrs. Claus.

But she is willing to enjoy the fame. And money. This summer Santa Claus is taking his comparitively petite, svelte wife, Debbie, the real Mrs. Claus, sort of, to Tuscany on his Santa earnings.

Ho! Ho! Ho! Way to go, Santa! Oh, I like this. Very American wouldn't you say? Business and idealism, mixed together. As American as apple pie.

Ho! Ho! Ho! Like oil and water, brother. But who cares? It is the delusion that counts, the delusion. On the way to reality we can always go to the hair stylist an get our beards colored white — again! Ho! Ho! Ho!

Ho! Ho! Ho! Scientists know that absolute objectivity has yet to be attained. So why not believe in Santa Claus?

Because Santa is not real. He is not poetic either.

Theologian Walter Bruggemann, in *The Poetic Imagination* writes, "To address the issue of a truth greatly reduced requires us to be poets that speak against a prose world. . . . By prose, I refer to a world that is organized in settled formulae. . . . By poetry, I mean language that moves, that jumps at the right moment, that breaks open old worlds with surprise, abrasion and pace. Poetic speech is the only proclamation worth doing in a situation of reductionism."[2]

I am all for poetry. But I am not for Santa. Santa is anything but objective. Nothing is objective or impartial about the Big Guy.

Are people better at making observations, discoveries, and decisions if they remain neutral and impartial? No. As Alice in the rabbit hole looking for truth learns, as the poet eloquently probes into the cosmos understands, truth is not dependent upon objectivity.

The problem with Santa, really, is that he requires no imagination at all. Nothing really is poetical about him. Jolly and fat and delusional as all get out, Santa is the perfect mascot for post-modern America.

Knowledge will be pursued and it will be found, but only by those who love and who find truth. Objectivity, as Alice found in her crisis, as the poet understands in his craft, is impossible. And undesirable. Are people better at making observations, discoveries, and decisions if they remain neutral and impartial? Absolutely not. And, by the way, Jesus Christ is the Way, the Truth, and the Life!

Santa is the way of delusion, narcissism, and subjectivity.

He spoke not a word, but went straight to his work,
and filled all the stockings, then turned with a jerk.
And laying his finger aside of his nose,
and giving a nod, up the chimney he rose.

He sprang to his sleigh, to his team gave a whistle,
And away they all flew like the down of a thistle.
But I heard him exclaim, 'ere he drove out of sight,
"Happy Christmas to all, and to all a good night!"

Whatever.

Science Test

The science test is a 40-question, 35-minute test that measures the skills required in the natural sciences: synthesis, interpretation, analysis, evaluation, critical thinking, and problem solving. You are not permitted to use a calculator on the science test.

The test assumes that you are in the process of taking the core science courses (earth science, biology, chemistry, physics) with special emphasis on earth science and biology.

The test presents seven sets of scientific information, each followed by a number of multiple-choice test questions. The scientific information is presented in one of three different formats:

- data representation (graphs, tables, and other schematic forms)
- research summaries (descriptions of one or more related experiments)
- conflicting viewpoints (expressions of several related theories)

The questions require you to:

- recognize and understand the basic features of, and concepts related to, the provided information
- examine critically the relationship between the information provided and the conclusions drawn or hypotheses developed
- generalize from given information and draw conclusions, gain new information, or make predictions. (from the ACT website)

> *Don't use words too big for the subject. Don't say 'infinitely' when you mean 'very'; otherwise you'll have no words left when you want to talk about something really infinite."[4]*
>
> — C.S. Lewis

W R I T I N G

Metaphor and Comparison

Compare each family member to an animal.

Describe the theory of relativity to a four year old.

■ ■ ■

A big debate among ACT coaches about writing on the ACT is "do I write about my personal experiences." The answer is yes — and no. Yes, write about your personal experience. But remember this: no ACT grader cares about what you ate last Thanksgiving. However, if you share an incident related to your topic, and at least three other examples from literature, history, and another discipline, you will no doubt enhance the veracity of your essay.

> *I stopped believing in Santa Claus when I was six. Mother took me to see him in a department store and he asked for my autograph."[5]*
>
> — Shirley Temple

M A T H

Word Problems

A cistern can he filled by two pipes in 3 hours and 5 hours respectively. What part of the cistern will be filled by both pipes running together for one hour?

> *Arithmetic is where the answer is right and everything is nice and you can look out of the window and see the blue sky — or the answer is wrong and you have to start over and try again and see how it comes out this time."[3]*
>
> —Carl Sandburg

ENGLISH

In these questions, choose the sentence that represents the best English usage.

A. Of the two runners, John is the worst.
B. Of the two runners, John is the better.
C. John is the worst of the two runners.
D. John is the best of the two runners.

A. We seldom ever receive this type of request anymore.
B. Neither of the employees are doing what is expected of him. Each of these regulations apply to your case.
C. I have enclosed a copy of the file you requested.

READING

Active Reading

The Adventures of Huckleberry Finn[6]
Mark Twain

YOU don't know about me without you have read a book by the name of *The Adventures of Tom Sawyer*; but that ain't no matter. That book was made by Mr. Mark Twain, and he told the truth, mainly. There was things which he stretched, but mainly he told the truth. That is nothing. I never seen anybody but lied one time or another, without it was Aunt Polly, or the widow, or maybe Mary. Aunt Polly — Tom's Aunt Polly, she is — and Mary, and the Widow Douglas is all told about in that book, which is mostly a true book, with some stretchers, as I said before.

Now the way that the book winds up is this: Tom and me found the money that the robbers hid in the cave, and it made us rich. We got six thousand dollars apiece — all gold. It was an awful sight of money when it was piled up. Well, Judge Thatcher he took it and put it out at interest, and it fetched us a dollar a day apiece all the year round — more than a body could tell what to do with.

The Widow Douglas she took me for her son, and allowed she would sivilize me; but it was rough living in the house all the time, considering how dismal regular and decent the widow was in all her ways; and so when I couldn't stand it no longer I lit out. I got into my old rags and my sugar-hogshead again, and was free and satisfied. But Tom Sawyer he hunted me up and said he was going to start a band of robbers, and I might join if I would go back to the widow and be respectable. So I went back.

The widow she cried over me, and called me a poor lost lamb, and she called me a lot of other names, too, but she never meant no harm by it. She put me in them new clothes again, and I couldn't do nothing but sweat and sweat, and feel all cramped up. Well, then, the old thing commenced again. The widow rung a bell for supper, and you had to come to time. When you got to the table you couldn't go right to eating, but you had to wait for the widow to tuck down her head and grumble a little over the victuals, though there warn't really anything the matter with them — that is, nothing only everything was cooked by itself. In a barrel of odds and ends it is different; things get mixed up, and the juice kind of swaps around, and the things go better.

After supper she got out her book and learned me about Moses and the Bulrushers, and I was in a sweat to find out all about him; but by and by she let it out that Moses had been dead a considerable long time; so then I didn't care no more about him, because I don't take no stock in dead people.

Pretty soon I wanted to smoke, and asked the widow to let me. But she wouldn't. She said it was a mean practice and wasn't clean, and I must try to not do it any more. That is just the way with some people.

They get down on a thing when they don't know nothing about it. Here she was a-bothering about Moses, which was no kin to her, and no use to anybody, being gone, you see, yet finding a power of fault with me for doing a thing that had some good in it. And she took snuff, too; of course that was all right, because she done it herself.

Her sister, Miss Watson, a tolerable

slim old maid, with goggles on, had just come to live with her, and took a set at me now with a spelling-book. She worked me middling hard for about an hour, and then the widow made her ease up. I couldn't stood it much longer. Then for an hour it was deadly dull, and I was fidgety. Miss Watson would say, "Don't put your feet up there, Huckleberry;" and "Don't scrunch up like that, Huckleberry — set up straight;" and pretty soon she would say, "Don't gap and stretch like that, Huckleberry — why don't you try to behave?" Then she told me all about the bad place, and I said I wished I was there. She got mad then, but I didn't mean no harm. All I wanted was to go somewheres; all I wanted was a change, I warn't particular. She said it was wicked to say what I said; said she wouldn't say it for the whole world; she was going to live so as to go to the good place. Well, I couldn't see no advantage in going where she was going, so I made up my mind I wouldn't try for it. But I never said so, because it would only make trouble, and wouldn't do no good. (chapter 1)

■ ■ ■

How does Twain create humor in this passage?

Twain is writing to an audience that does not have televisions or computers. Twain has to use language to paint a picture for his audience. Notice the descriptions that Twain uses. Write two here.

SCIENCE

Comparison

Which two leaf samples are similar?

VOCABULARY

The Fairie Queen[7]
Edmund Spenser

The Faerie Queene — as you probably know by now — is the longest narrative poem in the English language. It makes Milton's formidable *Paradise Lost* look like a walk in the park! Still, it is full of action and one of the seminal masterpieces of English literature, and it has influenced scholars since its completion in 1596. Nonetheless, its epic length, its wealth of incident and detail, and the complexity of its allegory and richness of its topical allusions make it one of the hardest texts to understand. By the way, letters *u* and *v* are rather interchangeable in Spenser's deliberately antique English — used to evoke a world of mystery.

Suggested Vocabulary Words

A. <u>Scarsely</u> had Phoebus in the <u>glooming</u> East / Yet <u>harnessed</u> his firie-footed teeme, / Ne reard aboue the earth his flaming creast, / When the last deadly smoke aloft did steeme, / That signe of last outbreathed life did seeme, / Vnto the watchman on the castle wall; / Who thereby dead that balefull Beast did deeme, / And to his Lord and Ladie lowd gan call, / To tell, how he had seene the Dragons fatall fall. (book 1, canto 12)

B. For all so soone, as Guyon thence was gon / Vpon his voyage with his trustie guide, / That wicked band of villeins fresh begon / That castle to assaile on euery side, / And lay strong siege about it far and wide. / So huge and infinite their numbers were, / That all the land they vnder them did hide; / So fowle and vgly, that <u>exceeding</u> feare / Their visages imprest, when they approched neare. (book 2, canto 11)

C. Who backe returning, told as he had seene, / That they were doughtie knights of <u>dreaded</u> name; / And those two Ladies, their two loues vnseene; / And therefore wisht them without blot or blame, / To let them passe at will, for dread of shame. / But Blandamour full of <u>vainglorious</u> spright, / And rather stird by his discordfull Dame, / Vpon them gladly would haue prov'd his might, / But that he yet was sore of his late lucklesse fight. (book 4, canto 3)

PROPHETIC IMAGINATION

SCRIPTURE

"Moses led the people out of the camp to meet with God, and they stood at the foot of the mountain. Mount Sinai was covered with smoke, because the LORD descended on it in fire. The smoke billowed up from it like smoke from a furnace, and the whole mountain trembled violently, and the sound of the trumpet grew louder and louder. Then Moses spoke and the voice of God answered him."

~ Exodus 19:17–19

PRAYER POINTS
JOY

"You became imitators of us and of the Lord; in spite of severe suffering, you welcomed the message with the joy given by the Holy Spirit."

~ 1 Thessalonians 1:6

Walter Brueggemann, in his book *The Prophetic Imagination*, traces the lines from the radical vision of Moses to the solidification of royal power in Solomon to the prophetic critique of that power with a new vision of freedom in the prophets. Here he traces the broad sweep from Exodus to Kings to Jeremiah to Jesus. He highlights that the prophetic vision not only embraces the ordinary world of the people but creates an energy and amazement (which he calls "imagination") based on the new thing that God is doing. Bruggemann's position is that the kingship in Israel is a step backward from the Mosaic "revolution" and that the prophets and then later Jesus called Israel away from kingship back to the original vision of Moses, the prophetic imagination. Bruggemann writes "to address the issue of a truth greatly reduced requires us to be poets that speak against a prose world. . . . By prose, I refer to a world that is organized in settled formulae. . . . By poetry, I mean language that moves, that jumps at the right moment, that breaks open old worlds with surprise, abrasion, and pace. Poetic speech is the only proclamation worth doing in a situation of reductionism."[1]

Bruggemann has his faults, but I think he says a few things that the 21st century evangelical community — especially my own community, the home school community — should incorporate into their vision. For one thing, we must maintain a prophetic, hopeful vision in a world that is embracing materialism and hopelessness. We must, at the same time, affirm objective truth in a post-modern world that is preaching subjectivity. We must not be post-modern hippies, wandering around spreading alternative communities, subversive narratives, and anti-secular sermons. Rather, as one social critic explains, "The Old Testament prophets came to announce to Israel their sin before God by going after other gods, playing the harlot to God-their-husband, revealing their liturgical and corruptions, and laying before them their sins. They were God's covenantal lawyers bringing to bear upon Israel the lawsuit of the covenant."[2] Our social criticism must be purposeful and constructive, not destructive. For example, we disagree with post-modern morality that argues that morality should be based in one's own subjective belief system, as long as that belief structure is sincerely held and harms no one. Our biblical, prophetic message must be that that is hog wash. Our feelings, our notions, of what is right are irrelevant unless it lines up with the Word of God.

Finally, basking in the bright light of biblical truth, we must show post-modern culture that, in Christ, and in Christ alone, there is hope and joy and a prophetic imagination.

ENGLISH

Punctuation

Punctuate these sentences as needed.

1. England in the eleventh century was conquered by the normans.

2. Amid the angry yells of the spectators he died.

3. For the sake of emphasis a word or a phrase may be placed out of its natural order.

4. In *The Pickwick Papers* the conversation of Sam Weller is spiced with wit.

5. New York on the contrary abounds in men of wealth.

6. It has come down by uninterrupted tradition from the earliest times to the present day.

Memorize

High-scoring ACT essays inevitably exhibit some quotes from notable sources. Memorize the following quotes so that you can use them on the ACT.[3]

- The future is purchased by the present. — Samuel Johnson

- The sober second thought is always essential, and seldom wrong. — Martin Van Buren

- Recollect that trifles make perfection, and that perfection is no trifle. — Michael Angelo

- Have more than thou showest, Speak less than thou knowest. — Shakespeare

- Sin has many tools, but a lie is the handle that fits them all. — O.W. Holmes

- Let all the end thou aim'st at be thy country's, Thy God's and truth's. — Shakespeare

- Our greatest glory is not in never falling, but in rising every time we fall.

- Honour and shame from no condition rise; act well your part, there all the honour lies. — Alexander Pope

- True happiness consists not in the multitude of friends, but in their worth and choice. — Ben Jonson

- One "do" is worth a thousand "don'ts" in the destruction of evil or the production of good. — Hughes

- I look upon the simple and childish virtues of veracity and honesty as the root of all that is sublime in character. — Emerson

- It is a low benefit to give me something; it is a high benefit to enable me to do something of myself. — Emerson

- Greatly begin! though thou hast time But for a line, be that sublime — Not failure, but low aim, is crime. — Lowell

- Push nobly on! The goal is near! Ascend the mountain! Breast the gale! Look upward, onward—never fear! He who has a thousand friends Has not a friend to spare; And he who has one enemy Will meet him everywhere. — Omar Khayyam

MATH

Quadratic Equations

Several ACT math questions test whether you are able to factor. Some of the expressions you should be able to factor are:

$w2 + aw = w(w + a)$ or $w2 + wy = w(w + y)$

$w2 - 1 = (w + 1)(w - 1)$ or $w2 - y2 = (w + y)(w - y)$

$w2 + 2w + 1 = (w + 1)(w + 1) = (w + 1)2$

$w2 - 3w - 4 = (w - 4)(w + 1)$

What is the solution set of the quadratic equation $2a2 + 7a - 4 = 0$?

A. (-2,1)
B. (-4,0.5)
C. (-0.5, 4)
D. (-6,1)
E. (-1,8)

Reading for Detail

The real trouble with most of the attempts that teachers and parents make, to teach children a vital relation to books, is that they do not believe in the books and that they do not believe in the children.

It is almost impossible to find a child who, in one direction or another, the first few years of his life, is not creative. It is almost impossible to find a parent or a teacher who does not discourage this creativeness. The discouragement begins in a small way, at first, in the average family, but as the more creative a child becomes the more inconvenient he is, as a general rule, every time a boy is caught being creative, something has to be done to him about it.

It is a part of the nature of creativeness that it involves being creative a large part of the time in the wrong direction. Half-proud and half-stupefied parents, failing to see that the mischief in a boy is the entire basis of his education, the mainspring of his life, not being able to break the mainspring themselves, frequently hire teachers to help them. The teacher who can break a mainspring first and keep it from getting mended, is often the most esteemed in the community. Those who have broken the most, "secure results." The spectacle of the mechanical, barren, conventional society so common in the present day to all who love their kind is a sign there is no withstanding. It is a spectacle we can only stand and watch — some of us — the huge, dreary kinetoscope of it, grinding its cogs and wheels, and swinging its weary faces past our eyes. The most common sight in it and the one that hurts the hardest, is the boy who could be made into a man out of the parts of him that his parents and teachers are trying to throw away. The faults of the average child, as things are going just now, would be the making of him, if he could be placed in seeing hands. It may not be possible to educate a boy by using what has been left out of him, but it is more than possible to begin his education by using what ought to have been left out of him. So long as parents and teachers are either too dull or too busy to experiment with mischief, to be willing to pay for a child's originality what originality costs, only the most hopeless children can be expected to amount to anything. If we fail to see that originality is worth paying for, that the risk involved in a child's not being creative is infinitely more serious than the risk involved in his being creative in the wrong direction, there is little either for us or for our children to hope for, as the years go on, except to grow duller together. We do not like this growing duller together very well, perhaps, but we have the feeling at least that we have been educated, and when our children become at last as little interested in the workings of their minds, as parents and teachers are in theirs, we have the feeling that they also have been educated. We are not unwilling to admit, in a somewhat useless, kindly, generalizing fashion, that vital and beautiful children delight in things, in proportion as they discover them, or are allowed to make them up, but we do not propose in the meantime to have our own children any more vital and beautiful than we can help. In four or five years they discover that a home is a place where the more one thinks of things, the more unhappy he is. In four or five years more they learn that a school is a place where children are expected not to use their brains while they are being cultivated. As long as he is at his mother's breast the typical American child finds that he is admired for thinking of things. When he runs around the house he finds gradually that he is admired very much less for thinking of things. At school he is disciplined for it.

In a library, if he has an uncommonly active mind, and takes the liberty of being as alive there, as he is outdoors, if he roams through the books, vaults over their fences, climbs up their mountains, and eats of their fruit, and dreams by their streams, or is caught camping out in their woods, he is made an example of. He is treated as a tramp and an idler, and if he cannot be held down with a dictionary he is looked upon as not worth educating. If his parents decide he shall be educated anyway, dead or alive, or in spite of his being alive, the more he is educated the more he wonders why he was born and the more his teachers from behind their dictionaries, and the other boys from underneath their dictionaries, wonder why he was born. While it may be a general principle that the longer a boy wonders why he was born in conditions like these, and the longer his teachers and parents wonder, the more there is of him, it may be observed that a general principle is not of very much comfort to the boy while the process of wondering is going on. There seems to be no escape from the process, and if, while he is being educated, he is not allowed to use himself, he can hardly be blamed for spending a good deal of his time in wondering why he is not someone else. In a half-seeing, half-blinded fashion he struggles on. If he is obstinate enough, he manages to struggle through with his eyes shut. Sometimes he belongs to a higher kind, and opens his eyes and struggles.[4] (Gerald Lee, *The Lost Art of Reading*).

The best title of this passage would be:

A. Childhood Reading Habits.
B. On Wondering Why One Was Born
C. Childhood Depression
D. Childhood Imagination and Reading

"It is a part of the nature of creativeness that it involves being creative a large part of the time in the wrong direction" means:

A. Creative children are often confused.
B. Creativeness involves much cognitive dissonance.
C. Creative children are necessarily lazy.
D. Creativity may appear, for a season, as aberrant behavior.

TEST-TAKING INSIGHT

Test Anxiety

Test anxiety is reduced in several ways.

- Memorize Scripture and pray Scripture during the test.

- Don't cram the night before. The best thing to do the night before the ACT exam is to sleep!

- Try to maintain a positive attitude while preparing for the test and during the test.

- Exercising for a few days before the test will help reduce stress.

- Arrive at the test site early so you won't have to worry about being late.

- Memorize the directions before the test.

- Be cognizant of the test numbers through the test so that you have a good idea how to pace yourself.

- Don't worry about how fast other people finish their test; just concentrate on your own test.

- If you don't know a question skip it for the time being (come back to it later if you have time), and remember that you don't have to always get every question right to do well on the test.

S CIENCE

Science Data

What can you conclude from the data below?

I. Fall time increases as height increases.
II. Fall time decreases as height increases.
III. Fall time decreases as height decreases.
IV. This object falls about .25 meters every .5 seconds

A. I
B. II
C. III
D. IV
E. I, II, IV
F. None
G. All

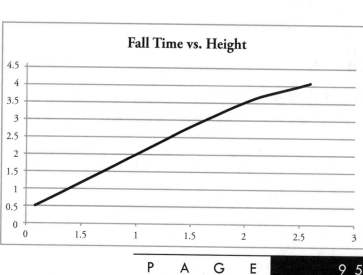

Fall Time vs. Height

VOCABULARY

The Sound and the Fury[5]
William Faulkner

The Sound and the Fury is the story of the fall of the Compson family, a wealthy Jackson, Mississippi, family in the early 1900s. The novel is divided into four sections, each told by a different character. The three Compson sons, Benjy, Quentin, and Jason Compson, and the family's black servant, Dilsey Gibson, each have their own section in which they tell their collective story.

Suggested Vocabulary Words

A. You can be <u>oblivious</u> to the sound for a long while, then in a second of ticking it can create in the mind unbroken the long diminishing parade of time you didn't hear. (June 2, 1910)

B. From then on until he had you completely subjugated he was always in or out of your room, <u>ubiquitous</u> and <u>garrulous</u>, though his manner gradually moved northward as his raiment improved, until at last when he had bled you until you began to learn better he was calling you Quentin or whatever. (June 2, 1910)

C. . . . and I suppose that with all his petty <u>chicanery</u> and <u>hypocrisy</u> he stank no higher in heaven's nostrils than any other. (June 2, 1910)

D. Suddenly I held out my hand and we shook, he gravely, from the <u>pompous</u> height of his municipal and military dream. (June 2, 1910)

E. . . . where only he and the gull, the one terrifically motionless, the other in a steady and measured pull and recover that partook of <u>inertia</u> itself. . . . (April 8, 1928)

F. . . . all I had felt suffered without visible form antic and perverse mocking without relevance <u>inherent</u> themselves with the denial of the significance they should have affirmed. . . . (April 8, 1928)

G. The air brightened, the running shadow patches were not the <u>obverse</u>, and it seemed to him that the fact the day was cleaning was another cunning stoke on the part of the foe. (April 8, 1928)

H. . . . and suddenly with an old <u>premonition</u> he clapped the brakes and stopped and sat perfectly still. . . . For a moment Benjy sat in an utter <u>hiatus</u>. (April 8, 1928)

WRITING

Writing Description

Close your eyes. Imagine that you are traveling on a road in a forest. What do you see?

Write down images evoked by the following.

Terror   Kindness   Hope

> "For every Southern boy fourteen years old, not once but whenever he wants it, there is the instant when it's still not yet two o'clock on that July afternoon in 1863, the brigades are in position behind the rail fence, the guns are laid and ready in the woods and the furled flags are already loosened to break out and Pickett himself with his long oiled ringlets and his hat in one hand probably and his sword in the other looking up the hill waiting for Longstreet to give the word and it's all in the balance, it hasn't happened yet, it hasn't even begun yet, it not only hasn't begun yet but there is still time for it not to begin against that position and those circumstances which made more men than Garnett and Kemper and Armistead and Wilcox look grave yet it's going to begin, we all know that, we have come too far with too much at stake and that moment doesn't need even a fourteen-year-old boy to think This time. Maybe this time with all this much to lose and all this much to gain: Pennsylvania, Maryland, the world, the golden dome of Washington itself to crown with desperate and unbelievable victory the desperate gamble, the cast made two years ago."[6]
>
> — William Faulkner

MODERNISM

Arising out of heady optimism in the early 1900s, modernism was a radical approach that tried to recreate the way modern civilization viewed culture, politics, and science. This new thinking engendered a sort of rebellion that merged in full force by the 1920s.

SCRIPTURE

"Raise your staff and stretch out your hand over the sea to divide the water so that the Israelites can go through the sea on dry ground. I will harden the hearts of the Egyptians so that they will go in after them. And I will gain glory through Pharaoh and all his army, through his chariots and his horsemen. The Egyptians will know that I am the LORD when I gain glory through Pharaoh, his chariots and his horsemen."

~ Exodus 14:16–18

There were certain assumptions that moderns made: Western culture was old-fashioned and dysfunctional. Society was bound by the facileness of a society that was too preoccupied with image and too recalcitrant or reticent to embrace needed change. This disillusionment with everything status quo led writers and artists to cross cultural boundaries heretofore ignored. The Puritans embraced neo-classicism. The romantics were nature lovers. The modernists examined and replicated the lifestyle of Amazon prehistoric culture. Ironically, everything that had emerged in Western culture for the last four hundred years was suspect but romantic motifs of pristine culture were cool!

This of course was impossible and laughable. Modernist subjects included primitive people groups who looked like they had just descended the steps of Macy's. In short, the emerging culture ultimately would undermine tradition and authority in the hopes of transforming contemporary society. They would try to replace Judeo-Christian morality with a "feel good" reductionist subjectivity.

They would fail abysmally, of course. They could not have their epistemological cake and eat their pneumatic icing in the same meal. It was like mixing oil and water. So, perhaps the best way to describe modernism is "nihilism." Nonetheless, modernism sets the stage for the chaotic 1960s, postmodernism, and absurdism. In other words, the worst was yet to come!

Nihilism was the questioning of all religious and moral enculturation principles as the only means of obtaining social progress. Ironically, a sort of modernist religion replaced the old orthodox religion and no progress was made at all. As one social critic explained, "Like poor Elmer Fudd and his futile quest to bag Bugs Bunny, there arrived a moment when Elmer exclaimed 'West and wewaxation at wast!' "[1] But poor Elmer and the modernists had neither bagged their prey nor knew how to rest!

At the same time that modernists embraced pastoral (nature) themes, they also embraced science. In the wake of the discovery of the theory of relativity, modernists were sure that they had arrived at Nirvana. Science, apparently, now, where religion had failed, would solve all the problems of society.

Science, being the cold and sterile thing that it is, invited modernists to repudiate the moral codes of the society in which they were living. In other words, the modernists ran from Victorian morality as quickly as they could! The reason that they did so was not necessarily because they did not believe in God, although there was a great majority of them who were atheists or agnostics. Rather, their rejection of conventional morality was based on its boring predictability, and

PRAYER POINTS

PERSEVERANCE

"No discipline seems pleasant at the time, but painful. Later on, however, it produces a harvest of righteousness and peace for those who have been trained by it."

~ Hebrews 12:11

its exertion of control over human feelings. In other words, it limited the human spirit or, to use later vernacular, traditional morality "cramped" one's style.

Conformity and tradition were anathema. And so, in the arts, for instance, at the beginning of the 20th century, artists flirted with many different styles: cubism, futurism, constructivism, dadaism, and surrealism. They broke new ground, so to speak.

Yet, is it really that new? Xerxes and Pharoah saw themselves as gods — now that is a metaphysical coup d'é·tat. Pretty modern, too. The builders of the Tower of Babel believed in science, too. Fervently, too. And we know what happened. But a few people got it right. Moses put his rod into the Red Sea and it parted. Hmm . . . not very "modern" — there is nothing cool about an old rod and old fashioned faith. The sea parted, too. And we know what happened to the most high and mighty Pharoah! I want my science to help me build my bridges but not my metaphysics!

V OCABULARY

Fathers and Children[3]
Ivan Turgenev

Ivan Turgenev was one of the giants of Russian literature, a literature that boasts Tolstoy, Chehkov, and Dostoevsky. This short novel was a 19th-century study of parent and children relations. It presages the "generation gap" that popularized the 1950s.

Suggested Vocabulary Words

A. The servant, from a feeling of <u>propriety</u>, and perhaps, too, not anxious to remain under the master's eye, had gone to the gate, and was smoking a pipe. Nikolai Petrovitch bent his head, and began staring at the crumbling steps; a big <u>mottled</u> fowl walked <u>sedately</u> towards him, treading firmly with its great yellow legs; a muddy cat gave him an unfriendly look, twisting herself <u>coyly</u> round the railing.

B. She used suddenly to go abroad, and suddenly return to Russia, and led an eccentric life in general. She had the reputation of being a <u>frivolous</u> <u>coquette</u>, abandoned herself eagerly to every sort of pleasure, danced to exhaustion, laughed and jested with young men, whom she received in the dim light of her drawing-room before dinner; while at night she wept and prayed, found no peace in anything, and often paced her room till morning, <u>wringing</u> her hands in anguish, or sat, pale and chill, over a psalter.

C. Nikolai Petrovitch had made Fenitchka's acquaintance in the following manner. He had once happened three years before to stay a night at an inn in a remote district town. He was agreeably struck by the cleanness of the room assigned to him, the freshness of the bed-linen. Surely the woman of the house must be a German? was the idea that occurred to him; but she proved to be a Russian, a woman of about fifty, neatly dressed, of a good-looking, sensible <u>countenance</u> and <u>discreet</u> speech.

M ATH

Solving Math Problems

- Read the problem very carefully. Most people answer a word problem incorrectly because they do not read the problem carefully — normally the math computation is easy.

- Draw a diagram if necessary but, if one is available, mark it up.

- Write an equation reflecting your problem.

- Solve the equation.

- Check your answer. Make sure it is in the right medium (i.e., x or so forth).

■ ■ ■

The length of the side of square B is double the width of rectangle A. The length of the rectangle is three times the width of the rectangle. The perimeter of the rectangle is 48 inches. Find the length of the side of the square.

> "If people do not believe that mathematics is simple, it is only because they do not realize how complicated life is."[3]
> — John Louis von Neumann

R E A D I N G

Tone and Inference

She used suddenly to go abroad, and suddenly return to Russia, and led an eccentric life in general. She had the reputation of being a frivolous coquette, abandoned herself eagerly to every sort of pleasure, danced to exhaustion, laughed and jested with young men, whom she received in the dim light of her drawing-room before dinner; while at night she wept and prayed, found no peace in anything, and often paced her room till morning, wringing her hands in anguish, or sat, pale and chill, over a psalter. Day came, and she was transformed again into a grand lady; again she went out, laughed, chattered, and simply flung herself headlong into anything which could afford her the slightest distraction. She was marvelously well-proportioned, her hair coloured like gold and heavy as gold hung below her knees, but no one would have called her a beauty; in her whole face the only good point was her eyes, and even her eyes were not good — they were grey, and not large — but their glance was swift and deep, unconcerned to the point of audacity, and thoughtful to the point of melancholy — an enigmatic glance. There was a light of something extraordinary in them, even while her tongue was lisping the emptiest of inanities. She dressed with elaborate care. . . . Her whole behaviour presented a series of inconsistencies; the only letters which could have awakened her husband's just suspicions, she wrote to a man who was almost a stranger to her . . . she ceased to laugh and to jest, she listened to him, and gazed at him with a look of bewilderment. Sometimes, for the most part suddenly, this bewilderment passed into chill horror; her face took a wild, death-like expression; she locked herself up in her bedroom, and her maid, putting her ear to the keyhole, could hear her smothered sobs. More than once, as he went home after a tender interview, Kirsanov felt within him that heartrending, bitter vexation which follows on a total failure. (Turgenev, *Fathers and Children*)

The tone of this passage is:

A. Serious
B. Moribund
C. Tepid
D. Whimsical

Turgenev characterizes this woman:

A. as a scatter-brained, silly female.
B. as an intelligent, iconoclastic character.
C. as a choleric, eccentric person.
D. as a reticent, sanguine person.

"Turgenev did for Russian literature what Byron did for English literature; he led the genius of Russia on a pilgrimage throughout all Europe. And in Europe his work reaped a glorious harvest of praise. Flaubert was astounded by him, George Sand looked up to him as to a master, Taine spoke of his work as being the finest artistic production since Sophocles. In Turgenev's work, Europe not only discovered Turgenev, but it discovered Russia, the simplicity and the naturalness of the Russian character; and this came as a revelation."[4] — M. Baring

"*If we wait for the moment when everything, absolutely everything is ready, we shall never begin.*"[5]
— Ivan Turgenev

SCIENCE

Analyzing Data

The most common causes of the common cold are viruses — rhinoviruses, coronaviruses, and the respiratory syncytial virus (RSV). The rhinovirus group causes 10% to 40% of colds. The coronaviruses and RSV are responsible for 20% and 10% of cases, respectively.

Rhinoviruses, the worst offenders, are most active in early fall, spring, and summer. More than 110 distinct rhinovirus types have been identified. These viruses grow best at temperatures of about 91 degrees, that perfect body temperature right inside the human nose. Most rhinoviruses seldom produce serious illnesses. Other cold viruses, such as parainfluenza and RSV, produce mild infections in adults but can lead to severe lower respiratory infections, such as pneumonia, in young children.

Scientists think coronaviruses cause a large percentage of adult colds. These cold viruses are most active in the winter and early spring. Of the more than 30 kinds of coronaviruses, three or four infect humans. The importance of coronaviruses as a cause of colds is hard to assess because, unlike rhinoviruses, they are difficult to grow in the laboratory.

About 10% to 15% of adult colds are caused by viruses also responsible for other, more severe respiratory illnesses. The causes of 30% to 50% of adult colds, presumed to be viral, remain unidentified. The same viruses that produce colds in adults appear to cause colds in children. The relative importance of various viruses in children's colds, however, is unclear because it's difficult to isolate the precise cause of symptoms in studies of children with colds.

There is no evidence that you can get a cold from exposure to cold weather or from getting chilled or overheated.

There is also no evidence that one's chances of getting a cold are related to factors such as exercise, diet, or enlarged tonsils or adenoids. On the other hand, research suggests that psychological stress and allergic diseases affecting your nose or throat may have an impact on your chances of getting infected by cold viruses.[6]

Which conclusion is correct?

On September 15, a four-year-old male is exhibiting flu-like symptons but his temperature is normal.

A. He most likely has problems with undiagnosed allergies.
B. He most likely has a cold instigated by the rhinovirus.
C. He most likely has a cold instigatged by RSV.
D. He most likely has the flu — not a cold.

On March 15, a 55-year-old female has a runny nose, slight cough, and very low grade temperature. She does not have the flu.

A. She mostly likely has a cold instigated by the rhinovirus.

B. She most likely has problems with undiagnosed allergies.
C. She most likely has a cold instigated by RSV.
D. She mostly likely has a cold instigated by the coronavirus.

On June 28, a very busy businessman walks into the emergency room with a splitting headache, a runny nose, and a high fever. His tonsils were inflamed. He tells the attending physician that he was out in the "weather" yesterday and had "chills." He is sure that he has a bad cold, or worse.

A. There is no evidence that one's chances of getting a cold are related to factors such as exercise, diet, or enlarged tonsils or adenoids. On the other hand, research suggests that psychological stress and allergic diseases affecting your nose or throat may have an impact on your chances of getting infected by cold viruses. Obviously the man was under stress, so he very well may have a cold. But, at the same time, his high fever points to a more serious cause.
B. There is evidence that one's chances of getting a cold are related to factors such as exercise, diet, or enlarged tonsils or adenoids. On the other hand, research suggests that psychological stress and allergic diseases affecting your nose or throat may have an impact on your chances of getting infected by cold viruses. Obviously the man was under stress, so he very well may have a cold.

But, at the same time, his high fever points to a more serious cause.

C. There is no evidence that one's chances of getting a cold are related to factors such as exercise, diet, or enlarged tonsils or adenoids. On the other hand, research suggests that psychological stress and allergic diseases affecting your nose or throat may have an impact on your chances of getting infected by cold viruses. Obviously the man was under stress, so he very well may have had allergies. But, at the same time, his high fever points to a more serious cause. Therefore, the allergies were merely a mask for more serious issues.

D. None of the above.

"Science does not know its debt to imagination."[7]
— Ralph Waldo Emerson

"The most exciting phrase to hear in science, the one that heralds the most discoveries, is not "Eureka!" (I found it!) but "That's funny. . . ."[8]
— Isaac Asimov

Below is a paragraph containing underlined portions. Alternate ways of stating the underlined portions follow the paragraphs. Choose the best alternative.

Several experienced African lion hunters strongly advise to take a "paradox," which in their parlance is affectionately called a "cripple-stopper." It looks like what one would suppose an elephant gun to look like. Its weight is staggering, and it shoots a solid ball, backed up by a fearful charge of cordite. They use it under the following conditions: Suppose that a big animal has been wounded and not instantly killed. It at once assumes the aggressive, and is savage beyond belief. The pain of the wound infuriates it and its one object in life is to get at the man who shot it. It charges in a well-nigh irresistible rush, and no ordinary bullet can stop it unless placed in one or two small vital spots. Under the circumstances the hunter may not be able to hold his rifle steady enough to hit these aforesaid spots. That is when the paradox comes in. The hunter points it in a general way in the direction of the oncoming beast, pulls the trigger and hopes for the best. The paradox bullet hits with the force of a sledge hammer, and stuns everything within a quarter of a mile, and the hunter turns several back somersaults from the recoil and fades into bruised unconsciousness.

1. A. taking a "paradox,"
   B. to took a "paradox,"
   C. bringing "a paradox,"
   D. No change

2. A. It at once assumed the aggressive and was savage beyond belief.
   B. It at once assumes an aggressiveness and savagery beyond belief.
   C. It at once assumes aggressive, and is savagely beyond belief.
   D. No change

3. A. That is when the paradox arrives.
   B. When the paradox comes in
   C. If the paradox comes in.
   D. No change

Developing an Argument with Examples

On the ACT writing section, you will develop your argument(s) by offering numerous examples. Analyze the way this author develops his argument. Which examples does he offer?

All this may be very true. But of what practical use will physical science be to me?

Let me ask in return: Are none of you going to emigrate? If you have courage and wisdom, emigrate you will, some of you, instead of stopping here to scramble over each other's backs for the scraps, like black-beetles in a kitchen. And if you emigrate, you will soon find out, if you have eyes and common sense, that the vegetable wealth of the world is no more exhausted than its mineral wealth. Exhausted? Not half of it — I believe not a tenth of it — is yet known. Could I show you the wealth which I have seen in a single Tropic island, not sixty miles square — precious timbers, gums, fruits, what not, enough to give employment and wealth to thousands and tens of thousands, wasting for want of being known and worked — then you would see what a man who emigrates may do, by a little sound knowledge of botany alone.

And if not. Suppose that any one of you, learning a little sound Natural History, should abide here in Britain to your life's end, and observe nothing but the hedgerow plants, he would find that there is much more to be seen in those mere hedgerow plants than he fancies now. The microscope will reveal to him in the tissues of any wood, of any seed, wonders which will first amuse him, then puzzle him, and at last (I hope) awe him, as he perceives that smallness of size interferes in no way with perfection of development, and that "Nature," as has been well said, "is greatest in that which is least." And more. Suppose that he went further still. Suppose that he extended his researches somewhat to those minuter vegetable forms, the mosses, fungi, lichens; suppose that he went a little further still, and tried what the microscope would show him in any stagnant pool, whether fresh water or salt, of Desmidiœ, Diatoms, and all those wondrous atomies which seem as yet to defy our classification into plants or animals.

Suppose he learnt something of this, but nothing of aught else. Would he have gained no solid wisdom? He would be a stupider man than I have a right to believe any of my readers to be, if he had not gained thereby somewhat of the most valuable of treasures — namely, that inductive habit of mind, that power of judging fairly of facts, without which no good or lasting work will be done, whether in physical science, in social science, in politics, in philosophy, in philology, or in history.

But more: let me urge you to study Natural Science, on grounds which may be to you new and unexpected — on social, I had almost said on political, grounds.

We all know, and I trust we all love, the names of Liberty, Equality, and Brotherhood. We feel, I trust, that these words are too beautiful not to represent true and just ideas; and that therefore they will come true, and be fulfilled, somewhen, somewhere, somehow. It may be in a shape very different from that which you, or I, or any man expects; but still they will be fulfilled.

But if they are to come true, it is we, the individual men, who must help them to come true for the whole world, by practising them ourselves, when and where we can. And I tell you — that in becoming scientific men, in studying science and acquiring the scientific habit of mind, you will find yourselves enjoying a freedom, an equality, a brotherhood, such as you will not find elsewhere just now.

Freedom: what do we want freedom for? For this, at least; that we may be each and all able to think what we choose; and to say what we choose also, provided we do not say it rudely or violently, so as to provoke a breach of the peace. That last was Mr. Buckle's definition of freedom of speech. That was the only limit to it which he would allow; and I think that that is Mr. John Stuart Mill's limit also. It is mine. And I think we have that kind of freedom in these islands as perfectly as any men are likely to have it on this earth.[9] (Charles Kingsley, *Town Geology*)

HOME

Larry King was gently scolding Al Gore. CNN's *Larry King Live* was blaring from my mother's opaque Panasonic 25-inch screen. Electrons danced across this colander of 21st century entertainment. Cable television munificence clashed with dancing electronic intruders. Bounteous contradictions were everywhere evident.

It did not matter, though, because my mother only accessed one-third of her available channels. The effort to ingress more exotic offerings in the upper channels was fatuous anyway. From Mom's perspective, she only needed CNN, the Weather Channel, and the History Channel. Even the local news did not interest her now. This was all the entertainment she needed and, to her, news was entertainment. Mom was dying of pancreatic cancer.

Lying under a brightly colored afghan knitted by her mother, who was affectionately called Big Momma by all other generations, Mom was obviously defeated by the cancer interlopers who had completely subdued her body and were now skirmishing with her spirit. With her blonde frosted wig slightly askew on her forehead, Mom very much appeared the defeated warrior.

She needed the bright color in the afghan to tease vigor from her emaciated frame and color from her pallid skin. Big Momma had shamelessly knit bright chartreuse, gold, and pinks into her afghan. Her cacophonic choices doomed the afghan to family coffers or to the most destitute recipient who had no ardor for natural, appealing, subtle hues or had no affordable choice anyway. My mother's body, naturally big boned but until recently pudgy, unnaturally jutted out from loose knitted afghan perimeters. Her angular right knee was lassoed by a frayed portion of Big Momma's much-used, little-appreciated afghan. It looked like a reptile peeking through the burnished flora of a viscous jungle thicket.

It suited my mother just fine now, though. She herself felt frayed, tattered, and very old. She also felt used and useless. In the dim hue of *Larry King Live*, the afghan and my mother had a bizarre, surrealistic demeanor that accurately depicted the environs of her crumbling world.

It started with a stomach ache. Ordinary in scope and sequence, this stomach ache nonetheless was an aberration in my mother's medical portfolio. Mom simply wasn't sick. Never. Her delusion of immortality was so endemic to her personality that sickness was beyond the realm of her possibilities.

Unfortunately, the stomach ache ended and the anemia began. In most medical communities anemia is a sure sign that something is amiss in the gastrointestinal cosmos. In the Southern Arkansas universe where my mother lived, medicine was more empathic than empirical, and anemia was perceived as too much fried chicken or turnip greens. This diagnosis worked

well enough, perhaps better, than conventional interventions in colds, flu, and the occasional gall bladder attack. However, in the really big things — like pancreatic cancer — normal rural Southern medical practice was hopelessly dilatory and inevitably, therefore, nugatory.

My mother, who walked three miles a day and regularly ate chicken gizzards fried in old lard, shrugged her shoulders and forgot about the whole thing. In fact, even after Geritol and BC Powders failed, she refused to visit her doctor. To question a doctor-friend's diagnosis was worse than a serious illness — it was downright unfriendly, something my mother manifestly refused to be. With confident sanguineness, old Dr. E.P. Donahue, throat reflector protruding from his head, oversized Masonic ring protruding from his left middle finger, pronounced mom to be in remarkably good health. Dr. Donahue, who had delivered all Mom's three boys, was infallible. The medical "pope" as it were, whose edicts, once promulgated, were infallible.

Mom's malady, however, was already fatal. Her stamina and obstinacy propelled her forward for almost a year, but the carcinoma had already ambushed her. No one could tell, though, because she was in such great health. Like a beautiful price mare whose robustness and wholesomeness camouflaged its metastasis malevolent concealed interior. "My health," my mother said as she ironically shrugged, "killed me."

By the time our family surgeon and good friend Dr. Johnny Joe Jones, one of Dr. Donahue's cardinals, called the hogs with mom one last time before she went into the operating room and opened her up with his scalpel, mom was mellifluent with metastatic carcinoma.

My mother did not know, but would find out an important truth: we are crucified with Christ, yet, it is not we who live, but Christ who lives in us. Mom did not know it, but that part of life that was hers, was ebbing, and that which was God's, was rising. Yet, in a sense, we all are dying physically, every day. But in Christ, we live forever — not metaphorically, but in reality.

My mother was walking onto the stage into a drama whose ending she could not control. She knew the ending, or at least she shortly would know the ending.

The question was, "Will it be a comedy or a tragedy? Will it have a happy ending, or a sad one?" It was never about cancer. It was about life. Life eternal. How about you? When you walk onto the stage of life, are you joining a drama with a happy or sad ending?

The truth is, the script had been written in eternity long before her physician found the carcinoma. And her script, as all our scripts, was written by a Creator God who loves us dearly.

"When you look into an abyss, the abyss also looks into you"[1] (Friedrich Nietzsche). *On Looking Into the Abyss: Untimely Thoughts on Culture and Society* by Gertrude Himmelfarb argues that the "abyss is the abyss of meaninglessness."[2] The interpreter takes precedence over the thing interpreted, and any interpretation goes. The most obvious aim of such a creed is to weaken our hold on reality, chiefly by denying that there is any reality for us

to get hold of; its most probable effect, if we were to take it seriously, would be to induce feelings of despair and dread. This view invites the tyranny of the subjective — anything goes so long as it does not hurt anyone and it is believed sincerely.

My poor mother had looked into the abyss. Even though she knew the Lord as Savior, it was precious little comfort to her as she faced pancreatic cancer. Yet, in the midst of this crisis, in the midst of her confusion, the clarity for her, as it is for us all, is the Cross at Calvary! I am crucified with Christ.

ENGLISH

Pick out the subject and the (direct) object:

1. This, and other measures of precaution, I took.

2. The pursuing the inquiry under the light of an end or final cause, gives wonderful animation, a sort of personality to the whole writing.

3. Why does the horizon hold me fast, with my joy and grief, in this center?

4. His books have no melody, no emotion, no humor, no relief to the dead prosaic level.

5. On the voyage to Egypt, he liked, after dinner, to fix on three or four persons to support a proposition, and as many to oppose it.

More ACT Test-taking Strategies

• In the math section, work from the middle out when you plug in answers.

• Don't forget your calculator and bring extra batteries.

• In the reading section, this is not space science. The answer is in the material! Find it. If you have followed my active reading suggestions, the answer will jump out at you. You will intuitively discern the question and the answer.

Test	Time	No. of Questions	Types
English	45	75	Grammar, Diction, Syntax, Organization, Style.
Math	60	60	Algebra (I mostly), Geometry, 4 questions on Trig, Arithmetic (and no calculus!)
Reading	35	40	Reading Comprehension, Main Idea, Inference
Science	35	40	Science Reasoning

WRITING

The Use of Contrasts

Antithesis, or contrast, is one of the two most effective devices at the disposal of any artist, whether he works with words or colors. Its skillful use often enables a newspaper writer to make a good item out of trifling material. The object of this week's work is to teach a little of the art of using antithesis effectively in reportorial work.

What contrasts exist in the following passages?

I. London, Dec. 25 — Mrs. Rebecca Clarke, who is 109 years of age, presided this morning at the wedding breakfast of her baby son, Harry, who is 67. This is Mr. Clarke's second venture on the matrimonial sea. His two brothers are sprightly bachelors of 70 and 73 years. Mrs. Clarke toasted the newly married couple and ate the first slice of the wedding cake. She attended the Christmas wedding celebration in the evening.

II. Commuters in Yonkers took advantage of the Christmas holiday to mow their lawns. The grass has been getting longer and longer, owing to the spring weather, until it just had to be cut.

The greens keeper at Dunwoodie says that the greens have been mowed four times since the latter part of September, when in ordinary seasons the grass is mowed for the last time until spring. The condition of the course is about the same as in May, according to the greens keeper.

Up in Bronx Park the grass has not been mowed recently, but it is unusually long for the time of year, and so it is in the other city parks. The same condition prevails in the nearby cemeteries. Out in New Jersey, a fine crop of grass is in evidence.

Farmers in the vicinity of New York are saving on their usual bills for winter fodder, for with the spring weather and the long grass the animals can pick up a living out of doors.

Writers enhance their writing by using sensory details: sight, smell, taste, touch, and hearing. For instance compare these two sentences.

> My shirt had dried food on it.

> My starched shirt had dried ketchup smudges with surrounding dirt rings.

Clearly the second sentence is better!

> "In the real world, you have classes, family obligations, sports practices. . . . How on earth are you going to study for the ACT? Just do it! Make it a priority."[3]
>
> — The ACT for Dummies

The Good Earth[4]
Pearl S. Buck

This moving novel is the story of a simple, humble, Chinese farmer who, in his own lifetime, became a wealthy, landed Chinese aristocrat. However, this farmer's hubris eventually destroys him.

Suggested Vocabulary Words

A. There was only this perfect <u>sympathy</u> of movement, of turning this earth of theirs over and over to the sun, this earth which formed their home and fed their bodies and made their gods. . . .

B. But Wang Lung thought of his land and <u>pondered</u> this way and that, with the sickened heart of <u>deferred</u> hope, how he could get back to it. He belonged, not to this scum which clung to the walls of a rich man's house; nor did he belong to the rich man's house. He belonged to the land and he could not live with any fullness until he felt the land under his feet and followed a plow in the springtime and bore a <u>scythe</u> in his hand at harvest.

> "If there's a book you really want to read, but it hasn't been written yet, then you must write it."[5]
>
> — Toni Morrison

Discerning the Argument

In order to demonstrate the primary role of women in *The Good Earth*, it is essential to discuss the women that exemplify each position and prototype. Representative of these roles are O'lan, as the first wife of the household, Lotus, as concubine, and Pear Blossom, as slave, serving as a servant to the family. O'lan was the first wife of Wang Lung and the foundation of family order and structure. Her role in the novel exemplified that of a farmer's wife, while revealing her as a definite influence upon Wang Lung's conscience, his fortune in life, and his life as a whole. Mother, farmer, and regulator of the household, O'lan in the *The Good Earth* is essential in every respect. For she radiated a strength both internal and physical, which remained the underlying base of the Wang family until her death. Thus, her presence is undoubtedly a principal contributor to the lives of her family since she embodies the position of first wife, the female figure at the top of the family structure in China. Lotus on the other hand played the role of concubine in the Wang household, further exemplifying a characteristic true to Chinese lifestyle. Although a notch below the first wife in status, she gained her power within the house through the manipulation of her master. Lotus employed this medium of control to obtain her material desires and hence, affect Wang Lung's psychological security.[6] (Janice E. Stockard, *Daughters of the Canton Delta*)

Which statement(s) are true?

I. The primary role of women is obvious. They are the strength that, in the background, by emotional and spiritual sustenance, support the male figures of the household.

II. Women are monolithic objects with no real value or importance.

III. Women are very important. They provide needed dynamic economic support in a household income that was static.

A. I	B. II
C. III	D. I & III
E. None	

Word Problem

I bought expensive 250 feet of gutter guard to keep leaves from clogging my gutter. It is exactly the amount of gutter guard I need. Exactly! The east and west gutters of the house are identical. The south and north gutters are also equal. However, the south gutter is double the length of the east gutter. Find the length of all four gutters.

SCIENCE

Extrapolation from Data

The breeding season of the buffalo is from the 1st of July to the 1st of October. The young cow does not breed until she is three years old, and although two calves are sometimes produced at a birth, one is the usual number. The calves are born in April, May, and June, and sometimes, though rarely, as late as the middle of August. The calf follows its mother until it is a year old, or even older. In May, 1886, the Smithsonian expedition captured a calf alive, which had been abandoned by its mother because it could not keep up with her. Unlike the young of nearly all other Bovidæ, the buffalo calf during the first months of its existence is clad with hair of a totally different color from that which covers him during the remainder of his life.

His pelage is a luxuriant growth of rather long, wavy hair, of a uniform brownish-yellow or "sandy" color (cinnamon, or yellow ocher, with a shade of Indian yellow) all over the head, body, and tail, in striking contrast with the darker colors of the older animals. On the lower half of the leg it is lighter, shorter, and straight. On the shoulders and hump the hair is longer than on the other portions, being 1½ inches in length, more wavy, and already arranges itself in the tufts, or small bunches, so characteristic in the adult animal.[7] (W. Hornaday, *The Extermination of the American Bison*)

■ ■ ■

The following conclusions may be extrapolated from the above information.

I.   The American bison is a mammal.
II. The American bison calf is helpless and totally dependent upon parents.
III. The American bison lives in a herd/group.
IV. The American bison female will occasionally abandon her calf.

A. I
B. II
C. III
D. IV
E. I and II
F. I and IV
G. All
H. None

If the bison herd was under attack by predators, when the calf was three weeks old, what do you conclude will happen?

I.   The herd, especially the parents, will protect the calf.
II. The calf can run, albeit at a slower pace than adult bisons.
III. The three-week-old calf would be the most likely victim to the predators.
IV. The color of the calf's coat will help him blend into the surroundings.

A. I
B. II
C. III
D. IV
E. I & II
F. I & IV
G. All
H. None

HISTORY

SCRIPTURE

"Therefore, since we have been justified through faith, we have peace with God through our Lord Jesus Christ."
~ Romans 5:1

Dr. Johnny Joe was the best surgeon in Arkansas. There was one — Dr. Robert P. Howell — who was as good, but it was rumored that he was a Unitarian. Besides, he enjoyed Jack Daniels too much. That was okay if one sought his services on a Wednesday. He was sober on Wednesdays out of respect for his Assembly of God mother who always went to church on Wednesdays. And it was Thursday. Besides, no one could trust a sober Unitarian anyway. Unitarians were as rare as Buddhists in 1990s Arkansas.

Trained in Houston, Texas — the medical school Mecca of the South; everyone wanted a doctor trained in Houston; he must be good if he was from Houston — Dr. Johnny Joe was a brilliant, skilled surgeon. He had assisted in the first heart transplant attempt (the patient died) in Arkansas. He was also a Presbyterian. Everyone knew that the best doctors were Presbyterians who went to medical school in Houston. In spite of one nasty habit — Dr. Johnny Joe chewed Red Chief Tobacco during surgery — he was much sought after. "Wipe my mouth, nurse," Dr. Johnny Joe often asked.

Dr. Jones loved the Razorbacks. When he had to miss the game, he nonetheless kept the radio blaring in the operating room. Once, while removing Mrs. Nickle's appendix, Texas intercepted a pass and ran back for a touchdown. Reacting to this tragedy, Dr. Jones' scalpel accidently cut out Mrs. Nickle's appendix and spleen. No one blamed him. Texas won the game.

No, my mother was fortunate to have him. He was pretty busy, but since he was a good friend of my mother's old neighbor Josephine Mae Stuart, he agreed to take my mom's case.

Five minutes after Dr. Johnny Joe opened my mother up, he determined that the villainous corporeality had begun in the pancreas but it had progressed too far too quickly and it was not worth it for him to do anything but remove a particularly nefarious and ripe-with-cancer gall bladder. This small token would be appreciated but would only slightly delay my mother's death sentence. Deep inside my mother's liver, with his rubber-clad left hand, Dr. Johnny Joe had rolled the marble-size tumors between his thumb and index finger. "Wipe my mouth, nurse," He sighed. "Nellie ain't going to make it to basketball season."

Mom's tumor-infected gall bladder was sent to Houston for tests, but Dr. Johnny Joe had already announced my mother's death sentence. It was over just that quickly. With buck season in full swing, Dr. Johnny Joe was still able to kill a four point later that afternoon. Mom went home to die. Mom did not know that her gall bladder had been removed until she received her hospital bill. She thought it would be impolite to say anything. Dr. Johnny Joe could have taken out her heart and she would have still been grateful.

PRAYER POINTS
COMPASSION

Therefore, as God's chosen people, holy and dearly loved, clothe yourselves with compassion, kindness, humility, gentleness and patience."
~ Colossians 3:12

Southern medicine was like that. Doctors politely did as they pleased. I am her son and I live in Pennsylvania. We Northerners want to know what our physicians do. We make them give us forms to sign and we ask for long lectures. We even get second opinions. We look at their diplomas on their walls and we want to know if they are board certified. All mom wanted was a smile, a nod, and a pat on her hand. "Johnny Joe is a good boy," mom said. "Josephine says he visits his mother every Saturday and he tithes."

For the first time, my mother was hedged in. She could not fight this thing. Her chances of survival, Dr. T.J. Jackson, the oncologist, whose nickname was "Stonewall," since he was himself named after the famous Confederate general, who was a Texas Longhorn fan — a grievous shortcoming only overcome by his obvious doctoring skills — adjudged, were zero. But she never wanted to hear the truth. Neither Dr. Johnny Joe nor Dr. Jackson told Mom. She did not want to know and they were too polite to tell her. My Yankee blood boiled. I smelled malpractice here. Mom only smelled okra gumbo stewing in the kitchen.

It turns out, however, the okra gumbo probably did her more good anyway. Virginia Maria, her childhood Catholic friend who gambled with her on the grounded riverboats at Greenville, Mississippi, told her, "Nelle, I am so sorry to hear you are going to die. And probably before the July Bonanza Night!"

"I'm sorry to hear that I'm going to miss the July Bonanza Night, too," Mom calmly responded.

As if she was sipping a new brand of orange pekoe tea, Mom tried a little chemotherapy. No one dared die of cancer in 1999 without having a little chemotherapy. Hospice care was for colored folks, my mom said, who did not have insurance. She meant to have all the medical care Blue Cross and Blue Shield owed her. Unfortunately, it only succeeded in destroying what hair she had left and caused her to discard her last pack of Winston Lights.

"Do you have, Mr. Vice President," Larry King leaned across his desk, "anything else to add?"

Although we did not know it, these were the last few weeks of her life. Mom sensed it. She had literally moved into her living room. She did not want to die in the backwaters of a bedroom. She did not want to die on the bed in which she and my father had made love and dreamed dreams that neither lived. She did not want to die on the periphery of life. She wanted to be in the middle of the action. Her living room controlled all accesses to her house.

She was the gatekeeper and planned to man her station until she literally dropped dead. A captain at her helm. With her CB radio scanning for police gossip, with practically every light burning, with her television running day and night, Mom wanted to feel the ebullience of life until the bitter end. She intended to watch *Larry King Live* until she took her last breath. It was Christmas and this was both the last Christmas I would be with my mother on this earth and the first one I had spent with her for two decades. The juxtaposition of these to portentous events seemed strangely ironical to me. I had lost my mother only to reclaim her in death.

I was not proud of the fact that I had not been home for Christmas in 22 years. I had too many kids, too many bills, and too little income to justify a two-day trip from my Pennsylvania farm to Southern Arkansas. Besides, who wanted to leave the postcard, snowy Pennsylvania Laurel Highlands to spend Christmas along the dirty black railroad ties of the Delta? Who wanted to replace the pristine Mennonite farms of Western Pennsylvania with the cotton-strewn roads of Southern Arkansas?

"I want to tell you a few things, Jimmy (my name), before I join your dad," she said. Mom never said that she was "dying" or even "passing away." She was always going to join dad or Big Momma or Aunt Mary, who all had died many years ago.

My mother told me some stories that changed my history. Not that history changed — my history changed. Those hours, those days before she died changed the way I saw my past, and therefore my present and future, forever. I began to write this story about my mother. But while she has a ubiquitous presence in my life, I realized I was unqualified to write about her life. I could barely talk about my own. What I discovered really, was that this is a story about both our lives. Lives that would be thrown together and torn apart in ancestral kinship, in hatred, and finally thrown together again in great love.

S CIENCE

Forming Conclusions

Malaria produces recurrent attacks of chills and fever. Caused by a parasite that's transmitted by mosquitoes, malaria kills over a million people each year.

While the disease is uncommon in colder climates, malaria is still prevalent in subtropical countries. There is no preventive medicine available, but a vaccine to prevent malaria is currently under development.

A malaria infection is generally characterized by recurrent attacks with the following signs and symptoms:

- severe shaking chills
- high fever
- profuse sweating

Other signs and symptoms may include:

- headache
- nausea
- diarrhea

Malaria signs and symptoms typically begin within a few weeks after a bite from an infected mosquito. However, some types of malaria parasites can lie dormant in the body for months or even years. Malaria is fatal, but only with patients who are weakened by malnutrition or other disease.

Fifty people went on a mission trip to Honduras. Fifteen were infected with malaria. Of those infected, 90% had visited a village in a remote area next to a river. What may you conclude?

I. Most of the infected persons had insomnia.
II. Many of the infected persons were bitten by malaria mosquitos near or in this village.
III. Most of the infected persons did not use mosquito netting.

A. I
B. II
C. III
D. II and III
E. All

Which of the following statements are true:

I. A mosquito becomes infected by feeding on a person who has malaria.
II. If you're the next person this mosquito bites, it can transmit malaria parasites to you.
III. The parasites can lie dormant for as long as a year.
IV. When the parasites mature, they leave the liver and infect your red blood cells. This is when people typically develop malaria symptoms.

V. If an uninfected mosquito bites you at this point in the cycle, it will become infected with your malaria parasites and can spread them to the next person it bites.

A. I
B. II
C. III
D. IV
E. V
F. All
G. None

Who would be most likely to die of malaria infection:

I. Young children and infants who are weakened by other diseases
II. Travelers coming from areas with no malaria
III. Pregnant women and their unborn children
IV. Athletes
V. Starving people

A. I
B. II
C. III
D. IV
E. V
F. I, I, III
G. All
H. I and V
I. I. None

" There is something fascinating about science. One gets such wholesale returns of conjecture out of such a trifling investment of fact."[1]

— Mark Twain

Special Circumstances

To level the playing field, the ACT creators have provided special dispensation for certain students. In other words, if you have a learning disability, physical disability, religious conflicts, or military duty, you can still have an equal opportunity to do well on this exam.

- Military duty: If you are an active military person, ask your Educational Services Officer about testing through DANTES (Defense Activity for Nontraditional Educational Support).

- Physical disability: Any physical disability will be compensated. If you are blind, ACT will provide a reader. If have a disease, untimed tests will be provided. I remember administering a test to a diabetic student who received an untimed test. She spent 20 hours, two days, taking a test that normally takes 3.5 hours.

- Religious conflicts: If your faith/religion does not permit you to take the ACT on Saturday, you may take it on an alternate date.

- Learning disability: If you have a diagnosed, provable learning disability you can take special tests with special accommodations. You can take an untimed test. You can have a reader. You can have a reader and an untimed test. My learning-disabled daughter, for instance, was able to take an untimed test with a reader!

Finally, and this is important, begin the process of special accommodation certification at least one year before you plan to take the ACT.

The national average ACT composite score for graduates is 21.1, unchanged from 2008 and 0.2 point higher than in 2005. The ACT is scored on a scale of 1 to 36, with 36 being the highest possible score. The average scores on the four subject-area tests were as follows: English — 20.6 (unchanged from 2008); mathematics — 21.0 (unchanged); reading — 21.4 (unchanged); science — 20.9 (up 0.1 point). The average scores in English, math, and reading are all higher than in 2005, while the average score in science is the same as it was in 2005.[2]

WRITING

Revision

Choose the best revision of the following paragraph:

The Russian empire is a state of such vast strength and boundless resources, that it is obviously destined to make a great and lasting impression on human affairs. Its progress has been slow, but it is Russian Empire has not, like the only on that account the more likely to be durable. It has not suddenly risen to greatness, like the empire of Alexander in ancient, or that of Napoleon in modern, times from the force of individual genius, or the accidents of casual fortune, but has slowly advanced, and been firmly consolidated during a succession of ages, from the combined influence of ambition skillfully directed and energy perseveringly applied.

A. Russia, with her vast strength and boundless resources, is obviously destined to exercise on the course of history a great and lasting influence. The czar is quite important too. And the reader should experience the winters! The slowness of her progress only renders her durability more probable. The Russian Empire has not, like the empires of Alexander the Great and Napoleon, been raised to sudden greatness by the genius of individuals or the accidents of fortune, but has been slowly enlarged and firmly consolidated by well-guided ambition and persevering energy, during a long succession of ages.

B. Russia, with her vast strength and boundless resources, is obviously destined to exercise on the course of history a great and lasting influence. The slowness of her progress only renders her durability more probable. The Russian Empire has not, like the empires of Alexander the Great and Napoleon, been raised to sudden greatness by the genius of individuals or by the accidents of fortune, but has been slowly enlarged and firmly consolidated by well-guided ambition and persevering energy, during a long succession of ages.

C. No change

When you evaluate the ACT prompt, be careful to evaluate the differences between the facts and the opinions represented in the statement. Statistics and historical events are all facts. Personal feelings, attitudes, and beliefs are opinions. The prompt may advance an opinion to support an argument but you must not do that. Be sure and write facts — not opinions — in support of an argument.

Great Expectations[3]
Charles Dickens

Dickens is one of the world's best-loved writers, in his age and today, and *Great Expectations*, if it is not his most popular book, may be Dickens's most autobiographical work. Although an earlier novel, *David Copperfield*, followed the facts of Dickens's life more closely, the narrator David seems a little too good to be true. The narrator of *Great Expectations*, Pip, is, in contrast, a man of many faults, who regularly manifests them!

Suggested Vocabulary Words

A. I could faintly make out the only two black things in all the prospect that seemed to be standing upright; one of these was the beacon by which the sailors steered — like an unhooped cask upon a pole — an ugly thing when you were near it; the other, a <u>gibbet</u>, with some chains hanging to it which had once held a pirate.

B. She concluded by throwing me — I often served as a <u>connubial</u> missile — at Joe, who, glad to get hold of me on any terms, passed me on into the chimney and quietly fenced me up there with his great leg.

C. My sister had a <u>trenchant</u> way of cutting our bread and butter for us. . . . Then she took some butter (not too much) on a knife and spread it on the loaf, in an *apothecary* kind of way, as if she were making a plaster — using both sides of the knife with a slapping dexterity . . . before separating from the loaf, hewed into two halves, of which Joe got one, and I the other.

D. My sister, having so much to do, was going to church <u>vicariously</u>, that is to say, Joe and I were going.

> [Dickens'] . . . books are full of baffled villains stalking out or cowardly bullies kicked downstairs. But the villains and the cowards are such delightful people that the reader always hopes the villain will put his head through a side window and make a last remark; or that the bully will say one more thing, even from the bottom of the stairs."[4]
>
> — G.K. Chesterton

Details

"[In *Great Expectations*] the comedy makes the serious elements stand out. It gives relief. The humorous chapters do not simply alternate with serious ones; the strands of comedy and tragedy are closely interwoven. . . . It is the fundamental irony of the book that makes this possible from the start: the fact that it was tragi-comic in its initial conception."[5] — K.J. Fielding

■ ■ ■

In the context of this passage "serio-comic" means:

A. halfway comic
B. melancholy
C. both serious and comic
D. none of the above

The central argument in this criticism is:

I. The humorous chapters do not simply alternate with serious ones; the strands of comedy and tragedy are closely interwoven.

II. The book is neither humorous nor serious, but a fruitless jab at both.

III. The book is full of irony, because from the start Dickens intertwines both humorous and serious themes.

A. I
B. II
C. III
D. I, II, III
E. I and II
F. I and III

ENGLISH

Usage and Writing Style

Choose the correct word usage.

1. Pleasure and excitement had more attractions for him <u>than his friend,</u> and the two companions became estranged gradually.

   A. than for his friend
   B. than that
   C. than he liked his friend
   D. no change

2. He soon grew tired of solitude even in that beautiful scenery, the pleasures of the retirement which he had once pined for, and leisure which he could use to no good purpose, being restless by nature.

   A. He soon grew tired of solitude even in that beautiful scenery, the pleasures of the retirement which he had once pined for, and leisure, being restless by nature, which he could use to no good purpose.
   B. He soon grew tired of solitude even in that beautiful scenery, the pleasures of the retirement for which he had once pined, and leisure which he could use to no good purpose, being restless by nature.
   C. Being restless by nature, he soon grew tired of solitude even in that beautiful scenery, the pleasures of the retirement for which he had once pined, and leisure which he could use to no good purpose.
   D. no change

3. The opponents of the government are naturally, and not without justification, elated at the failure of the bold attempt to return two supporters of the government at the recent election, which is certainly to be regretted.

   A. The opponents of the government, elated at the failure of the bold attempt to return two supporters of the government at the recent election, which is certainly to be regretted, are naturally, and not without justification.
   B. The opponents of the government are naturally, and not without justification, which is certainly to be regretted, elated at the failure of the bold attempt to return two supporters of the government at the recent election.
   C. The opponents of the government are naturally, and not without justification, which is certainly to be regretted, elated at the failure of the bold attempt to return two supporters of the government.
   D. No change

MATH

For every 8 cookies a man eats, his son eats 16. If the man eats 5 cookies, how many will his son eat?

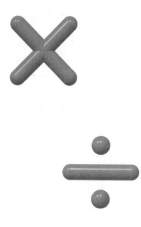

"*I never did very well in math — I could never seem to persuade the teacher that I hadn't meant my answers literally.*"[7]

— Calvin Trillin

"*Always dream and shoot higher than you know you can do. Don't bother just to be better than your contemporaries or predecessors. Try to be better than yourself.*"[6]

— William Faulkner

JAMES JESSE BAYNE

"He who covers over an offense promotes love, but whoever repeats the matter separates close friends."

~ Proverbs 17:9

PRAYER POINTS

R ESPONSIBILITY

"Each one should test his own actions. Then he can take pride in himself, without comparing himself to somebody else, for each one should carry his own load."

~ Galatians 6:4–5

My mother's father, James Jesse Bayne, I called him Big Daddy, ran away from his two-room, Louisiana pine barren home when he was 13. For the next seven years he lived in woods and swamps in the wild Delta bottoms. Living on the outskirts of early 20th-century southern towns, he experienced poverty that was sublime in its intensity.

Southern cuisine and lifestyle were the epitome of conservation and economy. Practically nothing was discarded from any animal: intestines, gizzards, stomachs — it all was eaten. There was precious little left for hoboes like Big Daddy, who ate crawdads and red-bellied brim.

There was not much that was big about Big Daddy. At 16, his blond-haired (almost white), blue-eyed head oversaw a body that was not symmetrical. His left arm was at least two inches longer than his right.

In those early years — far too early — Big Daddy lost all sentimentality and forgot the meaning of metaphor. Life was harsh and unforgiving. He learned to expect little from life and for that reason he seemed always to be content. At the same time, he never recognized the bird of good fortune when she happened to roost on his shoulder.

The first complete meal he had was when he was drafted into the army during World War I. While in the army, he drove steam-driven trains all over western Europe. He even enjoyed a little intrugue: he drove troops over to fight the Bolsheviks in 1919.

He returned to marry my grandmother who was a student at a Bastrop, Louisiana, finishing school for young ladies. Much impressed by his good looks, Big Momma, also ironically called Jessie Louise, married Big Daddy in the middle of the Great Flu Epidemic. They wore sanitary masks as they stood at the altar in their local Baptist church and exchanged vows.

Big Momma taught Big Daddy to read.

The marriage was shaky from the start. Big Momma, a Southern belle in consciousness if not by vocation, found it hard to adjust to the poverty that post-World War I railroad wages engendered. Besides, she had a potent temper and her husband was a closet alcoholic. This was a volatile combination and there was an undercurrent of tension in my mother's family.

They moved to McGehee where my mother and her eight siblings were born. Mom lived all of her 68 years in the same unpretentious, southeast Arkansas small town named McGehee. McGehee neither backed up to anything nor was it on anyone's corner. It lay halfway between Memphis, Tennessee, and Vicksburg, Mississippi.

McGehee had 4,081 residents when my mother was born in 1931. By that point she had four siblings ahead of her and three, all brothers, were still to come. Big Momma had five girls and then three boys. Like her husband, Big Momma's family was slightly off-center, but at least they came in a male and then female gender. This made housing assignments much easier. Alternative siblings could share the same room. One daughter, Patricia, the youngest, died, and while she was sorely missed, her presence set off an equilibrium that was critical to my mother's fragile household.

McGehee began at the railroad stockyard north of Edgar Dempsey's Pepsi Plant and ended at the railroad roundhouse south of Tip Pugh's rice dryer. When the railroads stopped depositing customers and picking up cotton bales, McGehee weakened and never really recovered. By the end of World War II huge combines replaced cotton pickers

McGehee was ill, but the illness was not fatal, however, and as I sat this last early December enjoying my mother's last few weeks, McGehee was still about 5,002. Big Daddy was gone, Big Momma was gone, and Mom apparently would be joining them soon.

By now the tired town had deteriorated to a critical mass of old people too tired to move and young children too young to think about it yet.

When my mother was growing up, in the 1930s, McGehee boasted of two hotels, the McGehee Hotel and the Graystone Hotel. If strangers stopped in McGehee, they were stranded between more comfortable boarding houses in Greenville, Mississippi, and Pine Bluff, Arkansas. Most gladly traded the ebullience of the Sam Peck Hotel in Little Rock for the pecan pies of the Graystone Cafe.

The Graystone Hotel was strategically placed between the train station and the pool hall. Its marble floor and chandeliers promised its patrons a luxurious evening with some equally roseate late evening activity at the pool hall.

My Uncle Cutter, married to my mother's oldest sister, Aunt Mary, ran the pool hall. Besides being one of the wealthiest men in town, and being an inveterate and successful bass fisherman, Uncle Cutter sold one of the best collections of girlie magazines in southeastern Arkansas and his pool hall was a veritable den of iniquity. As a young visitor (Uncle Cutter was careful not to let me look at the magazines) I never understood why it was called a pool hall — virtually no one played pool in it. So much of life was like that in McGehee — smoke and mirrors. The genuine article was hard to procure.

The Graystone Hotel looked like what I imagined a Little Rock or Vicksburg hotel to look like — it was a four-story white brick structure — the largest building in town. We were all proud that it greeted train visitors as they debarked from the train.

The McGehee Hotel, on the other hand, was a one-level ranch that looked like most of the houses in which we lived. That disappointed most of the local people — who wanted to stay in a hotel that looked like your house?

But many visitors found its modern facilities — the McGehee had toilets in each room; the Graystone asked its patrons to share one on each hall; and the McGehee even had a coffee peculator in each room — more appealing.

Nonetheless, both the Graystone and McGehee were approximately of the same species, but the McGehee Hotel had bragging rights — every Friday night the McGehee Owls, our high school football team ordered steaks, fries, and milk shakes before the big game. This blessed dispensation assured the proprietors of the McGehee Hotel that they would have a steady stream of customers. If the apex of McGehee power and prestige chose the McGehee, who in the general population would argue? To show solidarity with the football team, hundreds of residents would wait in line to eat black-eyed peas, gumbo, collard greens, and fried chicken before the game. They wanted to stand beside their heroes in body as well as spirit.

In addition to our two motels, there was one drugstore that gave credit and dispensed viscous chocolate sundaes to waiting patrons. The great attraction of the drugstore was the proprietor's daughter whose bosom was the lodestone for dozens of excessive testerone-endowed McGehee male youth. There were two department stores: Wolchanskies and the Wests.

Wolchanskies was run by Jewish survivors of the Holocaust. Dark, dreary, and always smelling different, like a scene from Casablanca, Wolchanskies had the latest fashions. Only stores in Greenville, Mississippi, could compete with

Wolchanskies. The Wests would be the equivalent of our present day Dollar Stores — long on variety and short on quality.

My mother grew up 10–12 blocks from Wolchanskies. Big Daddy's house was only a little bit better than a shack. Born in a rambling clapboard house next to the city sewage, mom always understood limitation and constraint. Her home sat on buckshot clay, a type of soil that blistered and cracked in the summer, and stuck eternally to every surface in the winter. The smell of feces and mildew intensified every hot summer afternoon. Behind her house was a wood lot too often the victim of unscrupulous foresters. Enchanted trails and moss-covered paths that would pique the imagination of most children were compromised in my mother's forest by young locust trees unimpeded by shade and larger competition. Sunlight was everywhere abundant. Since there was no reason to grow up and clasp sunlight, the young trees grew out, and selfishly deprived all the pretty things in the forest of light and life.

My mother's life, like all of our lives, was full of ambiguity, of pain, and of joy. In the midst of such turmoil, the best course of action is to evoke the love of God in the midst of tentativeness. It was not easy growing up in the Great Depression, it was not easy for Big Daddy to grow up before then, but love can cover a multitude of pain and failures. Young people, learn to love. Learn to forgive. And be quick to exhibit both with alacrity!

SCIENCE

Data Conclusions

Examine closely the following examples of wildflowers that grow in a Midwest cornfield. What conclusions can be drawn?

I. These species must be robust and resilient.
II. Since flowering corn plants compete with wildflowers for bee pollination, these species must be bright colors.
III. These wildflowers must not be bright; they will attract attention and this will lead to their destruction.
IV. These wildflowers must have a growing season very similar to the corn growing season.

    A. I
    B. II
    C. III
    D. IV
    E. I and II
    F. III and IV
    G. All
    H. None

We are soon at the hay field, and there is no mistake about the flowers being there, too. Close to the gate, where the wheat is not quite so thick as elsewhere, there is a splendid patch of scarlet poppies. This is perhaps the very brightest wild flower that we have.

Some plants, as we have seen, are annuals, others are perennials. An annual only lives for one year. The plant springs up from the seed, grows through the summer, and in the autumn or the winter dies. A perennial lives for many years. The flowers fade and fall as those of annuals do; even the leaves and stems may droop and die. The roots and lower part of the stem do not die; they live in the ground through the winter, and in the following year fresh stems appear. The White Clover which we found in Ashmead is a perennial, the Crimson Clover is an annual.

If you sowed a patch of your garden with Poppy seed you would have the flowers growing there year after year. You might therefore say, "Surely the Poppy is a perennial. I only sowed the seed one year, yet the poppies appear again and again." You would be wrong. Why?[1]

M A T H

Percentages

Bob is a real estate agent. He gets a 6% commission on a $458,000 sale; however, for some help, Bob gave another agent 1% of his commission. What was Bob's commission?

Somerset County Library patrons checked out the Bible 4,050 times last year. This represents 54% of all the annual book check outs. How many books were checked out?

V O C A B U L A R Y

Babbit[2]
Sinclair Lewis

Sinclair Lewis created two new words: Babbitt — an uncultured, conformist businessman; Babbittry — smugness, conventionality, and a desire for material success. Babbitt is about a middle-aged realtor: in George F. Babbitt he gave the world a character so unique that the name has come to stand not just for a single fictional character but for many American businessmen of that era as well. In some ways, Sinclair Lewis was himself much like Babbitt — Midwestern, ambitious, occasionally loud, sometimes obnoxious, and insecure. Babbitt is one of the most interesting and memorable characters in American literary history.

Suggested Vocabulary Words

A. Myra Babbitt — Mrs. George F. Babbitt — was definitely mature. She had creases from the corners of her mouth to the bottom of her chin, and her plump neck bagged. But the thing that marked her as having passed the line was that she no longer had <u>reticences</u> before her husband, and no longer worried about not having reticences. She was in a petticoat now, and corsets which bulged, and unaware of being seen in bulgy corsets. She had become so dully <u>habituated</u> to married life that in her full <u>matronliness</u> she was as sexless as an <u>anemic</u> nun. She was a good woman, a kind woman, a <u>diligent</u> woman, but no one, save perhaps Tinka, her ten-year-old, was at all interested in her or entirely aware that she was alive.

B. After a rather thorough discussion of all the domestic and social aspects of towels she apologized to Babbitt for his having an alcoholic headache; and he recovered enough to endure the search for a B.V.D. undershirt which had, he pointed out, <u>malevolently</u> been concealed among his clean pajamas.

C. He was fairly <u>amiable</u> in the conference on the brown suit.

E N G L I S H

Noun Clauses

Tell how each noun clause is used in these sentences:

1. I felt that I breathed an atmosphere of sorrow.

2. But the fact is, I was napping.

3. Shaking off from my spirit what must have been a dream, I scanned more narrowly the aspect of the building.

4. Except by what he could see for himself, he could know nothing.

5. Whatever he looks upon discloses a second sense.

READING

Description

"What do you think, Myra?" He pawed at the clothes hunched on a chair in their bedroom, while she moved about mysteriously adjusting and patting her petticoat and, to his jaundiced eye, never seeming to get on with her dressing. "How about it? Shall I wear the brown suit another day?"

"Well, it looks awfully nice on you."

"I know, but gosh, it needs pressing."

"That's so. Perhaps it does."

"It certainly could stand being pressed, all right."

"Yes, perhaps it wouldn't hurt it to be pressed."

"But gee, the coat doesn't need pressing. No sense in having the whole darn suit pressed, when the coat doesn't need it."

"That's so."

"But the pants certainly need it, all right. Look at them — look at those wrinkles — the pants certainly do need pressing."

"That's so. Oh, Georgie, why couldn't you wear the brown coat with the blue trousers we were wondering what we'd do with them?"

"Good Lord! Did you ever in all my life know me to wear the coat of one suit and the pants of another? What do you think I am? A busted bookkeeper?"

"Well, why don't you put on the dark gray suit today, and stop in at the tailor and leave the brown trousers?"

"Well, they certainly need — now where the devil is that gray suit? Oh, yes, here we are."

He was able to get through the other crises of dressing with comparative resoluteness and calm.

His first adornment was the sleeveless dimity B.V.D. undershirt, in which he resembled a small boy humorlessly wearing a cheesecloth tabard at a civic pageant. He never put on B.V.D.'s without thanking the God of Progress that he didn't wear tight, long, old-fashioned undergarments, like his father-in-law and partner, Henry Thompson. His second embellishment was combing and slicking back his hair. It gave him a tremendous forehead, arching up two inches beyond the former hairline. But most wonder-working of all was the donning of his spectacles.

Write a paragraph description of the Babbitt family.

WRITING

Which is the best paragraph?[3]

A. From the get go, you notice a rather curious fact, which sharply differentiates Russian literature from the literature of England, France, Spain, Italy, and even from that of vicious Germany. Germany really didn't have much literature, you know. Russia is old; her literature is new. Russian history goes back to the ninth century; Russian literature, so far as it interests the world, begins in the nineteenth. Russian literature and American literature are twins. But there is this strong contrast, caused partly by the difference in the age of the two nations.

In the early years of the nineteenth century, American literature started; Russian literature was pretty old. It is as though the world had watched this giant's deep slumber for a long time, wondering what he would say when he awakened.

B. At the start, we notice a rather curious fact, which sharply differentiates Russian literature from the literature of England, France, Spain, Italy, and even from that of Germany. Russia is old; her literature is new. Russian history goes back to the ninth century; Russian literature, so far as it interests the world, begins in the nineteenth. Russian literature and American literature are twins. But there is this strong contrast, caused partly by the difference in the age of the two nations. In the early years of the nineteenth century, American literature sounds like a child learning to talk, and then aping its elders; Russian literature is the voice of a giant, waking from a long sleep, and becoming articulate. It is as though the world had watched this giant's deep slumber for a long time, wondering what he would say when he awakened. And what he has said has been well worth the thousand years of waiting.

Why?

I. Choice A is full of colloquial language.

II. Choice A uses second person pronouns.

III. Choice A uses past tense

    A. I

    B. II

    C. I and II

    D. I and III

    E. None

UNCLE ROY

The forest near my mother's childhood home was hardly a forest at all — it was a tangle of bush-size trees — and since it was warm and dry enough on the western edge, cane rattlers loved to slither in the shadows of bushy ash trees to escape the torrid Arkansas summer sun. On the eastern edge, joining the sewage reservoir, moccasins hissed warnings at mockingbirds, snapping turtles, and inquisitive little girls. My mother learned very early the advantages of limitation and constraint. She learned to measure each step carefully, always looking at what was in front of her. Controlling, as much as possible, where her next step would land.

Not all snakes were my mother's enemies. One huge black and red king snake named Uncle Roy, lived under the old piano. Actually the piano didn't carry a tune at all. Big Momma kept it around to house Uncle Roy. An aggressive king snake brought all sorts of advantages to my mother's family — mice were noticeably absent. And no moccasin would dare bare his fangs near Big Momma's abode! Yes, reticent Uncle Roy, who would never bite a homo sapiens, was absolutely deadly murder for scores of unfortunate reptiles who invaded his territory. And, thankfully, was so proprietary that his domain was snake-free for most of my mother's young life.

Uncle Roy particularly enjoyed sleeping behind the family toilet during the inferno Arkansas afternoons. We all knew this and, as a result, mom and her siblings learned to look behind the toilet before they did their business. However, once, when Big Daddy was finishing his business and his *Field and Stream* magazine, Uncle Roy affectionately licked Big Daddy's right achilles' tendon, angled back to the right of the toilet.

Such unfeigned, if unsolicited affection was even too much even for Big Daddy, Uncle Roy's most fervent supporter. While his admiration for Uncle Roy's rodent venery skills were second to none, he could not tolerate this violation of his most private savoir faire. Advancing with no thought of modesty, Big Daddy, in all his sartorial splendor, quickly hopped out of the bathroom into the dining room where the whole family was gathered for supper. Then, with his pin-striped railroad overalls around his legs, he ignobly fell to the ground with his uncovered derriere signaling his unconditional surrender to man and to reptile alike. Uncle Roy coyly retreated behind an old ceramic garbage can.

With surprisingly little compunction, Big Daddy banned Uncle Roy not only from the bathroom but also from the house.

A king snake, however, was too valuable a thing to lose permanently, so Big Momma skillfully won forgiveness for Uncle Roy by depositing half-dead mice behind the ice box, which she had acquired from mouse traps. Eventually, Uncle Roy sullenly returned to the back of the ice box — a true ice box, full of block ice from Mr. Badgett's ice house. From this newly acquired launching point Uncle Roy effectively protected his and my mother's domicile. He occasionally protruded his nose from under the ice box, but only on the rarest occasions, like when a large roach wandered by. The naturally reticent Uncle Roy could not resist this delicacy. The family hardly knew he was there — although when the new kitten disappeared Uncle Roy allegedly was the miscreant who disposed of the feline pet. However, this was never proven and a good king snake was more difficult to replace than a kitten.

Despite Big Momma's approbation of reptiles, the downside of having Uncle Roy in the family was the growth of a pervasive herpetophobia that appeared in all my mother's clan.

My mother's childhood home was an old army officer barracks house, moved by huge six-wheeled trucks from a World War I Greenville, Mississippi, airfield. Placed incautiously on eight concrete cinder blocks, it was a nature refuge for a menagerie of unwelcome visitors. Nonetheless, during the Great Depression years, this abode was more the rule than the exception.

Unceremoniously, the movers had deposited this old barracks hut on hard buckshot ground by Macon Bayou, which also was the city sewage. The house was mortally wounded and exhibited a quarter inch crack all the way across its middle portion. During the winter, when the ground swelled with moisture, the crack closed. In the summer, when the buckshot soil cracked, so did the house. Over the years, the winters grew drier and the summers hotter until there was a permanent crack behind Big Momma's china cabinet to the edge of the screened-in back porch.

A generous house for most families, the old army barracks was never big enough for my mother's family. Three boys and five girls lived together in three bedrooms. Big Momma and Big Daddy lived in one room, the boys in another, and the girls in a final room. Gender, not chronology, determined commorancy. Mercifully, there were more girls than boys.

Ruth chose her God over her home. She understood that home is where we find sustaining relationships, not a place or location. I hope your home is a place of succor and hope. I hope the Lord is the Lord of your home. I hope also that you are fortunate to have a good friend like Uncle Roy living under your piano!

> *"A writer needs three things, experience, observation, and imagination, any two of which, at times any one of which, can supply the lack of the others."*[1]
>
> — William Faulkner

WRITING

The Beginning of the Composition

To choose a method of beginning a composition often causes trouble. Usually a simple, direct beginning is the best. But sometimes an introductory paragraph is necessary in order to explain the writer's point of view, or to indicate to what phases of the subject attention is to be given. How does the writer begin the following essays?

THE INDUSTRY OF LAWYER

Oddly enough, hardly any notice is taken of an industry in which the United States towers in unapproachable supremacy above all other nations of the earth. The census does not say a word about it, nor does there exist more than the merest word about it in all the literature of American self-praise.

MY CHILDHOOD FEAR OF GHOSTS

Nothing stands out more keenly in the recollection of my childhood than the feelings of terror I experienced when forced to go to bed without the protecting light of a lamp. Then it was that dread, indefinite ghosts lurked behind every door, hid in every clothespress, or lay in wait beneath every bed.

THE USES OF IRON

No other metal is put to so many uses and is so indispensable as iron.

The opening sentences of a composition should be able to stand alone; their meaning or clearness should not depend upon reference to the title.[2]

READING

Fact Versus Inference

"Now, what I want is Facts. Teach these boys and girls nothing but Facts. Facts alone are wanted in life. Plant nothing else, and root out everything else. You can only form the minds of reasoning animals upon Facts: nothing else will ever be of any service to them. This is the principle on which I bring up my own children, and this is the principle on which I bring up these children. Stick to Facts, sir!"

The scene was a plain, bare, monotonous vault of a school-room, and the speaker's square forefinger emphasized his observations by underscoring every sentence with a line on the schoolmaster's sleeve. The emphasis was helped by the speaker's square wall of a forehead, which had his eyebrows for its base, while his eyes found commodious cellarage in two dark caves, overshadowed by the wall. The emphasis was helped by the speaker's mouth, which was wide, thin, and hard set. The emphasis was helped by the speaker's voice, which was inflexible, dry, and dictatorial. The emphasis was helped by the speaker's hair, which bristled on the skirts of his bald head, a plantation of firs to keep the wind from its shining surface, all covered with knobs, like the crust of a plum pie, as if the head had scarcely warehouse-room for the hard facts stored inside. The speaker's obstinate carriage, square coat, square legs, square shoulders — nay, his very neckcloth, trained to take him by the throat with an unaccommodating grasp, like a stubborn fact, as it was — all helped the emphasis.

"In this life, we want nothing but Facts, sir; nothing but Facts!"

The speaker, and the schoolmaster, and the third grown person present, all backed a little, and swept with their eyes the inclined plane of little vessels then and there arranged in order, ready to have imperial gallons of facts poured into them until they were full to the brim.[3] (Dickens, *Hard Times*)

■ ■ ■

The principal and teacher in this school:

I. are in control and know it.
II. are very interested in teaching facts, and facts only.

    A. I
    B. II
    C. Both
    D. Neither

The text implies that:

I. the principal and teacher do not care about the children.
II. the principal and teacher discourage creativity.
III. the principal and teacher are grumpy, and outwardly appear rough, but down deep they love the children.

    A. I
    B. II
    C. I, II, & III
    D. I, II

MATH

Math Problems

A newspaper folding machine can fold the morning edition in two hours. The old folding machine, which still works, can fold the morning edition in three hours. How long will it take to fold the morning edition if both machines are working together?

TEST-TAKING INSIGHT

Repeating the Test

In an apptitude/IQ test there is no correlation between re-taking the exam and increased scores. That makes sense. I can't raise my IQ by taking 5 exams!

However, not so with the ACT! Your score could definitely, should definitely, improve every time you take it. What can you do to improve your scores?

• Review this book and other ACT preparation material. Were you ready academically?

• Review and memorize Scriptures. Were you prepared spiritually?

• Review test question types and individual instructions.

• Did you use your calculator too much? If you can determine a math answer without a calculator, do not waste time by using it!

• Were you sitting next to your best, well-intentioned, but talkative friend? Don't do that again.

• Did you bring a snack with you?

• Were you late?

• Were you sick?

Hard Times[4]
Charles Dickens

Hard Times, more than any other Dickens novel, is a critical assessment of the excesses of the Industrial Revolution. Coketown is a grimy, smelly industrial town in northern England, its houses and skies blackened by smoke from factory chimneys. One of its leading citizens is Thomas Gradgrind, future member of Parliament and governor of the local school. Gradgrind lives with his wife and five children, including the eldest, Louisa, and Tom Jr.

When we first see Gradgrind, he is observing a typical class in his school, taught by Mr. M'Choakumchild. Gradgrind lectures the teacher on the school's philosophy: "Facts" are important, nothing else but facts. All else is "fancy" — sentiment, imagination. The reader can discern the direction this book is heading.

Suggested Vocabulary Words

A. The square finger, moving here and there, lighted suddenly on Bitzer, perhaps because he chanced to sit in the same ray of sunlight which, darting in at one of the bare windows of the intensely white-washed room, <u>irradiated</u> Sissy.

B. Whether I was to do it or not, ma'am, I did it. I pulled through it, though nobody threw me out a rope. Vagabond, errand-boy, vagabond, labourer, porter, clerk, chief manager, small partner, Josiah Bounderby of Coketown. Those are the <u>antecedents</u>, and the <u>culmination</u>.

C. In truth, Mrs. Gradgrind's stock of facts in general was <u>woefully</u> defective; but Mr. Gradgrind in raising her to her high <u>matrimonial</u> position, had been influenced by two reasons.

D. "Whether," said Gradgrind, pondering with his hands in his pockets, and his <u>cavernous</u> eyes on the fire.

"The passages in *Hard Times* where Dickens most shows his genius, is most freely himself, are not those where he is most engaged with his moral fable or intent. . . . Rather, they appear when he comes near to being least engrossed with such things; when he is the Dickens who appears throughout the novels: the master of dialogue that, even through its stylization, crackles with life, perception, and sharpness, the master of drama in spectacle and setting and action."[5] — John Holloway.

E N G L I S H

Adjective Clauses

Pick out the adjective clauses, and tell what each one modifies; i.e., whether subject, object, etc.

1. There were passages that reminded me perhaps too much of Massillon.
2. I walked home with Calhoun, who said that the principles which I had avowed were just and noble.
3. Other men are lenses through which we read our own minds.

S C I E N C E

Comparison

Compare and contrast these two cells.[6]

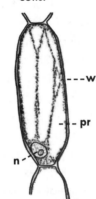

Fig. 1. — A single cell from a hair on the stamen of the common spiderwort (*Tradescantia*).
pr = protoplasm;
w = cell wall;
n = nucleus.

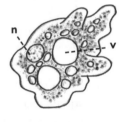

Fig. 2. — An amoeba. A cell without a cell wall.
n = nucleus;
v = vacuoles.

What could this illustration represent?

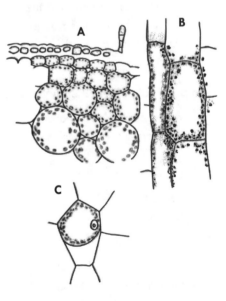

A. Cross section and longitudinal section of the leaf stalk of wild geranium, showing its cellular structure.
B. Meiosis
C. Mitosis

Redolent
GARDENS

SCRIPTURE

*"As long as the earth
endures, seedtime and
harvest, cold and heat,
summer and winter, day
and night will never
cease."*

~ Genesis 8:22

In the summer of 1965 I was 12 years old. On this particular morning my family was asleep. It was 6:30 a.m. when I stepped into our back yard.

The doughty St. Augustine grass irritated my virgin feet, too long the captive of black Keds. The uninvited crabgrass was surreptitiously invading our lawn, unobserved by our 68-year-old colored yard "boy" Aubry. Flexing my feet reminded me that neither I nor the crab grass belonged here this morning. This lawn belonged to my paternal grandmother, whom I cautiously called Mammaw, for she resented being called anything that remotely betrayed her caducity. My cousins called her Granny, but this cognomen was even more unappreciated.

Nonetheless, she was my grandmother and I had to call her something. Thus I tried my best to lay claim to my grandmother by calling her Mammaw but I knew that she really belonged to an era and could never really belong to one little boy, no matter how congenial and fervent his claim was. The rest of the white world called her Mammaw while the African-American world called her Mrs. Mammaw. I don't think I ever heard her called Mrs. Stobaugh (our last name).

Monday through Friday Aubry rode his bicycle to our property to care for Mammaw's lawn and flower garden. Today I would hug Aubry and call him friend. Then, he was another colored man, a man with no last name, under the employment of my moneyed family for wages that were scandalously low.

A Southern garden was both afflicted and blessed by a ten-month growing season. It was constantly battling interloping Johnson grass and ravenous rodents. As a result, while Northern flowers, shrubs, and perennials sported vivid colors and vigorous stems vitalized by cool summer evenings and short growing seasons, southern Arkansas begonias and roses had to endure endlessly long, hot summer days. Their paleness was the result of too much sun, not too little. However, commitment to task assured ardent redolence if not inspired accretion.

I loved flowers. I loved my grandmother's arsenal of yellow daffodils and I loved the skirmish line of black-eyed Susans that allegedly guarded my father's tomato patch from unscrupulous felines and their hygienic practices, as much as I loved our luscious poor boys. If anyone asked, with fervent self-righteousness we both lied that Mammaw made us do it.

My embarrassingly small feet would do very little damage to Mammaw's St. Augustine. Russell had size ten and Ricky had size eleven Ds! Russell could bench press 250 pounds and Ricky had run for over a thousand yards last football season. I only sported eight or maybe an eight and a half if I could stuff paper at the end, and I was cut from the football team. It was another of those things that made me different.

After less than two decades I already knew that I was different. For one thing, I liked to hunt game but not to kill game. This made me a human oxymoron. Among Southern notions of chivalry

PRAYER POINTS
FAITH

*"The apostles said to the Lord,
'Increase our faith!' He replied, 'If
you have faith as small as a mustard
seed, you can say to this mulberry
tree, "Be uprooted and planted in
the sea," and it would obey you.' "*

~ Luke 17:5–6

and manliness one planted gardens to raise crops, not flowers. One hunted to kill, not to admire nature. I had already displayed both derelictions.

It was in nature though, in my grandmother's yard, in the deepest most foreboding Arkansas duck-hunting swamp, that I found repose and insight that I so desperately needed in these halcyon days before the 1960 race riots and assassinations. The forest, the land, was immutable. As long as the earth endures, seedtime and harvest, cold and heat, summer and winter, day and night will never cease. I yearned to be part of this. And although I did not commit my life to Christ until five years later, I found His peace and solitude in this yard, in the surrounding forests, in loving relationships.

" *What I like in a good author is not what he says, but what he whispers.*"[1]
— Logan Pearsall Smith

SCIENCE

Observation Analysis

The name Protophytes (*Protophyta*) has been applied to a large number of simple plants, which differ a good deal among themselves. Some of them differ strikingly from the higher plants, and resemble so remarkably certain low forms of animal life as to be quite indistinguishable from them, at least in certain stages. Indeed, there are certain forms that are quite as much animal as vegetable in their attributes, and must be regarded as connecting the two kingdoms.

These curious organisms are among the most puzzling forms with which the botanist has to do, as they are so much like some of the lowest forms of animal life as to be scarcely distinguishable from them, and indeed they are sometimes regarded as animals rather than plants. At certain stages they consist of naked masses of protoplasm of very considerable size, not infrequently several inches in diameter. These are met with on decaying logs in damp woods, on rotting leaves, and other decaying vegetable matter.

However, why are these organisms plants or animals? How can a scientist prove what they are? Which of the following criteria are appropriate?[2]

I. Do they breathe?
II. Do they eat anything?
III. Do they create waste?
IV. Do they move independently?

    A. I
    B. II
    C. III
    D. IV
    E. All

WRITING

Slang

Rewrite the following sentences in a more formal style.

1. They can go everywheres.

2. He spends all his time grinding.

3. There ain't a sightlier town in the state.

4. He ate the whole hunk of cake.

5. Smith's new house is very showy.

ENGLISH

Adverb Clauses

Pick out the adverbial clauses in the following paragraph.

As I was clearing away the weeds from this epitaph, the little sexton drew me on one side with a mysterious air, and informed me in a low voice that once upon a time, on a dark wintry night, when the wind was unruly, howling and whistling, banging about doors and windows, and twirling weathercocks, so that the living were frightened out of their beds, and even the dead could not sleep quietly in their graves, the ghost of honest Preston was attracted by the well-known call of "waiter," and made its sudden appearance just as the parish clerk was singing a stave from the "mirrie garland of Captain Death."

Reading Between the Lines

In the old days Hortons Bay was a lumbering town. No one who lived in it was out of sound of the big saws in the mill by the lake. Then one year there were no more logs to make lumber. The lumber schooners came into the bay and were loaded with the cut of the mill that stood stacked in the yard. All the piles of lumber were carried away. The big mill building had all its machinery that was removable taken out and hoisted on board one of the schooners by the men who had worked in the mill. The schooner moved out of the bay toward the open lake, carrying the two great saws, the travelling carriage that hurled the logs against the revolving, circular saws and all the rollers, wheels,

belts, and iron piled on a hull-deep load of lumber. Its open hold covered with canvas and lashed tight, the sails of the schooner filled and it moved out into the open lake, carrying with it everything that had made the mill a mill and Hortons Bay a town.

The one-story bunk houses, the eating-house, the company store, the mill offices, and the big mill itself stood deserted in the acres of sawdust that covered the swampy meadow by the shore of the bay.

Ten years later there was nothing of the mill left except the broken white limestone of its foundations showing through the swampy second growth as Nick and Marjorie rowed along the shore. They were trolling along the edge of the channel-bank where the bottom dropped off suddenly from sandy shallows to twelve feet of dark water. They were trolling on their way to set night lines for rainbow trout.

"There's our old ruin, Nick," Marjorie said.

Nick, rowing, looked at the white stone in the green trees.

"There it is," he said.

"Can you remember when it was a mill?" Marjorie asked.

"I can just remember," Nick said.

"It seems more like a castle," Marjorie said.

Nick said nothing. They rowed on out of sight of the mill, following the shore line. Then Nick cut across the bay.

"They aren't striking," he said.

"No," Marjorie said. She was intent on the rod all the time they trolled, even when she talked. She loved to fish. She loved to fish with Nick.

Close beside the boat a big trout broke the surface of the water. Nick pulled hard on one oar so the boat would turn and the bait, spinning far behind, would pass where the trout was feeding. As the trout's back came up out of the water the minnows jumped wildly. They sprinkled the surface like a handful of shot thrown into the water. Another trout broke water, feeding on the other side of the boat.

"They're feeding," Marjorie said.[3]

Given this conversation between Marjorie and Nick, what can you infer about their relationship?

> "If you think dogs can't count, try putting three dog biscuits in your pocket and then giving Fido only two of them."[4]
> — Phil Pastoret

Geometry

Find the length of the missing side of a triangle with a longest side that measures 20 inches and a shortest side that measures 9 inches. The perimeter of the triangle is 46 inches.

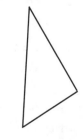

Double Check

The ACT for Dummies[5] suggests that there are nine points to double-check on your ACT:

1. Exponents: Add exponents when you multiply x or other bases.

2. Common sense: Does your answer match the question? If the question is asking you the weight of an automobile and your answer is 500 pounds, it is wrong. Common sense tells you it is wrong.

3. Decimal points: If a math question has three or more answers with the same digits but different decimal points watch out! Solve the problem and check very closely to see if you have your decimal point in the right place.

4. Operations: Did you put a + when you should have put a - ? Did you add when you should have subtracted? Inevitably there is a "sucker" answer that will grab you and cause you to miss the question.

5. Political correctness: Always write politically correct essays in the writing section. Unless the Holy Spirit tells you otherwise, find another venue to advance your religious convictions.

6. Usage: Careful! Lie and lay cannot be used interchangeably. The ACT essay graders want to give you a good score. Don't put obstacles in their way.

7. Context: When taking the English and reading tests, be careful to read the context around each passage.

8. Grammar: Most of you speak with decent grammar. Does the sentence you write or evaluate sound "right" to you?

9. Completed grid: I do not want to see any, not one, blank grid. Fill them in. All of them! Again, remember, there is no penalty for guessing.

VOCABULARY

Hamlet[6]
William Shakespeare

Hamlet, prince of Denmark, is at school in Wittenberg, Germany, when his father, King Hamlet, dies, or, as Hamlet discovers, is murdered. He comes home to Elsinore Castle to find his mother, Queen Gertrude, married to his Uncle Claudius, the late king's younger brother. Claudius has had himself crowned king. Soldiers guarding Elsinore report to Hamlet through his friend Horatio that his father's ghost has been seen on the battlements. Hamlet goes with them to see the ghost that Claudius has murdered the king by pouring poison in his ear and that he, Hamlet, must avenge his father's murder. Hamlet swears to do this.

Suggested Vocabulary Words

A. A <u>mote</u> it is to trouble the mind's eye.
In the most high and <u>palmy</u> state of Rome,
A little ere the mightiest Julius fell,
The graves stood tenantless, and the sheeted dead

Did squeak and gibber in the Roman streets;
As, stars with trains of fire and dews of blood,
Disasters in the sun; and the moist star,
Upon whose influence Neptune's empire stands,
Was sick almost to <u>doomsday</u> with <u>eclipse</u>:
And even the like precurse of fierce events —
As harbingers preceding still the fates,
And prologue to the <u>omen</u> coming on —
Have heaven and earth together demonstrated
Unto our climature and countrymen —
But, soft, behold! lo, where it comes again!

B. Think it no more:
For nature, <u>crescent</u>, does not grow alone.

C. Then weigh what loss your honour may <u>sustain</u>
If with too <u>credent</u> ear you list his songs,
Or lose your heart, or your chaste treasure open
To his unmaster'd <u>importunity</u>.

D. Out of the shot and danger of desire.
The chariest maid is <u>prodigal</u> enough.

E. And in the morn and liquid dew of youth
Contagious <u>blastments</u> are most <u>imminent</u>.
Be wary then; best safety lies in fear:
Youth to itself rebels, though none else near.

Man and BEAST

SCRIPTURE

"God is our refuge and strength, a very present help in trouble. Therefore we will not fear, though the earth give way and the mountains fall into the heart of the sea, though its waters roar and foam and the mountains quake with their surging."

~ Psalm 46:1–4

PRAYER POINTS
HEROISM

"All these people were still living by faith when they died. They did not receive the things promised; they only saw them and welcomed them from a distance."

~ Hebrews 11:13

As I stepped into our yard I quietly moved toward my dad's kennel. Dad's prize-winning bird dogs, Sandy and Jim (my namesake), were delighted to see me.

Jim was a pure-bred boxy male setter with caramel colored spots on a short white hair base. His most distinguishing feature was his voice that sounded more like a bloodhound than a prize-winning quail dog.

Sandy was an impressive black and white long hair bitch setter who my father claimed was smarter than my dim-witted Uncle Homer. Sandy could locate a covey of quail faster than any dog I had ever known; Uncle Homer diurnally could barely locate his false teeth.

Sandy deeply loved me. She was older than me and my father claimed that raising me had fulfilled her frustrated maternal instincts that had been cruelly terminated when my father spayed Sandy.

On this morning they wanted something I did not have: they supposed that I was a harbinger of a bird-hunting expedition or at least a romp over to Mr. Stalling's pasture to harass his two yearlings. While my father loved unconditionally and unimaginatively never wavered on that score, not even jokingly, Mammaw loved unconditionally in a whimsical, mischievous way. While Jim and Sandy were undeniably my father's dogs, they, like the rest of us, recognized and accepted Mammaw's peremptory influence over everything. They, unfortunately, had embraced Mammaw's teasing love rather than my father's steady, consistent love.

I sincerely apologized to Jim and Sandy and I vigorously scratched their prickly ears. Sincere appeasement accomplished nothing. Sandy and Jim rudely snubbed the young offspring of their master by turning their backs and growling.

They were my father's bird dogs; I was merely his son. They flaunted their advantage. They were acutely aware of the differences of our station and pushed it to their advantage at every occasion that offered itself. They knew full well that no little league game or school activity could compete with a bird-hunting excursion

There was no bird hunt planned this morning, however, and my father's canine wonders had nothing else to do with this pretentious interloper except ignore him.

I abandoned my station at the kennel and as I advanced across the yard I first heard and then saw an old army surplus red and white-striped biplane crop duster plane with "Weevil Killer" written in bright yellow Roman script on the side dropping DDT on old man Henley's nearby cotton field. Small sticky clear and odorless droplets accumulated on my arms and clothing. The oily residue left fading marks on all my shirts.

We were told never to walk on the lawn. Our yard was the final remnant of my grandmother's legacy to my father. She had given our mansion to my father, her youngest son, and to my mother as a wedding present. The house was hard enough to give up; her sacrosanct yard was impossible. In fact, Mammaw often walked along the edge of her creation next to the magnolia tree lusting for the hybrid St. Augustine that was no longer hers.

My father maintained loyal deference to her by guarding that yard. We all honored Mammaw by staying off the lawn. Today, though, I did not fear Mammaw. I knew that she had stayed up late last night to play bridge with her friends and rarely hazarded an early morning promenade after a bridge game.

My name is Jim, named after my Uncle Jim, my mother's brother, and the dog Jim, that is, the prize-winning bird dog my father really adored. I was proud to be named after Jim; he was a fine animal. And, my Uncle Jim, too, was okay, but never received any ribbons or anything. Like most southerners, I was never called by my Christian name: friends called me Jimbo and my Uncle Huey insisted on calling me Jimmy — a name I abhorred above all of them. My mother had experimented with calling me by my middle name — Parris — but thankfully she abandoned her efforts when she discovered that a two-syllable first name massacred our last name. Besides, it sounded like a pretentious Yankee.

The kennel was a large enclosure that bordered Jim Maier's house. It was surrounded mostly by privet hedge. Allegedly there was once a fence in there, too. In fact the fence was gone. There were wishful remnants, but the fence had long ago succumbed to damp rot and angry termites.

The dogs did not know that, so they never tried to escape. Within the confines of this phantom fence the ground was bare of grass, any kind of grass. My dad never overcame his guilt of slaughtering my Mammaw's beloved St. Augustine but he had to have a bigger pen when he borrowed T-Bone Arnold's black and tan deer-hunting hounds two winters ago. Only one section had any grass — the left corner where a cane rattler bite Jim last summer.

For one whole week Jim lay in the corner next to my father's grape vines — whose anemic fruits were regularly digested by Jim. Jim liked to eat the grapevines. They presented an illusion of coolness and privacy that was rare in Southern dog pens overrun with fetid dog feces and putrid dinner scraps. Occasionally, snake-bitten Jim staggered to his water bucket, a discarded Jim Dandy Lard container, but other than that Jim stayed absolutely still. Jim never stayed still. He moved around all the time. Not even 100+ July afternoons could keep him still. But he rarely moved and we were sure that he would die. After a week though, Jim limped over to the gate and licked my dad's hand. Since then we all — dogs and boy — avoided that corner — even though we had observed Dad mercilessly slaughter the snake with a kaiser blade.

After checking for rattlers, and moccasins — which sometimes crawled out of the bayou to warm themselves in Mammaw's St. Augustine — and for other snakes which were purported to be harmless but nonetheless gave me the creeps — I crawled among the green privet hedge foliage and disappeared from view. I needed to think.

Within the confines of the hedge itself, there was a surprisingly large amount of room to rest. I was completely hidden from sight. Only the dogs with their olfactory genius knew I was around.

Our real refuge is in the Lord, in the Lord alone. As the Psalmist proclaims, "God is our refuge and strength, a very present help in trouble. Therefore we will not fear, though the earth should change and though the mountains slip into the heart of the sea; though its waters roar and foam, though the mountains quake at its swelling pride" (Psalm 46: 1–4).

S C I E N C E

Drawing Conclusions

You are an archeologist and you have excavated an A.D. 45 Roman church building. This church "building" is really a home. You know that early church gatherings were held in homes. Speculate on how the following excavation develops into a church building.

I. A.D. 45 Roman houses looked very similar.

II. Later churches, outside of Rome, changed radically.

III. Church structure changed as churches became more episcopal (led by tertiary leadership)

IV. Because women lost influence in the Church, the buildings changed.

    A. I
    B. II
    C. III
    D. IV
    E. I, II, IV
    F. I, II, III
    G. All
    H. None

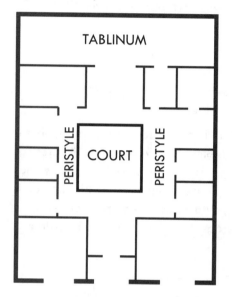

W R I T I N G

Grammar

Which sentence is correct?

A. There is not one of the company, but myself, who rarely speak at all, but speaks of him as that sort, etc.—Addison.

B. There is not one of the company, but ourselves, who rarely speak at all, but speaks of him as that sort, etc.—Addison.

C. There is not one of the company, but myself, who rarely speaks at all, but speaks of him as that sort, etc.—Addison.

D. There is not one of the company, but ourselves, who rarely speak at all, but speaks of him as that sort, etc.—Addison.

A. Let us be of good cheer, remembering that the misfortunes hardest to bear are this which never come.—Lowell.

B. Let us be of good cheer, remembering that the misfortune hardest to bear are those which never come.—Lowell.

C. Let us be of good cheer, remembering that the misfortunes hardest to bear are those which never come.—Lowell.

D. Let we be of good cheer, remembering that the misfortunes hardest to bear are those which never come.—Lowell.

M A T H

Rate and Time

A train leaves the station at 9 a. m. traveling east. Another train also leaves the station at 9 a. m. traveling west. At noon they are 465 miles apart. The train traveling east is averaging 25 fewer miles per hour than the train traveling west. Find the speed of each train.

Mark can swim freestyle at a speed of 4 mph. His average speed running is 9 mph, and he can bicycle 22 mph. At a triathlon competition in Albany, he completed the 68 mile race in 4.5 hours. He spent the same time swimming as running. How long was each part of the race?[1]

V O C A B U L A R Y

Our Town[2]
Thornton Wilder

The plot of *Our Town* is uncomplicated. In fact, some readers say there is no plot, that what passes for a story is simply a few anecdotes illustrating life in Grover's Corners. Straightforward as it is, the story has always had great appeal. In three acts, Wilder explores the meaning of life. Life and death, joy and sadness, hope and fear, all aspects of life are explored and presented with the tapestry of the average American town as a backdrop.

Suggested Vocabulary Words

A. That's what it was like to be alive. To move about in a cloud of ignorance; to go up and down <u>trampling</u> on the feelings of those . . . of those about you. To spend and waste time as though you had a million years. To be always at the mercy of one self-centered passion or another.

B. Never support two weaknesses at the same time. It's your combination sinners — your <u>lecherous</u> liars and your <u>miserly</u> drunkards — who dishonor the vices and bring them into bad <u>repute</u>.

C. He regarded love as a sort of cruel <u>malady</u> through which the elect are required to pass in their late youth and from which they emerge, pale and <u>wrung</u>, but ready for the business of living.

R E A D I N G

Main Idea

"Am I sure that there is no mind behind our existence and no mystery anywhere in the universe? I think I am. What joy, what relief there would be, if we could declare so with complete conviction. If that were so I could wish to live for ever. How terrifying and glorious the role of man if, indeed, without guidance and without consolation he must create from his own rituals the meaning for his existence and write the rules whereby he lives."[3]
(Thornton Wilder)

The main idea of this quote is:

A. God is in control and everything is fine in the world.

B. There is no "mind behind our existence" — no god. If one wishes to have "rituals" they must be created by each person.

C. There is no "mind behind our existence" — nor does there have to be. Life has no meaning.

D. One should live and let live.

E N G L I S H

Misplaced Modifiers

Fix misplaced modifiers.

1. The horse went into the barn with the rider holding a young girl.

2. Mary with its tank full of gas drove the automobile.

3. The dancer full of loyal patrons dazzled the audience.

DIVINE CONTRADICTION

"There is neither Jew nor Greek, slave nor free, male nor female, for you are all one in Christ Jesus."

~ Galatians 3:28

PRAYER POINTS

S ERVANT'S HEART

"Serve wholeheartedly, as if you were serving the Lord, not men, because you know that the Lord will reward everyone for whatever good he does, whether he is slave or free."

~ Ephesians 6:7–8

Southern Arkansas was a generous but exhausted land in the 1960s. Cotton grew to bountiful heights. Southwest winds permanently bent rice plants pregnant with pounds and pounds of offspring. Pecan trees cradled whole acres of antediluvian loam with their gigantic arms. Every spring, bayous and rivers perennially deposited a rich delta gift along the banks of grateful farm land. It was a gift from Minnesota and Ohio — freely given by the ubiquitous Mississippi River. This was really an unselfish land, a land that seemed to give more than it took.

The house in which I now lived was a natural addition to this bravura land. Built during the Great Depression years of cheap labor, the House — so named by Mammaw — reflected my grandparents' unbounded optimism. They shamelessly flaunted their prosperity in a culture that was painfully impoverished. No one seemed to mind. The South has always been kind to its elitists. They were a chosen people, or so they claimed with every offering of ebullience. No one questioned their credentials — especially when my grandmother imported bricks from New Orlean streets, painted wicker chairs from replete Havana shops, and crystal chandeliers from abandoned Liverpool mansions. I remember that the bricks surrounding our fireplace evoked a faint smell of horse manure every winter as we enjoyed our winter fires. This only enhanced the mystic of my southern mansion.

The House was a testimony both to my grandmother's generosity and to her eccentricity. Five thousand square feet, six bedrooms and five full baths, and a full, dry basement — the only full basement in my below-sea-level community — the house appeared in *Southern Living* in 1931 and 1932. The servant's quarters were above the kennel and they were better than many of our neighbor's houses. The kitchen was built of cool New Orleans bricks and attached to the house by a closed walkway.

Mammaw was a racist. Her racism was a blue-blooded paternalism variety that supposed the whole world must know and accept that African-Americans were inferior to the white race.

My mother's racism was much different. My mother was victimized by racism but not a victim of racism. Racism was a fad to her. It was her ticket into Southern respectability. Born into abject poor white poverty, Mom was only too glad to gain prestige through racism. Racism held sincerely and resolutely brought acceptance and, in a word, pedigree. Racism tied one's bloodlines to Southern ethos as surely as belonging to the Daughters of the Confederacy. In fact, she grasped it with gusto and vigor. Her manifestations of racism were particularly insidious and full of vigor. She did not hate African-Americans but loved the intrigue that they brought to her world. They made her life, her country, her land nonpareil. It was not the fear or the anger that drew her. It was the anger, and the intrigue that so much nonplused emotion brought her. Her racism was her own. Like a woman preparing for a debutante party, she nurtured it, refined it, savored it. It was her gentleman caller for whom she had waited all her life. She married that gentleman caller and passed her inheritance along to her three boys.

The problem for those who believe in the existence of races, particularly the superiority of one over another, is to demonstrate that real differences can be demonstrated objectively. White Arkansans in the 1960s were fascinated by race. There existed a paradox of pluralism: a land of ambivalent diversity. Everyone celebrates our diversity, but no one knows how to live with it.

In my own life, when I met the Lord I was faced with a quandary, an internal struggle, a battle of epic proportions. The author Shelby Foote says, "Everyone I loved was a racist."[1] So it was with me. My family, my church, my community — all of whom I deeply loved and respected — espoused a genteel and appetizing racism that was as smooth and nourishing as buttermilk and day-old cornbread. When I was born again I immediately was faced with a contradiction. "There is neither Jew nor Gentile" and, by inference, no black or white, in the Kingdom of God.

"*Lying stands on a different plane from all other moral offenses, not because it is intrinsically more heinous or less heinous, but simply because it is the only one that may be accurately measured.*"[2]
— H.L. Mencken

How Important Is the ACT, Reallty?

To a public or private school student, the ACT is very important. To a home-schooler the ACT is critical. In an era when public and, to a lesser degree, private education, varies from place to place, colleges are forced to give more weight to the objective ACT. Another consideration: college admission committees purchase the SAT and ACT writing essays from College Board and ACT. This means that your performance on these essays looms much larger. In fact, if you decide not to take the ACT writing section you should know that some colleges will view your decision adversely.

The ACT Website states: "ACT's College Readiness Benchmark scores are directly linked to ACT's College Readiness Standards, which define the knowledge and skills students need to succeed in college-entry courses based on empirical evidence."[3] Nonetheless, it is this author's belief that the ACT is more of a measure of high school performance, than a prediction of college performance. In that sense, then, the ACT is a predictor of college performance — but only that, "a predictor." As far as I know there is no study that proves that the ACT is an effective predictor.

ENGLISH

Pronoun Usage

Correct the following sentences.

1. Whom they were I really cannot specify.

2. Truth is mightier than us all.

3. If there ever was a rogue in the world, it is me.

4. They were the very two individuals whom we thought were far away.

5. "Seems to me as if them as writes must hev a kinder gift fur it, now."

SCIENCE

Matching

Match the primitive archeological implement with the letter in the pictures.

> flint skinning implement
> horn fish spear
> native copper drill
> native copper cutting knife
> flint skinning implement

Based on these implements, who can you speculate these Native Americans were?

I. hunters
II. farmers
III. tanners
IV. sailors

    A. I
    B. II
    C. III
    D. IV
    E. All
    F. None
    G. I, II, and III

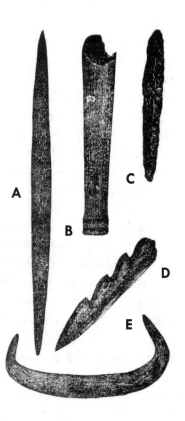

Speculate upon the purposes of this artifact.

I. motor oil container
II. water pot
III. hand basin
IV. toilet

    A. I
    B. II
    C. III
    D. IV
    E. All
    F. None
    G. I, II, and III
    H. I.II, III, IV

Credibility

Credibility is critical to your essay on the ACT writing section. What is the tone of this passage and how does the author use it to add to his credibility?

After five years of search I have been able to discover but one book in English upon the art of kissing, and that is a very feeble treatise by a savant of York, Pa., Dr. R. McCormick Sturgeon. There may be others, but I have been quite unable to find them. Kissing, for all one hears of it, has not attracted the scientists and literati; one compares its meager literature with the endless books upon the other phenomena of love, especially divorce and obstetrics. Even Dr. Sturgeon, pioneering bravely, is unable to get beyond a sentimental and trivial view of the thing he vivisects, and so his book is no more than a compendium of mush. His very description of the act of kissing is made up of sonorous gabble about heaving bosoms, red lips, electric sparks and such-like imaginings. What reason have we for believing, as he says, that the lungs are "strongly expanded" during the act? My own casual observation inclines me to hold that the opposite is true, that the lungs are actually collapsed in a pseudo-asthmatic spasm. Again, what is the ground for arguing that the lips are "full, ripe and red?" The real effect of the emotions that accompany kissing is to empty the superficial capillaries and so produce a leaden pallor. As for such salient symptoms as the temperature, the pulse and the rate of respiration, the learned pundit passes them over without a word.

Mrs. Elsie Clews Parsons would be a good one to write a sober and accurate treatise upon kissing. Her books upon "The Family" and "Fear and Conventionality" indicate her possession of the right sort of learning. Even better would be a work by Havelock Ellis, say, in three or four volumes. Ellis has devoted his whole life to illuminating the mysteries of sex, and his collection of materials is unsurpassed in the world. Surely there must be an enormous mass of instructive stuff about kissing in his card indexes, letter files, book presses, and archives.

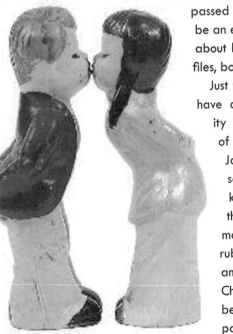

Just why the kiss as we know it should have attained to its present popularity in Christendom is probably one of the things past finding out. The Japanese, a very affectionate and sentimental people, do not practise kissing in any form; they regard the act, in fact, with an aversion matching our own aversion to the rubbing of noses. Nor is it in vogue among the Moslems, nor among the Chinese, who countenance it only as between mother and child. Even in parts of Christendom it is girt about by rigid taboos, so that its practise tends to be restricted to a few occasions. Two Frenchmen or Italians, when they meet, kiss each other on both cheeks. One used to see, indeed, many pictures of General Joffre thus bussing the heroes of Verdun; there even appeared in print a story to the effect that one of them objected to the scratching of his moustache. But imagine two Englishmen kissing! Or two Germans! As well imagined the former kissing the latter! Such a display of affection is simply impossible to men of Northern blood; they would die with shame if caught at it. The Englishman, like the American, never kisses if he can help it. He even regards it as bad form to kiss his wife in a railway station, or, in fact, anywhere in sight of a third party. The Latin has no such compunctions. He leaps to the business regardless of place or time; his sole concern is with the lady. Once, in driving from Nice to Monte Carlo along the lower Corniche road, I passed a hundred or so open taxicabs containing man and woman, and fully 75 per cent of the men had their arms around their companions, and were kissing them. These were not peasants, remember, but well-to-do persons. In England such a scene would have caused a great scandal; in most American States the police would have charged the offenders with drawn revolvers.[4] (H.L. Mencken).

The Grapes of Wrath[5]
John Steinbeck

This is the story of the Joads, a family of Oklahoma sharecroppers, whose lives are tangled up with something bigger than themselves. In fact, they are living in the Great Depression. They are tough people, but not insensitive. At the beginning of the novel, the Joads have been thrown off their farm by the bank that owns the land. A long drought has made farming unprofitable, and so the Joads, who have occupied the land for more than a generation, cannot stay. So they join thousands of other poor families on an 1800-mile trek west. This book is thick with journey motifs and socialism that Steinbeck so much wanted to dominate in American economic policy.

Suggested Vocabulary Words

A. Is a tractor bad? Is the power that turns the long <u>furrows</u> wrong? If this tractor were ours, it would be good — not mine, but ours. We could love that tractor then as we have loved this land when it was ours. But this tractor does two things — it turns the land and turns us off the land. There is little difference between this tractor and a tank. The people were driven, <u>intimidated</u>, hurt by both. We must think about this.

B. And the great owners, who must lose their land in an <u>upheaval</u>, the great owners with access to history, with eyes to read history and to know the great fact: when property <u>accumulates</u> in too few hands it is taken away.

C. How can you frighten a man whose hunger is not only in his own <u>cramped</u> stomach but in the <u>wretched</u> bellies of his children? You can't scare him — he has known a fear beyond every other.

M ATH
Money Problems

An investment banker invests for a client. The client wants $200 more money invested in an account with a fixed simple interest rate of 6% than the money invested in a technology fund. After a year, the technology fund averages 9% simple interest and earned $333. What was the total amount invested and how much did the client invest in each account?[6]

R EADING
Inferences

"And the great owners, who must lose their land in an upheaval, the great owners with access to history, with eyes to read history and to know the great fact: when property accumulates in too few hands it is taken away. And that companion fact: when a majority of the people are hungry and cold they will take by force what they need. And the little screaming fact that sounds through all history: repression works only to strengthen and knit the repressed."

"How can you frighten a man whose hunger is not only in his own cramped stomach but in the wretched bellies of his children? You can't scare him — he has known a fear beyond every other."

"The migrant people, scuttling for work, scrabbling to live, looked always for pleasure, dug for pleasure, manufactured pleasure, and they were hungry for amusement."

"In the souls of the people the grapes of wrath are filling and growing heavy, growing heavy for the vintage."

"Whenever they's a fight so hungry people can eat, I'll be there. Whenever they's a cop beatin' up a guy, I'll be there. . . . I'll be in the way guys yell when they're mad an' I'll be in the way kids laugh when they're hungry an' they know supper's ready. An' when our folks eat the stuff they raise an' live in the houses they build — why, I'll be there."

Based on these quotes from *The Grapes of Wrath*, which inferences must be true?

I. The weak die, the strong survive, and that is the way it should be.

II. Socialism would be a more just government.

III. John Steinbeck voted for Herbert Hoover in the 1932 presidential election.

A. I

B. II

C. III

D. I & II

E. I, II, & III

CONVENIENT DELUSIONS

No one knew how to live with race in a just way, although justice never really was a topic of anyone's conversation. Benjamin Franklin wrote, "So convenient a thing it is to be a reasonable creature." Franklin is intimating that one can create his own reality to justify almost any action or opinion. In other words, many modern people suspend beliefs; pretend, in other words, to obtain their desires. Convenient delusions.

We have created a language to describe American people groups. "White trash" were poor white people. "N-----" were African-Americans who "misbehaved" and "Nigras" were African-Americans who conformed to what we considered a proper African-American to be. In the minds of my mother, my grandmother, and countless other community members, the idea of race, then, emerged from the ways that social meaning becomes attached to physical differences. "Black" meant subservient; "White" meant domination.

The White community pursued power and convinced themselves they were entitled to it.

Racial discussions were complicated by the myth of homogeneity — as if there were a pure white and black race. But, ironically, American racial homogeneity was an illusion. Very few white southerners in my community were 100 percent black or white. Miscegenation had been epidemic for over a century.

Nonetheless, most of my white neighbors normally described their racial identity in homogeneous terms. The reality was that individuals and their racial communities were not homogeneous. When one was classified white, one enjoyed the privileges of the dominant caste. Non-whites did not enjoy these privileges. So the whole discussion of American racism was made even more complicated by the ambiguous defining apparatus of American racial language. But my white community needed this language and needed a language that was homogeneous and antiseptic.

The problem was, as I intimated, my grandparents wanted to build their mansion too close to what my community called "N--- Town." At least Mammaw wanted to build it there; my grandfather most assuredly did not. He wanted to build his house in the new Wolf Project where all sensible, prosperous, blue-blooded white southerners lived. But he lacked imagination and he knew it, so he dutifully submitted the decision to Mammaw. Not that he could do anything else. No one ever denied Mammaw anything that she really wanted.

SCRIPTURE

"When the Counselor comes, whom I will send to you from the Father, the Spirit of truth who goes out from the Father, he will testify about Me."

~ John 15:26

PRAYER POINTS
HOPE

"May the God of hope fill you with all joy and peace as you trust in him, so that you may overflow with hope by the power of the Holy Spirit."

~ Romans 15:13

Mammaw was no Civil Rights activist nor did she pretend that she had any high moral standards. Mammaw was no hypocrite. She was a cold realist and she cared for no one more than herself. Her egotism was unalloyed with any idealism. She loved us, her family, dearly but she loved herself more. She knew a propitious place to build a house and was not going to let the absence of money or the pretension of Southern society stop her.

Old man John John Parker at the bank at first denied her request. But Mammaw walked into his business, the Fitzgerald County Stock Exchange, sat on his lap, kissed him on the cheek, and asked in her most polished and sophisticated Southern accent, "Please, Mr. John John, will you loan me the money to build my house?"

Whether from warm enticement of further benefits, like homemade pecan pie and fried squirrel brains or from cold fear that she would do something else to embarrass him, Old Man Parker loaned her the money at no interest. The deal was sealed when Mammaw promised to bake him a Christmas pecan pie for the rest of his life. And she did. Parker ate pecan pie every Christmas until he died. (In fact, it may have killed him — when he died he weighed a whopping 330 pounds.) Only once did Mammaw fail to live up to her bargain — one season the pecan crop was abysmally bad and she had to substitute Vermont walnuts. Old Man Parker hardly noticed because Mammaw compensated the loss with her 100-proof rum cake! Mammaw did not like to cook — nor did she

have to cook — she always had servants. But when she did anything, cooking, building a house, playing hide and seek with her grandchildren, she played and cooked to win.

Married when she was 15 and divorced when she was 16, Mammaw was truly an iconoclast. She was the first unrepentant divorced woman my small Southern railroad town had ever known. Her first husband abused her once and she nearly killed him. In fact, she would have killed him but the shotgun with which she shot him was loaded with number eight shot and only made him lame for life. She merely walked away from the marriage and the man. It was beneath her to file for divorce — but Judge Johnstown knew what she wanted, everyone did, so he filed and granted divorce within the week. Her first husband never remarried and suffered in ebullient regret for the rest of his life. For penance, he became a United Pentecostal pastor. As far as I know, Mammaw never spoke or thought of the man again.

> "It is the misfortune of humanity that its history is chiefly written by third-rate men. The first-rate man seldom has any impulse to record and philosophise; his impulse is to act; life, to him, is an adventure, not a syllogism or an autopsy."[1]
> — H.L. Mencken.

Writing Essays

- Write with an outline. Think before you write!

- Pace yourself. Typically, allow 2–4 minutes to organize the essay and 2–4 minutes to proofread it. The rest of the time is for writing!

- Do not use words that are misspelled.

- Do not write the way you speak. Write in formal English.

- Don't be a wimp. Take a position and argue it thoroughly.

- Spend extra time on the introduction. It is the most important part.

- State a thesis in the introduction and repeat it several times.

WRITING

Writing with Emotion

This essay is about a very emotional incident, the death of a helpless dog. Answer the questions that follow this poem.

Dog's Death

She must have been kicked unseen or brushed by a car.
Too young to know much, she was beginning to learn
To use the newspapers spread on the kitchen floor
And to win, wetting there, the words, "Good dog! Good dog!"
We thought her shy malaise was a shot reaction.
The autopsy disclosed a rupture in her liver.
As we teased her with play, blood was filling her skin
And her heart was learning to lie down forever.
Monday morning, as the children were noisily fed
And sent to school, she crawled beneath the youngest's bed.
We found her twisted and limp but still alive.
In the car to the vet's, on my lap, she tried
To bite my hand and died. I stroked her warm fur
And my wife called in a voice imperious with tears.
Though surrounded by love that would have upheld her,
Nevertheless she sank and, stiffening, disappeared.
Back home, we found that in the night her frame,
Drawing near to dissolution, had endured the shame
Of diarrhea and had dragged across the floor
To a newspaper carelessly left there. Good dog.[2]

John Updike

■ ■ ■

1. What is the tone or mood of this poem?

2. How does he create the tone or mood of this poem?

READING

Tone

What is the tone of the following passage? Highlight verbal clues that determine what this tone is.

She rolled up her knitting when she had said those words, and presently took the rose out of the handkerchief that was wound about her head. Either Saint Antoine had an instinctive sense that the objectionable decoration was gone, or Saint Antoine was on the watch for its disappearance; howbeit, the Saint took courage to lounge in, very shortly afterwards, and the wine-shop recovered its habitual aspect.

In the evening, at which season of all others Saint Antoine turned himself inside out, and sat on door-steps and window-ledges, and came to the corners of vile streets and courts, for a breath of air, Madame Defarge with her work in her hand was accustomed to pass from place to place and from group to group: a Missionary — there were many like her — such as the world will do well never to breed again.

All the women knitted. They knitted worthless things; but, the mechanical work was a mechanical substitute for eating and drinking; the hands moved for the jaws and the digestive apparatus: if the bony fingers had been still, the stomachs would have been more famine-pinched.

But, as the fingers went, the eyes went, and the thoughts. And as Madame

Defarge moved on from group to group, all three went quicker and fiercer among every little knot of women that she had spoken with, and left behind.

Her husband smoked at his door, looking after her with admiration. "A great woman," said he, "a strong woman, a grand woman, a frightfully grand woman!"

Darkness closed around, and then came the ringing of church bells and the distant beating of the military drums in the Palace Courtyard, as the women sat knitting, knitting. Darkness encompassed them. Another darkness was closing in as surely, when the church bells, then ringing pleasantly in many an airy steeple over France, should be melted into thundering cannon; when the military drums should be beating to drown a wretched voice, that night all potent as the voice of Power and Plenty, Freedom and Life. So much was closing in about the women who sat knitting, knitting, that they their very selves were closing in around a structure yet unbuilt, where they were to sit knitting, knitting, counting dropping heads.[3] (Charles Dickens, *A Tale of Two Cities*)

■ ■ ■

Diction Clues: Syntax Clues:

_____

_____

_____

_____

_____

> "Outside of a dog, a book is man's best friend. Inside of a dog, it's too dark to read."[4]
> — Groucho Marx

The Old Man and the Sea[5]
Ernest Hemingway

In *The Old Man and the Sea*, most of the action occurs during three days and three nights on the sea. There is also a "day before" and part of a "day after." Consider the demands this makes on the writer. Three days in the life of one person — with no other people around. Remarkable! Hemingway does a fantastic job of making a statement about almost all aspects of life.

Suggested Vocabulary Words

A. The old man was thin and <u>gaunt</u> with deep wrinkles in the back of his neck. The brown <u>blotches</u> of the benevolent skin cancer the sun brings from its reflection on the tropic sea were on his cheeks. The blotches ran well down the sides of his face and his hands had the deep-creased scars from handling heavy fish on the cords. But none of these scars were fresh. They were as old as <u>erosions</u> in a fishless desert.

B. The clouds were building up now for the trade wind and he looked ahead and saw a flight of wild ducks <u>etching</u> themselves against the sky over the water, then <u>blurring</u>, then etching again and he knew no man was ever alone on the sea.

> "The secret about the novel, Ernest explained, was that there wasn't any symbolism. Sea equaled sea, old man was old man, the boy was a boy, the marlin was itself, and the sharks were no better and no worse than other sharks."[6]
> — Carlos Baker

Graphs

Which graph best exhibits the relationship between increased temperature and increased melting rate of ice?

Increased Temp Melting Rate

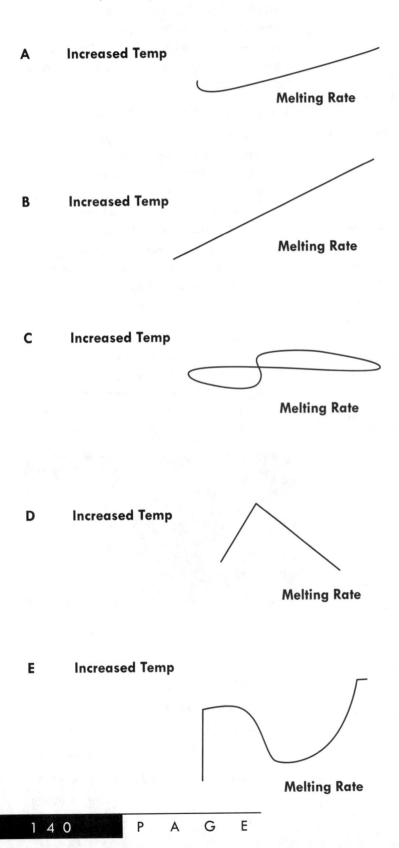

A   **Increased Temp**

Melting Rate

B   **Increased Temp**

Melting Rate

C   **Increased Temp**

Melting Rate

D   **Increased Temp**

Melting Rate

E   **Increased Temp**

Melting Rate

M ATH

Variable Omission

You must be careful with this next problem. Do not omit a variable.

> In a crate of 60 apples, there are 5 red apples for every green apple. How many green apples are in the crate?

E NGLISH

Agreement

Correct the following sentences.[6]

"Neither of the sisters were very much deceived." — Thackeray

"Every one must judge of their own feelings." — Byron

"Had the doctor been contented to take my dining tables, as anybody in their senses would have done." — Austen

"If the part deserve any comment, every considering Christian will make it themselves as they go." — Defoe

"Every person's happiness depends in part upon the respect they meet in the world. — Paley

"Every nation have their refinements." — Sterne

"Neither gave vent to their feelings in words." — Scott

"Each of the nations acted according to their national custom." — Palgrave

"I find television to be very educating. Every time somebody turns on the set, I go in the other room and read a book." — Groucho Marx

The ICONOCLAST

SCRIPTURE

"There is no fear in love. But perfect love drives out fear, because fear has to do with punishment. The one who fears is not made perfect in love."

~ 1 John 4:18

Mammaw was an enigma that greatly bothered our arcane Southern society. Again, Mammaw was an iconoclast. She cared nothing about what others thought — except to irritate potential critics. For instance, Mammaw, a fourth-generation Methodist, loved to visit the Presbyterian Church because the pastor's wife wore stylish dresses. Mammaw wore scandalous short dresses and, while she refused to inhale, she nonetheless carried a lit cigarette in her right hand to pique scurrilous busybodies.

She had to be punished. Banished from the country club, most felt that she was sufficiently castigated. But Mammaw was not penitent. In fact, when she married my grandfather — the wealthiest and most eligible bachelor in town — the town was only too happy to invite my grandmother back into the country club. She refused and all her offspring and generations following grew up as pariahs — without the benefit of Southern country club amenities. Mammaw never again set a foot in the Fitzgerald County Country Club — although she loved to have garden parties and social events in the House.

Mammaw had three sons. My dad was the youngest. Uncle Sammy was one of the most prosperous landowners in the area. Uncle Bobby went to Harvard and later became a Harvard Business School professor. My dad, who loved the House and Mammaw and black-eyed peas on New Years Day, stayed at the House.

Daddy Bobby, my grandfather, owned the House, but Mammy Lee ran it. Mammy Lee was in a long line of distinguished women of color who had raised us — what Lee called — white boys.

Armed with collard greens, black-eyed peas, and a sturdy dusting cloth, my Mammy Lee single-handedly maintained this fragile world that was 1965 Arkansas. Mammy Lee was parent, servant, and benevolent despot all rolled up into one. This 250-pound, five-foot tall, black woman was an awesome presence. Chewing tobacco, limping slightly, and occasionally rubbing a lucky Mercury-head dime tied around her foot with kite string, Lee enveloped us in her arms and propelled us forward through all adversity; she protected us from reality, and gave us false security garnished with pecan pies and encouraging words. Lee set perimeters for all our lives. "Mistah Jim," she often scolded me, "I'se gonna spank yo' bottom if you don't pick up yo' toys." And many times she did exactly that!

I loved my Mammy Lee. I can still feel her as she held me and squeezed — as if a hug and a shake could cure anything! Lee showed me where to find the fattest fishing worms; she helped me dig for pirate treasure.

There was a desperation about Lee. Her world was changing quickly — too quickly — and her discomfort grew. I loved Lee, I loved my homeland, this way of life, and, in a way, they — Lee

PRAYER POINTS

CREATIVITY

"Whatever you do, work at it with all your heart, as working for the Lord, not for men."

~ Colossians 3:23

and my South — were one and the same. They were both grotesquely generous and subtly selfish at the same time. My mother could see it. Walter Cronkite could see it. Lyndon Baynes Johnson could see it. I could see it.

The Brown decision and federal soldiers entering Little Rock's Central High School marched through our quiet land with as much destructive force as Sherman's march through Georgia. This appealing, seductive land was mercilessly, if slowly, being ripped open for the whole world to see. And inside this enlarging cauldron, a young white boy and a sweet black lady were growing up together — and apart — at the same time.

In spite of the fact that Mammy took care of all of us, she was not allowed to sleep in our house. She had a very comfortable apartment next to our garage. I once asked my mother, "Can Mammy Lee sleep in my room? I need her!" My mother gently responded, "Nigras do not sleep in white people's houses. Little boys sleep upstairs, Nigras must sleep downstairs."

This was the beginning of the end of my world. I was learning very quickly that I was part of an upstairs/downstairs world.

Segregated schools, segregated churches, segregated doctors' offices — we all knew our place, too. Mammy Lee never prepared me for the world that I had to enter once I left the placenta-like fairyland she had created for me within my home. Lee never warned me that I would sing, "Jesus Loves the Little Children," in my fourth-grade Sunday school class. "Red and yellow, black and white, they are precious in His sight. . . ." The words still painfully lurk in my memory. Where was this world of which I so enthusiastically sang? Mammy Lee never told me that I would wipe the steam from my school-bus window and see African-American children standing with their tattered books — some of which I had discarded only the year before. As I peered into their consuming brown eyes, I felt a part of me die, I felt my innocence departing. Poor Mammy Lee could no longer solve all my problems with Vick's rub and castor oil.

Maturity, young people, draws us into a place of cognizant reflection. I had no control over where I was born, or how I was raised. But there came a time when I had to take control of my life. In my case, that was in 1971 when I gave my life to Christ, when I was reborn. I took control of my life, and then I lost it. I devoted my life to advance the Kingdom of God on this earth as it is in heaven! There is no fear in love. But perfect love drives out fear, because fear has to do with punishment. The one who fears is not made perfect in love.

MATH

Solve:

$$(3x + y)(x - 2y) =$$

"*The only excuse for making a useless thing is that one admires it intensely.*"[1]

— Oscar Wilde

VOCABULARY

The Picture of Dorian Gray[2]
Oscar Wilde

The Picture of Dorian Gray is the only published novel by Oscar Wilde, whose specialty was other literary genres. This haunting novel tells of a young man named Dorian Gray, the subject of a painting by artist Basil Hallward. Basil is impressed by Dorian's beauty and becomes infatuated with him, believing his beauty is responsible for a new mode in his art. Dorian meets Lord Henry Wotton, a friend of Basil's, and is impressed by Lord Henry's hedonism. Lord Henry suggests the only things worth pursuing in life are beauty and fulfillment of the senses. Realizing that one day his beauty will fade, Dorian sarcastically and flippantly expresses a desire to sell his soul to ensure the portrait Basil has painted would age rather than himself. Dorian's wish is fulfilled, plunging him into ungodly acts. The portrait serves as a reminder of the effect each act has upon his soul, with each sin displayed as a disfigurement of his form, or through a sign of aging.

Suggested Vocabulary Words

A. No, you don't feel it now. Some day, when you are old and wrinkled and ugly, when thought has <u>seared</u> your forehead with its lines, and passion branded your lips with its <u>hideous</u> fires, you will feel it, you will feel it terribly.

B. It cannot be questioned. It has its divine right of <u>sovereignty</u>. It makes princes of those who have it.

C. Every month as it wanes brings you nearer to something <u>dreadful</u>.

D. Don't squander the gold of your days, listening to the tedious, trying to improve the hopeless failure, or giving away your life to the ignorant, the common, and the vulgar.

E. We <u>degenerate</u> into <u>hideous</u> puppets, haunted by the memory of the passions of which we were too much afraid, and the exquisite temptations that we had not the courage to yield to. Youth! Youth! There is absolutely nothing in the world but youth!

F. A few wild weeks of happiness cut short by a hideous, <u>treacherous</u> crime. Months of voiceless agony, and then a child born in pain.

G. Behind every <u>exquisite</u> thing that existed, there was something tragic. There was something terribly <u>enthralling</u> in the exercise of influence.

WRITING

Persuasive Techniques

Persuasive writers and speakers try to persuade the reader of the value of a particular position, attitude, or action. The reader is not interested in fairness or objectivity.

Match these statements with the persuasive technique.:

_____ Harvard students are all snobs.

_____ Either I will go to college or I will fail at everything I try.

_____ I drive a car that only the richest people drive.

_____ Students will do well on the SAT I if they will only take five or six practice exams.

_____ I know that the election of our president is the cause of my pastor leaving our church.

Persuasive Techniques:

A. Faulty Reasoning: Writers makes statements that draw readers to a conclusion that is not supported by facts.

B. Stereotype: A writer makes unsubstantiated generalizations about groups of people.

C. Cause and Effect: A writer suggests that some cause leads to an effect that in fact is erroneous.

D. Snob Appeal: A writer encourages his reader to adopt a position with the promise that the reader will be joining an "elite group."

E. Either/or Fallacy: A writer argues that the reader must accept his position or there will be an effect, when in fact the outcome is far more complicated.

Data Research

Researchers examined meat before it was brought into the factory. They found nearly half of the meat and poultry samples, 47 percent, were contaminated with dangerous levels of bacteria.

What conclusions are plausible:

I. The meat was mishandled in the factory.
II. The meat was contaminated in the transportation mode.
III. The meat was contaminated on the farm.
IV. The meat is unsafe to eat.

A. I
B. II
C. III
D. IV
E. I, II, IV
F. II, III, IV
G. None
H. All

Main Idea and Supporting Details

The development of Cuba's commerce since the withdrawal of Spain, and the substitution of a modern fiscal policy for an antiquated and indefensible system, has been notable. It is, however, a mistake to contrast the present condition with the condition existing at the time of the American occupation, in 1899. The exact accuracy of the record is questionable, but the returns for the year 1894, the year preceding the revolution, show the total imports of the island as $77,000,000, and the total exports as $99,000,000. The probability is that a proper valuation would show a considerable advance in the value of the imports. The statement of export values may be accepted. It may be assumed that had there been no disorder, the trade of the island, by natural growth, would have reached $90,000,000 for imports and $120,000,000, for exports, in 1900. That may be regarded as a fair normal. As it was, the imports of that year were $72,000,000, and the exports, by reason of the general wreck of the sugar business, were only $45,000,000. With peace and order fairly assured, recovery came quickly. The exports of 1905, at $99,000,000, equaled those of 1894, while the imports materially exceed-

ed those of the earlier year. In 1913, the exports reached $165,207,000, and the imports $132,290,000. This growth of Cuba's commerce and industry is due mainly to the economic requirements of the American people. We need Cuba's sugar and we want its tobacco. These two commodities represent about 90 percent of the total exports of the island. We buy nearly all of its sugar, under normal conditions, and about 60 per cent of its tobacco and cigars. On the basis of the total commerce of the island, the records of recent years show this country as the source of supply for about 53 percent of Cuba's total imports, and as the market for about 83 percent, of its exports. A comparison of the years 1903 and 1913 shows a gain of about $87,000,000 in Cuba's total exports. Of this, about $75,000,000 is represented by sugar. The crop of 1894 a little exceeded a million tons. Such a quantity was not again produced until 1903. With yearly variations due to weather conditions, later years show an enormous and unprecedented increase. The crops of 1913 and 1914 were approximately 2,500,000 tons each. The tobacco industry shows only a modest gain. The average value of the exports of that commodity has risen, in ten years, from about $25,000,000 to about $30,000,000. The increase in the industry appears largely in the shipment of leaf tobacco. The cigar business shows practically no change in that time, as far as values are concerned.

By the operation of the Platt Amendment of these instruments the United States virtually underwrites the

political stability and the financial responsibility of the Cuban Government. That Government cannot borrow any important sums without the consent of the United States, and it has agreed that this country "may exercise the right to intervene for the preservation of Cuban independence, the maintenance of a government adequate for the protection of life, property, and individual liberty, and for discharging the obligations with respect to Cuba imposed by the Treaty of Paris on the United States." This assumption of responsibility by the United States inspired confidence on the part of capital, and large sums have been invested in Cuban bonds, and in numerous public and private enterprises. Railways and trolley lines have been built and many other works of public utility have been undertaken. The activities of old sugar plantations have been extended under improved conditions, and many new estates with costly modern equipment have been created. The cultivation of large areas, previously lying waste and idle, afforded both directly and indirectly employment for an increased population, as did the numerous public works. The other force, perhaps no less effective, appears in the reciprocity treaty of 1903. This gave to Cuba's most important crop a large though by no means absolute control of the constantly increasing sugar market of the United States, as far as competition from other foreign countries was concerned. The sugar industry of the island may be said to have been restored to its normal proportions in 1903. Our imports for the five-year period 1904–1908 averaged 1,200,000 tons a year. For the five-year period

1910–1914 they averaged 1,720,000 tons. In 1914, they were 2,200,000 tons as compared with 1,260,000 tons in 1904. It is doubtful if the treaty had any appreciable influence on the exports of Cuban tobacco to this country. We buy Cuba's special tobacco irrespective of a custom-house advantage that affects the box price only a little, and the price of a single cigar probably not at all. On the other side of the account, that of our sales to Cuba, there also appears a large increase since the application of the reciprocity treaty. Using the figures showing exports from the United States to Cuba, instead of Cuba's records showing imports from this country, it appears that our sales to the island in the fiscal year 1903, immediately preceding the operation of the treaty, amounted to $21,761,638. In the fiscal year 1913 they were $70,581,000, and in 1914 were $68,884,000.[3]

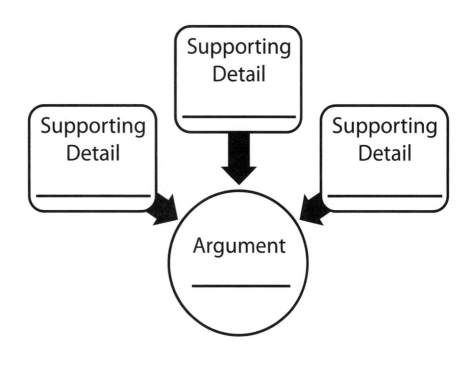

ENGLISH

Usage

Change each of the following sentences to accord with standard usage.[4]

1. "And sharp Adversity will teach at last Man — and, as we would hope — perhaps the devil, That neither of their intellects are vast." — Byron
2. "Both death and I am found eternal." — Milton
3. "How each of these professions are crowded." — Addison
4. "Neither of their counselors were to be present." — Id
5. "Either of them are equally good to the person to whom they are significant." — Emerson

A GATHERED INHERITANCE

A transplanted Arkansas boy who now lives in the often-frigid Allegheny Mountains of western Pennsylvania, I like my apple cider to be steaming and my house to be about 78 degrees. An anthracite coal-burning stove does the job, but there is one problem with coal heat, and it occurs about three o'clock every morning: the fire dies down to the point where the house is dangerously cold.

Is 21st century evangelicalism growing cold? I think not.

Old Testament Levitical priests had a duty to tend the fire in the tent of meeting, to keep it roaring and bright. The fire on the altar, the eternal flame on which sacrifices were offered to God, was not to go out. Other tasks could be deferred, but the fire on the altar was never to go out (Lev. 6:8–13).

Through the centuries believers have served well as fire tenders. "The secret things belong to the LORD our God, but the things revealed belong to us and to our children forever" (Deut. 29:29). This is a gathered inheritance kept alive by men and women of faith. In our own Christian homeschool history, for instance, the honor belongs to Hulsey, Harris, Ferris, and countless others.

Truth is restated; more than that, the reader will observe that saints throughout the ages have built on the faith of those who preceded them. Jesus Christ is the way, the truth, and the life: that is true, and truth is the same forever. Revelation of truth, though, is forever becoming better understood, we hope. The previous generation of believers passes the torch to us, and we pass it to the next, and so on. Each generation builds on the illumination of the previous generation. We trust that the world is better for it.

On my farm grows an oak tree that began its life 30 years ago, full of potential, and it was beautiful in its own right. Today it is so much more beautiful than it was 30 years ago. It is the same tree, but oh, how much larger and fuller are its branches and fruits! Diurnally I remove acorns and leaves deposited on my truck. It is the same tree, still full of potential, but producing more fruit than ever. A vicious blight or uncaring gypsy moth may kill it someday, but I already see a new oak seedling growing in its redolent shadow.

I look at this new generation of Christian young people and I know that we are not going to run out of fuel. The Holy Spirit is still here to encourage, to inspire every generation. There is, I have no doubt, a new C.S. Lewis or Oswald Chambers alive today. Fear is dissipated by promises; evil is overcome by good. A gathered

SCRIPTURE

"The secret things belong to the LORD our God, but the things revealed belong to us and to our children forever, that we may follow all the words of this law."

~ Deuteronomy 29:29

PRAYER POINTS
LOVE FOR GOD

"My soul clings to you; your right hand upholds me."

~ Psalm 63:8

WRITING

Spelling

Spelling is critical on the ACT writing essay. It will make the difference between a 4 or a 5. If you can't be sure that you know how to spell a word, choose another one! These are some of the most common misspelled words.

inheritance. We again recognize that the secret things belong "to the LORD our God, but the things revealed belong to us and to our sons forever" (Deut. 29:29). A gathered inheritance!

Theologian Paul Tillich wrote, "The lightning illuminates all and then leaves it again in darkness. So faith in God grasps humanity, and we respond in ecstasy. And the darkness is never again the same . . . but it is still the darkness."[1]

All of God's saints — past, present, and future — are flashes of lightning in the sky. And the darkness is never the same again, because the light reveals what life can be in Jesus Christ. "Memory allows possibility," theologian Walter Brueggemann writes.[2] A gathered inheritance. We bring memory. You young people bring possibility.

accede	woolly
descend	village
pressure	already
accident	forty
fascinate	villain
misspelled	all right
accommodate	foreign
mischievous	till
possession	preceptor
accordance	disappearance
miscellaneous	immediately
accuracy	accommodation
muscle	fiend
recollection	choose
succeed	succeed
susceptible	usually
dispelled	amateur
occasional	formally
inflammation	perpetual
yielding	grandeur
boundary	formerly
recommend	persuade
elementary	perspiration
summary	fulfill
seize	apparatus
symmetrical	willful
receive	police
final	appetite
committee	policies
receipt	approximate
finally	guardian
occur	opportunity
existence	guessing
monosyllable	presence
experience	opposite
intellectual	precede
across	disappoint
sentence	imminent
parallel	on
amount	siege
embellishment	chosen
apart	grammar
foregoing	friend
wholly	legible
arouse	proceed
forehead	ledger

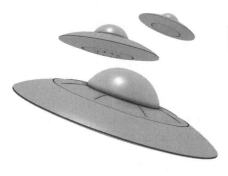

VOCABULARY

The War of the Worlds[3]
H.G. Wells

The War of the Worlds (1898) is a science fiction novel by H.G. Wells. It describes the experiences of a narrator who travels through the suburbs of London as England is invaded by Martians. It is one of the earliest stories that details a conflict between mankind and an alien race. At the same time, in this naturalist novel, as he travels from place to place, escaping the Martians, the protagonist learns much about himself and the world.

Suggested Vocabulary Words

A. The growing crowd, he said, was becoming a serious <u>impediment</u> to their excavations, especially the boys. They wanted a light railing put up, and help to keep the people back. He told me that a faint stirring was occasionally still audible within the case, but that the workmen had failed to unscrew the top, as it afforded no grip to them. The case appeared to be enormously thick, and it was possible that the faint sounds we heard represented a noisy <u>tumult</u> in the interior.

B. I was very glad to do as he asked, and so become one of the privileged spectators within the <u>contemplated</u> <u>enclosure</u>. I failed to find Lord Hilton at his house, but I was told he was expected from London by the six o'clock train from Waterloo; and as it was then about a quarter past five, I went home, had some tea, and walked up to the station to <u>waylay</u> him.

C. Two large dark-coloured eyes were regarding me <u>steadfastly</u>. The mass that framed them, the head of the thing, was rounded, and had, one might say, a face. There was a mouth under the eyes, the lipless brim of which quivered and panted, and dropped saliva. The whole creature <u>heaved</u> and <u>pulsated</u> convulsively. A lank tentacular <u>appendage</u> gripped the edge of the cylinder, another swayed in the air.

D. Those who have never seen a living Martian can scarcely imagine the strange horror of its appearance. The peculiar V-shaped mouth with its pointed upper lip, the absence of brow ridges, the absence of a chin beneath the wedgelike lower lip, the <u>incessant</u> <u>quivering</u> of this mouth, the <u>Gorgon</u> groups of tentacles, the tumultuous breathing of the lungs in a strange atmosphere, the evident heaviness and painfulness of movement due to the greater gravitational energy of the earth.

TEST-TAKING INSIGHT

Writing Section Tips

- Choose a position and defend it. Don't be a wimp! The ACT test inevitably offers a prompt that will require you to take a position and to defend it well. Do not equivocate; do not elaborate; do not flip flop. Take a position and defend it with multiple evidence types. Repeat, at least three times, your main position or thesis.

- Stay focused. In every paragraph, restate the thesis in some form or another. "As the reader sees, so and so is true." Or "Clearly the above evidence proves . . ." Or "Thus the reader understands. . . ."

- Organize! Organize! Organize! Make sure that the graders sense that you have a beginning point and a closing point — and that you are taking them somewhere!

- Use appropriate (i.e., formal) diction (grammar) and syntax (style). Do not write the way you speak. Write more formally. Do not become your readers' friend — graders do not want to be your friend. They want you to change their lives with an inspired insight on a topic.

- Remember: longer is always better. I don't care what you hear, what you read, that is always the case.

Tone and Mood

The end of the cylinder was being screwed out from within. Nearly two feet of shining screw projected. Somebody blundered against me, and I narrowly missed being pitched onto the top of the screw. I turned, and as I did so the screw must have come out, for the lid of the cylinder fell upon the gravel with a ringing concussion. I stuck my elbow into the person behind me, and turned my head towards the Thing again. For a moment that circular cavity seemed perfectly black. I had the sunset in my eyes.

I think everyone expected to see a man emerge — possibly something a little unlike us terrestrial men, but in all essentials a man. I know I did. But, looking, I presently saw something stirring within the shadow: greyish billowy movements, one above another, and then two luminous disks — like eyes. Then something resembling a little grey snake, about the thickness of a walking stick, coiled up out of the writhing middle, and wriggled in the air towards me — and then another.

A sudden chill came over me. There was a loud shriek from a woman behind. I half turned, keeping my eyes fixed upon the cylinder still, from which other tentacles were now projecting, and began pushing my way back from the edge of the pit. I saw astonishment giving place to horror on the faces of the people about me. I heard inarticulate exclamations on all sides. There was a general movement backwards. I saw the shopman struggling still on the edge of the pit. I found myself alone, and saw the people on the other side of the pit running off, Stent among them. I looked again at the cylinder, and ungovernable terror gripped me. I stood petrified and staring.

A big greyish rounded bulk, the size, perhaps, of a bear, was rising slowly and painfully out of the cylinder. As it bulged up and caught the light, it glistened like wet leather.

Two large dark-coloured eyes were regarding me steadfastly. The mass that framed them, the head of the thing, was rounded, and had, one might say, a face. There was a mouth under the eyes, the lipless brim of which quivered and panted, and dropped saliva. The whole creature heaved and pulsated convulsively. A lank tentacular appendage gripped the edge of the cylinder, another swayed in the air.

Those who have never seen a living Martian can scarcely imagine the strange horror of its appearance. The peculiar V-shaped mouth with its pointed upper lip, the absence of brow ridges, the absence of a chin beneath the wedgelike lower lip, the incessant quivering of this mouth, the Gorgon groups of tentacles, the tumultuous breathing of the lungs in a strange atmosphere, the evident heaviness and painfulness of movement due to the greater gravitational energy of the earth — above all, the extraordinary intensity of the immense eyes — were at once vital, intense, inhuman, crippled, and monstrous. There was something fungoid in the oily brown skin, something in the clumsy deliberation of

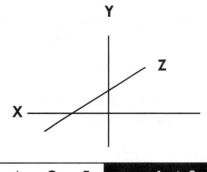

the tedious movements unspeakably nasty. Even at this first encounter, this first glimpse, I was overcome with disgust and dread.

Suddenly the monster vanished. It had toppled over the brim of the cylinder and fallen into the pit, with a thud like the fall of a great mass of leather. I heard it give a peculiar thick cry, and forthwith another of these creatures appeared darkly in the deep shadow of the aperture.

I turned and, running madly, made for the first group of trees, perhaps a hundred yards away; but I ran slantingly and stumbling, for I could not avert my face from these things.

What is the tone or mood of this passage and how does the author create this tone?

Parallel and Perpendicular Lines

Which of the following could represent an equation of a line perpendicular to the graph of line Z?

A. $y = x + 1$

B. $y = 2x + 4$

C. $y = 5$

D. $y = -x + 2$

E. $y = -10x + 2$

S CIENCE

Goddard proves that mentally challenged individuals whose intelligence has reached its full development continue to test at exactly the same mental age by the Binet scale, year after year. In their case, familiarity with the tests does not in the least improve the responses. At each retesting the responses given at previous examinations are repeated with only the most trivial variations. Of 352 mentally challenged children tested at Vineland, three years in succession, 109 gave absolutely no variation, 232 showed a variation of not more than two fifths of a year, while 22 gained as much as one year in the three tests. The latter, presumably, were younger children whose intelligence was still developing.[4]

Which diagram best represents the above conclusions?

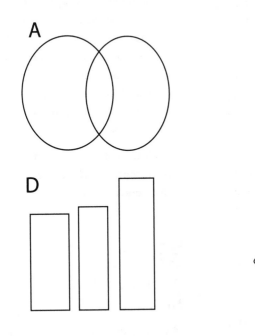

A

B

D

C

E NGLISH

Grammar

Correct the following sentences:[5]

1. 1. They crowned him long ago;/But who they got to put it on/Nobody seems to know.

2. I experienced little difficulty in distinguishing among the pedestrians they who had business with St. Bartholomew.

3. The great difference lies between the laborer who moves to Yorkshire and he who moves to Canada.

4. It can't be worth much to they that hasn't larning.

5. To send me away for a whole year — I who had never crept from under the parental wing — was a startling idea.

Do you not know? Have you not heard? The LORD is the everlasting God, the Creator of the ends of the earth. He will not grow tired or weary, and his understanding no one can fathom. He gives strength to the weary and increases the power of the weak. Even youths grow tired and weary, and young men stumble and fall; but those who hope in the LORD will renew their strength. They will soar on wings like eagles; they will run and not grow weary, they will walk and not be faint (Isa. 40:28–31).

Rewriting HISTORY

SCRIPTURE

"From one man he made every nation of men, that they should inhabit the whole earth; and he determined the times set for them and the exact places where they should live."

~ Acts 17:26

The writing of history is the selection of information and the synthesis of this information into a narrative that will stand the critical eye of time. History, though, is never static. One never creates the definitive theory of a historical event. History invites each generation to reexamine its own story and to reinterpret past events in light of present circumstances.

The creation of this story is more difficult than it seems. From the beginning the historian is forced to decide what sort of human motivation matters most: Economic? Political? Religious? Social?

For instance, what caused the American Revolution? The historian Bernard Bailyn argues that ideology or the history of thought caused the American Revolution.[1] No, the historian Oscar Handlin argues, the Revolution was caused by social upheaval (i.e., the dislocation of groups and classes of people).[2] Sydney Ahlstrom argues that religion was an important cause of the American Revolution.[3] And so forth. Students will look at several theories of history, primary source material, and then decide for themselves what really happened. "Every true history is contemporary history," historian Gerald Billias writes.[4]

After everything is said and done, historians are only studying the past. They cannot really change the past. Theories about the past come and go, and change with each generation. However, the past is past. It is over.

Historians will debate about history, but they can never change history. Only God can change history.

God alone can change history. When persons are reborn in Christ, their present, future, and, yes, even their past is changed. History is literally rewritten. They are new creations. That bad choice, that sin, that catastrophe, is placed under the blood of the Lamb and everything starts fresh and new. A new history for new people.

Let me illustrate. My great-great-great grandfather, whose passion was to kill Yankees, was a slave owner in eastern Tennessee 170 years ago. From that inheritance, like most white southerners who grew up in the 1960s, I grew up to mistrust, even to hate African-Americans. Like so many people captured by their history and culture, present and future became my past. However, when I was a senior in high school, I was saved, Jesus Christ became my Lord and Savior. My attitudes changed. It took time, but prejudices disappeared. Ultimately, I married my New Jersey wife, Karen, and we adopted three African-American children — whose ancestors, by the way, may have been owned by my great-great-great uncle! Three of my children are African-American. Imagine! Quite literally, my history was rewritten. It has been changed irrevocably by my decision to invite Jesus Christ to be Savior of my life. In a real sense, family prejudice and death existing for generations ended in my generation. The destructive, historical cycle that was part of my history has ended. No one,

PRAYER POINTS
DISCIPLINE

"The proverbs of Solomon son of David, king of Israel . . . for acquiring a disciplined and prudent life."

~ Proverbs 1:3

nothing can do that but the Lord. History has been rewritten!

My prayer is that if you do not know this God who can change history — even your history — this history text might encourage you to invite Jesus Christ into your heart as Savior.

E N G L I S H

Usage

Correct these sentences.[5]

1. Let you and I look at these, for they say there are none such in the world.

2. "Nonsense!" said Amyas, "we could kill every soul of them in half an hour, and they know that as well as me."

3. Markland, who, with Jortin and Thirlby, Johnson calls three contemporaries of great eminence.

4. They are coming for a visit to she and I.

W R I T I N G

Rules for the Use and Arrangement of Words

The following rules for the use and arrangement of words will be found helpful in securing clearness and force.

1. Use words in their proper sense.

2. Avoid useless circumlocution and "fine writing." Simplicity and cogency are always virtues in good writing.

3. Avoid exaggerations.

4. Be careful in the use of ambiguous words, e. g., certain.

5. Write with precision.

6. Be careful in the use of he, it, they, these, etc.

7. Report a speech in the first person where necessary to avoid ambiguity.

8. Use the third person if possible. It gives a formal air to your essay.

9. Do not mix metaphor with literal statement.

10. Adverbs and adjectives should be placed next to the words they are intended to qualify.

Often authors do not state overtly all their conclusions. Readers are forced to read carefully and to draw their own conclusions about the plot, setting, or characters. Readers do this by inferring, or figuring out, ideas that emerge from the facts. For instance, if a friend ignores your phone calls for six straight days, you might infer that he is not your friend anymore! You could be wrong — he might just be busy — but you will make some sort of inference. You will need to make a lot inferences on the ACT!

S C I E N C E

Observation Conclusion

The left half of a field of clover was fertilized with lime; the right half was not. What conclusions can be drawn from the picture of this field of clover?

I. Lime made no difference on the growth potential of the field.

II. Lime made a great deal of difference on the growth potential of the field.

III. From the information provided, no conclusion may be drawn.

    A. I

    B. II

    C. III

    D. I and II

    E. None

VOCABULARY

Around the World in 80 Days[6]
Jules Verne

When Phileas Fogg accepts a challenge from his fellow members at the Reform Club to travel around the world in 80 days — no small feat in the 1880s — the reader is warned to hold on to his seat! — and sets off to prove that you can travel around the world in a mind-boggling 80 days. He sets off by train to Paris with his new valet Passepartout, but then is forced to continue the trip by balloon, arriving next in Spain where Passepartout has an interesting encounter in the bullfighting ring. They continue. Throughout the voyage, they are followed by a detective, Mr. Fix, who is convinced that Fogg is responsible for the recent £55,000 theft at the bank of England. The thrill of seeing all these exotic sights is reason enough to read this novel!

Suggested Vocabulary Words

A. It would be <u>rash</u> to predict how Passepartout's lively nature would agree with Mr. Fogg. It was impossible to tell whether the new servant would turn out as absolutely methodical as his master required; experience alone could solve the question. Passepartout had been a sort of vagrant in his early years, and now <u>yearned</u> for <u>repose</u>; but so far he had failed to find it, though he had already served in ten English houses. But he could not take root in any of these; with <u>chagrin</u>, he found his masters <u>invariably</u> <u>whimsical</u> and irregular, constantly running about the country, or on the look-out for adventure.

B. Fix had heard this conversation. A little while before, when there was no prospect of proceeding on the journey, he had made up his mind to leave Fort Kearney; but now that the train was there, ready to start, and he had only to take his seat in the car, an <u>irresistible</u> influence held him back.

C. The engineer whistled, the train started, and soon disappeared, mingling its white smoke with the <u>eddies</u> of the densely falling snow.

D. The weather was <u>dismal</u>, and it was very cold. Aouda, despite the storm, kept coming out of the waiting room, going to the end of the platform, and <u>peering</u> through the tempest of snow, as if to pierce the mist which narrowed the horizon around her, and to hear, if possible, some welcome sound. She heard and saw nothing. Then she would return, chilled through, to issue out again after the <u>lapse</u> of a few moments, but always in vain.

E. The commander of the fort was anxious, though he tried to conceal his <u>apprehensions</u>. As night approached, the snow fell less plentifully, but it became intensely cold. Absolute silence rested on the plains. Neither flight of bird nor passing of beast troubled the perfect calm.

F. Throughout the night Aouda, full of sad <u>forebodings</u>, her heart stifled with <u>anguish</u>, wandered about on the <u>verge</u> of the plains.

> "For a child will be born to us, a son will be given to us; and the government will rest on His shoulders; and His name will be called Wonderful Counselor, Mighty God, Eternal Father, Prince of Peace" (Isaiah 9:6).

"Anything one man can imagine, other men can make real."[7]

— Jules Verne

R E A D I N G

Inference

Colonel Proctor and Mr. Fogg, revolvers in hand, hastily quitted their prison, and rushed forward where the noise was most clamorous. They then perceived that the train was attacked by a band of Sioux.

This was not the first attempt of these daring Indians, for more than once they had waylaid trains on the road. A hundred of them had, according to their habit, jumped upon the steps without stopping the train, with the ease of a clown mounting a horse at full gallop.

The Sioux were armed with guns, from which came the reports, to which the passengers, who were almost all armed, responded by revolver-shots.

The Indians had first mounted the engine, and half stunned the engineer and stoker with blows from their muskets. A Sioux chief, wishing to stop the train, but not knowing how to work the regulator, had opened wide instead of closing the steam-valve, and the locomotive was plunging forward with terrific velocity.

The Sioux had at the same time invaded the cars, skipping like enraged monkeys over the roofs, thrusting open the doors, and fighting hand to hand with the passengers. Penetrating the baggage-car, they pillaged it, throwing the trunks out of the train. The cries and shots were constant. The travellers defended themselves bravely; some of the cars were barricaded, and sustained a siege, like moving forts, carried along at a speed of a hundred miles an hour.

Aouda behaved courageously from the first. She defended herself like a true heroine with a revolver, which she shot through the broken windows whenever a savage made his appearance. Twenty Sioux had fallen mortally wounded to the ground, and the wheels crushed those who fell upon the rails as if they had been worms. Several passengers, shot or stunned, lay on the seats.

It was necessary to put an end to the struggle, which had lasted for ten minutes, and which would result in the triumph of the Sioux if the train was not stopped. Fort Kearney station, where there was a garrison, was only two miles distant; but, that once passed, the Sioux would be masters of the train between Fort Kearney and the station beyond.

The conductor was fighting beside Mr. Fogg, when he was shot and fell. At the same moment he cried, "Unless the train is stopped in five minutes, we are lost!"

■ ■ ■

Which of the following conclusions can be inferred from this passage?

I. Native Americans are bloodthirsty, ruthless savages.

II. Native Americans are noble, courageous warriors.

A. I

B. II

C. I and II

D. None

As you react to ACT reading selections, or as you write a response to an ACT writing prompt, you will have to make judgments. To make a judgment you must compare the conclusions of the prompt or the text to a standard, or criteria. You will weigh the veracity of the argument, or the conclusion, to a corpus of information (e.g.., the Bible) or other criteria (e.g., exigencies). This is where it gets sticky for Christian ACT test takers. We must be careful not to be "preachy" when we state our case. In any event, always offer well-supported opinions and logical factual arguments.

M A T H

Word Problem

At what time between 1 o'clock and 2 o'clock are the hands of a clock (1) together? (2) at right angles? (3) opposite to each other? How far does the hour hand move while the minute hand goes around the whole circle? How far while the minute hand goes half around? What part of the distance that the minute hand moves in a given time does the hour hand move in the same time?

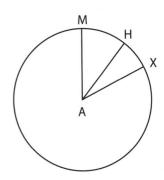

DADDY

"For you did not receive a spirit that makes you a slave again to fear, but you received the Spirit of sonship. And by him we cry, 'Abba, Father.' "

~ Romans 8:15

By my estimation I have preached 35 Easter sermons. This year, wishing to be different, I chose to preach on Romans 8. I alluded to the Easter narrative, but I preached on Romans 8. Why? Because everything about this chapter screams "He is risen!"

The truth is, I bet the disciples were suffering that morning. Certainly the ladies who visited the grave were suffering. They had come to prepare the body for burial, not to meet a risen Lord.

When Paul speaks of the spiritual life in Romans 8 he speaks much of suffering. We who are in Christ need not suffer from guilt or fear, for our sins have all been forgiven. There is no condemnation for those who are in Christ Jesus (Rom. 8:1–4). When we sin as Christians, we need never doubt that we are justified by faith because God's Spirit dwells within us, bearing witness that we are God's sons. Further, because the Spirit of God indwells us, He not only leads us to do the will of God, but He empowers our dead bodies to do so (Rom. 8:5–17).

But the best thing I like about Romans 8:15 is when we are invited to call God "Abba" or "Daddy." I don't know about you, but beyond age four or five, I never called my dad "Daddy." It was not cool. In fact, I wanted to be extra cool, so I tried calling Dad "Father," but that only got a scowl from my mother. I compromised and called him "Dad." I know my son-in-law, who is really cool, calls me "Jim." Coolness not withstanding, that is too much. I would like to be called "Dad" or at least "Big Daddy," but Karen refuses to be a "Big Momma" and how can you have a Big Daddy without a Big Momma? But I digress.

Can you imagine, the pedantic, choleric, ex-Pharisee Paul, who until recently did not even pronounce the name of God — YHWH — now invited the Roman Church to call God "Daddy"? Imagine the old stuffed shirt Jewish Christians in the congregation praying "Our Daddy, who art in heaven, hallowed be thy name!" Ha! It is embarrassing.

"For you have not received a spirit of slavery leading to fear again, but you have received a spirit of adoption as sons by which we cry out, 'Abba! Father!' " The Spirit Himself testifies with our spirit that we are children of God, and if children, heirs also, heirs of God and fellow heirs with Christ, if indeed we suffer with Him so that we may also be glorified with Him.

PRAYER POINTS
H EART OF PRAYER

"Pray in the Spirit on all occasions with all kinds of prayers and requests. With this in mind, be alert and always keep on praying for all the saints."

~ Ephesians 6:18

"For you did not receive the spirit of slavery leading again to fear, but you received the Spirit of adoption, by whom we cry, 'Abba, Father.' The Spirit himself bears witness to our spirit that we are God's children. And if children, then heirs (namely, heirs of God and also fellow heirs with Christ) if indeed we suffer with him so we may also be glorified with him" (Romans 8:15–17; Net Bible).

But it is true. He is our Daddy, Abba, Father. It is not cool, but it is true. God, the Creator of the universe, is so intimate, so wonderful, so loving, that He invites us to call Him Daddy. Wow! Now that is an Easter message. And that really is cool!

TEST-TAKING INSIGHT

The Reading Test

There will be four passages. The topics will include:

Prose Fiction: These passages are based on readings in classical, fictional literature of all genres — novels, plays, poetry. Remember! The single most important preparation that you can do for the ACT is to read great books! If you need a guide, consult my book, *Companion to 50 Classics*. Also, it wouldn't hurt to use my literature books in your regular English courses (Encouraging Thoughtful Christians to be World Changers for Christ Series). My courses will teach you how to do literary analysis, the single most important skill that you will bring to the ACT.

Social Sciences: The social science passages will include sociology, history, antropology, political science, and economics. Again, the content of these courses is unimportant — these passages are measuring your reading/comprehension ability — but it doesn't hurt to be familiar with some of the terminology in the passages.

Humanities: I generally find these passages to be daunting, tedious, and generally boring. And reading something boring decreases one's comprehension! Humanities includes music, theater, art, and architecture. If you share my aversion to these subjects, it would benefit you to read some secondary sources — even encyclopedias — on these subjects.

Pure Science: These passages are based on science, including chemistry, biology, physics, and other physical sciences. Try to take chemistry, biology, and physics in your regular class work around and during taking the ACT. Again, the best time to take the ACT is in the spring of your junior year (so you can retake it in the fall of your senior year if you need to do so).

When you read a passage, or a literary work, it is critical that you notice details. These "details" reveal the essence, the purpose, of the passage or literary work. For example, details about the physical environment or the social, cultural, and moral influences affect the outcome of a character. You need to discern these.

Data Analysis

Analyze the two orchids — a warm environment orchid and a colder environment orchid. What conclusions can you draw?

Warm Weather Orchid

Cold Weather Orchid

I. Harsh, warm climates cause the orchids to have less foliage but a more sturdy stem structure to store water.

II. Colder weather orchids naturally have large flowers to attract bees. They have less time for pollination.

III. Warm weather orchids do not live as long as cold weather orchids.

A. I
B. II
C. III
D. None
E. I and II
F. II and III

READING

Main Concept

No one knows for sure if there really was a King Arthur. Most historians, however, believe there really was a Briton king named Arthur, or a combination of Briton kings whose exploits were summed up in the life of one man.

Arthur was allegedly the son of King Pendragon, a Briton Welsh king during the Roman occupation. Legend states that the departing Roman army asked Arthur to protect Britons from the warring Anglo-Saxons pouring into England.

Inevitably, like all national heroes (e.g., Roland, Siegfried, El Cid, George Washington), King Arthur became more of a myth than a historical man. In apocryphal stories Arthur manifests superhuman strength and abilities. In fact, legends suggest that Arthur is not dead but only sleeping in one of numerous caves waiting to return and lead his people.

Serving with King Arthur were the Knights of the Round Table. The knights themselves were the heroes of many of the stories. The most important ones are Sir Bedivere, Sir Gawain, and Sir Kay. Later surpassed by Sir Lancelot.

According to early legends, Excalibur was the name of the famous sword of King Arthur. According to this account, King Arthur obtains a sword called "Caliburn," which was made on the Isle of Avalon. Later legends have the sword being returned to the Lady of the Lake on the mortal wounding of King Arthur at Camlann. It was not until Robert de Boron created the character Merlin (c. 1200) that the story of the young King Arthur drawing the sword Excalibur from a rock emerged.

Arthur's knights perennially embark on quests for the Holy Grail. The Holy Grail is the cup from which Christ drank at the Last Supper and which was used by Joseph of Arimathea to catch Christ's blood as he died on the Cross.

English 19th century poet Alfred Lord Tennyson had the greatest influence on the conception of the Holy Grail quest through his *Idylls of the King*, and his short poem "Sir Galahad."

How did Arthur die? In some accounts, King Arthur was taken to the Isle of Avalon to be healed, and what happened to him after reaching the island is a mystery. Some say he lies in a cave awaiting the day he is needed again by his country; others say King Arthur died at Avalon. Apart from the somewhat dubious claim by some medieval monks to have found King Arthur's grave, no real evidence has emerged for an Arthurian grave.

In summary, King Arthur was probably a folk tale, based roughly on a historic, figure. He was portrayed as a "Protector of Britain" who wanders across Britain with his band of chivalrous knights. Perhaps there was a great king who saved Briton from Saxon hands for a time. Perhaps not.

■ ■ ■

Based on this passage which is true? The author:

   I. strongly believes that King Arthur was a historical figure.
   II. is fairly certain that King Arthur was only a folk tale.
   III. has found historical evidence to prove King Arthur was a real historical figure

   A. I
   B. II
   C. III
   D. All
   E. None

How did Arthur die?

   A. No one knows.
   B. In a sword fight.
   C. In some accounts, King Arthur was taken to the Isle of Avalon to be healed, and what happened to him after reaching the island is a mystery.

MATH

A courier who travels at the rate of 6 miles an hour is followed 5 hours later, by another who travels at the rate of 8½ miles an hour. In how many hours will the second overtake the first?

"Today a reader, tomorrow a leader."

— Margaret Fuller

WRITING

Evaluating Essays

Score the following ACT essay using the criteria from the next two pages and then rewrite it at a higher score level.

The prompt is: "Choices are costly. Agree or disagree and give some examples."

Throughout history, life has presented people with difficult choices. ~~Some~~ Some choose bad responses, and others choose good. Good choices often come with a price. They can be costly, but they are for the greater good.

Good decisions are often costly. For example, Rodion in <u>Crime and Punishment</u> gives all of his remaining money to a widow for her husband's funeral. This decision cost him his money while benefitting the widow.

Although making good choices can be costly, they are for the greater good. The Allied invasion of Normandy in World War II costed them a lot of troops, but resulted in the greater good of reclaiming France.

Good decisions are rarely easy. They often have a large price. Sometimes they are made because it is the right thing to do, and others because a greater good will result from their decision. Either way, they can be difficult and costly.

Scoring Guidelines

These are the descriptions of scoring criteria that the trained readers will follow to determine the score (1–6) for your essay. Papers at each level exhibit all or most of the characteristics described at each score point.

Score = 6: Essays within this score range demonstrate effective skill in responding to the task.

The essay shows a clear understanding of the task. The essay takes a position on the issue and may offer a critical context for discussion. The essay addresses complexity by examining different perspectives on the issue, or by evaluating the implications and/or complications of the issue, or by fully responding to counterarguments to the writer's position. Development of ideas is ample, specific, and logical. Most ideas are fully elaborated. A clear focus on the specific issue in the prompt is maintained. The organization of the essay is clear: the organization may be somewhat predictable or it may grow from the writer's purpose. Ideas are logically sequenced. Most transitions reflect the writer's logic and are usually integrated into the essay. The introduction and conclusion are effective, clear, and well developed. The essay shows a good command of language. Sentences are varied and word choice is varied and precise. There are few, if any, errors to distract the reader.

Score = 5: Essays within this score range demonstrate competent skill in responding to the task.

The essay shows a clear understanding of the task. The essay takes a position on the issue and may offer a broad context for discussion. The essay shows recognition of complexity by partially evaluating the implications and/or complications of the issue, or by responding to counterarguments to the writer's position. Development of ideas is specific and logical. Most ideas are elaborated, with clear movement between general statements and specific reasons, examples, and details. Focus on the specific issue in the prompt is maintained. The organization of the essay is clear, although it may be predictable. Ideas are logically sequenced, although simple and obvious transitions may be used. The introduction and conclusion are clear and generally well developed. Language is competent. Sentences are somewhat varied and word choice is sometimes varied and precise. There may be a few errors, but they are rarely distracting.

Score = 4: Essays within this score range demonstrate adequate skill in responding to the task.

The essay shows an understanding of the task. The essay takes a position on the issue and may offer some context for discussion. The essay may show some recognition of complexity by providing some response to counterarguments to the writer's position. Development of ideas is adequate, with some movement between general statements and specific reasons, examples, and details. Focus on the specific issue in the prompt is maintained throughout most of the essay. The organization of the essay is apparent but predictable. Some evidence of logical sequencing of ideas is apparent, although most transitions are simple and obvious. The introduction and conclusion are clear and somewhat developed. Language is adequate, with some sentence variety and appropriate word choice. There may be some distracting errors, but they do not impede understanding.

Score = 3: Essays within this score range demonstrate some developing skill in responding to the task.

The essay shows some understanding of the task. The essay takes a position on the issue but does not offer a context for discussion. The essay may acknowledge a counterargument to the writer's position, but its development is brief or unclear. Development of ideas is limited and may be repetitious, with little, if any, movement between general statements and specific reasons, examples, and details. Focus on the general topic is maintained, but focus on the specific issue in the prompt may not be maintained. The organization of the essay is simple. Ideas are logically grouped within parts of the essay, but there is little or no evidence of logical sequencing of ideas. Transitions, if used, are simple and obvious. An introduction and conclusion are clearly discernible but underdeveloped. Language shows a basic control. Sentences show a little variety and word choice is appropriate. Errors may be distracting and may occasionally impede understanding.

Score = 2: Essays within this score range demonstrate inconsistent or weak skill in responding to the task.

The essay shows a weak understanding of the task. The essay may not take a position on the issue, or the essay may take a position but fail to convey reasons to support that position, or the essay may take a position but fail to maintain a stance. There is little or no recognition of a counterargument to the writer's position. The essay is thinly developed. If examples are given, they are general and may not be clearly relevant. The essay may include extensive repetition of the writer's ideas or of ideas in the prompt. Focus on the general topic is maintained, but focus on the specific issue in the prompt may not be maintained. There is some indication of an organizational structure, and some logical grouping of ideas within parts of the essay is apparent. Transitions, if used, are simple and obvious, and they may be inappropriate or misleading. An introduction and conclusion are discernible but minimal. Sentence structure and word choice are usually simple. Errors may be frequently distracting and may sometimes impede understanding.

Score = 1: Essays within this score range show little or no skill in responding to the task.

The essay shows little or no understanding of the task. If the essay takes a position, it fails to convey reasons to support that position. The essay is minimally developed. The essay may include excessive repetition of the writer's ideas or of ideas in the prompt. Focus on the general topic is usually maintained, but focus on the specific issue in the prompt may not be maintained. There is little or no evidence of an organizational structure or of the logical grouping of ideas. Transitions are rarely used. If present, an introduction and conclusion are minimal. Sentence structure and word choice are simple. Errors may be frequently distracting and may significantly impede understanding.

No Score: Blank, off-topic, illegible, not in English, or void. (ACT Website)

The Connecticut Yankee in King Arthur's Court
Mark Twain

Hank Morgan finds himself transported back to England's Dark Ages — where he is immediately captured and sentenced to death at Camelot. Fortunately, he's quick-witted, and in the process of saving his life he turns himself into a celebrity — winning himself the position of prime minister as well as the lasting enmity of Merlin. The introduction of modern technology into medieval England is intriguing and keeps the reader spellbound.

Suggested Vocabulary Words

A. Camelot — Camelot," said I to myself. "I don't seem to remember hearing of it before. Name of the <u>asylum</u>, likely."

B. It was a soft, <u>reposeful</u> summer landscape, as lovely as a dream, and as lonesome as Sunday.

C. She walked <u>indolently</u> along, with a mind at rest, its peace reflected in her innocent face.

D. She was going by as <u>indifferently</u> as she might have gone by a couple of cows; but when she happened to notice me, then there was a change! Up went her hands, and she was turned to stone; her mouth dropped open, her eyes stared wide and timorously, she was the picture of astonished curiosity touched with fear. And there she stood gazing, in a sort of <u>stupefied</u> fascination.

E. I couldn't make head or tail of it. And that she should seem to consider me a spectacle, and totally overlook her own merits in that respect, was another puzzling thing, and a display of <u>magnanimity</u>, too, that was surprising in one so young.

F. As we approached the town, signs of life began to appear. At intervals we passed a <u>wretched</u> cabin, with a thatched roof, and about it small fields and garden patches in an indifferent state of cultivation.

G. In the town were some substantial windowless houses of stone scattered among a wilderness of thatched cabins; the streets were mere crooked alleys, and unpaved; troops of dogs and nude children played in the sun and made life and noise; hogs roamed and rooted contentedly about, and one of them lay in a reeking wallow in the

middle of the main thoroughfare and suckled her family. Presently there was a distant blare of military music; it came nearer, still nearer, and soon a noble <u>cavalcade</u> wound into view, glorious with plumed helmets and flashing mail and flaunting banners and rich doublets and horse-cloths and gilded spearheads; and through the muck and swine, and naked brats, and joyous dogs, and shabby huts, it took its gallant way, and in its wake we followed.

Usage

"Another way of referring to an antecedent which is a distributive pronoun or a noun modified by a distributive adjective, is to use the plural of the pronoun following. This is not considered the best usage, the logical analysis requiring the singular pronoun in each case; but the construction is frequently found when the antecedent includes or implies both genders. The masculine does not really represent a feminine antecedent, and the expression his or her is avoided as being cumbrous."

Correct the following sentences.

1. "Neither of the sisters were very much deceived." — Thackeray

2. "Every one must judge of their own feelings." — Byron

3. "Had the doctor been contented to take my dining tables, as anybody in their senses would have done." — Austen

4. "If the part deserve any comment, every considering Christian will make it themselves as they go." — Defoe

■ ■ ■

Literary passages that you will read have a chronological order, or a sequence in which they occur. Look for clues that signal transitions between two events: during, next, first, second, last.

JEREMIAH

SCRIPTURE

"So I bought the field at Anathoth from my cousin Hanamel and weighed out for him seventeen shekels of silver."

~ Jeremiah 32:9

This is the word that came to Jeremiah from the LORD in the tenth year of Zedekiah king of Judah, which was the eighteenth year of Nebuchadnezzar. The army of the king of Babylon was then besieging Jerusalem, and Jeremiah the prophet was confined in the courtyard of the guard in the royal palace of Judah.

Now Zedekiah king of Judah had imprisoned him there, saying, "Why do you prophesy as you do? You say, 'This is what the LORD says: I am about to hand this city over to the king of Babylon, and he will capture it. Zedekiah king of Judah will not escape out of the hands of the Babylonians but will certainly be handed over to the king of Babylon, and will speak with him face to face and see him with his own eyes. He will take Zedekiah to Babylon, where he will remain until I deal with him, declares the LORD. If you fight against the Babylonians, you will not succeed.' "

Jeremiah said, "The word of the LORD came to me: Hanamel son of Shallum your uncle is going to come to you and say, 'Buy my field at Anathoth, because as nearest relative it is your right and duty to buy it.'

"Then, just as the LORD had said, my cousin Hanamel came to me in the courtyard of the guard and said, 'Buy my field at Anathoth in the territory of Benjamin. Since it is your right to redeem it and possess it, buy it for yourself.'

"I knew that this was the word of the LORD; so I bought the field at Anathoth from my cousin Hanamel and weighed out for him seventeen shekels of silver. I signed and sealed the deed, had it witnessed, and weighed out the silver on the scales. I took the deed of purchase — the sealed copy containing the terms and conditions, as well as the unsealed copy — and I gave this deed to Baruch son of Neriah, the son of Mahseiah, in the presence of my cousin Hanamel and of the witnesses who had signed the deed and of all the Jews sitting in the courtyard of the guard.

"In their presence I gave Baruch these instructions: 'This is what the LORD Almighty, the God of Israel, says: Take these documents, both the sealed and unsealed copies of the deed of purchase, and put them in a clay jar so they will last a long time. For

PRAYER POINTS
DISCERNMENT

"I know your deeds, your hard work and your perseverance. I know that you cannot tolerate wicked men, that you have tested those who claim to be apostles but are not, and have found them false."

~ Revelation 2:2

this is what the LORD Almighty, the God of Israel, says: Houses, fields and vineyards will again be bought in this land' " (Jeremiah 32:1–15).

Jeremiah, knowing full well that he was going to die in captivity, without ever enjoying his homeland again, bought property in that homeland. His investment was not for himself; it was for his children, his grandchildren, his nation. Can you do that? Can you live your life knowing that you might never enjoy your field at Anathoth? Can you invest in the lives of things and people, knowing you may never live to see the fruit grow on the bushes in the fields that you bought but will not enjoy?

MATH

Simultaneous Equations

Solve

$$x + 3y = 17,$$
$$2x + y = 9.$$

SCIENCE

Drawing Conclusions from Data

Examine the following picture of the density of the Western Hemisphere (1911).[1]

What conclusions can you draw?

I. Climate has an impact on population growth.
II. Geography has an impact on population growth
III. Geo-political influence has an impact on population growth

  A. I
  B. II
  C. III
  D. None
  E. I and II
  F. All

> "You don't have to burn books to destroy a culture. Just get people to stop reading them."[2]
> — Ray Bradbury

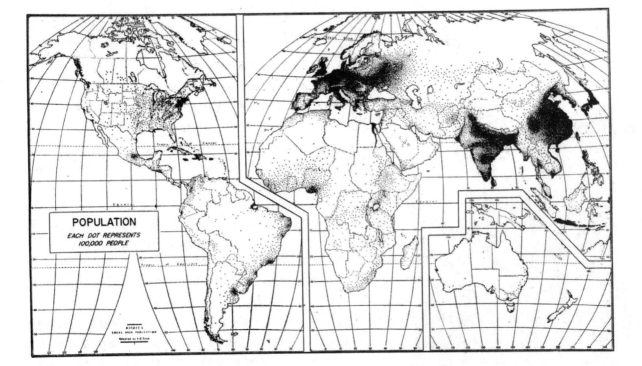

POPULATION
EACH DOT REPRESENTS 100,000 PEOPLE

Psychology of the ACT

The ACT, like the SAT, is a critical-thinking exam, which is to say that it is based on Bloom's Taxonomy, or a cognitive developmental theory of education, particularly analysis, synthesis, and evaluation questions.

BLOOM'S TAXONOMY (Argues that people learn in stages.)

1. KNOWLEDGE: Remembering the material without understanding, using, or changing the material.

2. COMPREHENSION: Understanding the material being given without comparing it to anything else.

3. APPLICATION: Using a general concept to solve a problem.

4. ANALYSIS: Taking something apart.

5. SYNTHESIS: Creating something new by putting different ideas together to make a new whole.

6. EVALUATION: Judging the value of material.

Clearly, your high school courses must teach you to do the above higher, critical thinking. In other words, the more challenging your high school curricula, the higher your ACT score will be. Generally, whole book, classical approaches to education (with emphasis on English and math), will generate much higher scores on the ACT than other curricula. Memorizing the state capitals will do nothing to increase your ACT; however, analyzing why certain places were chosen as state capitals, and then evaluating if these locations were good, will most certainly increase ACT scores! In other words, avoid wimpy high school courses!

W R I T I N G

Evaluating Essays

Score the following ACT essay and then discuss how it could be improved. Some people believe that there is only one foolproof plan, perfect solution, or correct interpretation. But nothing is ever that simple. For better or worse, for every so-called final answer there is another way of seeing things. There is always a "however." Assignment: Is there always another explanation or another point of view? Plan and write an essay in which you develop your point of view on this issue. Support your positioning with reasoning and examples taken from your reading, studies, experience, or observations.

In the world, people always have a perfect solution or a truly foolproof plan. There is the right choice to make or the wrong choice. This can be seen in three examples. One is the narrative poem, *Sir Gawain and the Green Knight*. Second is the study of medicine and specifically treating an ill patient. Thirdly is Charlie, the main character in *Charlie and the Chocolate Factory*. Although one is faced with two different options when making a decision, in the end there is only one perfect solution.

In the medieval poem *Sir Gawain and the Green Knight*, the knight Gawain, a brave, kind, and loyal man is tempted by a beautiful lady. He has a choice of falling into her snare or standing strong and resisting her. These choices are clearly right versus wrong. In the end, this knight remains strong and resists her. As the poem concludes, one sees that Gawain made the right choice, or perfect solution.

The field of medicine represents another reason why there is always just one correct interpretation. When treating a sick patient and working to find the right cure, a doctor will be faced with many options. However, as he learns more about the illness and the possible cures, the doctor will eventually find the only one right cure to the disease. Whatever the number of other available medications, they will not all cure the patient. It's the one right medication that is the foolproof plan for that specific patient.

The third example that supports this viewpoint is the characters in Ronald Dahl's *Charlie and the Chocolate Factory*. Five children are given a tour of a chocolate factory. Four of these children, in one way or another, disobey Willy Wonka, the owner of the factory, by making a choice. This choice is simply going against Mr. Wonka's set rules. However, Charlie follows all the rules, which makes him the winner of a certain prize. In this children's story, the presented rules set the line between right and wrong. Four children, realizing the rules, walk onto the wrong side. Charlie, though, stays in the boundaries, and makes the right decision by following Mr. Wonka's rules.

In both the worlds of science and literature, there is always just one right choice, although there may be multiple wrong choices. One sees a definite bright line between the perfect solution and the wrong decision, without any "howevers." (From a student)

VOCABULARY

King Solomon's Mines[3]
H. Rider Haggard

Guide Allan Quatermain, the original Indiana Jones, helps a young lady (Beth) find her lost husband somewhere in Africa. It's a spectacular adventure story with romance, because while they fight with ferocious beasts and natives, they fall in love. Will they find the lost husband or skip town for parts unknown?

Suggested Vocabulary Words

A. With the first light we were up and making ready for the <u>fray</u>.

B. With great difficulty, and by the promise of a present of a good hunting-knife each, I succeeded in persuading three <u>wretched</u> natives from the village to come with us for the first stage, twenty miles, and to carry a large gourd holding a gallon of water apiece. My object was to enable us to refill our water-bottles after the first night's march, for we determined to start in the cool of the evening. I gave out to these natives that we were going to shoot ostriches, with which the desert abounded. They <u>jabbered</u> and shrugged their shoulders, saying that we were mad and should perish of thirst, which I must say seemed probable; but being <u>desirous</u> of obtaining the knives, which were almost unknown treasures up there, they consented to come, having probably <u>reflected</u> that, after all, our <u>subsequent</u> <u>extinction</u> would be no affair of theirs.

C. . . . if indeed there are any other such in the world, measuring each of them at least fifteen thousand feet in height, standing not more than a dozen miles apart, linked together by a <u>precipitous</u> cliff of rock, and towering in awful white <u>solemnity</u> straight into the sky.

D. These mountains placed thus, like the pillars of a gigantic gateway, are shaped after the fashion of a woman's breasts, and at times the mists and shadows beneath them take the form of a <u>recumbent</u> woman, veiled mysteriously in sleep. The stretch of cliff that connects them appears to be some thousands of feet in height, and perfectly <u>precipitous</u>, and on each flank of them, so far as the eye can reach, extent similar lines of cliff, broken only here and there by flat table-topped mountains, something like the world-famed one at Cape Town; a formation, by the way, that is very common in Africa.

ENGLISH

Grammar: Complex Sentences

Change each compound sentence below to a complex sentence. Relate the ideas in each part of the sentence by using the subordinating conjunction or relative pronoun given in parenthesis.

1. Mary plays the guitar beautifully, and so we will ask her to play for church. (who)

2. My homework needs some attention, so I asked my mother to help me. (because)

3. I gathered as much coal as I could, and the winter storm struck. (before)

4. We slowed down, and we saw the roadblock. (when)

■ ■ ■

Rewrite the following paragraph, which consists wholly of simple and compound sentences. To vary the style, change or combine some of the sentences.

My friends could hear the enemy growing closer, and they were talking. Finally we could see the enemy emerge around the bend. The captain was motioning with his hand to be quiet and the soldiers were laughing. One blew his nose and coughed and stumbled. All my friends were staring and waiting and the enemy soldiers came forward.

READING

Idea Stated

David Livingston was born into a Christian Scottish family outside Glasgow and he made a commitment to Christ when he was young. He studied medicine and theology at the University of Glasgow. He tried to go to China as a missionary in 1838, but was unable to do so. Contact with Robert Moffat, pioneer missionary to Africa, prompted Livingstone to dedicate his life to African missions. On December 8, 1840, Livingstone sailed for Africa for the first time. He had a burden that all natives should have an opportunity to embrace Christianity, and he wanted to go where no missionary had gone. On his first mission trip he was almost eaten by a lion! It was not a propitious beginning.

In 1844 he was married to Mary Moffat, oldest daughter of Robert and Mary Moffat. Sadly, Dr. Livingston's work took him away from his beloved wife Mary and their five children too much.

Livingstone was more convinced than ever of his mission to reach unsaved people groups in the interior of Africa and introduce them to Christianity, and, at the same time, freeing them from slavery. Normally slave traders were hesitant to buy converted African captives. They were harder to sell to American traders.

In 1849 and 1851, he traveled across the Kalahari, on the second trip sighting the upper Zambezi River.

In 1842, he began a four-year expedition to find a route from the upper Zambezi to the coast. This filled huge gaps in western knowledge of central and southern Africa. In 1855, Livingstone discovered a spectacular waterfall that he named "Victoria Falls." He reached the mouth of the Zambezi on the Indian Ocean in May 1856, becoming the first European to cross the width of southern Africa.

Returning to Britain, where he was now a national hero, Livingstone did many speaking tours and published his best selling *Missionary Travels and Researches in South Africa* (1857). In 1862, while Livingstone was in Africa, his wife died.

He returned to Africa. This expedition lasted from 1866 until Livingstone's death in 1873. After nothing was heard from him for many months, Henry Stanley, an explorer and journalist, set out to find Livingstone. This resulted in their meeting near Lake Tanganyika in October 1871 during which Stanley uttered the famous phrase: "Dr Livingstone, I presume?" With new supplies from Stanley, Livingstone continued his efforts to find the source of the Nile. He discovered it late in his life.

His health had been poor for many years and he died on May 1, 1873. His body was taken back to England and buried in Westminster Abbey. His heart, it is purported, was buried in Africa.[4] (James Stobaugh, *British History*)

What best describes the author's attitude toward David Livinston?

A. David Livingston was one of the most important, seminal figures in English colonial history.

B. David Livingston's greatness was somewhat tarnished by his shabby treatment of his family.

C. David Livingston was an unorthodox, troublesome religious fanatic.

D. David Livingston was more an ambassador for English culture than Christianity.

David Livingston is best known for:

A. His discovery of Victorian Falls.

B. His encounter with Henry Stanley.

C. His translation of the Bible into a native Language.

D. His participation in World War I.

No matter how long a writing passage is, authors vary their sentence types. Each writer uses different sentences to keep his reader's attention. One effective technique is to use transitions — for instance, in spite of, therefore, etc. Another strategy is to combine sentences together: "The world will little note nor long remember what we say here, but it can never forget what they did here." — Abraham Lincoln, "The Gettysburg Address"

Read a
GOOD BOOK

SCRIPTURE

"Blessed are they whose transgressions are forgiven, whose sins are covered. Blessed is the man whose sin the Lord will never count against him."

~ Romans 4:7–8

The British evangelical Dorothy Sayers writes:

The Christian faith is the most exciting drama that ever staggered the imagination of man — and the dogma is the drama. [The central doctrine of Christianity is a tale of] the time when God was the underdog and got beaten, when he submitted to the conditions he had laid down and became a man like the men He had made, and the men He had made broke Him and killed Him. Nobody is compelled to believe a single word of this remarkable story. But the divine Dramatist has set out to convince us.[1]

How true Dorothy Sayers' words are! I am preparing for my sermon this weekend, Romans 4, and I am struck again at how rich is the story surrounding our faith! We say in a negative way, "Don't make so much drama!" But no matter what drama life may hold, we can never eclipse the drama we read in the gospel.

But we try. Television has become the command center of our new epistemology. It promotes shallow thinking and has pretty well killed reading and rhetoric. The clearest way to see through a culture is to see how it speaks to itself. The television has dramatically and irreversibly shifted the content and meaning of public discourse. Truth is not and can never be show business, and Americans want show business. This is one danger of our facile Christian culture.

Neil Postman writes, "We are by now into a second generation of children for whom television has been their first and most accessible teacher and, for many, their most reliable companion and friend. To put it plainly, television is the command center of the new epistemology . . . there is no subject of public interest . . . that does not find its way into television. Which means that all public understanding of these subjects is shaped by the biases of television . . . television has gradually become our culture."

Postman continues, "Television has become, so to speak, the background radiation of the social and intellectual universe, the all-but-imperceptible residue of the electronic big bang of a century past, so familiar and so thoroughly integrated with American culture that we no longer hear its faint hissing in the background or see the flickering grey light. This, in turn, means that its epistemology goes largely unnoticed. And the peekaboo world it has constructed around us no longer seems even strange."

"There is no more disturbing consequence of the electronic and graphic revolution than this: that the world as given to us through television seems natural, not bizarre. For the loss of the sense of the strange is a sign of adjustment, and the extent to which we have

PRAYER POINTS

STAND FIRM IN PERSECUTION

"You have persevered and have endured hardships for my name, and have not grown weary."

~ Revelation 2:3

adjusted is a measure of the extent to which we have changed. Our culture's adjustment to the epistemology of television is by now almost complete; we have so thoroughly accepted its definitions of truth, knowledge, and reality that irrelevance seems to us to be filled with import, and incoherence seems eminently sane."[2]

Young people! Turn off the television and read a good book! It will inspire your heart and increase your ACT score!

VOCABULARY

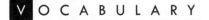

Democracy in America[3]
Alexis de Tocqueville

Coming from old, sedentary Europe, 25-year-old Tocqueville was fascinated by America's relatively free and egalitarian society. Having never had an aristocracy, America had taken democracy to its natural limits. In America, he saw Europe's future; indeed, the world's future!

Suggested Vocabulary Words

Through their means man acquires a kind of <u>preternatural</u> power over the future lot of his fellow-creatures. When the legislator has regulated the law of inheritance, he may rest from his labor. The machine once put in motion will go on for ages, and advance, as if self-guided, towards a given point. When framed in a particular manner, this law unites, draws together, and vests property and power in a few hands: its tendency is clearly <u>aristocratic</u>. On opposite principles its action is still more rapid; it divides, distributes, and disperses both property and power. Alarmed by the rapidity of its progress, those who despair of <u>arresting</u> its motion endeavor to obstruct it by difficulties and <u>impediments</u>; they vainly seek to counteract its effect by contrary efforts; but it gradually reduces or destroys every obstacle, until by its incessant activity the bulwarks of the influence of wealth are ground down to the fine and shifting sand which is the basis of democracy.

When the law of inheritance permits, still more when it decrees, the equal division of a father's property amongst all his children, its effects are of two kinds: it is important to <u>distinguish</u> them from each other, although they tend to the same end.

In virtue of the law of <u>partible</u> inheritance, the death of every <u>proprietor</u> brings about a kind of revolution in property; not only do his possessions change hands, but their very nature is altered, since they are parcelled into shares, which become smaller and smaller at each division. This is the direct and, as it were, the physical effect of the law. It follows, then, that in countries where equality of inheritance is established by law, property, and especially landed property, must have a tendency to <u>perpetual</u> <u>diminution</u>. The effects, however, of such legislation would only be perceptible after a lapse of time, if the law was abandoned to its own working; for supposing the family to consist of two children (and in a country people as France is the average number is not above three), these children, sharing amongst them the fortune of both parents, would not be poorer than their father or mother.

TEST-TAKING INSIGHT

Tricks of the Trade

While the IQ type SAT is full of tricks and illusions, the knowledge-based ACT is pretty straightforward. However there are a few techniques you should master.

Levels of difficulty: There are different types of questions — easy ones, hard ones, long ones, short ones. Feel free to skip around, but be sure and coordinate your answer sheet with the questions.

Identify deal makers: A little bell should ring in your mind when you read words like "but," "although," "in spite of," "however," and "nonetheless." It means a deal is being made, a change is occurring. Don't be left at the station when the train leaves and goes in another direction!

Clock watching: Watch the clock. Pace yourself. Write in the test book. For example, you have 45 minutes to answer 45 questions. The test begins at 11:00 A.M. At the first item write "11:00." Now, move to the end, to question 45, and write "11:35." Next to question 23 write "11:18." Your goal is to attain these benchmarks. This leaves you ten minutes to check your answers. Remember: scores in the high 20s and low 30s inevitably emerge from thorough proofreading.

What you see is what you get: Don't be fancy. Answer the question. Don't look for trickery or intrigue. If it seems easy, well, maybe it is. This test-taking strategy is much different from the SAT, which is full of subtleties that don't exist in the ACT.

Idea Stated

In America, not only do municipal bodies exist, but they are kept alive and supported by public spirit. The township of New England possesses two advantages which infallibly secure the attentive interest of mankind, namely, independence and authority. Its sphere is indeed small and limited, but within that sphere its action is unrestrained; and its independence gives to it a real importance which its extent and population may not always ensure.

It is to be remembered that the affections of men generally lie on the side of authority. Patriotism is not durable in a conquered nation. The New Englander is attached to his township, not only because he was born in it, but because it constitutes a social body of which he is a member, and whose government claims and deserves the exercise of his sagacity. In Europe the absence of local public spirit is a frequent subject of regret to those who are in power; everyone agrees that there is no surer guarantee of order and tranquility, and yet nothing is more difficult to create. If the municipal bodies were made powerful and independent, the authorities of the nation might be disunited and the peace of the country endangered. Yet, without power and independence, a town may contain good subjects, but it can have no active citizens. Another important fact is that the township of New England is so constituted as to excite the warmest of human affections, without arousing the ambitious passions of the heart of man. The officers of the country are not elected, and their authority is very limited. Even the State is only a second-rate community, whose tranquil and obscure administration offers no inducement sufficient to draw men away from the circle of their interests into the turmoil of public affairs. The federal government confers power and honor on the men who conduct it; but these individuals can never be very numerous. The high station of the Presidency can only be reached at an advanced period of life, and the other federal functionaries are generally men who have been favored by fortune, or distinguished in some other career. Such cannot be the permanent aim of the ambitious. But the township serves as a centre for the desire of public esteem, the want of exciting interests, and the taste for authority and popularity, in the midst of the ordinary relations of life; and

the passions which commonly embroil society change their character when they find a vent so near the domestic hearth and the family circle.[4]

■ ■ ■

An appropriate thesis for this passage would be:

A. The American president is mostly ineffectual.
B. Democracy, at least in the local setting, is a delusion.
C. Most Americans are loyal to their local setting rather than the federal setting.
D. Americans are great patriots.

??? Are you reading 50 to 100 pages a day ???

" We are all inventors, each sailing out on a voyage of discovery, guided each by a private chart, of which there is no duplicate. The world is all gates, all opportunities."[5]
— Ralph Waldo Emerson

W R I T I N G

Evaluating Essays

Score the following unpublished, student-produced ACT essay and then discuss how it could be improved.

Think carefully about the issue presented in the following excerpt and the assignment below.

Traditionally the term "heroism" has been applied to those who have braved physical danger to defend a cause or to protect others. But one of the most feared dangers people face is that of disapproval by their family, peers, or community. Sometimes acting courageously requires someone to speak out at the risk of such rejection. We should consider those who do so true heroes. Should heroes be defined as people who say what they think when we ourselves lack the courage to say it?

Heroes are not only people who perform physically dangerous deeds on behalf of others. Many heroes are simply people who stand up and defend what they believe through their actions and words no matter what the consequence. Sometimes those consequences are danger, and sometimes the consequences are rejection. People like Mother Teresa and Dietrich Bonhoeffer are examples of such heroes.

Mother Teresa is known all over the world for her acts of charity. However, had she not stood up for what she believed in, she would have never had an opportunity to serve the poor. Throughout her time in India, Mother Teresa faced rejection and hardships. Her bishop and the pope told her she could not leave her convent to work in the slums and rejected both her and her proposals multiple times. The Indian government tore down her work on more than one occasion. Sometimes she was threatened by angry Hindus because they thought that she wanted to convert Hindus to Christianity. Often they would not even allow her to defend her position. Yet in every situation she faced, Mother Teresa stood up for what she believed to be right. She didn't receive much recognition until the end of her life, but she was truly a hero for the poorest of the poor all over the world.

Dietrich Bonhoeffer is another such hero. Bonhoeffer was a pastor in his native Germany. In the 1930s, when Adolf Hitler was gaining power in Germany, Bonhoeffer sensed trouble brewing and went to England and then the United States. He returned to Germany just before the borders were closed because he felt that he needed to stand up for what he believed was right. Bonhoeffer worked against Hitler's Third Reich. He was rejected by many of his fellow countrymen and his church members. He was involved in a plot to assassinate Hitler and was put in a concentration camp. Bonhoeffer stood firm in his convictions. He was hanged at the camp in April 1945, shortly before Germany surrendered.

People like Mother Teresa and Dietrich Bonhoeffer are heroes because they were willing to stand upon their personal convictions. That bravery is what truly makes a hero.

M A T H

Algebra

1. $5x^2 - 12 = 33$

2. $3x^2 + 4 = 16$

3. $4x^2 + 11 = 136 - x^2$

4. $5(3x^2 - 1) = 11(x^2 + 1)$

5. $2/5x^2 - 1/3x^2 = 4/15$

E N G L I S H

Grammar: Adverb Placement, Part 1

In the following citations, see if the adverbs can be placed before or after the infinitive and still modify it as clearly as they now do:[6]

1. "There are, then, many things to be carefully considered, if a strike is to succeed." — Laughlin

2. "That the mind may not have to go backwards and forwards in order to rightly connect them." — Herbert Spencer

3. "It may be easier to bear along all the qualifications of an idea . . . than to first imperfectly conceive such idea." — Id

4. "In works of art, this kind of grandeur, which consists in multitude, is to be very cautiously admitted." — Burke

5. "That virtue which requires to be ever guarded is scarcely worth the sentinel." — Goldsmith

SCIENCE

Drawing Conclusions

Scientists typically examine data and draw conclusions from that data. Examine the following map and information and evaluate the veracity of the proposed conclusions. Remember: these conclusions are merely inferences (or not) that you have to evaluate.[7]

Which conclusions are defensible by the data on the map?

I. The modern colonial movements which have been genuine race expansions have shown a tendency not only to adhere to their zone, but to follow parallels of latitude or isotherms. The stratification of European peoples in the Americas, excepting Spanish and Portuguese, coincides with heat zones.

II. The movement of Europeans into the tropical regions of Asia, Australasia, Africa, and America, like the American advance into the Philippines, represents commercial and political, not genuine ethnic expansion.

III. The rapid inland advance from the coast of oversea colonists is part of that restless activity which is fostered by contact with the sea and supported by the command of abundant resources conferred by maritime superiority. The Anglo-Saxon invasion of England, as later the English colonization of America, seized the rim of the land, and promptly pushed up the rivers in sea-going boats far into the interior. But periphery may give to central region something more than conquerors and colonists. From its active markets and cosmopolitan exchanges there steadily filter into the interior culture and commodities, carried by peaceful merchant and missionary, who, however, are often only the harbingers of the conqueror. The accessibility of the periphery tends to raise it in culture, wealth, density of population, and often in political importance, far in advance of the center.

IV. People of color naturally prefer the temperate climates.

A. I
B. II
C. III
D. IV
E. I and II
F. I, II, and III
G. None
H. All

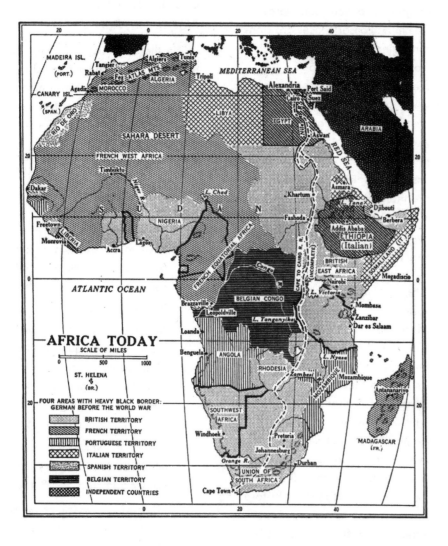

AFRICA TODAY
SCALE OF MILES
0   500   1000

ST. HELENA
(BR.)

FOUR AREAS WITH HEAVY BLACK BORDER:
GERMAN BEFORE THE WORLD WAR

- BRITISH TERRITORY
- FRENCH TERRITORY
- PORTUGUESE TERRITORY
- ITALIAN TERRITORY
- SPANISH TERRITORY
- BELGIAN TERRITORY
- INDEPENDENT COUNTRIES

Peanut Butter
AND JELLY

I am at the Ohio Homeschool Convention. This is their 25th anniversary this year. I have been a part of 19 of these conventions, 150 over the last two decades. Congratulations to Ohio Homeschoolers!

My wife, Karen, and my son Peter have graciously excused me from my vendor duties so that I can write.

SCRIPTURE

"And as if this were not enough in your sight, O God, you have spoken about the future of the house of your servant. You have looked on me as though I were the most exalted of men, O LORD God."

~ 1 Chronicles 17:17

As I write and meditate I look around me. To the right of me a family is spreading its homemade paraphernalia on a table. Bologna, whole grain bread, apples, and water are carefully placed on the obviously aged table cloth that graces an otherwise beat up old chipped round wooden table. This family honors the old table and this old veteran with its presence. We both are blessed. The family of six corporately bows its head and gives thanks to our God.

To my left is a child gleefully throwing a red rubber ball with a corner torn out to his father. The child is screaming in joy. The dad is smiling. A little innocent game gives so much joy to its owners. And to this quiet observer who loves both of them for their gift.

Behind me is a mom quietly weeping. Around her table are four children eating peanut butter and jelly sandwiches. I don't know why that mom is weeping. I see she is speaking on an ancient Nokia phone. No iPhone for this mom! Suddenly she stops and prays. All four children, their grape jelly and peanut butter sandwiches hanging in mid-air waving to God, stop and pray, too. Obviously the kids don't know what their mom is saying or why she is crying but they are neither upset or curious — they grasp the import of the moment and join their mom in this sacred moment. I can't help feeling like God is answering their prayers.

In the corner is a teen quietly reading my worldview devotional *Fire That Burns But Does not Consume* that my son Peter no doubt sold her.

PRAYER POINTS
OVERCOME FAILURE

"Though he stumble, he will not fall, for the LORD upholds him with his hand."

~ Psalm 37:24

As I look around me on this late summer morning, I can't help but feel that history is being made. Quietly, unpretentiously, with no cynicism, a people gathers in places all over this nation. Peoria, Columbus, St. Charles, Pottstown, and Boise. Indianapolis, Phoenix, Knoxville, and Birmingham. In a hundred places, thousands strong, they are changing history. And they are my people, my community, because I too am a homeschooler. I bow my head with them, I eat my peanut butter and jelly, and I dream dreams with them. I see history being made.

ENGLISH

Grammar: Adverb Placement, Part 2

A very careful writer will so place the modifiers of a verb that the reader will not mistake the meaning.

The rigid rule in such a case would be to put the modifier in such a position that the reader not only can understand the meaning intended, but cannot misunderstand the thought. Now, when such adverbs as only, even, etc., are used, they are usually placed in a strictly correct position, if they modify single words; but they are often removed from the exact position, if they modify phrases or clauses: for example, from Irving, "The site is only to be traced by fragments of bricks, china, and earthenware." "Here" only modifies the phrase by fragments of bricks, etc., but it is placed before the infinitive. This misplacement of the adverb can be detected only by analysis of the sentence.[1]

Tell what the adverb modifies in each quotation, and see if it is placed in the proper position:[2]

1. "Only the name of one obscure epigrammatist has been embalmed for us in the verses of his rival." — Palgrave

2. "Do you remember pea shooters? I think we only had them on going home for holidays." — Thackeray

3. "Irving could only live very modestly. He could only afford to keep one old horse." — Id

4. "The arrangement of this machinery could only be accounted for by supposing the motive power to have been steam." — Wendell Phillips

5. "Such disputes can only be settled by arms." —Id

WRITING

Evaluating Essays

Score the following ACT essay and then discuss how it could be improved.

Has today's abundance of information only made it more difficult for us to understand the world around us?

In today's society, information, more information than could fit in any library, is available instantaneously, easily, and cheaply. Just moments after turning on a computer, one can arrive at millions of pages about giant salamanders, the principality of Monaco, or any other subject imaginable. But is this good for us? Does an abundance of information actually translate into greater understanding of the world around us? No, it does not and, in fact, it has quite the opposite effect: with so much information, we are actually less able to make sense of the world.

"Truth" in the Internet age is often shaky at best. Wikipedia, an online encyclopedia that anyone can edit, has become a commonplace reference for many. It contains volumes upon volumes of information, more than any print encyclopedia, and important articles are often current to the day. Wikipedia articles are always changing, and edit wars among groups of disagreeing editors can erupt on controversial articles. "Truth" on Wikipedia, unlike scholarly circles, is often a democracy. The side with the most numerous or most active editors, not necessarily the side with the most solid facts, wins out. Other areas of the Internet exhibit these same tendencies, although often to a much greater degree.

Furthermore, the pages that appear at the top of Internet searches are often not the most reputable, scholarly, or even factual, but rather those that match the search term best or receive the greatest number of visits. It is often difficult to sort out the worthy sources from the rest.

So much information makes it quite difficult to sort out any decent approximation of truth.

"I did very well on the ACT because I practiced several weeks and then spent some time in prayer where I got in touch with God and myself. Finally, I memorized Scripture that really helped me calm down on test day." — a testimony from a student who made 32 on the ACT.

Science Test

Several scientific tests have proven that familiarity alone with a test will increase your score. No portion of the ACT is more responsive than the science section. To that end, there are three parts of the ACT science test.

Data analysis: The ACT has three data analysis passages with 5 questions each for a total of 15 questions. The data analyzed is a table, diagram, or graph followed with a minimum of text. You will be asked to analyze the data in the table, diagram, or graph. Strategy: it does not matter if you are analyzing shoes or microbes, the data is all that interests you. Typically, data is measured in a graph that includes a Y and an X axis. A diagram or table is merely a modification of that concept.

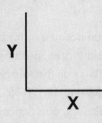

Research analysis: The ACT has three research summary passages with six questions each. In other words, this section is about one-half of the entire science section of the ACT. Research analysis questions, like data analysis questions, include tables, diagrams, and graphs. Now, however, you are asked to evaluate the veracity of the research. This research will also include the purpose of the study, the design of the experiment, and the results itself.

Experimental design: In an experimental design question all factors remain constant — except one — and you will need to determine the outcome. For instance, if you have a block of ice in an ice chest, and the outside temperature rises 50 percent, you will need to predict the result. Everything else is the same — the ice is the same and the ice chest is the same — but the outside temperature rises. Be sure and predict changes that are unequivocally related to the rise in temperature. For instance, if you said that the water was "salty," that change would not be related to the temperature rise.

M A T H

Word Problems

1. Matthew had three times as many stamps as Herman, but after he had lost 70, and Herman had bought 90, they put what they had together, and found that they had 540. How many had each at first?

2 It is required to divide the number 139 into four parts, such that the first may be 2 less than the second, 7 more than the third, and 12 greater than the fourth.

3. In an election, 7,105 votes were cast for three candidates. One candidate received 614 votes less, and the other 1,896 votes less, than the winning candidate. How many votes did each receive?

4. There are four towns, A, B, C, and D, in a straight line. The distance from B to C is one-fifth of the distance from A to B, and the distance from C to D is equal to twice the distance from A to C. The whole distance from A to D is 72 miles. Record the distance from A to B, B to C, and C to D.

Life on the Mississippi[3]
Mark Twain

Released in 1883 by James R. Osgood & Co., the first edition had 624 pages and 316 illustrations. Twain incorporated passages from other books on the river when he discovered he didn't have enough material to fill out the book; he also included a portion from his unfinished *Huckleberry Finn* manuscript.

In the early 1870s, Twain wanted to write an account of his piloting days in an effort to preserve the memory of the rapidly disappearing steamboat era on the Mississippi. The result was the "Old Times on the Mississippi" serial, published in seven installments in the *Atlantic Monthly* in 1875. This novel is full of several genres: essays, biography (non-fiction), and fictional narrative. You will surely enjoy it!

Suggested Vocabulary

(Young Mark Twain is learning about how to be a riverboat pilot on the Mississippi River. Mr. Bixby is his captain.)

Now and then Mr. Bixby called my attention to certain things. Said he, "This is Six-Mile Point." I <u>assented</u>. It was pleasant enough information, but I could not see the bearing of it. I was not conscious that it was a matter of any interest to me. Another time he said, "This is Nine-Mile Point." Later he said, "This is Twelve-Mile Point." They were all about level with the water's edge; they all looked about alike to me; they were <u>monotonously</u> <u>unpicturesque</u>. I hoped Mr. Bixby would change the subject. But no; he would crowd up around a point, hugging the shore with affection, and then say: "The slack water ends here, abreast this bunch of China-trees; now we cross over." So he crossed over. He gave me the wheel once or twice, but I had no luck. I either came near chipping off the edge of a sugar plantation, or I yawed too far from shore, and so dropped back into disgrace again and got abuse.

The watch was ended at last, and we took supper and went to bed. At midnight the glare of a lantern shone in my eyes, and the night watchman said, "Come! Turn out!"

And then he left. I could not understand this extraordinary procedure; so I presently gave up trying to, and dozed off to sleep. Pretty soon the watchman was back again, and this time he was gruff. I was annoyed. I said: "What do you want to come bothering around here in the middle of the night for. Now as like as not I'll not get to sleep again to-night."

The watchman said, "Well, if this an't good, I'm blest."

The "off-watch" was just turning in, and I heard some <u>brutal</u> laughter from them, and such remarks as "Hello, watchman! an't the new cub turned out yet? He's delicate, likely. Give him some sugar in a rag and send for the chambermaid to sing rock-a-by-baby to him."

About this time Mr. Bixby appeared on the scene. Something like a minute later I was climbing the pilot-house steps with some of my clothes on and the rest in my arms. Mr. Bixby was close behind, commenting. Here was something fresh — this thing of getting up in the middle of the night to go to work. It was a detail in piloting that had never occurred to me at all. I knew that boats ran all night, but somehow I had never happened to reflect that somebody had to get up out of a warm bed to run them. I began to fear that piloting was not quite so romantic as I had imagined it was; there was something very real and work-like about this new phase of it.

It seemed to me that I had put my life in the keeping of a <u>peculiarly</u> reckless outcast. Presently he turned on me and said: "What's the name of the first point above New Orleans?"

I was gratified to be able to answer promptly, and I did. I said I didn't know.

"Don't KNOW?"

This manner <u>jolted</u> me. I was down at the foot again, in a moment. But I had to say just what I had said before.

"Well, you're a smart one," said Mr. Bixby. "What's the name of the NEXT point?"

Once more I didn't know.

"Well, this beats anything. Tell me the name of ANY point or place I told you."

I studied a while and decided that I couldn't.

"Look here! What do you start out from, above Twelve-Mile Point, to cross over?"

"I — I — don't know."

"You — you — don't know?" mimicking my drawling manner of speech. "What DO you know?"

"I — I — nothing, for certain."

"By the great Caesar's ghost, I believe you! You're the stupidest dunderhead I ever saw or ever heard of, so help me Moses! The idea of you being a pilot — you! Why, you don't know enough to pilot a cow down a lane."

Oh, but his <u>wrath</u> was up! He was a nervous man, and he shuffled from one side of his wheel to the other as if the floor was hot. He would boil a while to himself, and then overflow and scald me again.

"Look here! What do you suppose I told you the names of those points for?"

I tremblingly considered a moment, and then the devil of temptation provoked me to say: "Well — to — to — be entertaining, I thought."

This was a red rag to the bull. He raged and stormed so (he was crossing the river at the time) that I judge it made him blind, because he ran over the steering-oar of a trading-scow. Of course the traders sent up a volley of red-hot profanity. Never was a man

so grateful as Mr. Bixby was: because he was brim full, and here were subjects who would TALK BACK. He threw open a window, thrust his head out, and such an irruption followed as I never had heard before. The fainter and farther away the scowmen's curses drifted, the higher Mr. Bixby lifted his voice and the weightier his adjectives grew. When he closed the window he was empty. You could have drawn a seine through his system and not caught curses enough to disturb your mother with. Presently he said to me in the gentlest way, "My boy, you must get a little memorandum book, and every time I tell you a thing, put it down right away. There's only one way to be a pilot, and that is to get this entire river by heart. You have to know it just like A B C."

R E A D I N G

Idea Stated

Twain describes Bixby as:

I. a grumpy, choleric man who no one likes.
II. a cruel, sadistic man.
III. a kind, gentle, even patient man.
IV. a man who was demanding of himself and his students but was nonetheless a fair man.

A. I
B. II
C. III
D. IV
E. All
F. None
G. I and III

S C I E N C E

Drawing Conclusions

The following bone implements were discovered in a cave in Europe. Which conclusions are appropriate?

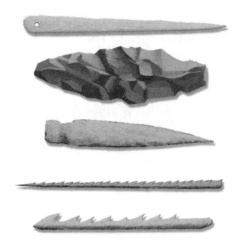

I. These cave dwellers were mostly farmers.
II. These cave dwellers were carnivores.
III. These cave dwellers were omnivores.
IV. These cave dwellers killed animals and perhaps people.

A. I
B. II
C. III
D. IV
E. I and II
F. I, II, and III
G. None
H. All

MAKING DO

My wife Karen often scolds me for avoiding perfection by "making do." She means it, I know, as a pejorative comment. Of course she is hyper-critical (!) (not really); she should learn to compromise more (but alas, she is cursed by her oldest sibling perfectionist syndrome — she is the oldest of 12 children/siblings).

Seriously though, Karen is right (but don't tell her I said this!). Too often I am too lazy, or too busy, to seek perfection in what I do. I compromise too often, I fear.

And compromise is not all bad. We compromise about what restaurant we frequent — that is a good compromise.

Here is a bad compromise.

In the 1950s I remember my mother voting for Governor Orville Faubus (a notorious segregationist). "Why," a friend asked mom, "would you vote for a man who is diametrically opposed to your worldview?" (Mom was opposed to Faubus's racial views.)

"Because," Mom softly responded, "he is in favor of widening Highway 65 [an important road in our small Arkansas town]."

Do you see what I mean? Mom, a good woman really, principled in her own way, voted against her conscience to advance a laudable, even necessary improvement: expansion of an important roadway. This roadway would bring life and prosperity to our region. No doubt, Highway 65 was a good thing.

But Faubus was elected and Faubus tried to stop desegregation at Central High School in Little Rock, Arkansas. President Eisenhower had to mobilize the American army. How awful!

But we also got a beautiful new road!

SCRIPTURE

"Whoever eats my flesh and drinks my blood has eternal life, and I will raise him up at the last day."

~ John 6:54

PRAYER POINTS
KIND PROVIDENCE

"For the LORD loves justice and does not forsake His godly ones."

~ Psalm 37:28

Friends, twice in the last 50 years pro-choice administrations were elected by a solid majority of Americans. If one examines closely the voting patterns, the administration won support — overwhelming support — from some pro-life evangelical groups. Come by me again? That is right — a ton of us (but not me!) pro-lifers voted for a pro-choice candidate for . . . well, perhaps we needed Highway 65 built. And Highway 65 will bring us prosperity and nothing is wrong with prosperity, is there?

Pray about it.

" *A children's story that can only be enjoyed by children is not a good children's story in the slightest.*"[1]

— C.S. Lewis

VOCABULARY

The Scarlet Pimpernel[2]
Baroness Orczy

The Scarlet Pimpernel was first a classic play and then it became an adventure novel, both by Baroness Emmuska Orczy. The novel occurs during the Reign of Terror following the start of the French Revolution. The story is a precursor to the "disguised superhero" tales such as Spiderman and Superman.

Suggested Vocabulary Words

I. A <u>surging</u>, <u>seething</u>, <u>murmuring</u> crowd of beings that are human only in name, for to the eye and ear they seem naught but savage creatures, <u>animated</u> by <u>vile</u> passions and by the lust of vengeance and of hate.

II. During the greater part of the day the <u>guillotine</u> had been kept busy at its ghastly work: all that France had boasted of in the past centuries, of ancient names, and blue blood, had paid toll to her desire for liberty and for <u>fraternity</u>. The carnage had only ceased at this late hour of the day because there were other more interesting sights for the people to witness, a little while before the final closing of the <u>barricades</u> for the night.

III. Their ancestors had oppressed the people, had crushed them under the scarlet heels of their dainty buckled shoes, and now the people had become the rulers of France and crushed their former masters — not beneath their heel, for they went shoeless mostly in these days — but a more <u>effectual</u> weight, the knife of the guillotine.

TEST-TAKING
INSIGHT

Science Counter Arguments

The ACT science section has one nasty passage that concerns conflict viewpoints. In other words, the passage will have a reading from one scientist on a relevant subject. Next, there will be a reading from another, opposing scientist, on the same subject. You will be asked to identify each scientific argument. For instance, one scientist argues that radical changes in temperature will exacerbate cold symptoms. Another scientist will argue the opposite. Your job is to analyze both arguments, and while you will not be asked to choose one viewpoint over another, you will have to identify each scientist's evidence and argument. You will need to identify assumptions made by each scientist and ultimately tease out each scientist's point of view. Finally, perhaps the most difficult questions on the ACT occur at this point. You will be asked to strengthen or support a scientist's argument. For instance, if a scientist argues that radical changes in temperature exacerbate the symptoms of the common cold, you could suggest that his argument would be strengthened if he could show statistically that a vast majority of people with colds who experience radical temperature shifts in fact experience more detrimental cold symptoms. Remember: as you answer questions, be sure and mark up each scientist's argument/main points. Also, remember, it really doesn't matter which scientist is right.

Evaluating Essays

Score the following essay and then discuss how it could be improved.

What can we learn from failure?

I agree that success requires failure. Throughout history, there have been many great men who had to fail before they savoured the sweet taste of success. I will use four examples of men who failed before succeeding.

Firstly, IFBB bodybuilder Ronnie Coleman holds the title of winning Mr. Olympia eight years in a row. However, prior to his eight-year winning streak, he placed in 14th, 9th, and 4th. His success came because he learned from his failures and improved for the following competitions.

In the same way, the Wright brothers, inventors of the airplane, failed to create and fly their prototype for years. Therefore, had they not failed so many times, they would have not been able to improve their mistakes.

Lastly, there are two men known for their many failures before they succeeded. William Wilberforce and Martin Luther King Jr. Both failed many times before their success was reached. Wilberforce fought for the abolishment of the slave trade in England and King fought for the abolishment of segregation and racism. Both of these men failed countless times and they both gave their lives until they succeeded, literally.

In conclusion, whether you are a pro bodybuilder, an inventor, or public activist fighting and protesting to the death, success requires failure to come true.

Christoper Columbus would have used a map like this. This made him conclude that he could reach China by sailing West in a couple of months. He was wrong. What are some possible explanations:

NOVAE INSVLAE, XVII·NOVA TABVLA·

I.   Cartographers and Columbus considered the world to be much smaller than it really is.
II. There was an unknown continent between Europe and China.
III. Sea monsters caused Columbus to avoid the West Indian Trade winds.
IV. Cartographers and Columbus considered the world to be much larger than it really is.

A. I
B. II
C. III
D. IV
E. I and II
F. III and IV
G. None

Inference

A surging, seething, murmuring crowd of beings that are human only in name, for to the eye and ear they seem naught but savage creatures, animated by vile passions and by the lust of vengeance and of hate. The hour, some little time before sunset, and the place, the West Barricade, at the very spot where, a decade later, a proud tyrant raised an undying monument to the nation's glory and his own vanity.

During the greater part of the day the guillotine had been kept busy at its ghastly work: all that France had boasted of in the past centuries, of ancient names, and blue blood, had paid toll to her desire for liberty and for fraternity. The carnage had only ceased at this late hour of the day because there were other more interesting sights for the people to witness, a little while before the final closing of the barricades for the night.

And so the crowd rushed away from the Place de la Greve and made for the various barricades in order to watch this interesting and amusing sight.

It was to be seen every day, for those aristos were such fools! They were traitors to the people of course, all of them, men, women, and children, who happened to be descendants of the great men who since the Crusades had made the glory of France: her old NOBLESSE. Their ancestors had oppressed the people, had crushed them under the scarlet heels of their dainty buckled shoes, and now the people had become the rulers of France and crushed their former masters — not beneath their heel, for they went shoeless mostly in these days — but a more effectual weight, the knife of the guillotine.

And daily, hourly, the hideous instrument of torture claimed its many victims — old men, young women, tiny children until the day when it would finally demand the head of a King and of a beautiful young Queen.[3] — *The Scarlet Pimpernel*

■ ■ ■

Based on this passage, the following inferences are true:

I. The French Revolution, while it had it excesses, was a necessary evil.
II. While there were injustices, the excesses of the French Revolution made the Revolution worse than the injustices.
III. The guillotine, while it was intended to be a merciful execution device, was in fact, in the hand of the terrorists, a cruel, inhumane tool.

   A. I
   B. II
   C. III
   D. All
   E. None
   F. I and III

Grammar

Which part of each of the following sentences is wrong?

(A) Last year, we spent our vacation in California(B), this year we plan to go to Disney World.

(A) While I washed the car, (B)my black dog took his bone, and (C) went swimming.

(A) Today I learned a lot about the Pilgrims (B), especially the parts about John Winthrop and Squanto.

Word Problems

1. William paid eight times as much for a dictionary as for a thesaurus. If the difference in price was $6.30, how much did he pay for each?

2. The sum of two numbers is 4,256, and one is 37 times as great as the other. What are the numbers?

3. Aleck has 48 cents more than Arthur, and seven times Arthur's money equals Aleck's. How much has each?

4. The sum of the ages of a mother and daughter is 32 years, and the age of the mother is seven times that of the daughter. What is the age of each?

5. John's age is three times that of Mary, and he is ten years older. What is the age of each?

Humans Cannot Bear
MUCH REALITY

The church lies bereft,
Alone, desecrated, desolated.
And the heathen shall build
On the ruins.[1] — T.S. Eliot

These haunting words punctuate the lowest point of British playwright and poet T.S. Eliot's *Murder in the Cathedral*. The iconic Archbishop of Canterbury, Samuel Beckett, will die, martyred by the malevolent, selfish King Henry II. But not for any nostalgic reason. Not for any sentimental purpose. Beckett will die in obedience to our Lord God's purposes. He defies hyperbole.

As we struggle to make sense of all the hard times we face, of all the good things we can do. Let us choose the obedient thing to do, not the thing that may seem right in our own eyes. "Yet we have gone on living, living and partly living," Beckett muses.[2]

There is a crisis of ethics in our time. The sagacious Beckett, as he contemplates his future, muses, "Only the fool, fixed in his folly, may think he can turn the wheel on which he turns."[3] And even worse, "The last temptation is the greatest treason: To do the right deed for the wrong reason." To do the right deed for the wrong reason. . . . in this age of compromises, of good intentions, it is critical that we follow Beckett's example. Thy will be done on earth as it is in heaven.

Human kind cannot bear very much reality.
The church shall be open, even to our enemies.
We are not here to triumph by fighting, by stratagem, or by resistance,
Not to fight with beasts as men. We have fought the beast
And have conquered. We have only to conquer
Now, by suffering. This is the easier victory. . . .
For every life and every act
Consequence of good and evil can be shown.
And as in time results of many deeds are blended
So good and evil in the end become confounded. . . .
In life there is not time to grieve long. . . .
And the heathen shall build on the ruins
Their world without God. I see it. I see it.[4]

Oh, young people, children of my God, if you only knew how much I believe in you! I believe God will do great things in and through you!

The biggest problem among my evangelical friends is not that they turned their backs on God, it is that they replaced Him with other gods. They lost their passion. They were tamed.

Let us not be of the world; let us be in that world. In fact, let us create a new world!

READING

Main Idea

The modern world is not evil; in some ways the modern world is far too good. It is full of wild and wasted virtues. When a religious scheme is shattered (as Christianity was shattered at the Reformation), it is not merely the vices that are let loose. The vices are, indeed, let loose, and they wander and do damage. But the virtues are let loose also; and the virtues wander more wildly, and the virtues do more terrible damage. The modern world is full of the old Christian virtues gone mad. The virtues have gone mad because they have been isolated from each other and are wandering alone. Thus some scientists care for truth; and their truth is pitiless. Thus some humanitarians only care for pity; and their pity (I am sorry to say) is often untruthful. For example, Mr. Blatchford attacks Christianity because he is mad on one Christian virtue: the merely mystical and almost irrational virtue of charity. He has a strange idea that he will make it easier to forgive sins by saying that there are no sins to forgive. Mr. Blatchford is not only an early Christian, he is the only early Christian who ought really to have been eaten by lions. For in his case the pagan accusation is really true: his mercy would mean mere anarchy. He really is the enemy of the human race — because he is so human. As the other extreme, we may take the acrid realist, who has deliberately killed in himself all human pleasure in happy tales or in the healing of the heart. Torquemada tortured people physically for the sake of moral truth. Zola tortured people morally for the sake of physical truth. But in Torquemada's time there was at least a system that could to some extent make righteousness and peace kiss each other. Now they do not even bow. But a much stronger case than these two of truth and pity can be found in the remarkable case of the dislocation of humility.[5] — G.K. Chesterton, *Orthodoxy*

■ ■ ■

What does Chesterton mean when he says, "The modern world is not evil; in some ways the modern world is far too good. It is full of wild and wasted virtues"?

I.   He doesn't mean it. He is only joking.
II. He laments the loss of "orthodoxy," or "balanced religion," by excessive emphasis on one doctrine or Christian truth.
III. Heresy is not an aberrant truth; it is the over emphasis of a real truth.

A. I
B. II
C. III
D. I and III
E. II and III
F. None
G. All

???

Are you reading

50 to 100 pages

a day

???

SCIENCE

Observations

Pretend that you are an anthropologist and visiting New Guinea. You see these men. What do you conclude about their environment? Of course you may be wrong, but make some conclusions.

I.   This society is pre-historic (does not practice writing).
II. The adults in this society do not live long.
III. The main source of food in this society is agricultural products.

    A. I
    B. II
    C. III
    D. All
    E. None
    F. I and II
    G. I, II, and III

WRITING

Evaluating Essays

Score the following essay and then discuss how it could be improved.

How does adversity shape who we are?

I support that ease does not challenge us and that we must face adversity to discover who we are. I have three examples of how we need adversity to discover ourselves. Firstly, when I was 14 years old, I struggled with being over-weight. However, I started to exercise and eat healthier, then I lost a lot of weight. Had I not had the challenge of being overweight, I would not have known that I was a disciplined person.

Secondly, I have an aunt who, over a period of years, has been having health problems. She has went away to seek medical treatment on numerous occasions, and most of the time she was disappointed. However, if she did not have this health issue, she would not have known that she is a determined person. My final example that adversity helps us to discover who we are is the story of Hercules. Hercules was the son of the chief god Zeus. He had had to be given 12 tasks in order to be seen as a true hero. Had he not gone through the grueling ordeals, he may have not discovered who he truly was, a hero. In conclusion, adversity and challenges make us look at ourselves and discover who we are; whether we are an overweight teen, a sick woman, or just a Greek myth.

V O C A B U L A R Y

Orthodoxy, The Romance of Faith[6]
G.K. Chesterton

If G.K. Chesterton's *Orthodoxy: The Romance of Faith* is, as he called it, a "slovenly autobiography," then we need more slobs in the world. This quirky, slender book describes how Chesterton came to view orthodox Catholic Christianity as the way to satisfy his personal emotional needs in a way that would also allow him to live happily in society. Chesterton argues that people in western society need a life of "practical romance, the combination of something that is strange with something that is secure. We need so to view the world as to combine an idea of wonder and an idea of welcome." Drawing on such figures as Fra Angelico, George Bernard Shaw, and Paul to make his points, Chesterton argues that submission to ecclesiastical authority is the way to achieve a good and balanced life. The whole book is written in a style that is as majestic and down-to-earth as C.S. Lewis at his best. The final chapter, called "Authority and the Adventurer," is especially persuasive. It's hard to imagine a reader who will not close the book believing, at least for the moment, that the Church will make you free.[7]
— Michael Joseph Gross

Suggested Vocabulary Words

I mean hope, courage, poetry, <u>initiative</u>, all that is human. For instance, when materialism leads men to complete <u>fatalism</u> (as it generally does), it is quite idle to pretend that it is in any sense a liberating force. It is absurd to say that you are especially advancing freedom when you only use free thought to destroy free will. The <u>determinists</u> come to bind, not to loose. They may well call their law the "chain" of causation. It is the worst chain that ever <u>fettered</u> a human being. You may use the language of liberty, if you like, about materialistic teaching, but it is obvious that this is just as <u>inapplicable</u> to it as a whole as the same language when applied to a man locked up in a mad-house. You may say, if you like, that the man is free to think himself a poached egg.

In passing from this subject I may note that there is a queer fallacy to the effect that <u>materialistic</u> fatalism is in some way favourable to mercy, to the <u>abolition</u> of cruel punishments or punishments of any kind. This is startlingly the reverse of the truth. It is quite <u>tenable</u> that the doctrine of necessity makes no difference at all; that it leaves the flogger flogging and the kind friend exhorting as before.

M A T H

Word Problems

1. A had seven times as many apples, and B three times as many as C had. If they all together had 55 apples, how many had each?

2. The difference between two numbers is 36, and one is four times the other. What are the numbers?

3. In a company of 48 people there is one man to each five women. How many are there of each?

4. A man left $1400 to be distributed among three sons in such a way that James was to receive double what John received, and John double what Henry received. How much did each receive?

5. A field containing 45,000 feet was divided into three lots so that the second lot was three times the first, and the third twice the second. How large was each lot?

E N G L I S H

Grammar: General to Specific

Arrange the words in each of the following lists in descending order of general to specific.

1. fish, animal, creature, goldfish.

2. foreigner, woman, person, German

3. chicken, main dish, food, meat

When you write, always use specific, precise language.

What Is LOVE?

Love is forgiveness.

A 16-year-old Westbury, Long Island, boy was picked up by the police several years ago for defacing a synagogue. It seems that the boy went on a Halloween tear with some friends. They sprayed obscenities on the front door of the synagogue while a service was going on.

The young man, a Christian, was caught. He was fined $150 and ordered to give one hundred hours of service to his hometown church. His parents publicly deplored what their son had done. Their pain drew letters of sympathy support from people near and far.

But most touching of all was a letter that had to do with court costs and expenses of legal counsel. The family incurred a deficit of $1,000 to defend their son. They were finding it hard to come up with the money. One day a letter arrived. It contained a check for $1,000. It was from a Jewish lawyer in Manhattan.

A train pulls into Auschwitz concentration camp. Even before the steam has ceased hissing from the brakes of the engine, the hapless, forlorn Jews are being unloaded. An SS captain stands erect with two ominous police dogs at his side. A motion with his right hand means life in  the work camp nearby, called Birkenau, that supplied labor for the I.G. Farben chemical factory. A motion with his left hand means instant death in the gas chambers.

The Jews knew this. No one could ignore the ominous, acrid smoke billowing from the stacks of the crematorium. The awful stench of flesh burning was unmistakable. Yet no one could move. Everyone had to wait to accept his/her fate. The line moved ever so slowly toward the captain. Right, right, and then a whole series of people were sent left.

A Jewish couple was perceivably nervous as the line moved closer to the captain. The couple had been newly married only a month before. What a honeymoon! The persons ahead of them were sent to the right. They felt hope! And then, the horror of hopelessness hit them. The woman was sent to the right and the man, slightly injured on the train, to the left.

Suddenly a Catholic priest, a prisoner, formerly part of the resistance, approached the SS captain. He interjected, "Excuse me, Herr Captain, that young man is injured but he will get better. I am feeble and will obviously not be much good in the factory. May I take the place of the young man you are sending to the left?"

The SS captain, while he was obviously irritated, had to agree.

He yanked the young man from the left and threw him next to his wife.

The priest was gassed.

Recently, the man and his bride, now old people, attended a ceremony where the young prisoner, a priest, was honored.

We consciously, deliberately, choose to love or to hate; love is not something we unconsciously wander into. It is a willful act and costs us a great deal, perhaps even our lives.

S CIENCE

Observations

Which of the following interventions could stop the spread of malaria?

I. Draining surrounding wet lands
II. Spray insecticide on remaining open water sources
III. Promote a nutritional campaign.
IV. Quarantine patients.
V. Introduce carp — a fish species that consumes thousands of mosquito larvae.

A. I
B. II
C. III
D. IV
E. V
F. I and II
G. I, II, and III
H. I, II, and V
I. None
J. All

Cool Phrases

The following are cool phrases and will impress your grader (Greenville Kleiser, *Fifteen Thousand Useful Phrases*).[1]

abandoned hope	cautious skepticism
abated pride	cavernous gloom
abbreviated visit	ceaseless vigilance
abiding romance	celebrated instance
abject submission	celestial joy
abjured ambition	censorious critic
able strategist	diabolical passion
abnormal talents	damaging admission
abominably perverse	dampened ardor
abounding happiness	dancing sunshine
abridged statement	dangerous temerity
abrogated law	dappled shadows
abrupt transition	daring candor
absolutely irrevocable	dark superstition
capricious allurements	dashing gallantry
centralized wealth	dastardly injustice
careless parrying	dauntless courage
caressing grasp	dawning instinct
carping critic	dazed brain
casual violation	dazzling triumph
cataclysmic elements	captivating speech
causelessly frightened	cardinal merit
caustic remark	

■ ■ ■

Replace these ordinary sentences with cool sentences, using expressions from the above list.

1. The poor shipwrecked sailor gave up all hope of being saved.

2. Good health requires unstoppable attention.

3. That Super Bowl win was a memorable victory.

Use of Double Negative

Do not use double negatives in formal English. Rewrite the following sentences.[2]

1. "The red men were not so infrequent visitors of the English settlements." — Hawthorne

2. "Huldy was so up to everything about the house, that the doctor didn't miss nothin' in a temporal way." — Mrs. Stowe

3. "Her younger sister was a wide-awake girl, who hadn't been to school for nothing." — Holmes

4. "You will find no battle which does not exhibit the most cautious circumspection." — Bayne

5. "Not only could man not acquire such information, but ought not to labor after it." — Grote

6. "There is no thoughtful man in America who would not consider a war with England the greatest of calamities." — Lowell

7. "In the execution of this task, there is no man who would not find it an arduous effort." — Hamilton

8. " 'A weapon,' said the King, 'well worthy to confer honor, nor has it been laid on an undeserving shoulder.' " — Scott

VOCABULARY

Kim[3]
Rudyard Kipling

Kim is the orphaned son of a British soldier and a white mother who have both died in poverty. Living a vagabond existence in India under British rule in the late 19th century, Kim earns his living by begging and running small errands on the streets of Lahore, what is now Pakistan. He occasionally works for Mahbub Ali, a Pathan horse trader who is one of the native operatives of the British secret service. Kim is so immersed in the local culture, few realize he is a white child, though he carries a packet of documents from his father entrusted to him by an Indian woman who cared for him.

Kim is recruited by a British officer to carry a message to the British commander in Umballa. Kim's trip with the Lama along the Grand Trunk Road is the first great adventure in the novel. The rest of the novel is one adventure after another as Kim and his British allies fight renegade Indians and evil Russian spies.

Recommended Vocabulary Words

A. But Kim did not suspect that Mahbub Ali, known as one of the best horse-dealers in the Punjab, a wealthy and enterprising trader, whose caravans <u>penetrated</u> far and far into the Back of Beyond, was registered in one of the locked books of the Indian Survey Department as C.25.1B. Twice or thrice yearly C.25 would send in a little story, badly told but most interesting, and generally — it was checked by the statements of R.17 and M.4 — quite true. It concerned all manner of out-of-the-way mountain <u>principalities</u>, explorers of nationalities other than English, and the gun trade — was, in brief, a small portion of that vast mass of "information received" on which the Indian Government acts. But, recently, five <u>confederated</u> Kings, who had no business to confederate, had been informed by a kindly Northern Power that there was a leakage of news from their territories into British India. So those Kings' Prime Ministers were seriously annoyed and took steps, after the Oriental fashion. They suspected, among many others, the bullying, red-bearded horsedealer whose caravans ploughed through their fastnesses belly-deep in snow. At least, his caravan that season had been ambushed and shot at twice on the way down, when Mahbub's men accounted for three strange <u>ruffians</u> who might, or might not, have been hired for the job. Therefore Mahbub had avoided halting at the <u>insalubrious</u> city of Peshawur, and had come through without stop to Lahore, where, knowing his country-people, he anticipated curious developments.

B. Dynamite was milky and innocuous beside that report of C.25; and even an Oriental, with an Oriental's views of the value of time, could see that the sooner it was in the proper hands the better. Mahbub had no particular desire to die by violence, because two or three family blood-feuds across the Border hung unfinished on his hands, and when these scores were cleared he intended to settle down as a more or less <u>virtuous</u> citizen. He had never passed the serai gate since his arrival two days ago, but had been ostentatious in sending telegrams to Bombay, where he banked some of his money; to Delhi, where a sub-partner of his own clan was selling horses to the agent of a Rajputana state; and to Umballa, where an Englishman was excitedly demanding the <u>pedigree</u> of a white stallion.

MATH

Word Problems

1. A man had 95 sheep in three flocks. In the first flock there were 23 more than in the second, and in the third flock 12 less than in the second. How many sheep in each flock?

2. In an election in which 1,073 ballots were cast, Mr. A receives 97 votes less than Mr. B, and Mr. C 120 votes more than Mr. B. How many votes did each receive?

3. A man owns three farms. In the first there are 5 acres more than in the second and 7 acres less than in the third. If there are 53 acres in all the farms together, how many acres are there in each farm?

4. Divide 111 into three parts so that the first part shall be 16 more than the second and 19 less than the third.

5. Three firms lost $118,000 by fire. The second firm lost $6000 less than the first and $20,000 more than the third. What was each firm's loss?

R E A D I N G

Details

For the same reason the First Anglo-Afghan War occurred the Second Anglo-Afghan War began. The competing empires of Britain and Russia were bound to clash in central Asia at some point, with Russia's eventual goal being the invasion and seizure of Britain's prize possession, India. British strategy was focused on keeping Russian influence out of Afghanistan, which could become Russia's stepping-stone to India.

The British government decided to launch a war in late 1878. British troops from India invaded Afghanistan in late 1878, with a total of about 40,000 troops advancing in three separate columns. The British Army met resistance from Afghan tribesmen, but was able to control a large part of Afghanistan by the spring of 1879. With a military victory in hand, the British arranged for a treaty with the Afghan government. It seemed that Britain had accomplished its objectives.

The Afghan leader agreed to accept a permanent British mission which would essentially conduct Afghanistan's foreign policy. Britain also agreed to defend Afghanistan against any foreign aggression, meaning any potential Russian invasion.

Relations with the Afghans began to sour, and in September a rebellion against the British broke out in Kabul. Again, the British army in Kabul was slaughtered. A British column commanded by General Frederick Roberts, one of the most capable British officers of the period, marched on Kabul to take revenge.

After fighting his way to the capital in October 1879, Roberts had a number of Afghans captured and hanged. There was allegedly a sort of reign of terror in Kabul as the British avenged the September massacre.

General Roberts appointed himself military governor of Afghanistan. With his force of approximately 6,500 men, he settled in for the winter. In early December 1879 Roberts and his men had to fight a substantial battle against attacking Afghans. The British moved out of the city of Kabul and took up a fortified position nearby. Roberts wanted to avoid a repeat of the disaster of the British retreat from Kabul in 1842, and remained in fortified positions. In the spring of 1880 a British column marched to Kabul and relieved General Roberts. But when news came that British troops at Kandahar were surrounded and facing grave danger, General Roberts embarked on what would become a legendary military feat.

With 10,000 men, Roberts marched from Kabul to Kandahar, a distance of about 300 miles, in just 20 days. The British march was generally unopposed, but being able to move that many troops 15 miles a day in the brutal heat of Afghanistan's summer was a remarkable example of discipline, organization, and leadership. When General Roberts reached Kandahar he linked up with the British garrison of the city, and the combined British forces inflicted a defeat on the Afghan forces. This marked the end of hostilities in the Second Anglo-Afghan War.[4]
— Stobaugh, *British History*

■ ■ ■

What statement(s) is (are) true?

I. General Roberts was a capable general and governor who unwisely executed many rogue Afghans.

II. General Roberts was a typical, British aristocratic snob.

III. General Roberts did not retreat from Kabal, even though he was greatly outnumbered, because he did not want to repeat a disastrous retreat of 35 years before.

A. I

B. II

C. III

D. All

E. I and II

F. II and III

G. I and III

H. None

The ANOINTED ELITE

SCRIPTURE

*"But you his son, O Belshazzar,
have not humbled yourself,
though you knew all this
Instead, you have set yourself
up against the Lord of heaven.
You had the goblets from his
temple brought to you, and
you and your nobles, your
wives and your concubines
drank wine from them. You
praised the gods of silver and
gold, of bronze, iron, wood
and stone, which cannot see or
hear or understand. But you
did not honor the God who
holds in his hand your life and
all your ways."*

~ Daniel 5:22–23

PRAYER POINTS
STAND FIRM IN PERSECUTION

*"All men will hate you because
of me, but he who stands firm
to the end will be saved."*
~ Matthew 10:22

Young people, as you have heard me say many times, you are replacing the old guard in our society. Many of you, partly because of this book, no doubt (to God be the glory!), will do well on the ACT, will be admitted to prestigious colleges, and will become the next leadership group in this country. In short, you will become the new "elite" or the new "culture creators."

Since the 1920s (when the Scopes Trial successfully drove most evangelical intellectuals from the university and active culture creating), a singularly secular elite group, mostly anti-Christian, has governed America and created much of its culture.

French social theorist Bertrand de Jouvenel[1] tried to explain the anti-Christian bias of many in the intellectual community. He suggested the following reasons for this tendency.

First, intellectuals — particularly those in academic life — devote a good part of their time building analytical models of the world — models in which the intellectual creates conceptions of hypothetically orderly and ideal conditions for man in society. Never mind what the Word of God says. They try to rearrange the human condition to match their more perfect model. There is, then, among reigning intellectuals, a penchant toward utopia and to a certain degree toward excellence. But overall, the people making decisions in the United States today have nothing but disdain for objective truth.

Second, the intellectual is often deeply disturbed by the fact that the world seems to be governed and guided by what seems to them to be irrational hierarchies of value. The intellectual, with his conception of the well-ordered and designed society, is revolted by the fact that objective truth, morality, and virtue do not advance their understanding of justice. To tag truth with authorship by an unseen deity is insane.

Christian sociologist and social critic Thomas Sowell's newest book *The Vision of the Anointed* takes this reigning elite to the shed. Sowell has abandoned the notion of a human-centered utopia for the biblical notion of the Kingdom of God. Sowell calls this "a tragic view of man."[2] By the constrained or tragic view of man, Sowell means the acceptance that there are natural and inherent limitations upon man — physical, mental, social — that will always prevent the possibility of creating a utopia on earth. Life is a never-ending struggle of using limited means to satisfy our numerous ends, with the necessity of having to accept tradeoffs that we hope will make us better off but never fully satisfied. And among those limited means are our own imperfections of knowledge that make it impossible for us to have either the ability or the wisdom to make a perfect world. Sowell, like yours truly, understands that we need God's help.

The emerging evangelical elite must be entirely different. You must humble yourself before the Lord and see His guidance and His favor. The unconstrained vision of the present, secular anointed is the view that there are some who have been able to rise above the limitations of the existing social order and who are able to design plans for the ameliorating of man and the human condition. They see themselves as superior in wisdom and understanding in comparison to the ordinary, average man. They want power to remold the world to fit their model of how they think the rest of us should live and act and what we should believe in and value.

So strongly do these "anointed" feel about their visions, they are willing to do everything to shield themselves from any evidence that might contradict and undermine their utopian fantasies.

"Without a sense of the tragedy of the human condition, and of the painful tradeoffs implied by inherent constraints," Sowell argues, "the anointed are free to believe that the unhappiness they observe and the anomalies they encounter are due to the public's not being as wise or virtuous as themselves. . . . It is a world of victims, villains, and rescuers, with the anointed cast in the last and most heroic of these roles."[3] This is why political correctness in politics, education, culture, history, and literature is so important to these anointed social engineers. Through this means, they hope, the human mind can be wiped clean and filled with the preconceived ideas and myths that will enable them to control those whom they desire to have mastery over. If they succeed, our world as we know it will cease to exist. But they shall not succeed.

But you his son, O Belshazzar . . . have set yourself up against the Lord of heaven. You had the goblets from his temple brought to you, and you and your nobles, your wives and your concubines drank wine from them. You praised the gods of silver and gold, of bronze, iron, wood and stone, which cannot see or hear or understand. But you did not honor the God who holds in his hand your life and all your ways. Therefore he sent the hand that wrote the inscription.

This is the inscription that was written:
MENE, MENE, TEKEL, PARSIN
This is what these words mean:
Mene: God has numbered the days of your reign and brought it to an end.
Tekel: You have been weighed on the scales and found wanting.
Peres: Your kingdom is divided and given to the Medes and Persians."

. . . That very night Belshazzar, king of the Babylonians, was slain (Daniel 5:22–30).

ENGLISH

Use of Conjunctions

Which part of the following sentences are incorrect?

1. (A) I discovered that bears (B) while traveling in Yellowstone National Park (C) were not as dangerous as I thought.

2. (A)He could have (B)been seriously injured.

3. Mom called the doctor (A)because I wasn't feeling (B) good.

4. (A) Next time, (B) when you bake a cake, (C) use less eggs.

5. (A) Beside the wonderful chocolate cake, (B) there were numerous other (C) appetizing desserts.

Avoid using "tired" words like: nice, good, wonderful, and great. Use more robust words like complete, fulfilling, stupendous, and rewarding.

WRITING

Three Essentials

The three essentials of the English language are: *purity, perspicuity* and *precision.*

By *purity* is signified the use of good English. It precludes the use of all slang words, vulgar phrases, obsolete terms, foreign idioms, ambiguous expressions or any ungrammatical language whatsoever. Neither does it sanction the use of any newly coined word until such word is adopted by the best writers and speakers. Remember: your graders are English teachers with attitude! They do not want to be "entertained' by your idioms. Keep your English clean and clear.

Perspicuity demands the clearest expression of thought conveyed in unequivocal language, so that there may be no misunderstanding whatever of the thought or idea the speaker or writer wishes to convey. All ambiguous words, words of double meaning, and words that might possibly be construed in a sense different from that intended, are strictly forbidden. Perspicuity requires a style at once clear and comprehensive and entirely free from pomp and pedantry and affectation or any straining after effect.

Precision requires concise and exact expression, free from redundancy and tautology, a style terse and clear and simple enough to enable the hearer or reader to comprehend immediately the meaning of the speaker or writer. It forbids, on the one hand, all long and involved sentences, and, on the other, those that are too short and abrupt. Its object is to strike the golden mean in such a way as to rivet the attention of the hearer or reader on the words uttered or written.[4] (Abbott, *How to Write Clearly*)

■ ■ ■

Rewrite these sentences giving attention to purity, perspicuity, and precision.

1. I am no sure why you'all folks ain't paying attention to "moi."

2. Well, yeah — I guess so — what else could that mean?!?

3. You really mean that? Whatever!

SCIENCE

Observation

What is true?

I. I. An ordinary mosquito looks very much like a malaria mosquito.

II. II. One can probably kill both mosquitos in the same way.

III. III. One will have to kill both to kill one if they are in the same place.

IV. IV. Both prefer moist, damp areas.

A. I
B. II
C. III
D. IV
E. I and II
F. I, II, and III
G. None
H. All

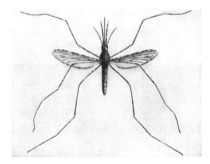

Ordinary mosquito

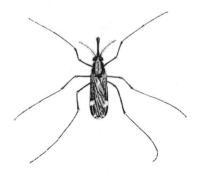

Malaria mosquito

Argument

The French and Indian War was part of a world war called the "seven years' war." France, England, and Spain were all belligerents. However, for our purposes, we will concentrate on the North American phase.

The French and Indian War took more lives than the American Revolution. In fact, this war was the bloodiest 18th-century war on North American soil. "It erased France's political influence from the continent and established English dominance east of the Mississippi and in Canada. And it set the stage for the American Revolution and the establishment of the United States of America."[5]

The conflict between England and France in North America centered on the fur trade and control of inland waterways.

When European people began settling on the coast of North America in the early 17th century, the French occupied the most convenient route to the interior — the St. Lawrence River. From their posts at Quebec and Montreal they rapidly moved up the St. Lawrence River to explore the continent and trade for furs with the Native peoples. But this movement westward was blocked by the pro-British Iroquois.

The Iroquois, perhaps the most politically powerful group of Native people in the history of North America, had early confrontations with the French. Their hostility lasted until the French had been driven from North America.

To restore the balance of power in favor of their allies, the French began selling firearms and ammunition in limited numbers to the Huron and Algonquin. These weapons, as well as steel hatchets and knives, soon spread to other tribes, and the British responded by providing guns to the Iroquois. An arms race developed, in which tribes providing the most fur had a military advantage over those which did not.[6]

Two other minor wars occurred before the decisive conflict opened in 1754. General Braddock led an army of British regulars and colonial irregulars (including George Washington) to attack Fort Duquesne. Braddock was annihilated.

It took the English several years, but eventually they won this war. In 1758, British General Forbes captured Fort Duquesne and renamed it Fort Pitt. In 1759, General James Wolfe took Quebec but he lost his own life. Finally, General William Johnson captured Montreal and New France fell.[7]

The main argument of this passage is:

I. The French caused the French and Indian War by attacking English colonial posts.
II. The English caused the French and Indian War by inciting the Native Americans to violence.
III. The American colonists caused the French and Indian War by refusing to accept British rule.

A. I
B. II
C. III
D. None
E. All

The results of the French and Indian War include:

I. It erased France's political influence from the continent and established English dominance east of the Mississippi and in Canada. It also set the stage for the American Revolution and the establishment of the United States of America.
II. It made Spanish domination of South America possible.

A. I
B. II
C. None
D. All
E. I and II

VOCABULARY

The Last of the Mohicans[8]
James Fenimore Cooper

The setting is the 18th century French and Indian War, one of the first world wars in history. As the English and French soldiers battle for control of the North American colonies in the 18th century, the settlers and Native Americans are forced to take sides. Cora and her sister Alice unwittingly walk into trouble but are saved by Hawkeye, a colonial settler adopted by the last of the Mohicans. Cora and Alice are two daughters of a British colonel, who have been targeted by Magua, one of the most infamous villains in American literature, a sadistic and vengeful Native American who has dedicated his life to destroying the girls' father for a past injustice.

Suggested Vocabulary Words

A. The officer proceeded, without affecting to hear the words which escaped the <u>sentinel</u> in his surprise; nor did he again pause until he had reached the low strand, and in a somewhat dangerous vicinity to the western water <u>bastion</u> of the fort. The light of an <u>obscure</u> moon was just sufficient to render objects, though dim, <u>perceptible</u> in their outlines. He, therefore, took the precaution to place himself against the trunk of a tree, where he leaned for many minutes, and seemed to contemplate the dark and silent mounds of the English works in profound attention. His gaze at the <u>ramparts</u> was not that of a curious or idle spectator; but his looks wandered from point to point, <u>denoting</u> his knowledge of military usages, and betraying that his search was not unaccompanied by distrust.

B. Just then a figure was seen to approach the edge of the rampart, where it stood, apparently <u>contemplating</u> in its turn the distant tents of the French encampment. Its head was then turned toward the east, as though equally anxious for the appearance of light, when the form leaned against the mound, and seemed to gaze upon the glassy expanse of the waters, which, like a submarine firmament, glittered with its thousand mimic stars. The melancholy air, the hour, together with the vast frame of the man who thus leaned, musing, against the English ramparts, left no doubt as to his person in the mind of the observant spectator. Delicacy, no less than <u>prudence</u>, now urged him to retire; and he had moved cautiously round the body of the tree for that purpose, when another sound drew his attention, and once more <u>arrested</u> his footsteps.

It was a low and almost <u>inaudible</u> movement of the water, and was succeeded by a grating of pebbles one against the other.

??? Are you reading 50 to 100 pages a day ???

MATH

Algebra Word Problems

1. A man sold a lot of wood for B dollars, and received in payment a barrel of flour worth E dollars. How many dollars remain due?

2. A man sold a cow for I dollar, a calf for 4 dollars, and a sheep for M dollars, and in payment received a wagon worth X dollars. How much remains due?

3. A box of raisins was bought for A dollars, and a firkin of butter for B dollars. If both were sold for C dollars, how much was gained?

4. At a certain election, 1,065 ballots were cast for two candidates, and the winning candidate had a majority of 207. How many votes did each receive?

5. A merchant started the year with M dollars; the first month he gained X dollars, the next month he lost Y dollars, the third month he gained B dollars, and the fourth month lost Z dollars. How much had he at the end of that month?

HOME

S C R I P T U R E

"When the LORD your God brings you into the land he swore to your fathers, to Abraham, Isaac and Jacob, to give you — a land with large, flourishing cities you did not build, houses filled with all kinds of good things you did not provide, wells you did not dig, and vineyards and olive groves you did not plant—then when you eat and are satisfied, be careful that you do not forget the LORD, who brought you out of Egypt, out of the land of slavery."

~ Deuteronomy 6:10–12

PRAYER POINTS
STEWARDSHIP
H A B I T S

"Others, like seed sown on good soil, hear the word, accept it, and produce a crop —thirty, sixty, or even a hundred times what was sown."

~ Mark 4:20

In *The Odyssey*, Homer emphasizes the importance of family and home. After being absent from his home and family in Ithaca for almost 20 years, Odysseus sits daily on the shores of Calypso's island, Ogygia, wearing out his soul with lamentation and tears because he longs to return to his home. The goddess Athena, who argues with Zeus to allow Odysseus to go home against the wishes of Poseidon tries her best to help him. "Even his griefs are a joy long after to one that remembers all that he wrought and endured."[1] (Homer, *Odyssey*)

I have lived for six weeks on the road — literally, six weeks. I have not laid in my bed or scratched my dog's ears in six weeks, and I miss home terribly. I "wear out my soul with lamentation."

That feeling was more than mitigated, however, last week when I had the privilege to stay with a home school family outside San Francisco. They are some of the finest people in the world. Hospitable, generous, and loving, they made their home my home. And I am grateful.

Home to Odysseus, as it is to me, is a place, true, but it is also people. Relationships. Family.

Most Americans today don't really know where home is. We contextualize our lives in ways that have no connection to place. Where do we live? Where does one place begin and another end? It is now clear that a sense of place is a human hunger which our present society has not met.

Because Americans have lost a sense of belonging to a time and a place, as Odysseus does, we have lost our sense of destiny. A sense of destiny is derived from a sense of belonging. The problem is, technically speaking, a Christian is never at home until he or she goes to heaven.

Still we do new things — like going to college. We are called to leave what is known and secure — Ur and Egypt — and to go to an unknown place wrought with danger and risk. "Go forth from your country, and from your relatives and from your father's house" (Gen. 12:1) and "I am the LORD who brought you out of Ur of the Chaldeans" (Gen. 15:7). Time and time again God reminds us that we are sojourners with no promise that times will be easy.

"Sojourner" is a technical word usually described as resident alien. It means to be in a place, perhaps for an extended time, to live there and take some roots, but always to be an outsider, never belonging, always without rights, title, or voice in the decisions that seem to matter.

We find ourselves wandering in the wilderness. The buoyant faith of the fathers is much less evident. Now the stress is upon being without resources and necessities. The dreams end. For 40 years Moses' generation wandered — always at the disposal of the elements, drought, hunger, or the Amalekites. The wanderer is not a sojourner because the wanderer is merely going to die in the desert; the sojourner is going into the Promised Land — even if it takes a long time. In some

ways we are like the wandering Jews: faith is for those who remember the land but see no way to it.

The promise of God is kept. It was a new generation that entered the land. But the admonition of the Lord in Deuteronomy 6:10–11 held true. Remember this, saints: it is the emptiness of Israel, exposed and without resources, that promises are received with power, that risks are run, and hope is energizing.

Once in the land, or even near it, the traditions of the wilderness prevent us from romanticizing landlessness as a time of resourceful faith. The wilderness to Israel is a sentence of death (Num. 32:13) and a route to the Promised Land. When Israel stopped journeying, they were enslaved.

TEST-TAKING INSIGHT
Math Test Overview

The math test contains 60 questions to be completed in 60 minutes. You don't need to be a rocket scientist to figure that you will have one minute for each question. Wow, that's ideal. Well, that is not how it really works. You will find that some questions will take only seconds to answer, while others will take more than a minute.

Just keep in mind that if you find you are really having trouble on a particular question, go on to the next one. Don't waste time on questions you cannot figure out. If you return to a difficult question and you still cannot answer it, just guess. Remember that the answer is there. Try to eliminate at least two that seem obviously wrong. (TCA website. If you want more help, visit http://forsuchatimeasthis.com.)

R EADING

Tone and Mood

What is the tone and mood of this passage?

"Peter Blood, hold up your hand!"

Abruptly he was recalled to his position by the harsh voice of the clerk of arraigns. His obedience was mechanical, and the clerk droned out the wordy indictment which pronounced Peter Blood a false traitor against the Most Illustrious and Most Excellent Prince, James the Second, by the grace of God, of England, Scotland, France, and Ireland King, his supreme and natural lord. It informed him that, having no fear of God in his heart, but being moved and seduced by the instigation of the Devil, he had failed in the love and true and due natural obedience towards his said lord the King, and had moved to disturb the peace and tranquility of the kingdom and to stir up war and rebellion to depose his said lord the King from the title, honour, and the regal name of the imperial crown — and much more of the same kind, at the end of all of which he was invited to say whether he was guilty or not guilty.

He answered more than was asked.

"It's entirely innocent I am." (Rafael Sabatini, *Captain Blood*)

I. serious
II. mock serious
III. humorous
IV. satirical
V. pensive

A. I
B. II
C. none
D. all
E. I and II
F. II, III, and IV

V OCABULARY

Captain Blood[2]
Rafael Sabatini

The protagonist, Dr. Peter Blood, an Irish soldier who is now a medical doctor, is nonetheless (in the beginning of the novel) attending to his geranium while the town prepares to fight the British. He wants no part in the rebellion, but while attending to some of the wounded Irish rebels, Peter is arrested by the British. And the adventure begins! Eventually Peter Blood becomes Captain Blood and, suffice it to say that the British rue the day that they messed with Peter Blood!

Suggested Vocabulary Words

A. There were dark stains of suffering or sleeplessness under the low-lidded eyes, heightening their brilliance and their gentle <u>melancholy</u>. The face was very pale, save for the vivid colour of the full lips and the hectic flush on the rather high but <u>inconspicuous</u> cheekbones. It was something in those lips that <u>marred</u> the perfection of that countenance; a fault, <u>elusive</u> but undeniable, lurked there to belie the fine sensitiveness of those nostrils, the tenderness of those dark, liquid eyes and the noble calm of that pale brow.

B. The physician in Mr. Blood regarded the man with peculiar interest knowing as he did the agonizing malady from which his lordship suffered, and the amazingly irregular, <u>debauched</u> life that he led in spite of it — perhaps because of it. "Peter Blood, hold up your hand!"

C. Abruptly he was recalled to his position by the harsh voice of the clerk of arraigns. His obedience was mechanical, and the clerk <u>droned</u> out the wordy indictment.

E NGLISH

Use of Subordinate Conjunctions

In the following sentences,[3] substitute *that, but,* or *but that* for the words *but what.*

1. "The doctor used to say 'twas her young heart, and I don't know but what he was right." — S.O. Jewett

2. "At the first stroke of the pickax it is ten to one but what you are taken up for a trespass." — Bulwer

3. "There are few persons of distinction but what can hold conversation in both languages." — Swift

4. "Who knows but what there might be English among those sun-browned half-naked masses of panting wretches?" — Kingsley

5. "No little wound of the kind ever came to him but what he disclosed it at once." — Trollope

6. "They are not so distant from the camp of Saladin but what they might be in a moment surprised." — Scott

M ATH

Algebra Expressions

Arrange according to the descending powers of a:

$$\backslash -80a^3 b^3 + 60a^4 b^2 + 108ab^5 + 48a^5 b + 3a^6 - 27b^6 - 90a^2 b^4$$

Data Analysis

An Inquiry into the Causes and Effects of the Variolae Vaccinae[4]
Edward Jenner

The following are case studies from a 1778 study conducted by English scientists. What can one conclude from these cases? The punctuation and spelling has been retained for authenticity. At this time "cow pox" was the same as "small pox."

CASE I

JOSEPH MERRET, now an Under Gardener to the Earl of Berkeley, lived as a Servant with a Farmer near this place in the year 1770, and occasionally assisted in milking his master's cows. Several horses belonging to the farm began to have sore heels, which Merret frequently attended. The cows soon became affected with the Cow Pox, and soon after several sores appeared on his hands. Swellings and stiffness in each axilla followed, and he was so much indisposed for several days as to be incapable of pursuing his ordinary employment. Previously to the appearance of the distemper among the cows there was no fresh cow brought into the farm, nor any servant employed who was affected with the Cow Pox.

In April, 1795, a general inoculation taking place here, Merret was inoculated with his family; so that a period of twenty-five years had elapsed from his having the Cow Pox to this time. However, though the variolous matter was repeatedly inserted into his arm, I found it impracticable to infect him with it; an efflorescence only, taking on an erysipelatous look about the centre, appearing on the skin near the punctured parts. During the whole time that his family had the Small Pox, one of whom had it very full, he remained in the house with them, but received no injury from exposure to the contagion.

It is necessary to observe, that the utmost care was taken to ascertain, with the most scrupulous precision, that no one whose case is here adduced had gone through the Small Pox previous to these attempts to produce that disease.

Had these experiments been conducted in a large city, or in a populous neighbourhood, some doubts might have been entertained; but here, where population is thin, and where such an event as a person's having had the Small Pox is always faithfully recorded, no risk of inaccuracy in this particular can arise.

■ ■ ■

CASE II

SARAH PORTLOCK, of this place, was infected with the Cow Pox, when a Servant at a Farmer's in the neighbourhood, twenty-seven years ago.

In the year 1792, conceiving herself, from this circumstance, secure from the infection of the Small Pox, she nursed one of her own children who had accidentally caught the disease, but no indisposition ensued. During the

Smallpox: Oval yellow blisters depressed or umbilicated in the center.

time she remained in the infected room, variolous matter was inserted into both her arms, but without any further effect than in the preceding case.

■ ■ ■

CASE III

JOHN PHILLIPS, a Tradesman of this town, had the Cow Pox at so early a period as nine years of age. At the age of sixty-two I inoculated him, and was very careful in selecting matter in its most active state. It was taken from the arm of a boy just before the commencement of the eruptive fever, and instantly inserted. It very speedily produced a sting-like feel in the part. An efflorescence appeared, which on the fourth day was rather extensive, and some degree of pain and stiffness were felt about the shoulder; but on the fifth day these symptoms began to disappear, and in a day or two after went entirely off, without producing any effect on the system.

■ ■ ■

I. Smallpox can naturally be controlled by the infected human host through proper hygiene.
II. Smallpox can be controlled by inoculations of harmless quantities of the disease. The host develops an immune response.
III. Smallpox is highly contagious.

A. I
B. II
C. III
D. All
E. None
F. I and III
G. II and III
H. I and II

Arrangement of Words in a Sentence

Of course in simple sentences the natural order of arrangement is subject — verb — object. In many cases, no other form is possible. Thus in the sentence "The cat has caught a mouse," we cannot reverse it and say "The mouse has caught a cat" without destroying the meaning, and in any other form of arrangement, such as "A mouse, the cat has caught," we feel that while it is intelligible, it is a poor way of expressing the fact.

In longer sentences, however, when there are more words than what are barely necessary for subject, verb, and object, we have greater freedom of arrangement and can so place the words as to give the best effect. The proper placing of words depends upon perspicuity and precision. These two combined give style to the structure.

Most people are familiar with Gray's line in the immortal Elegy — "The ploughman homeward plods his weary way." This line can be paraphrased to read 18 different ways. Here are a few variations:

Homeward the ploughman plods his weary way.

The ploughman plods his weary way homeward.

Plods homeward the ploughman his weary way.

Homeward his weary way plods the ploughman.

Plods the ploughman his weary way homeward.

His weary way homeward the ploughman plods.

The ploughman plods homeward his weary way.

. . . and so on. It is doubtful if any of the other forms are superior to the one used by the poet. Of course his arrangement was made to comply with the rhythm and rhyme of the verse. Most of the variations depend upon the emphasis we wish to place upon the different words.

In arranging the words in an ordinary sentence we should not lose sight of the fact that the beginning and end are the important places for catching the attention of the reader. Words in these places have greater emphasis than elsewhere. This is especially true for the ACT essay. The graders are usually tired and harassed, and will often pay more attention to the beginning and the end of sentences and paragraphs.

In Gray's line, the general meaning conveyed is that a weary ploughman is plodding his way homeward, but according to the arrangement a very slight difference is effected in the idea. Some of the variations make us think more of the ploughman, others more of the plodding, and still others more of the weariness.

As the beginning and end of a sentence are the most important places, it naturally follows that small or insignificant words should be kept from these positions. Of the two places, the end one is the more important, therefore, it really calls for the most important word in the sentence. Never commence a sentence with *and, but, since, because*, and other similar weak words and never end it with prepositions, small, weak adverbs, or pronouns.

The parts of a sentence which are most closely connected with one another in meaning should be closely connected in order also. By ignoring this principle many sentences are made, if not nonsensical, really ridiculous and ludicrous. For instance: "Ten dollars reward is offered for information of any person injuring this property by order of the owner." "This monument was erected to the memory of John Jones, who was shot by his affectionate brother."

In the construction of all sentences the grammatical rules must be inviolably observed. The laws of concord, that is, the agreement of certain words, must be obeyed. The amusing effect of disregarding the reference of pronouns is well illustrated by Burton in the following story of Billy Williams, a comic actor who thus narrates his experience in riding a horse owned by Hamblin, the manager:

"So down I goes to the stable with Tom Flynn, and told the man to put the saddle on him."

"On Tom Flynn?"

"No, on the horse. So after talking with Tom Flynn awhile I mounted him."

"What! mounted Tom Flynn?"

"No, the horse; and then I shook hands with him and rode off."

"Shook hands with the horse, Billy?"

"No, with Tom Flynn; and then I rode off up the Bowery, and who should I meet but Tom Hamblin; so I got off and told the boy to hold him by the head."

"What! hold Hamblin by the head?"

"No, the horse; and then we went and had a drink together."

"What! you and the horse?"

"No, me and Hamblin; and after that I mounted him again and went out of town."

"What! mounted Hamblin again?"

"No, the horse; and when I got to Burnham, who should be there but Tom Flynn — he'd taken another horse and rode out ahead of me; so I told the hostler to tie him up."

"Tie Tom Flynn up?"

"No, the horse; and we had a drink there."

"What! you and the horse?"

"No, me and Tom Flynn."

Finding his auditors by this time in a horse laugh, Billy wound up with: "Now, look here — every time I say horse, you say Hamblin, and every time I say Hamblin you say horse: I'll be hanged if I tell you any more about it."[5] (Abbott, *How to Write Clearly*)

An Excuse to be
REDEEMED

Friedrich Nietzsche is one of my favorite philosophers. No, I do not agree with his worldview, but even unsaved pagans can be prophetic! In particular, I really appreciate that he called the hand of the naturalists.

S C R I P T U R E

"I have been crucified with Christ and I no longer live, but Christ lives in me."

~ Galatians 2:20

Neitzsche correctly argued that if life is a struggle for existence in which the fittest survive, then strength is the ultimate virtue. This is absolutely true, but naturalists, who naturally embraced social Darwinism and evolutionary theory, preferred to think of themselves as "ammoral." Jack London, Stephen Crane, and Edward A. Robinson, among other naturalists, with almost religious fervor created literary figures and promoted literary themes, that purported to be morally neutral. After all, Buck, in *Call of the Wild* merely responded to the forces of nature, "the call of the wild."

Buck though was really virtuous! He was loyal, kind — more human than the humans! He was also the strongest dog in the pack. To call "strength" a virtue truly was too radical to the naturalists/evolutionists.

No, Nietzsche argued, there is a need to turn away from orthodox virtue altogether. The superman is someone who in discovering himself also discovers that it is in his best interests to reject any outside notions about values, trusting rather what he finds within himself. He creates his own good and evil, based on that which helps him to succeed or fail. In this way, good is something which helps one to realize his or her potential, and evil is whatever hampers or stands in the way of this effort. Since to Nietzsche everything in the world, including good and evil, is mutable, everything is being continually reinvented. The superman embraces this idea of change and he understands that since there is nothing in the world which is permanent, whatever exists must eventually be overcome by something else which comes along. In that sense, to Nietzsche, the naturalists got it right.

Seeing himself and his values in the same light, he knows that these aspects must also be overcome by something stronger. The superman therefore is the ideal of someone who has mastered the practice of overcoming himself.

The source of his strength lies in the cherishing of the same natural desires restricted in Christianity. Selfishness is healthy. He sees these insatiable desires as the best of all possible good since they act as the driving force behind his need to overcome.

The Christians, to Nietzsche, are just wrong; the naturalists are wrong and hypocrites.

Neitzsche was right about naturalism. For the first time, virtue is not connected to knowledge (Plato). Good is what survives, which wins; bad is what gives way and falls. The naturalists were brave enough to reject religion, Nietzsche said, but too cowardly to reject Christian morality. They replaced Judeo-Christian morality with a

PRAYER POINTS
A T T E N T I V E
TO GOD'S VOICE

"We proclaim to you what we have seen and heard, so that you also may have fellowship with us. And our fellowship is with the Father and with his Son, Jesus Christ."

~ 1 John 1:3

sort of humanist morality. Henry Fleming in *The Red Badge of Courage* shows virtue and courage by charging the enemy position. Wrought with irony, the "red badge of courage" was really Fleming's realization that the world was controlled by an impersonal, bordering on malevolent, deity.

But Nietzsche correctly pointed out that one can't have it both ways. One can't replace one religion — Christianity — with another one — naturalism/ evolution — without creating an intolerable anachronism. If one does that sort of thing, one creates a sort of metaphysical critical mass that could very well blow up in one's face!

Nietzsche warned us that with the collapse of religion, that is Christianity, and the rise of nascent unsatisfactory naturalism, Hegelian (based on the struggle) totalitarianism was inevitable. We see in the life of Joseph Stalin and Adolf Hitler the dark fulfillment of that prophecy.

The good news, however, is that there is strength in weakness, in Christ. We are crucified with Christ nonetheless we live (Gal. 2:20). Nietzsche got it right with naturalism — it is a paradox, a contradictory worldview. But he got it wrong with Christianity, too — it was not a faith for weak people. Christianity is not an excuse to be powerless but an excuse to be redeemed. Within that theological concept — something that cannot be duplicated philosophically — the believer is more fulfilled that Nietzsche tauted superman.

WRITING

Redundancy: Wordiness

In the following examples, place the word or words in parentheses that are uncalled for and that should be omitted:

1. Fill the glass full.

2. They appeared to be talking together on private affairs.

3. I saw the boy and his sister both in the garden.

4. He went into the country last week and returned back yesterday.

5. The subject matter of his discourse was excellent.

6. You need not wonder that the subject matter of his discourse was excellent; it was taken from the Bible.

7. They followed after him, but could not overtake him.

8. The same sentiments may be found throughout the whole of the book.

9. I was very ill every day of my life last week.

10. That was the sum and substance of his discourse.[1]

(Joseph Devlin, *How to Speak and Write Correctly*)

One can argue, correctly, that the entire ACT is a reading test! In fact, as it is true with the SAT, so it is true with the ACT: reading good books is the single best preparation for the ACT. The reading section of the ACT will include four passages, and after each passage you will answer several questions. The passages will be fiction and non-fiction. You have 35 minutes to finish.

Spend about six minutes reading a each passage. This should leave you about two or three minutes to answer the question on each passage. If you are prepared, you should be able to identify the questions as you read the passage. In any event, do not waste time looking at the questions before you read the passage.

How you read the passage is the key to doing well on this test. The questions will not be hard to answer if you have read the passages well.

To review, you are not reading the passage if you are not marking it up. First read a passage very quickly. Understand the general context of the passage. Then read the passage for more in-depth comprehension. Pay particular attention to the topic sentences of paragraphs and the thesis of the essay. Focus on the introduction and conclusion. What is the argument? How is it developed?

Whatever you do, don't be thinking about the questions as you are reading. Concentrate on the passage you are reading. I repeat: you should be spending most of your time reading and not answering questions.

S CIENCE

Drawing Conclusions

Based upon this treatment for diphtheria, what assumptions can be made about this disease?

PERSONAL AND BEDSIDE HYGIENE.

1. (a) All discharges from the nose and mouth should be gathered in soft, clean cloths or rags or papers and destroyed by burning. (b) The patient should cover the mouth and nose when coughing or sneezing, for a cough or sneeze will throw droplets of mucus to a distance of 10 or 12 feet.

2. The attendant should wear a washable gown that completely covers her clothing. It should be put on when entering the room of the patient and taken off immediately on leaving it.

3. A basin of water, together with a cake of castile soap (or where possible an antiseptic solution), should be placed in a convenient place, so that the doctor and nurse attending the patient may wash their hands whenever leaving the room, and even before touching the door handle.

4. All eating utensils that the patient uses should be washed in boiling hot water separately from other dishes and used exclusively by the patient.

5. All bedclothes and bedding should be boiled in soap and water, or they should be exposed to the sunshine. Direct sunshine kills disease germs.

6. The person attending the patient should wear a double layer of gauze or other soft thin cloth across the mouth and nose as a face mask whenever near the patient so as to prevent the droplets containing the germs coming from the patient's mouth from entering and lodging on the lining of the mouth or throat of the attendant. Always remember that even though you may not get the disease, if the germs lodge in your throat they may grow there and you may carry the disease to another person who may catch it.

7. There should be but one attendant wherever possible.

8. No visitors should be permitted in the sick room — not even during convalescence.

9. The one who attends the sick should not prepare or handle the food of others. Sometimes it is impossible to take this precaution, as very often it is the mother who must take care of the patient, cook, and do all the housework. In such cases the one attending the sick must never neglect whenever near the patient:

1. To wear a face mask.

2. To wear a washable gown (which is to be taken off on leaving the room).

3. To wash her hands when leaving the sick room.

■ ■ ■

Every attendant on the sick should know how disease germs are carried from the sick to the well. This knowledge should make her more careful, and thus help to prevent the spread of the disease.[2]

I. Diptheria is a highly contagious disease.
II. Diptheria is an airborne disease.
III. Diptheria is spread through bodily fluids.
IV. It is easier to prevent diptheria than to cure it.

A. I
B. II
C. III
D. IV
E. I and II
F. I, II, and III
G. None
H. All

Details

"My soul followeth hard after thee: thy right hand upholdeth me" (Ps. 63:8).

Christian theology teaches the doctrine of prevenient grace, which briefly stated means this — that before a man can seek God, God must first have sought the man.

Before a sinful man can think a right thought of God, there must have been a work of enlightenment done within him; imperfect it may be, but a true work nonetheless, and the secret cause of all desiring and seeking and praying which may follow.

We pursue God because, and only because, He has first put an urge within us that spurs us to the pursuit. "No man can come to me," said our Lord, "except the Father which hath sent me draw him," and it is by this very prevenient drawing that God takes from us every vestige of credit for the act of coming. The impulse to pursue God originates with God, but the outworking of that impulse is our following hard after Him; and all the time we are pursuing Him we are already in His hand: "Thy right hand upholdeth me."

In this divine "upholding" and human "following" there is no contradiction. All is of God, for as von Hügel teaches, God is always previous. In practice, however, (that is, where God's previous working meets man's present response) man must pursue God. On our part there must be positive reciprocation if this secret drawing of God is to eventuate in identifiable experience of the Divine. In the warm language of personal feeling this is stated in the Forty-second Psalm: "As the hart panteth after the water brooks, so panteth my soul after thee, O God. My soul thirsteth for God, for the living God: when shall I come and appear before God?" This is deep calling unto deep, and the longing heart will understand it.

The doctrine of justification by faith — a biblical truth, and a blessed relief from sterile legalism and unavailing self-effort — has in our time fallen into evil company and been interpreted by many in such manner as actually to bar men from the knowledge of God. The whole transaction of religious conversion has been made mechanical and spiritless. Faith may now be exercised without a jar to the moral life and without embarrassment to the Adamic ego. Christ may be "received" without creating any special love for Him in the soul of the receiver. The man is "saved," but he is not hungry nor thirsty after God. In fact he is specifically taught to be satisfied and encouraged to be content with little.

The modern scientist has lost God amid the wonders of His world; we Christians are in real danger of losing God amid the wonders of His Word. We have almost forgotten that God is a Person and, as such, can be cultivated as any person can. It is inherent in personality to be able to know other personalities, but full knowledge of one personality by another cannot be achieved in one encounter. It is only after long and loving mental intercourse that the full possibilities of both can be explored.

All social intercourse between human beings is a response of personality to personality, grading upward from the most casual brush between man and man to the fullest, most intimate communion of which the human soul is capable. Religion, so far as it is genuine, is in essence the response of created personalities to the Creating Personality, God. "This is life eternal, that they might know thee the only true God, and Jesus Christ, whom thou hast sent."

God is a Person, and in the deep of His mighty nature He thinks, wills, enjoys, feels, loves, desires and suffers as any other person may. In making Himself known to us He stays by the familiar pattern of personality. He communicates with us through the avenues of our minds, our wills and our emotions. The continuous and unembarrassed interchange of love and thought between God and the soul of the redeemed man is the throbbing heart of New Testament religion.

This intercourse between God and the soul is known to us in conscious personal awareness. It is personal: that is, it does not come through the body of believers, as such, but is known to the individual, and to the body through the individuals which compose it. And it is conscious: that is, it does not stay below the threshold of consciousness and work there unknown to the soul (as, for instance, infant baptism is thought by some to do), but comes within the field of awareness where the man can "know" it as he knows any other fact of experience.

You and I are in little (our sins excepted) what God is in large. Being made in His image we have within us the capacity to know Him. In our sins we lack only the power. The moment the Spirit has quickened us to life in regeneration our whole being senses its kinship to God and leaps up in joyous recognition. That is the heavenly birth without which we cannot see the Kingdom of God. It is, however, not an end but an inception, for now begins the glorious pursuit, the heart's happy exploration of the infinite riches of the Godhead. That is where we begin, I say, but where we stop no man has yet discovered, for there is in the awful and mysterious depths of the Triune God neither limit nor end.[3] (A.W. Tozer, *The Pursuit of God*)

■ ■ ■

A title for this passage would be:

A. Justification by Faith
B. Following Hard After God
C. Obeying Scripture
D. Walking the Talk

The phrase "you and I are in little (our sins excepted) what God is in large" means:

A. We are made in the image of God but we are not as powerful.
B. We are separated from God by sins.
C. God is a mystery, unable to be comprehended.
D. None of these

The theme of this essay is summarized by which quote:

A. God is a Person, and in the deep of His mighty nature He thinks.
B. No man has yet discovered the complete infinite riches of God.
C. God so loved the world that He sent his only begotten Son.
D. None of these

Prevenient grace means:

A. God's providence protects the believer.
B. God's mercy creates painful knowledge.
C. Before man can see God, he first must be sought by God.
D. None of these

Miscellaneous Examples for Correction

1. Can you imagine Indians or a semi-civilized people engaged on a work like the canal connecting the Mediterranean and the Red seas?

2. In the friction between an employer and workman, it is commonly said that his profits are high.

3. None of them are in any wise willing to give his life for the life of his chief.

4. Art is neither to be achieved by effort of thinking, nor explained by accuracy of speaking.

■ ■ ■

"Like" is a preposition, introducing a prepositional phrase. In informal English, "like" is often used as a conjunction; but in formal English (as you will be writing!) "as" is always preferable.

❝ *What comes into our minds when we think about God is the most important thing about us.*❞[4]

A.W. Tozer

The Pursuit of God[5]
A.W. Tozer

A.W. Tozer remains one of the most popular and important Christian teachers of this and the last century. His unabashed call to intimacy with God is peculiar to most Protestant teachers. This a remarkable book that will no doubt change your life!

Suggested Vocabulary Words

A. Before the Lord God made man upon the earth He first prepared for him by creating a world of useful and pleasant things for his <u>sustenance</u> and delight. In the Genesis account of the creation these are called simply "things." They were made for man's uses, but they were meant always to be external to the man and <u>subservient</u> to him. In the deep heart of the man was a shrine where none but God was worthy to come. Within him was God; without, a thousand gifts which God had showered upon him.

B. Men have now by nature no peace within their hearts, for God is crowned there no longer, but there in the moral dusk stubborn and aggressive <u>usurpers</u> fight among themselves for first place on the throne.

C. This is not a mere metaphor, but an accurate analysis of our real spiritual trouble. There is within the human heart a tough <u>fibrous</u> root of fallen life whose nature is to possess, always to possess. It covets "things" with a deep and fierce passion. The pronouns "my" and "mine" look innocent enough in print, but their constant and universal use is significant.

M A T H

Rate Word Problems

1. If x represent the number of miles a man can row in an hour in still water, how far can the man row in 5 hours down a stream which flows y miles an hour? How far up the same stream in 4 hours?

2. A can reap a field in 7 hours, and B can reap the same field in 5 hours. How much of the field can they do in one hour, working together?

3. A tank can be filled by two pipes in a hours and b hours respectively. What part of the tank will be filled by both pipes running together for one hour?

ELEVATORS

I like elevators. I really do. They are so nice! I mean I would much prefer riding elevators to walking up stairs. Especially in 18-floor buildings.

My wife, Karen, prefers to walk up stairs. It is good exercise for one thing, and she seems never to be in a hurry. Also, I wonder if it is because I kiss her in the elevator (it is a tradition), but I really think it is because she wants some exercise. Go figure. We will talk about kissing later.

I like to exercise, too. But I like my exercise to be on straightaways and short. And I guess I look like it, too. I like my exercise to be short, sweet, and manageable. A little suffering is okay, but walking up 18 floors of stairs? Too much for me.

I like God to keep me on straightaways and easy walking, too. But, like Karen, He often does not always do what I want Him to do. He makes me walk up the stairs. But that is another issue.

I like elevators. I am a "punch the button four or five times" sort of guy. Those of you who know me could have guessed that. Karen reminds me that I only need to punch the button once. And she is right. The things lights up — or not — after one punch. But it still feels good to me to do it three or four times. And if the elevator is delayed I give it three or four more punches for good measure. Never causes the darn thing to go any faster though.

Karen sighs and tells me that it really doesn't make the elevator move any faster. She is probably right.

And she is probably right when she tells me that my worrying doesn't help either. It is like punching an elevator button multiple times in order to change my situation. Neither thing works I suppose — but, honestly, it still feels good sometimes!

Am I right, fellow worriers?

But I like to be with my wife alone even more. Now, I don't know about other married people, and sundry other loving couples, but Karen and I are inveterate surreptitious elevator smoochers. Rarely do I get a kiss on the lips, I admit — after all we must not mess up the lipstick thing — but we certainly do kiss. And I most certainly am not a picky kisser when it comes to my wife — really, I am of the school that believes all kisses are special. After almost 40 years of marriage, I am grateful for the most innocent kiss. Karen and I are absolutely wicked though. With no guilt, we kiss on that empty elevator. That is, if we are all alone on the elevator. If we are not I just wink and smile at my honey and she does her best to ignore me.

Rarely, but occasionally, I stay in hotels with six or eight elevators. In my present hotel, I avoid the last of three elevators on the right. The button for the lobby does not light up. Do you know how frustrating it is to push a button that is supposed to light up but it doesn't? Is it really pushed? Should I try again and push harder? I like my elevator buttons to light up. Don't you? You sit there and wait — not knowing if it is working. I like my elevator buttons to light up.

I am old enough to remember elevator wardens — nicely dressed, uniformed guys who pushed all the buttons for you. Pushing elevator buttons is pretty important stuff. These guys always were able to push their elevator buttons.

Yes, elevator buttons that don't light up can be a problems. Now really, how can you be sure you are going to land on L level? What if the mischievous thing decides to drop you off on level 4 or 3 — how will you know? How will you know when you arrive at the lobby if the button does not light up?

Serving God sometimes feels that way. You know? He sets me on a path and He does not always light up all the floors as we travel. I have to sort of trust Him to get me to the lobby, to the destination. In fact, I often don't know I have arrived until I arrive. But I know when I arrive. Maybe that is what faith is all about. Maybe.

TEST-TAKING INSIGHT

Science Test

As with the reading test, you will be asked 40 questions in 35 minutes. Here is a news flash: the science test is really a reading test. All the answers are in front of you. Simply read the science questions well and you will have your answers.

Quickly read the passage and analyze the tables, graphs, or figures. Then carefully read the passage and try to comprehend any other data illustrated. What sort of data is it? How is it presented? In bar graphs? In a pie graph?

After about two or three minutes of careful reading, answer the question. Spend 20 to 30 seconds per question.

Practice brings perfection! Practice reading these passages and understanding the data presented. Practice! Practice! Practice! The more you work with this type of passage, the faster you will be able to comprehend the data.

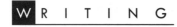

WRITING

Redundancy: Wordiness

In the following examples, place the word or words in parentheses that are uncalled for and that should be omitted:[2]

1. He took wine and water and mixed them both together.

2. He descended down the steps to the cellar.

3. He fell down from the top of the house.

4. I hope you will return again soon.

5. The things he took away he restored again.

(Joseph Devlin, *How to Speak and Write Correctly*)

> "*The elevator to success is out of order. You'll have to use the stairs . . . one step at a time.*"[1]
>
> — Joe Girard

The Sea Wolf[3]
Jack London

The protagonist and narrator, Humphrey Van Wyden, is a wealthy, educated dandy who does not work. While traveling to see friends, his boat is rammed by another boat and sinks. Van Wyden is rescued by the *Ghost*, a schooner that hunts seals, and is forced to become the cabin boy. Life on the *Ghost* is hard. The captain, Wolf Larsen, and others are cruel to Van Wyden. Van Wyden adjusts to his new surroundings by learning how to run a ship, and by becoming stronger. Miss Brewster, a woman the *Ghost* rescues, and Van Wyden become friends. Miss Brewster and Van Wyden escape from the *Ghost* on a small boat and land on an island. Life on the island is hard and Miss Brewster and Van Wyden become self-sufficient and fall in love. This is a strange plot twist for the naturalist London — romantic love in the desolate, Darwinist universe that is their deserted island! The *Ghost*, in disrepair and abandoned except for Captain Larsen, arrives at the island one day. Van Wyden attempts to fix the ship and in spite of Larsen's attempts to sabotage his work he succeeds. Larsen is slowly dying of a brain tumor. Miss Brewster and Van Wyden set sail on the *Ghost* and Larsen dies of the brain tumor shortly afterward. Miss Brewster and Van Wyden are rescued by an American ship. The interplay between Wolf Larsen and Humphrey Van Wyden is a remarkable literary event. In many ways, like Buck in *Call of the Wild*, Van Wyden gives into his own "call of the wild" and manages to survive in the most difficult surroundings.

Suggested Vocabulary Words

I seemed swinging in a mighty rhythm through <u>orbit</u> <u>vastness</u>. Sparkling points of light <u>spluttered</u> and shot past me. They were stars, I knew, and flaring comets, that peopled my flight among the suns. As I reached the limit of my swing and prepared to rush back on the counter swing, a great gong struck and thundered. For an immeasurable period, lapped in the rippling of <u>placid</u> centuries, I enjoyed and pondered my <u>tremendous</u> flight.

But a change came over the face of the dream, for a dream I told myself it must be. My rhythm grew shorter and shorter. I was jerked from swing to counter swing with irritating haste. I could scarcely catch my breath, so fiercely was I <u>impelled</u> through the heavens. The gong thundered more frequently and more furiously. I grew to await it with a nameless dread. Then it seemed as though I were being dragged over *rasping* sands, white and hot in the sun. This gave place to a sense of <u>intolerable</u> anguish. My skin was scorching in the torment of fire. The gong clanged and <u>knelled</u>. The sparkling points of light flashed past me in an interminable stream, as though the whole <u>sidereal</u> system were dropping into the void. I gasped, caught my breath painfully, and opened my eyes. Two men were kneeling beside me, working over me. My mighty rhythm was the lift and forward plunge of a ship on the sea. The terrific gong was a frying-pan, hanging on the wall, that rattled and clattered with each leap of the ship. The rasping, scorching sands were a man's hard hands <u>chafing</u> my naked chest. I squirmed under the pain of it, and half lifted my head. My chest was raw and red, and I could see tiny blood globules starting through the torn and inflamed cuticle.

R EADING

Argument

A metaphysician (i.e., scientist/philosopher who studies the universe) whose worldview requires God (if a decidedly anemic God), and who respected the cultural role of religious institutions. Contrasted to existentialists and naturalists, A.N. Whitehead preferred to work within society's institutions. Nonetheless, Whitehead appealed to direct experience. Like many romantics, Whitehead saw harmony in nature and all human experience. Similar to the empiricists, Whitehead leaned toward rationalism. Whitehead's story is a modern story — he became an agnostic. He also took some radical tangents in his world view.

In his book *Process and Reality*,[4] A.N. Whitehead abandoned the notion, strong in Western philosophy since Plato, that what is most unchanging is most real. Instead he conceived the structure of reality in dynamic terms. Whitehead set out a radical metaphysics based not on entities but on events — on an infinite series of "actual occasions." Reality was not based on Platonic "forms" but on "fluid experience." All entities are "momentary constituents of the processes of reality"; unchangingness is a property of what is "dead, past, abstract or purely formal." The emphasis is on becoming, on development in time, rather than on static being, and by implication, absolute truth. Whitehead embraced the modernist notion of process thought. The central metaphor for process thought is that of organism, rather than that of machine. The formation of each event is a function of the nature of the entities involved, their context and interdependence in a way more characteristic of biological organisms than of inanimate objects; their "experience" and their effort to "fulfill their possibilities to the full" in the given event; language deriving not merely from biology but from the analogy of human mentality. Whitehead's agnosticism is most evident in his understanding of suffering. God "the fellow-sufferer who understands," who does not coerce but merely seeks to persuade other beings in the direction of love, seems profoundly attractive in the light of the Holocaust. Process schemes subvert the notion of the omnipotence of God, and therefore escape some of these tensions.

■ ■ ■

What is the central problem that the author has with Whitehead's worldview?

A. Whitehead is a romantic.
B. Whitehead is a Darwinist.
C. Whitehead's pursuit of empathy dilutes the omnipotence of God.
D. Whitehead is an agnostic.

E NGLISH

Vague and Commonplace Words

Rewrite the following sentences with more vigor and precision. Note: precision may or may not mean "shorter." Take as many words as necessary to ensure that your reader gets your point.

1. He hit the ball over the fence.
2. He ate all the cake that was left.
3. She called for help.

■ ■ ■

Another common cause of sentence dullness is lack of variety in the kinds of sentences in a paragraph. Too many simple or compound sentences can make your style just as monotonous as too many subject-first sentences.

M ATH

Expand

1. $(5 - x)(3 - x)$
2. $(6 - x)(7 + x)$
3. $(11 - x)(3 + x)$
4. $(x - 3)(x + 3)$
5. $(y + 5)(y - 5)$

"*Art is the imposing of a pattern on experience, and our aesthetic enjoyment is recognition of the pattern.*"[5]
— Alfred North Whitehead

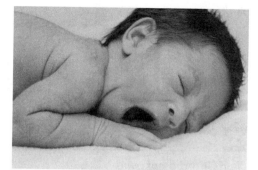

SCIENCE

Faulty Logic

What is wrong with the conclusion in this 1850 health manual?

HOW OFTEN SHOULD CHILDBIRTH TAKE PLACE?

It is most important that the childbearing wife and mother have a long period of rest between births. At least one year should separate a birth and the conception following it. This means that about two years should elapse between two births. If this rule be followed, the wife will retain her health, and her children will also be healthy. It is far better to give birth to seven children who will live and be healthy, than to bear fourteen, of whom seven are likely to die, while the numerous successive births wear out and age the unfortunate mother.

I. It is most important that the childbearing wife and mother have a long period of rest between births.

II. This means that about two years should elapse between two births. If this rule be followed, the wife will retain her health, and her children will also be healthy.

III. It is far better to give birth to seven children, who will live and be healthy, than to bear fourteen, of whom seven are likely to die, while the numerous successive births wear out and age the unfortunate mother.

A. I
B. II
C. III
D. All
E. None

What is a false assumption?

A. Childbirth is painful.
B. Rest between childbirth will produce laudable results.
C. Childbirth wears out the mother.

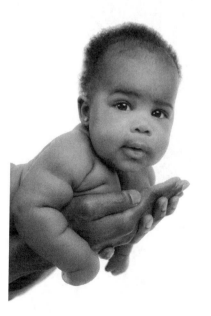

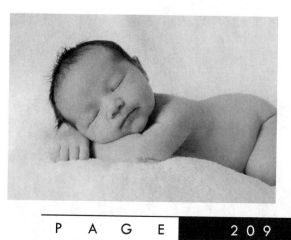

A New
CREATION

SCRIPTURE

"For God did not send his Son into the world to condemn the world, but to save the world through him. Whoever believes in him is not condemned, but whoever does not believe stands condemned already because he has not believed in the name of God's one and only Son."

~ John 3:17–18

PRAYER POINTS
BOLDNESS

"The wicked man flees though no one pursues, but the righteous are bold as a lion."

~ Proverbs 28:1

Rainer Hoess was just a boy when he discovered that his grandfather was Rudolf Hoess, the Death Dealer of Auschwitz. Hoess was in charge of Auschwitz Concentration camp from 1940 to 1943. Under his tenure an estimated 2.5 million people were executed. Rudolf Hoess, then, was history's greatest mass murderer, the architect and SS Kommandant of the largest killing center ever created, the death camp Auschwitz. To Rainer's father, though, Hoess was a mild-mannered, happily married Roman Catholic who enjoyed normal family life with his five children, despite his view of the crematoria chimney stacks 150 yards from his bedroom window. At peak efficiency Auschwitz had the capacity to murder and to burn ten thousand people in 24 hours.

What is poor Rainer Hoess to do?

No matter who our family is, who we are, in Christ we are new creations!

Rudolf Hoess's final letter to Rainer's father before he was executed in 1947:

You, my dear, good children!

Your daddy has to leave you now. For you, poor ones, there remains only your dear, good Mommy. . . .

The biggest mistake of my life was that I believed everything faithfully which came from the top, and I didn't dare to have the least bit of doubt about the truth of that which was presented to me. Walk through life with your eyes open. Don't become one-sided; examine the pros and cons in all matters. In all your undertakings, don't just let your mind

speak, but listen above all to the voice in your heart. . . . Once more from my heart I ask you all, my dear good children, take to heart my last words. Think of them again and again.

Keep in loving memory, Your Dad.

The Jewish Children of Izieu

The number of children killed by Hitler and his Nazis is not fathomable and full statistics for the tragic fate of the children will never be known. Estimates range as high as 1.5 million murdered children during the Holocaust. This figure includes more than 1.2 million Jewish children, tens of thousands of Gypsy children, and thousands of institutionalized handicapped children.

One particularly tragic story is the story of the children of Izieu. In 1944 the Nazis from Lyon sent three vehicles to the tiny French village to exterminate the children of the orphanage known as La Maison d'Izieu. Here 44 Jewish children in age from 3 to 18 were hidden away from the Nazi terror that surrounded them.

On the morning of April 6, 1944, the little children were deported to the Nazi death camp Auschwitz and murdered immediately upon arrival. Of the 44 children kidnapped by the Nazis in Izieu, not a single one survived. Hoess was not present but the concentration camp he built murdered the children of Izieu.[1]

??? Are you reading 50 to 100 pages a day ???

Writing Style

Which version is better? Why?

A. It will not be impertinent nor unnatural to this present discourse, to set down in this place the present temper and constitution of both Houses of Parliament, and of the court itself, that it may be the less wondered at, that so prodigious an alteration should be made in so short a time, and the crown fallen so low, that it could neither support itself nor its own majesty, nor those who would appear faithful to it.

B. And now, in order to explain, as far as possible, how so prodigious an alteration could take place in so short a time, and how the royal power could fall so low as to be unable to support itself, its dignity, or its faithful servants, it will be of use to set down here, where it comes most naturally, some account of the present temper and composition, not only of both Houses of Parliament, but also of the court itself.[2] (Edwin A. Abbott, *How to Write Clearly*)

E N G L I S H

Agreement

Find the problem in these sentences and identify by the letter(s).

1. (A) Cells in your body (B) needs vitamins.

2. Roger (A) drove (B) their car (C) into the ocean.

3. (A) According to Plato, (B) nobody except evil people (C) rejoice at the misfortune of others.

Essay Scoring

Two trained readers — I call them "English teachers with attitude" will score your essay. The readers will use a detailed scoring guide to evaluate your essay. This guide uses a 6-point scale, with 1 being the lowest and 6 being the highest. The scores from your two readers are then combined for a total score of 2 to 12.

Study Guide ACT Essay Scoring Guide
(property of ACT)

6 = Effective

Critical Thinking: The essay takes a clear position on the subject and critically examines it from different perspectives, considers the implications of the topic, and/or responds to counterarguments. The writer uses specific, detailed examples to fully develop the argument.

Organization and Focus: The essay is well organized and stays focused on the topic. Ideas are logically and clearly developed, and paragraphs are carefully constructed and organized. The essay is a unified presentation of the thesis and has a clear introduction, body, and conclusion.

Use of Language: The writer has versatility and mastery in use of language and a comprehensive vocabulary.

Sentence Structure: The writer uses variety in sentence structure to enhance communication.

Grammar, Usage, and Mechanics: The essay has very few if any errors that detract from meaning.

5 = Competent

Critical Thinking: The essay takes a clear position on the subject and critically examines it from different perspectives, considers the implications of the topic, and/or responds to counterarguments to some extent. The writer uses specific, detailed examples to fully develop the argument.

Organization and Focus: The essay is well organized and focused. Ideas are logically developed. Paragraphs are generally well developed and unified. Transitions are effective though they may be simple and predictable. For the most part, the introduction and conclusion are clear and well developed.

Use of Language: The essay demonstrates competent use of language and vocabulary.

Sentence Structure: The essay generally uses a variety of sentence structures.

Grammar, Usage, and Mechanics: The essay has only a few minor errors.

4 = Adequate

Critical Thinking: The essay takes a position on the subject and may examine the implications of the topic and respond to counter-arguments. The writer adequately develops the argument.

Organization and Focus: The essay is generally well organized and focused. Ideas are logically developed for the most part. Transitions are generally effective though most are simple and predictable. The introduction and conclusion are clearly stated and somewhat developed.

Use of Language: The essay demonstrates adequate use of language and vocabulary.

Sentence Structure: The essay uses some variety in sentence structure.

Grammar, Usage, and Mechanics: There are occasional minor errors, but they do not interfere with meaning.

3 = Inadequate

Critical Thinking: The essay takes a position on the subject but does not examine the implications of the topic. It may respond to counterarguments, but the development is limited.

Organization and Focus: The essay may be somewhat arbitrarily organized or lack focus. Ideas may be organized in sections of the essay, but transitions are not effectively used to provide overall coherence. The essay does contain an introduction and conclusion, but development is inadequate.

Use of Language: The essay shows a basic grasp of use of language.

Sentence Structure: The essay uses somewhat varied sentence structure.

Grammar, Usage, and Mechanics: Errors occasionally interfere with meaning.

2 = Seriously Limited

Critical Thinking: The essay may not take a position on the subject or may fail to support the position. Counter-arguments are not adequately addressed. Development of the topic is weak.

Organization and Focus: Some organization exists, but transitions are simple and sometimes incorrectly used. Focus on the general subject is evident but may not be apparent on the specific issues. The essay contains an introduction and a conclusion, but development is minimal.

Use of Language: The essay uses simple word choice.

Sentence Structure: The essay uses simple sentence structure.

Grammar, Usage, and Mechanics: There are frequent errors that sometimes interfere with meaning.

1 = Fundamentally Lacking

Critical Thinking: There is either no sustainable position on the subject or a lack of examples or reasoning to support the position. Development is minimal.

Organization and Focus: The essay contains little or no organization. Use of transitions is rare. Focus on the general subject is evident but may not be apparent on the specific issues. The essay may contain an introduction and conclusion, but development is minimal.

Use of Language: The essay uses simple word choice.

Sentence Structure: The essay uses simple sentence structure.

Grammar, Usage, and Mechanics: There are frequent errors that significantly interfere with meaning.

M A T H

Word Problems

1. An army was drawn up with x men in front and y men deep. How many men were there in the army?

2. In how many minutes will a train go x miles at the rate of a miles an hour?

3. How many apples at x cents apiece can be bought for b dollars?

S C I E N C E

Reading for Detail

No mind retains consciously everything that has ever impressed it. It is necessary that it put aside what ceases to be of importance or value and make way for new impressions. We found early in our study that the subconscious never forgets, but harbors the apparently forgotten throughout the years, allowing it to modify our thinking, our reactions. But the conscious mind cannot be cluttered with the things of little importance when the more essential is clamoring. So there is a forgetting that is very normal. We forget numberless incidents of our childhood and youth; we may forget the details of much that we have learned to do automatically; but the subconscious mind is attending to them for us.

Do you know how to skate? and if so, do you remember just how you did it the first time? Probably all you recall is that you fell again and again because your feet would slip away from where you meant them to be. When you glide over the ice now it is as natural as walking, and as easy. You cannot remember in detail at all how you first "struck out," nor the position of your feet and arms and legs, which you felt forced to assume. At the time there was very real difficulty with every stroke — each one was an accomplishment to be attempted circumspectly, in a certain definite way. All you remember now is, vaguely, a tumble or two, soreness, and lots of fun.[3]

■ ■ ■ ■

The main idea of this passage is:

A. People forget things as they get older.
B. The unconscious mind prompts us to do involuntary learned activities.
C. We forget a lot of things.
D. None of the above

VOCABULARY

Suggested Vocabulary Words

In spite of the fact that Germany had one of the best democracies in world history, the Weimar republic, Germans enthusiastically embraced <u>totalitarianism</u> during the period between the two world wars. Both the fear of communism and the hope of economic prosperity drove Germans into the Nazi Party.

The Nazi Party was one of the many right-wing parties formed by the <u>monarchist reactionaries</u> who supported the Kaiser's rule and <u>conversely</u> hated the Weimar Republic. Many of these right-wing parties disappeared in the 1920s, but the Nazi Party was an exception. Under the brilliant leadership of Adolf Hitler, it grew as an important political party. It appealed to the unemployed masses and the <u>nationalistic</u> industrialists.

<u>Ironically</u>, the leader of Nazi Germany was an Austrian. Adolf Hitler, born in 1899, was the son of an Austrian minor customs official. Hitler was an undistinguished boy. After unsuccessful attempts to become a student of art in the Vienna College of Fine Art, he failed in many jobs.

During the First World War, Hitler served in the German army. He fought bravely and was awarded an Iron Cross for his bravery. He was wounded and while he was recovering in the hospital, he learned of Germany's defeat. He believed that the defeat was due to betrayal by Jewish people.

When he was discharged from the hospital, Hitler joined the National Socialist German Workingmen's Party (abbreviated as Nazi). By his skill as an orator and organizer, Hitler became the führer (leader) of the Nazi Party in 1921. The party adopted an emblem, a salute, and a greeting as its <u>distinctives</u>. It had a newspaper through which Hitler fiercely <u>denounced</u> the Treaty of Versailles and the Jews. He also organized the Stormtroopers (S.A. or the Brown Shirts) to disrupt the meetings of opposition parties. In November 1923, Hitler and his small party tried to overthrow the government. He failed. In April 1924, Hitler was put on trial and was sentenced to five years' imprisonment. While in prison he wrote *Mein Kampf*.

Hitler was an able leader. He was able to convince the Germans that he was a man of action and of ideals. Hitler promised everything to everybody. To the landowner and the industrialists, Hitler promised to stop communism. To the middle classes, he promised to abolish the Treaty of Versailles and relieve them of the burden of <u>reparations</u> payment. To the army, he promised military victory. Hitler was also a gifted orator. His speeches, though they contained little truth, always made successful appeals to the masses. Moreover, the Nazi Party, with its huge parades, attracted the younger generation. Most Germans followed Hitler with religious <u>fervor</u>. By 1933, Hitler was firmly in control.[4] (James Stobaugh, *World History*)

READING

Details

Which facts below can be supported by the above passages?

I. Adolf Hitler was a murderer.
II. Adolf Hitler came to power by supporting the middle class and industrialists.
III. Adolf Hitler was an Austrian.
IV. Adolf Hitler was an effective chancellor.

A. I
B. II
C. III
D. IV
E. None
F. All
G. I and IV
H. II, III, and IV

TOLERATION

My son, who was a student at a very strict Christian university, was forbidden to leave campus on the weekend to visit his brother who lived off campus. Now, in fact, the reason my youngest son wanted to visit my oldest son was that they wanted to participate in a community mission outreach. My son was irritated and frustrated, but he was not confused. The decision of the university was exactly consistent with its worldview.

That university's policy was clearly stated and justified by its mission statement. My son knew this. Within those reasonable limits, the university offered much freedom and grace.

The problem is many modern institutions — some universities, some businesses — celebrate "freedom" and "permissiveness" with a sobriquet of "toleration." But it is only toleration in the way that they define it. For instance, Messiah College in 2011 sought to maintain its biblical stand concerning homosexuality. Messiah College has had a consistent, long-standing policy of asking its students to desist from participating in anti-biblical behavior. Within that very reasonable policy lies much toleration and freedom. However, some students claimed that Messiah was "intolerant."

If anything and everything is allowed, without any moral base, then nihilism quickly emerges. Justice is sacrificed on the altar of facile toleration. Relativistic toleration makes justice impossible. Both Plato and the Apostle Paul agree, justice requires both a moral and an epistemological base. One cannot do justice unless one knows the difference between right and wrong. The fact is, many American institutions are in a headlong pursuit of toleration that ultimately is victimized by both injustice and relativism that ironically leads to intolerance!

Most secular universities have concluded that abstract concepts like grace, hope, and especially faith are indefinable, immeasurable, and above all unreasonable. Not that God or the uniqueness of Jesus Christ can be proved or disproved. There are certain issues that the order of the intellect simply cannot address, so we must rise above that to the order of the heart. Faith is our

SCRIPTURE

"If your very own brother, or your son or daughter, or the wife you love, or your closest friend secretly entices you, saying, 'Let us go and worship other gods' . . . do not yield to him or listen to him. Show him no pity. Do not spare him or shield him."

~ Deuteronomy 13:6–8

PRAYER POINTS
GENEROSITY

"He and all his family were devout and God-fearing; he gave generously to those in need and prayed to God regularly."

~ Acts 10:2

consent to receive the good that God would have for us. Evangelicals believe that God can and does act in our world and in our lives. Human needs are greater than this world can satisfy and therefore it is reasonable to look elsewhere. The university has forgotten or ignores this fact.[1]

In the midst of so much uncertainty, it is good to serve a God who loves His creation. The American secular university would try to convince us that it is fun to be living in clashing relativities where the foundations and structures of thoughts are up for grabs. Every truth is negotiated. Truth emerges by virtue of persuasion and consent. Truth is democratized. Morality is based on objective truth from an inspired corpus of information (i.e., the Bible); morality is an outcome of human interchange.[2]

In the years ahead, the Church will be called to maintain its firm commitment to the efficacy of the Word of God and to belay all attempts to impose false toleration in order to maintain its coziness with modern culture.

Scoring

Unlike in the SAT, in the ACT the questions do not follow a specific order of difficulty. If you feel stumped by a difficult question, quickly move on to the next question.

Remember, you get the same number of points for an easy question as for a hard one, so try to answer as many questions as you can.

Each section is scored on a scale of 1 to 36. The four sections are averaged together to get the composite score. If you write the optional ACT essay, you will receive an essay score from 2 to 12 and a combined essay and English score from 1 to 36.

According to the Triumph College Admissions website, Here are some rough estimates of how many questions you need to answer correctly in order to get a particular score.

ENGLISH

18 (40 of 75) — about 53% right

21 (48 of 75) — about 64% right

24 (56 of 75) — about 75% right

27 (63 of 75) — about 84% right

READING

18 (20 of 40) — about 50% right

21 (23 of 40) — about 58% right

24 (26 of 40) — about 65% right

27 (29 of 40) — about 73% right

MATH

18 (26 of 60) — about 43% right

21 (32 of 60) — about 53% right

24 (38 of 60) — about 63% right

27 (45 of 60) — about 75% right

SCIENCE

18 (17 of 40) — about 43% right

21 (24 of 40) — about 60% right

24 (29 of 40) — about 73% right

27 (34 of 40) — about 85% right

What is your target score?

"*Books are the quietest and most constant of friends; they are the most accessible and wisest of counselors, and the most patient of teachers.*"[3]

— Charles W. Eliot

W R I T I N G

Writing Style

Rewrite the following stringy sentence.

I read the assignment, and then I began making notes on cards, for I wanted to memorize the main points in the lesson, but the bell rang, and I was not through, and so I had to carry my heavy books home.

M A T H

Cube Roots

Find the cube root of each of the following:[4]

1. $27x^3 - 27x^2y + 9xy^2 - y^3$

2. $15x^2 - 1 - 75x^4 + 125x^6$

3. $144a^2 b^2 + 27b^6 + 108ab4 + 64a^3$

4. $x^6 - 8y^6 + 12x^2 y^4 - 6x^4 y^2$

5. $1 + 9x + 27x^2 + 27x^3$

Analysis

In what we may term "prescientific days," people were in no uncertainty about the interpretation of dreams. When they were recalled after awakening they were regarded as either the friendly or hostile manifestation of some higher powers, demoniacal and Divine. With the rise of scientific thought the whole of this expressive mythology was transferred to psychology; today there is but a small minority among educated persons who doubt that the dream is the dreamer's own psychical act.

But since the downfall of the mythological hypothesis an interpretation of the dream has been wanting. The conditions of its origin; its relationship to our psychical life when we are awake; its independence of disturbances which, during the state of sleep, seem to compel notice; its many peculiarities repugnant to our waking thought; the incongruence between its images and the feelings they engender; then the dream's evanescence, the way in which, on awakening, our thoughts thrust it aside as something bizarre, and our reminiscences mutilating or rejecting it — all these and many other problems have for many hundred years demanded answers which up till now could never have been satisfactory. Before all there is the question as to the meaning of the dream, a question which is in itself double-sided. There is, firstly, the psychical significance of the dream, its position with regard to the psychical processes, as to a possible biological function; secondly, has the dream a meaning — can sense be made of each single dream as of other mental syntheses?

Three tendencies can be observed in the estimation of dreams. Many philosophers have given currency to one of these tendencies, one which at the same time preserves something of the dream's former over-valuation. The foundation of dream life is for them a peculiar state of psychical activity, which they even celebrate as elevation to some higher state. Schubert, for instance, claims: "The dream is the liberation of the spirit from the pressure of external nature, a detachment of the soul from the fetters of matter."

Not all go so far as this, but many maintain that dreams have their origin in real spiritual excitations, and are the outward manifestations of spiritual powers whose free movements have been hampered during the day. A large number of observers acknowledge that dream life is capable of extraordinary achievements — at any rate, in certain fields.

In striking contradiction with this, the majority of medical writers hardly admit that the dream is a psychical phenomenon at all. According to them, dreams are provoked and initiated exclusively by stimuli proceeding from the senses or the body, which either reach the sleeper from without or are accidental disturbances of his internal organs. The dream has no greater claim to meaning and importance than the sound called forth by the ten fingers of a person quite unacquainted with music running his fingers over the keys of an instrument. The dream is to be regarded, says Binz, "as a physical process always useless, frequently morbid." All the peculiarities of dream life are explicable as the incoherent effort, due to some physiological stimulus, of certain organs, or of the cortical elements of a brain otherwise asleep.

But slightly affected by scientific opinion and untroubled as to the origin of dreams, the popular view holds firmly to the belief that dreams really have got a meaning, in some way they do foretell the future, whilst the meaning can

be unravelled in some way or other from its oft bizarre and enigmatical content. The reading of dreams consists in replacing the events of the dream, so far as remembered, by other events. This is done either scene by scene, according to some rigid key, or the dream as a whole is replaced by something else of which it was a symbol. Serious-minded persons laugh at these efforts — "Dreams are but seafoam!"[5] (Sigmund Freud, *Dream Psychology*)

■ ■ ■

Which statements are true (according to this passage)?

I. We obtain matter enough for the resolution of every dream if we especially direct our attention to the unbidden associations which disturb our thoughts — those which are otherwise put aside by the critic as worthless refuse.

II. Some think of dreams as a spiritual experience.

III. Dreams foretell the future.

   A. I

   B. II

   C. III

   D. All

   E. None

VOCABULARY

At Agincourt[6]
G.A. Henty

The long and bloody feud between the houses of Orleans and Burgundy — which for many years devastated France, caused a prodigious destruction of life and property, and was not even relaxed in the presence of a common enemy — is very fully recorded in the pages of Monstrelet and other contemporary historians. I have here only attempted to relate the events of the early portion of the struggle — from its commencement up to the astonishing victory of Agincourt, won by a handful of Englishmen over the chivalry of France. Here the two factions, with the exception of the Duke of Burgundy himself, laid aside their differences for the moment, only to renew them while France still lay prostrate at the feet of the English conqueror.

At this distance of time, even with all the records at one's disposal, it is difficult to say which party was most to blame in this disastrous civil war, a war which did more to cripple the power of France than was ever accomplished by English arms. Unquestionably Burgundy was the first to enter upon the struggle, but the terrible vengeance taken by the Armagnacs — as the Orleanists came to be called — for the murders committed by the mob of Paris in alliance with him, was of almost unexampled atrocity in civil war, and was mainly responsible for the terrible acts of cruelty afterwards perpetrated upon each other by both parties. I hope some day to devote another volume to the story of this desperate and unnatural struggle.

Suggested Vocabulary Words

A. In 1402 the king, influenced by his wife, Isobel, and his brother, the Duke of Orleans, who were on terms of the closest alliance, placed the entire government in the hands of the <u>latter</u>, who at once began to abuse it to such an extent, by imposing enormous taxes upon the clergy and the people, that he paved the way for the return of his uncle of Burgundy to power.

B. The change was <u>disastrous</u> for France. John was violent and utterly <u>unscrupulous</u>, and capable of any deed to gratify either his passions, jealousies, or hatreds.

C. When he recovered, the two princes went to mass together, dined at their uncle's, the Duke of Berri, and together entered Paris; and the Parisians fondly hoped that there was an end of the <u>rivalry</u> that had done so much harm.

D. The Duke of Burgundy at first affected grief and <u>indignation</u>, but at the council the next day he boldly avowed that Orleans had been killed by his orders. He at once took a horse and rode to the frontier of Flanders, which he reached safely, though hotly chased by a party of the Duke of Orleans' knights.

E. The duke's widow, who was in the country at the time, hastened up to Paris with her children, and <u>appealed</u> for justice to the king, who declared that he regarded the deed done to his brother as done to himself. The Dukes of Berri and Bourbon, the Constable and Chancellor, all assured her that she should have justice; but there was no force that could hope to cope with that which Burgundy could bring into the field, and when, two months later, Burgundy entered Paris at the head of a thousand men-at-arms, no attempt was made at resistance, and the murderer was received with <u>acclamations</u> by the <u>fickle</u> <u>populace</u>.

ENGLISH

Miscellaneous Examples for Correction

Correct these sentences.

(A) I use to want a pet monkey (B) who could do tricks.

(A) About a year ago, (B) I sat in the park and (C) sulked.

The trouble (A) started when I went into the house (B) to lay down.

READING

Details

The arrival and conquest of William and the Normans radically altered the course of English history. William instituted a brand of feudalism in England that strengthened the monarchy. Villages and manors were given a large degree of autonomy in local affairs. Although he began the invasion with papal support, William refused to let the church dictate policy within English and Norman borders. William died as he had lived: a warrior.

The next noteworthy king was Henry Plantagenet, Henry II. Among other things, Henry II developed common law. No longer were the feudal lords and the churches in sole control of judicial matters. Now the state was in control of judicial matters. This naturally gave a central government and its monarch more control than ever.

There was opposition from the church. Notably, Saint Thomas à Becket, opposed his king's actions. Henry II had Becket assassinated in 1170.

Henry II was a capable general as well as monarch. Henry's domain included more than half of France, all of Ireland, and most of Scotland.

Eventually the throne passed to Richard I, the Lionhearted, who ruled only briefly until he went to the Crusades. His younger brother, John, replaced him. John was a shrewd but cruel monarch, who won the scorn of English noblemen. The nobles forced John in 1215 to accept the Magna Carta, or Great Charter, by which he admitted his errors and promised to respect English law. The Magna Carta of 1215 required King John of England to proclaim certain liberties, and accept that his will was not arbitrary, for example by explicitly accepting that no freeman could be punished except through the law of the land, a right which is still in existence today.

The Magna Carta influenced later constitutional documents, including the United States Constitution. When John died in 1216, King Henry III assumed the throne and confirmed the Magna Carta in 1225. The monarchy continued to affirm the Magna Carta throughout British history. In England certain fundamental rights limited government's power. At this time no other nation could make that claim.

England prospered in the 12th and 13th centuries. The population doubled from about 1.5 million to more than 3 million.

Several kings later, Edward I assumed the British throne. Edward I created the Parliament, which was essentially the king's enlarged advisory council with a new name. Later, Parliament divided into two houses, Lords and Commons, and controlled fiscal matters. Edward conquered Wales and tried to conquer Scotland. Neither Edward nor his son, Edward II, could conquer Scotland. In 1314, at the Battle of Bannockburn, King Robert Bruce confirmed Scotland's claim to independence. Later, Edward gained consensual right to rule Scotland but he never really conquered it.

Next, Henry V won a brilliant victory at Agincourt, France, in 1415 and had his success confirmed in the Treaty of Troyes (1420). He married the daughter of the mad French king, Charles VI, and claimed control of both kingdoms (although Henry never controlled all of France).

In 1422 both Henry and Charles VI died, bringing the nine-month-old Henry VI to the throne of both countries. It was during this time that the French nationalist/religious mystic Joan of Arc was active.

Ultimately, Henry VI was an awful, if not insane, king and he lost control of the government. England lost all their possessions in France and this set the stage for the Wars of the Roses (1455–1485).[7] (James Stobaugh, *British History*)

■ ■ ■

One noteworthy development in the English Plantagenet reign was:

A. The claim to the French throne
B. The defeat of Spain in the War of the Spanish Succession
C. The founding of the English colony of Jamestown
D. The Reformation

The following facts can be inferred from this passage:

I. Henry II was a ruthless, pragmatic monarch.
II. England prospered because of an abundant harvest.
III. Henry V won a brilliant victory at Agincourt, France, because of the superiority of the English long bow.
IV. Scotland was a very hard country to conquer.

A. I
B. II
C. III
D. IV
E. None
F. All
G. I and IV
H. II and III

The Cry of
MODERN MAN

" 'Where, O death, is your victory? Where, O death, is your sting?' The sting of death is sin, and the power of sin is the law. But thanks be to God! He gives us the victory through our Lord Jesus Christ."

~ 1 Corinthians 15:55–57

Because I could not stop for Death,
He kindly stopped for me;
The carriage held but just ourselves
And Immortality.

We slowly drove, he knew no haste,
And I had put away
My labor, and my leisure too,
For his civility.

We passed the school where children played
At wrestling in a ring;
We passed the fields of gazing grain,
We passed the setting sun.

We paused before a house that seemed
A swelling of the ground;
The roof was scarcely visible,
The cornice but a mound.

Since then it is centuries; but each
Feels shorter than the day
I first surmised the horses' heads
Were toward eternity.[1]

Emily Dickinson, a 19th century recluse, was the first modern American poet. She wrote in free verse and she discussed topics often ignored (e.g., birds on sidewalks). She also wrote about death.

Many think that Dickinson refused to commit her life to Christ. Perhaps that haunted her for her whole life. I think so. When I read her poems I hear that forlorn cry.

Dickinson presages the cry of modern man's cry for relevance and meaning and life in the midst of inhumanity.

If I should die,
And you should live,
And time should gurgle on,
And morn should beam,
And noon should burn,
As it has usual done;
If birds should build as early,
And bees as bustling go,
One might depart at option
From enterprise below!
It is sweet to know that stocks will stand

PRAYER POINTS
K IND WORDS

"We proclaim to you what we have seen and heard, so that you also may have fellowship with us. And our fellowship is with the Father and with his Son, Jesus Christ."

~ 1 John 1:3

When we with daisies lie,
That commerce will continue,
And trades as briskly fly.
It makes the parting tranquil
And keeps the soul serene,
That gentlemen so sprightly
Conduct the pleasing scene![2]

I am so glad I know who my Redeemer is! He snatches me from the tentativeness and hopelessness of modernity!

R E A D I N G

Main Idea

In 1800, for the first time in history, a democratically elected government peacefully replaced an entirely different ideological government. The major political parties we know today did not exist in 1800. That contest was Democratic Republicans vs. Federalists. Nonetheless, it is remarkable and a credit to the American civilization that two candidates could vigorously debate issues and remain friends and colleagues after one was elected. Though Federalists lost and the Democratic-Republicans won, the whole world won when the young nation transferred its power without bloodshed. Contrast this with what was happening in France! France decapitated its deposed king; the United States honorably retired its losing president.

Nation-building invites dissension, discord, and violence. These elements were remarkably absent from the young American nation, 1800–1828. Let's look more closely at the 1800 election.

The Federalist John Adams had been elected in 1796 without much opposition. But in 1800, the Republicans left no stone unturned in their efforts to discredit the Federalist candidate. President Adams, blamed for the unpopular Alien and Sedition laws, made a poor campaign. Federalists tried to discredit Thomas Jefferson with epithets of "Jacobin" and "Anarchist." When the vote was counted, it was found that Adams had been defeated; the Republicans had carried the entire South and New York and secured 8 of the 15 electoral votes cast by Pennsylvania.

Jefferson's election, however, was still uncertain. By a strange provision in the Constitution, presidential electors were required to vote for two persons without indicating which office each was to fill, the one receiving the highest number of votes to be president and the candidate standing next to be vice president. Remember, there were no political parties. Aaron Burr, the Republican candidate for vice president, had received the same number of votes as Jefferson; as neither had a majority the election was thrown into the House of Representatives, where the Federalists held the balance of power. Although it was well known that Burr was not even a candidate for president, his friends and many Federalists promoted his election to that high office. Had it not been for vigorous opposition by Alexander Hamilton, Aaron Burr (later convicted of treason) would have

been the third president of the United States. Not until the 36th ballot on February 17, 1801, was Jefferson officially president.[4] (James Stobaugh, *American History*)

■ ■ ■

The best title for this passage is:

A. The Revolution of 1800
B. Jefferson Steals the Election
C. Hamilton Is the Hero
D. President Aaron Burr?

VOCABULARY

A Man Without a Country and Other Tales
Edward Hale

Philip Nolan was as fine a young officer as there was in the "Legion of the West," as the Western division of our army was then called. When Aaron Burr made his first dashing expedition down to New Orleans in 1805, at Fort Massac, or somewhere above on the river, he met, as the Devil would have it, this gay, dashing, bright young fellow, at some dinner-party, I think. Burr marked him, talked to him, walked with him, took him a day or two's voyage in his flat-boat, and, in short, fascinated him. For the next year, barrack-life was very tame to poor Nolan. He occasionally availed himself of the permission the great man had given him to write to him. Long, high-worded, stilted letters the poor boy wrote and rewrote and copied. But never a line did he have in reply from the gay deceiver. The other boys in the garrison sneered at him, because he sacrificed in this unrequited affection for a politician the time which they devoted to Monongahela, hazard, and high-low-jack. Bourbon, euchre, and poker were still unknown. But one day Nolan had his revenge. This time Burr came down the river, not as an attorney seeking a place for his office, but as a disguised conqueror. He had defeated I know not how many district-attorneys; he had dined at I know not how many public dinners; he had been heralded in I know not how many Weekly Arguses, and it was rumored that he had an army behind him and an empire before him. It was a great day — his arrival — to poor Nolan. Burr had not been at the fort an hour before he sent for him. That evening he asked Nolan to take him out in his skiff, to show him a canebrake or a cotton-wood tree, as he said — really to seduce him; and by the time the sail was over, Nolan was enlisted body and soul. From that time, though he did not yet know it, he lived as *A Man Without a Country.*[5]

Suggested Vocabulary Words

A. That story shows about the time when Nolan's <u>braggadocio</u> must have broken down. At first, they said, he took a very high tone, considered his imprisonment a mere <u>farce</u>, affected to enjoy the voyage, and all that; but Phillips said that after he came out of his stateroom he never was the same man again.

B. When Captain Shaw was coming home — if, as I say, it was Shaw — rather to the surprise of every body they made one of the Windward Islands, and lay off and on for nearly a week. The boys said the officers were sick of salt-junk, and meant to have turtle-soup before they came home. But after several days the Warren came to the same <u>rendezvous</u>.

C. He looked very blank when he was told to get ready to join her. He had known enough of the signs of the sky to know that till that moment he was going "home." But this was a <u>distinct</u> evidence of something he had not thought of, perhaps — that there was no going home for him, even to a prison.

Use context clues to determine meaning. For instance, what is the meaning of the underlined word in this sentence?

<u>Organ</u> transplants are often rejected by the host.

(A) a musical instrument, (B) a part of a symphony, (C) part of a body. Clearly the answer is C. An organ, of course, is a musical instrument but its context demands another definition. Another one: The judge questioned the witness's <u>character</u>. (A) an actor in a play, (B) integrity, (C) a badge of honor. The answer is B.

Ten Wrong Assumptions

Here are three wrong ACT assumptions:

1. You can't study for the ACT. That is wrong. The ACT, an achievement, knowledge-based test is particularly responsive to ACT preparation and coaching.

2. Different states have different ACTs. Different states have different assessment tests but there is only ONE ACT that everyone takes.

3. The ACT has a passing score. Americans score about 21.1 on the ACT, so if you score higher than that you are in gravy! Schools like to see above 26 before they give scholarships, but that is all relative.

W R I T I N G

Writing Style

Which part of the sentence below is wrong?

The spirit of Liberty and the spirit of Nationality were once for all dead; (A) it might be for a time a pious duty, but it could not continue always expedient or (B) profitable to (C) mourning (D) for their loss. Yet this is the (E) feeling of the age of Trajan.[6]

M A T H

Word Problems

1. A merchant bought a bale of cloth containing just as many pieces as there were yards in each piece. The whole number of yards was 1,089. What was the number of pieces?

2. A regiment, consisting of 5,476 men, is to be formed into a solid square. How many men must be placed in each rank?

3. What is the depth of a cubical cistern which contains 5,000 gallons of water? (1 gallon = 231 cubic inches)

4. A farmer plants an orchard containing 8,464 trees, and has as many rows of trees as there are trees in each row. What is the number of trees in each row?[7]

"*You think your pain and your heartbreak are unprecedented in the history of the world, but then you read. It was books that taught me that the things that tormented me most were the very things that connected me with all the people who were alive, or who had ever been alive.*"[8]

— James Baldwin

E N G L I S H

Usage

Which part of the passage below is wrong?

God never wrought a miracle to refute atheism, because His ordinary works refute it. (A) A little philosophy inclines man's mind to atheism: depth in philosophy brings men's minds back to religion. (B) While the mind of man looks upon second causes, it may sometimes rest in them; (C) when it beholds the chain of them confederate and linked together, it must acknowledge a Providence. (D) That school which is most accused of atheism most clearly demonstrates the truth of religion.[9]

■ ■ ■

Use semicolons and colons with alacrity and sparingly.

Drawing Conclusions

It is in the second and third years of the child's life that the rapidity of the development of the mental processes is most apparent, and it is with that age that we may begin a closer examination. At first sight it might seem more reasonable to adopt a strictly chronological order, and to start with the infant from the day of his birth. Since, however, we can only interpret the mind of the child by our knowledge of our own mental processes, the study of the older child and of the later stages is in reality the simpler task. The younger the infant, the greater the difficulties become, so that our task is not so much to trace the development of a process from simple and early forms to those which are later and more complex, as to follow a track which is comparatively plain in later childhood, but grows faint as the beginnings of life are approached.

At the age, then, of two or three, the first quality of the child which may arrest our attention is his extreme imitativeness. Not that the imitation on his part is in any way conscious; but like a mirror he reflects in every action and in every word all that he sees and hears going on around him. We must recognise that in these early days his words and actions are not an independent growth, with roots in his own consciousness, but are often only the reflection of the words and actions of others. How completely speech is imitative is shown by the readiness with which a child contracts the local accent of his birthplace. The London parents awake with horror to find their baby an indubitable Cockney; the speech of the child bred beyond the Tweed proclaims him a veritable Scot. Again, some people are apt to adopt a somewhat peremptory tone in addressing little children. Often they do not trouble to give to their voices that polite or deferential inflection which they habitually use when speaking to older people. Listen to a party of nurses in the Park addressing their charges. As if they knew that their commands have small chance of being obeyed, they shout them with incisive force. "Come along at once when I tell you," they say. And the child faithfully reflects it all back, and is heard ordering his little sister about like a drill sergeant, or curtly bidding his grandmother change her seat to suit his pleasure. If we are to have pretty phrases and tones of voice, mothers must see to it that the child habitually hears no other. Again, mothers will complain that their child is deaf, or, at any rate, that he has the bad habit of responding to all remarks addressed

to him by saying, "What?" or, worse still, "Eh?" Often enough the reason that he does so is not that the child is deaf, nor that he is particularly slow to understand, but simply that he himself speaks so indistinctly that no matter what he says to the grown-up people around him, they bend over him and themselves utter the objectionable word.

We all hate the tell-tale child, and when a boy comes in from his walk and has much to say of the wicked behaviour of his little sister on the afternoon's outing, his mother is apt to see in this a most horrid tendency towards tale-bearing and currying of favour. She does not realise that day by day, when the children have come in from their walk, she has asked nurse in their hearing if they have been good children; and when, as often happens, they have not, the nurse has duly recounted their shortcomings, with the laudable notion of putting them to shame, and of emphasising to them the wickedness of their backsliding — and this son of hers is no hypocrite, but speaks only, as all children speak, in faithful reproduction of all that he hears. Those grown-up persons who are in charge of the children must realise that the child's vocabulary is their vocabulary, not his own. It is unfortunate, but I think not unavoidable, that so often almost the earliest words that the infant learns to speak are words of reproof, or chiding, or repression. The baby scolds himself with gusto, uttering reproof in the very tone of his elders: "No, no," "Naughty," or "Dirty," or "Baby shocked."[10]

■■ ■ ■

According to this passage, what is true?

I. Nervous boys can aggravate their parents.

II. Nervousness is congenital

III. Nervousness is a bio-chemical issue, not a psychological issue

A. I
B. II
C. III
D. All
E. None

The STRANGER

The Stranger is a novel by Albert Camus, published in 1942. Camus's first novel, it is perhaps his best-known work, and a key text of 20th-century philosophy. It is also a perennial favorite among freshman college English teachers. It is an example of existentialism, an aberrant and very appealing worldview that emphasizes the subjective.

The protagonist is Meursault, a French man (characterized by being largely emotionally detached, innately stoic, and iconic, who irrationally murders an Arab man whom he recognizes in French Algiers. The story is divided into parts one and two: Meursault's first-person narrative view before and after the murder.

Meursault lives completely in the present. As an existentialist, he has no reason to regret what he does because it is done; regret is redundant. It is a dishonest emotion. In this state of mind, Meursault lives fully in the present: he feels joy and frustration like every other human; he has a soul in that he is reflective about metaphysical, abstract reality. The difference is that his feelings are sensual; they are experienced and explained through his senses. In prison, while awaiting the execution of his death sentence by the guillotine, Meursault meets with a chaplain, but rejects his proffered opportunity of turning to God, explaining that God is a waste of his time. Although the chaplain persists in attempting to lead Meursault from his atheism, Meursault finally attacks him in a rage.

Meursault ultimately grasps the universe's indifference toward humankind (coming to terms with his execution):

> As if this great outburst of anger had purged all my ills, killed all my hopes, I looked up at the mass of signs and stars in the night sky and laid myself open for the first time to the benign indifference of the world. And finding it so much like myself, in fact so fraternal, I realized that I'd been happy, and that I was still happy. For the final consummation and for me to feel less lonely, my last wish was that there should be a crowd of spectators at my execution and that they should greet me with cries of hatred.[1]

Thematically, the absurd overrides responsibility; the notion of taking "responsibility" for one's acts is irrelevant. In fact, much like Henry Fleming in *The Red Badge of Courage*, despite his physical terror, Meursault is satisfied with his death; his discrete sensory perceptions only physically affect him, and thus are relevant to his being. Death gives Meursault revelation and happiness in the passive indifference of the world. To the existentialist, this is a sort of "peace." Central to that happiness is his pausing after the first, fatal gunshot when killing the Arab man. Interviewed by the magistrate, he mentions it did not matter that he paused and then shot four more times. Meursault is objective, there was no resultant, tangible difference: the Arab man died of one gunshot, and four more gunshots did not render him "more dead."

The absurdity is in society's creating a justice system to give meaning to his action via capital punishment: The fact that the death sentence had been read at eight o'clock at night and not at five o'clock . . . the fact that it had been handed down in the name of some vague notion called the French (or German, or Chinese) people — all of it seemed to detract from the seriousness of the decision.

Do you see why this book is so appealing and yet so dangerous? It places humankind at the center of the story, at the center of the universe. Sensory reality is holy empiricism, but without so much as a nod to the "gods" (as the empiricist Aristotle does). Existentialists invite humankind to embrace a rabid narcicism that is at once facile and deductive.

Nothing — nothing! — is meaningless. God has planned everything. He is in absolute control and everything He does is altogether good.

As if that blind rage has washed me clean, rid me of hope; for the first time, I that night alive with signs and stars, I opened myself to the gentle indifference of the world. Finding it so much life myself — so like a brother, really — I felt that I had been happy and that I was happy again. For everything to be consummated, for me to feel less alone, I had only to wish that there be a large crowd of spectators the day of my execution and that they greet me with cries of hate.[2]

M AT H

Word Problems

What rate of interest is implied in an offer to sell a house for $2,700 cash, or in annual installments each of $1,000 payable 1, 2, and 3 years from date?

Hint: The amount of $2,700 with interest for 3 years should be equal to the sum of the first payment with interest for 2 years, the amount of the second payment with interest for 1 year, and the third payment. Hence if r is the rate of interest and we write x for 1 + r, we have

$$2,700 \, x^3 = 1,000 \, x^2 + 1,000 \, x + 1,000.$$

Find the rate of interest implied in an offer to sell a house for $3,500 cash, or in annual installments each of $1,000 payable 1, 2, 3, and 4 years from date.

Find the rate of interest implied in an offer to sell a house for $3,500 cash, or $4,000 payable in annual installments each of $1,000, the first payable now.

The Writing Section
Essay

Bring something new or unique to the essay.

Remember that the graders are reading hundreds, maybe thousands of these on the same topic. So use an example or story that will make your essay memorable.

Grab their attention.

You have to count on the first few sentences to make the grader want to read more. You have about 15 seconds to persuade the grader to give you a 6 — which he will only do if he reads the whole thing carefully — instead of a safe 3 — which he will do if he doesn't like the beginning and he skims the essay.

Narrow your focus.

Your essay should prove a single point, allowing the reader to find the main idea and follow it from beginning to end.

More is always better.

While you want your syntax to be precise and cogent, the essay itself needs to fill the pages you are given!

Don't forget to proofread.

Spelling and grammatical errors can be interpreted as careless or bad writing. Don't rely on your computer's spell check — it has a way of making the odd correction go astray.

VOCABULARY

The Legend of Sleepy Hollow[3]
Washington Irving

The Legend of Sleepy Hollow, by New Yorker Washington Irving, is one of the most enduring and memorable short novels in American literary history. The inimical Ichabod Crane rides across the dark nights of all our imaginations.

Suggested Vocabulary Words

In this by-place of nature there abode, in a <u>remote</u> period of American history, that is to say, some thirty years since, a worthy wight of the name of Ichabod Crane, who sojourned, or, as he expressed it, "tarried," in Sleepy Hollow, for the purpose of instructing the children of the <u>vicinity</u>. He was a native of Connecticut, a State which supplies the Union with pioneers for the mind as well as for the forest, and sends forth yearly its legions of frontier woodmen and country schoolmasters. The cognomen of Crane was not inapplicable to his person. He was tall, but exceedingly <u>lank</u>, with narrow shoulders, long arms and legs, hands that dangled a mile out of his sleeves, feet that might have served for shovels, and his whole frame most loosely hung together. His head was small, and flat at top, with huge

ears, large green glassy eyes, and a long snipe nose, so that it looked like a weather-cock perched upon his <u>spindle</u> neck to tell which way the wind blew. To see him striding along the profile of a hill on a windy day, with his clothes bagging and fluttering about him, one might have mistaken him for the genius of famine descending upon the earth, or some scarecrow <u>eloped</u> from a cornfield.

His schoolhouse was a low building of one large room, rudely constructed of logs; the windows partly glazed, and partly patched with leaves of old copybooks. It was most <u>ingeniously</u> secured at vacant hours, by a withe twisted in the handle of the door, and stakes set against the window shutters; so that though a thief might get in with perfect ease, he would find some embarrassment in getting out — an idea most probably borrowed by the architect, Yost Van Houten, from the mystery of an eelpot.

The schoolhouse stood in a rather lonely but pleasant situation, just at the foot of a woody hill, with a brook running close by, and a <u>formidable</u> birch-tree growing at one end of it. From hence the low murmur of his pupils' voices, conning over their lessons, might be heard in a drowsy summer's day, like the hum of a beehive; interrupted now and then by the authoritative voice of the master, in the tone of menace or command, or, peradventure, by the <u>appalling</u> sound of the birch, as he urged some tardy loiterer along the flowery path of knowledge. Truth to say, he was a conscientious man, and ever bore in mind the golden maxim, "Spare the rod and spoil the child." Ichabod Crane's scholars certainly were not spoiled.

I would not have it imagined, however, that he was one of those cruel <u>potentates</u> of the school who joy in the smart of their subjects; on the contrary, he administered justice with <u>discrimination</u> rather than severity; taking the burden off the backs of the weak, and laying it on those of the strong. Your mere puny stripling, that winced at the least flourish of the rod, was passed by with <u>indulgence</u>; but the claims of justice were satisfied by inflicting a double portion on some little tough wrong-headed, broad-skirted Dutch urchin, who sulked and swelled and grew dogged and sullen beneath the birch. All this he called "doing his duty by their parents"; and he never inflicted a <u>chastisement</u> without following it by the assurance, so <u>consolatory</u> to the smarting <u>urchin</u>, that "he would remember it and thank him for it the longest day he had to live."

To the untrained eye, the stars and the planets are not distinguishable. It is customary to call them all alike "stars." But since the planets more or less rapidly change their places in the sky, in consequence of their revolution about the sun, while the stars proper seem to remain always in the same relative positions, the latter are spoken of as "fixed stars." In the beginnings of astronomy it was not known that the "fixed stars" had any motion independent of their apparent annual revolution with the whole sky about the earth as a seeming center. Now, however, we know that the term "fixed stars" is paradoxical, for there is not a single really fixed object in the whole celestial sphere. The apparent fixity in the positions of the stars is due to

stand fast in their tracks. Jupiter's speed in his orbit is about eight miles per second, Neptune's is less than three and one-half miles, and the earth's is about eighteen and one-half miles; while there are "fixed stars" which move two hundred or three hundred miles per second. They do not all, however, move with so great a velocity, for some appear to travel no faster than the planets. But in all cases, notwithstanding their real speed, long-continued and exceedingly careful observations are required to demonstrate that they are moving at all. No more overwhelming impression of the frightful depths of space in which the stars are buried can be obtained than by reflecting upon the fact that a star whose actual motion across the line of sight amounts to two hundred miles per second does not change its apparent place in the sky, in the course of a thousand years, sufficiently to be noticed by the casual observer of the heavens!

their immense distance, combined with the shortness of the time during which we are able to observe them. It is like viewing the plume of smoke issuing from a steamer, hull down, at sea: if one does not continue to watch it for a long time it appears to be motionless, although in reality it may be traveling at great speed across the line of sight. Even the planets seem fixed in position if one watches them for a single night only, and the more distant ones do not sensibly change their places, except after many nights of observation. Neptune, for instance, moves but little more than two degrees in the course of an entire year, and in a month its change of place is only about one-third of the diameter of the full moon.

Yet, fixed as they seem, the stars are actually moving with a speed in comparison with which, in some cases, the planets might almost be said to

There is one vast difference between the motions of the stars and those of the planets to which attention should be at once called: the planets, being under the control of a central force emanating from their immediate master, the sun, all move in the same direction and in orbits concentric about the sun; the stars, on the other hand, move in every conceivable direction and have no apparent center of motion, for all efforts to discover such a center have failed. At one time, when theology had finally to accept the facts of science, a grandiose conception arose in some pious minds, according to which the Throne of God was situated at the exact center of His Creation, and, seated there, He watched the magnificent spectacle of the starry systems obediently revolving around Him. Astronomical discoveries and speculations seemed for a time to afford some warrant for this view, which was, moreover, an acceptable substitute for the abandoned geocentric theory in minds that could only conceive of God as a superhuman artificer, constantly admiring his own work. No longer ago than the middle of the nineteenth century a German astronomer, Maedler, believed that he had actually found the location of the center about which the stellar universe revolved. He placed it in the group of the Pleiades, and upon his authority an extraordinary imaginative picture was sometimes drawn of the star Alcyone, the brightest of the Pleiades, as the very seat of the Almighty. This idea even seemed to gain a kind of traditional support from the mystic significance, without known historical origin, which has for many ages, and

among widely separated peoples, been attached to the remarkable group of which Alcyone is the chief. But since Maedler's time it has been demonstrated that the Pleiades cannot be the center of revolution of the universe, and, as already remarked, all attempts to find or fix such a center have proved abortive. Yet so powerful was the hold that the theory took upon the popular imagination, that even today astronomers are often asked if Alcyone is not the probable site of "Jerusalem the Golden."

If there were a discoverable center of predominant gravitative power, to which the motions of all the stars could be referred, those motions would appear less mysterious, and we should then be able to conclude that the universe was, as a whole, a prototype of the subsidiary systems of which it is composed. We should look simply to the law of gravitation for an explanation, and, naturally, the center would be placed within the opening enclosed by the Milky Way. If it were there the Milky Way itself should exhibit signs of revolution about it, like a wheel turning upon its hub. No theory of the star motions as a whole could stand which failed to take account of the Milky Way as the basis of all. But the very form of that divided wreath of stars forbids the assumption of its revolution about a center.

Even if it could be conceived as a wheel having no material center it would not have the form which it actually presents. As was shown in Chapter 2, there is abundant evidence of motion in the Milky Way; but it is not motion of the system as a whole, but motion affecting its separate parts. Instead of all moving one way, the galactic stars, as far as their movements can be inferred, are governed by local influences and conditions. They appear to travel crosswise and in contrary directions, and perhaps they eddy around foci where great numbers have assembled; but of a universal revolution involving the entire mass we have no evidence. (Garrett P. Serviss,[4] *Curiosities of the Sky*)

■ ■ ■

The chief purpose of this essay is:

A. to examine stars and planets
B. to explore the causes of sun spots
C. to compare and contrast the apparent motion of planets and stars
D. none

Drawing Conclusions

Ichabod Crane had a soft and foolish heart towards the sex; and it is not to be wondered at that so tempting a morsel soon found favor in his eyes, more especially after he had visited her in her paternal mansion. Old Baltus Van Tassel was a perfect picture of a thriving, contented, liberal-hearted farmer. He seldom, it is true, sent either his eyes or his thoughts beyond the boundaries of his own farm; but within those everything was snug, happy, and well-conditioned. He was satisfied with his wealth, but not proud of it; and piqued himself upon the hearty abundance, rather than the style in which he lived. His stronghold was situated on the banks of the Hudson, in one of those green, sheltered, fertile nooks in which the Dutch farmers are so fond of nestling. A great elm tree spread its broad branches over it, at the foot of which bubbled up a spring of the softest and sweetest water, in a little well formed of a barrel; and then stole sparkling away through the grass, to a neighboring brook, that babbled along among alders and dwarf willows. Hard by the farmhouse was a vast barn, that might have served for a church; every window and crevice of which seemed bursting forth with the treasures of the farm; the flail was busily resounding within it from morning to night; swallows and martins skimmed twittering about the eaves; and rows of pigeons, some with one eye turned up, as if watching the weather, some with their heads under their wings or buried in their bosoms, and others swelling, and cooing, and bowing about their dames, were enjoying the sunshine on the roof. Sleek unwieldy porkers were grunting in the repose and abundance of their pens, from whence sallied forth, now and then, troops of sucking pigs, as if to snuff the air.

A stately squadron of snowy geese were riding in an adjoining pond, convoying whole fleets of ducks; regiments of turkeys were gobbling through the farmyard, and Guinea fowls fretting about it, like ill-tempered housewives, with their peevish, discontented cry. Before the barn door strutted the gallant cock, that pattern of a husband, a warrior and a fine gentleman, clapping his burnished wings and crowing in the pride and gladness of his heart — sometimes tearing up the earth with his feet, and then generously calling his ever-hungry family of wives and children to enjoy the rich morsel which he had discovered.

■ ■ ■

What is true about this character?

I. Crane is an outgoing, popular man.
II. Crane is a hardworking man.
III. Crane is a good teacher.
IV. Crane is a reticent, private person.

    A. I
    B. II
    C. III
    D. IV
    E. None
    F. All
    G. I and IV
    H. II and IV

Writing Style

Which part of the sentence below is wrong?

It cannot be doubted (A) that the minds of a vast number of men would be left poor shrunken things, soldiers and the like, if (B) there were taken out of men's minds vain opinions, false valuations, imaginations as one (C) would, and the (D) like.

Correct Sentences

(A) On one occasion, I heard someone say "he is bigger than(B) him."

(A) Sometimes it is hard to recognize (B) who is having the better time, (C) him or me.

(A) I could hear (B) them speaking (C) to he and to she.

Elaboration — Effective writers include information in their arguments that support their main ideas. This is called elaboration. Elaboration includes facts, statistic, sensory details, anecdotes, examples, and quotes. Methods of elaboration include questioning, exploring, and research.

Is There ANYTHING ELSE?

My life closed twice before its close; It yet remains to see
If Immortality unveil A third event to me,
So huge, so hopeless to conceive, As these that twice befell.
Parting is all we know of heaven, And all we need of hell.[1]

Emily Dickinson uses the metaphor of death to describe the catastrophe that two terrible events caused. Were these the deaths of two friends? Two unrequited loves? We really don't know. What matters is that the pain of these events was so sharp that Dickinson feels as if her life ended. Loss exacerbates Dickinson's already fragile metaphysics.

What happens after death, in immortality? Well we know, don't we?

The last two lines of this poem present a powerful paradox; parting is heaven to some and hell to others. We part with those who die and — hopefully — go to heaven, which is, ironically, an eternal happiness for them; however, we who are left behind suffer the pain (hell) of their deaths (parting).

Is there any comfort in this poem? Not if one is the realist Emily Dickinson whose cold New England intellectualism offers scant protection against the frigid exigencies of death! It is fun to talk about birds walking on sidewalks as long as one does not have to think about ultimate things.

But we all have to think about ultimate things once in a while. In "a while" for most of us is death. Where will you spend eternity? If the Lord Jesus is your Savior, you know where you will spend eternity.

Contrast this tentativeness with Dickinson's New England predecessor Puritan Edward Taylor (From "I Prepare a Place"):

But thats not all: Now from Deaths realm, erect,
Thou gloriously gost to thy Fathers Hall:
And pleadst their Case preparst them place well dect
All with thy Merits hung. Blesst Mansions all.
Dost ope the Doore locks fast 'gainst Sins that so
These Holy Rooms admit them may thereto.[2]

I like to read Emily Dickinson's poems. I like to drink vanilla milk shakes, too. But not too many and never for nourishment and life. How about you?

"Life like a dream is lived alone . . ." (Marlow in *Heart of Darkness*).[3] I know someone who believes that to be true. One of my students rarely speaks. Indeed, he seems virtually unable to do anything. He is frozen in time. Last year he tried to commit suicide. Thankfully, he failed. When he was driving home from the hospital with his obviously irritated mom, this young man sat sullen and broken. His mom, furious, stopped the car, looked at her son, opened the car pocket and said, "Here is a loaded gun, finish the job."

Thankfully, my poor student could not finish the job; but the loss of trust he experienced more or less ended his life as he knew it. Over the next year, slowly, steadily he made progress. Finally, thanks to the love of a young lady, the young man has blossomed! Life like a dream is lived alone. . . . But in those magical moments when a friend, a spouse, a kindred spirit joins us — we experience hope and life.

No one likes to be on the losing side — unless one is breaking up a fight in public high school. We teachers are taught, when breaking up a fight, to hold the losing student — why? Because the losing student wants an excuse to quit. You give him the excuse. Well, I chose the winning side last week and it nearly killed me! I rushed from in front of my door to break up a fight. I go to the doctor tomorrow to see how much damage the winner did to my artificial hip. Life is like that, isn't it? We find sometimes that grabbing the losing cause can bring us winning. Think about it.

V OCABULARY

Through the Iron Bars[4]
Emile Cammaerts

Every war causes excesses and atrocities, but World War I created more than its share. In particular, as Germany rushed across the lowlands of neutral Belgium to conquer France, it subjugated Belgium and occupied it as an unfriendly government for the next four years. There is much debate about how bad the Germans really were, but propaganda, among the allies, was magnificent.

M A T H

Graphs

Solve graphically:

1. $x^2 - 5x + 4 = 0$

2. $x^2 + 5x + 4 = 0$

3. $x^2 + 5x - 4 = 0$

4. $x^2 - 5x - 4 = 0$

5. $x^2 - 4x + 4 = 0$

Suggested Vocabulary Words

A. The German occupation of Belgium may be roughly divided into two periods: Before the fall of Antwerp, when the hope of prompt deliverance was still <u>vivid</u> in every heart and when the German policy, in spite of its frightfulness, had not yet assumed its most <u>ruthless</u> and <u>systematic</u> character; and after the fall of the great fortress, when the yoke of the conqueror weighed more heavily on the <u>vanquished</u> shoulders and when the Belgian population, grim and <u>resolute</u>, began to struggle to preserve its honour and loyalty and to resist the ever increasing pressure of the enemy to bring it into complete submission and to use it as a tool against its own army and its own King.

B. I am only concerned here with the second period. The story of the German <u>atrocities</u> committed in some parts of the country at the beginning of the occupation is too well known to require any further comment. Every honest man, in Allied and neutral countries, has made up his mind on the subject. No unprejudiced person can hesitate between the evidence brought forward by the Belgian Commission of Enquiry and the vague denials, paltry excuses and <u>insolent calumnies</u> opposed to it by the German Government and the Pro-German Press.

C. Besides, in a way, the atrocities committed during the last days of August 1914 ought not to be considered as the culminating point of Belgium's <u>martyrdom</u>. They have, of course, appealed to the imagination of the masses, they have filled the world with horror and <u>indignation</u>, but they did not extend all over the country, as the present oppression does; they only affected a few thousand men and women, instead of involving hundreds of thousands.[5]

WRITING

Active Voice

Always write in active voice. Change the passive voice sentences to active voice sentences.

1. In the large room some forty or fifty students were walking about while the parties were preparing.

2. This was done by taking off the coat and vest and binding a great thick leather garment on, which reached to the knees.

3. We were joined by the crowd, and used our lungs as well as any.[7]

ENGLISH

Writing Style

Which part of the sentence below is wrong?

His (A) bravery during this painful operation and the (B) fortitude he had shown in heading the last charge in the recent action (C); though, he was wounded at the time and had been unable to use his right arm, and was the only officer left in his regiment, out of twenty who were alive the day before, (D) inspired every one with admiration.

SCIENCE

Calculations

The following is a chart of tidal levels after sunset (and as the moon rises):

Hour of moon's transit after sunset:

0	1	2	3	4	5	6	7	8	9	10	11

Tidal position:

0	-20m	-30m	-50m	-60m	-60m	-60m	-40m	-10m	+10m	+20m	+10m

If sunset is 5:45 p.m., and at that time the tide is at X m, what is the approximate tidal level at 11 p.m.?

A. -60m   B. -35m   C. -65m   D. +10m

READING

Credibility

By the Waters of Babylon . . .

"By the waters of Babylon, there we sat down, yea, we wept, when we remembered Zion."

What prophetic spirit inspired Cardinal Mercier when he chose this psalm for the text of his sermon, on the occasion of the second anniversary of their Independence (July 21st, 1916), which the Belgians celebrated in exile and captivity? It was in the great Gothic church, in Brussels, under the arches of Ste. Gudule, at the close of a service for the soldiers fallen during the war, the very last patriotic ceremony tolerated by the Germans. Socialists, Liberals, Catholics crowded the nave, forgetting their old quarrels, united in a common worship, the worship of their threatened country, of their oppressed liberties.

"How shall we sing the Lord's song in a strange land?" His audience imagined that the preacher alluded only to a spiritual captivity, that he meant: "How shall we celebrate our freedom in this German prison?" And they listened, like the first Christians in the catacombs, dreading to hear the tramp of the soldiers before the door. The Cardinal pursued his fearless address: "The psalm ends with curses and maledictions. We will not utter them against our enemies. We are not of the Old but of the New Testament. We do not follow the old law: an eye for an eye, a tooth for a tooth, but the new law of Love and Christian brotherhood. But we do not forget that even above Love stands Justice. If our brother sins, how can we pretend to love him if we do not wish that his sins should be punished. . . ."

Such was the tenor of the Cardinal's address, the greatest Christian address inspired by the war, uttered under the most tragic and moving circumstances. For the people knew by then the danger of speaking out their minds in conquered Belgium; they knew that some German spies were in the church taking note of every word, of every gesture. Still, they could not restrain their feelings, and, at the close of the sermon, when the organ struck up the Brabançonne, they cheered and cheered again, thankful to feel, for an instant, the dull weight of oppression lifted from their shoulders by the indomitable spirit of their old leader.

What strikes us now, when recalling this memorable ceremony, is not so much the address itself as the choice of its text: "For they that carried us away captive required of us a song."

Many of those who listened to Cardinal Mercier on July 21st, 1916, have no doubt been "carried away" by now, and they have sung. They have sung the Brabançonne and the "Lion de Flandres" as a last defiance to their oppressors whilst those long cattle trains, packed with human cattle, rolled in wind and rain towards the German frontier. And the echo of their song still haunts the sleep of every honest man.[9]

How does the author influence the reader?

I. By using facts.
II. By referencing an emotive scriptural passage
III. By using archetypical villain types
IV. By offering pejorative motifs

   A. I
   B. II
   C. III
   D. IV
   E. None
   F. All
   G. I and IV
   H. II, III, and IV

How does the author influence the reader through this picture?

I. By using facts.
II. By referencing an emotive scene; a man attacking a child
III. By using caricatures
IV. By offering pejorative motifs
V. By appealing to religion

   A. I
   B. II
   C. III
   D. IV
   E. V
   F. All
   G. I, II, IV, V
   H. II, III, and IV

Life, Like a Dream, Is

LIVED ALONE

Joseph Conrad's *Heart of Darkness* is a story of a histrionic English official named Marlowe who visits the most uncivilized parts of late 19th-century Africa to discover what happened to an erudite, arcane English station chief named Kurtz. The journey is nothing less than a naturalistic journey into the human soul. We journey deeper and deeper into the heart of darkness. It was very quiet there.

Marlowe comments, "At night sometimes the roll of drums behind the curtain of trees would run up the river and remain sustained faintly, as if hovering in the air high over our heads, till the first break of day. Whether it meant war, peace, or prayer we could not tell. The dawns were heralded by the descent of a chill stillness; the wood-cutters slept, their fires burned low; the snapping of a twig would make you start. We were wanderers on a prehistoric earth, on an earth that wore the aspect of an unknown

planet. We could have fancied ourselves the first of men taking possession of an accursed inheritance, to be subdued at the cost of profound anguish and of excessive toil. But suddenly, as we struggled round a bend, there would be a glimpse of rush walls, of peaked grass-roofs, a burst of yells, a whirl of black limbs, a mass of hands clapping, of feet stamping, of bodies swaying, of eyes rolling, under the droop of heavy and motionless foliage. The steamer toiled along slowly on the edge of a black and incomprehensible frenzy. The pre-historic man was cursing us, praying to us, welcoming us — who could tell? We were cut off from the comprehension of our surroundings; we glided past like phantoms, wondering and secretly appalled, as sane men would be before an enthusiastic outbreak in a madhouse. We could not understand because we were too far and could not remember because we were travelling in the night of first ages, of those ages that are gone, leaving hardly a sign — and no memories."[1]

Kurtz, apparently has gone off the deep end — he has, in effect, given into his "darker side" and become a savage. The irony in this turn of events is obvious: Kurtz, the civilized man seeking to civilize the savage, becomes, instead, a savage himself. Poor Kurtz, full of hope and faith, has lost it all. "One evening coming in with

a candle I was startled to hear him say a little tremulously, 'I am lying here in the dark waiting for death.' The light was within a foot of his eyes. I forced myself to murmur, 'Oh, nonsense!' and stood over him as if transfixed." Anything approaching the change that came over his features I have never seen before, and hope never to see again. Oh, I wasn't touched. I was fascinated. It was as though a veil had been rent. I saw on that ivory face the expression of sombre pride, of ruthless power, of craven terror — of an intense and hopeless despair. Did he live his life again in every detail of desire, temptation, and surrender during that supreme moment of complete knowledge? He cried in a whisper at some image, at some vision — he cried out twice, a cry that was no more than a breath: "'The horror! The horror!' The horror! The horror!"[2]

Poor Kurtz. Poor 21st-century America. They (we) have looked into the abyss, and we see no loving God. What is the horror to Kurtz? He has lost his faith in a loving God. His world is a naturalistic, impersonal, cruel jungle. "I thought his memory was like the other memories of the dead that accumulate in every man's life — a vague impress on the brain of shadows that had fallen on it in their swift and final passage; but before the high and ponderous door, between the tall houses of a street as still and decorous as a well-kept alley in a cemetery, I had a vision of him on the stretcher, opening his mouth voraciously, as if to devour all the earth with all its mankind. He lived then before me; he lived as much as he had ever lived — a shadow insatiable of splendid appearances, of frightful realities; a shadow darker than the shadow of the night, and draped nobly in the folds of a gorgeous eloquence. The vision seemed to enter the house with me — the stretcher, the phantom-bearers, the wild crowd of obedient worshippers, the gloom of the forests, the glitter of the reach between the murky bends, the beat of the drum, regular and muffled like the beating of a heart — the heart of a conquering darkness. It was a moment of triumph for the wilderness, an invading and vengeful rush which, it seemed to me, I would have to keep back alone for the salvation of another soul. And the memory of what I had heard him say afar there, with the horned shapes stirring at my back, in the glow of fires, within the patient woods, those broken phrases came back to me, were heard again in their ominous and terrifying simplicity. I remembered his abject pleading, his abject threats, the colossal scale of his vile desires, the meanness, the torment, the tempestuous anguish of his soul. And later on I seemed to see his collected languid manner, when he said one day, 'This lot of ivory now is really mine. The Company did not pay for it. I collected it myself at a very great personal risk. I am afraid they will try to claim it as theirs though. H'm. It is a difficult case. What do you think I ought to do — resist? Eh? I want no more than justice.' . . . He wanted no more than justice — no more than justice. I rang the bell before a mahogany door on the first floor, and while I waited he seemed to stare at me out of the glassy panel — stare with that wide and immense stare embracing, condemning, loathing all the universe. I seemed to hear the whispered cry, 'The horror! The horror!' "[3]

My friends, brothers, and sisters, I have looked into the abyss and I see a God. A real, loving God. A God who loved the world so much that He sent His only begotten Son. Do you? To the naturalist, as Marlow muttered, life like a dream is lived alone. To a Christian, there is life, and life more abundant than we can imagine!

ENGLISH

Usage: Shall and Will

Traditionally, shall is used for the future tense with the first-person pronouns I and we: I shall, we shall. Will is used with the first-person (again, I refer to traditional usage) only when we wish to express determination. The opposite is true for the second-person (you) and third-person (he, she, it, they) pronouns: Will is used in the future tense, and shall is used only when we wish to express determination or to emphasize certainty.

Although this is the traditional distinction between shall and will, many linguists and grammarians have challenged this rule, and it is often not observed, even in formal writing. Personally, I still try to remember to follow it, even though the use of shall seems to be declining.

Here are some examples, applying the traditional rule.

First-person pronouns:

> I shall attend the meeting. (Simple future tense)

> I will attend the meeting. (Simple future tense but with an added sense of certainty or determination)

> Regardless of the weather, we shall go to the city. (Simple future tense)

> Regardless of the weather, we will go to the city. (Simple future tense but with an added sense of certainty or determination)

Second-person pronoun:

> You will receive a refund. (Simple future tense)

> You shall receive a refund. (Simple future tense but with an added sense of certainty or determination)

Third-person pronoun:

> It will be done on time. (Simple future tense)

> It shall be done on time. (Simple future tense but with an added sense of certainty or determination)

Will is usually the better choice with second- and third-person pronouns. If we wish to express certainty or determination, we do not need to use shall but can provide emphasis by using an adverb, such as certainly or definitely. However, the distinction between shall and will that I mention above is useful with first-person pronouns.[4]

Examine the following sentences, and justify the use of shall and will, or correct them if wrongly used:

1. Thou shalt have a suit, and that of the newest cut; the wardrobe keeper shall have orders to supply you.

2. "I shall not run," answered Herbert stubbornly.

An idiom is a phrase whose meaning is not immediately apparent from the meanings of its individual words. Occasionally the ACT will include some idioms that you will need to interpret in the context of the reading passage. For example, "Watching my grandchildren was no effort to the eye" means "watching my grandchildren was easy, even pleasant."

Math Test Breakdown

Arithmetic: 20%

Basic Math — Definitions and Principles
Variable Linear Equations
Signed Numbers/Absolute Value
Averages
Multiples and Factors
Ordering Numbers
Percents
Probability
Proportions
Ratios
Powers and Roots
Substitution
Factoring Quadratic Equations

Beginning Algebra: 20%

Polynomials
Variables to Relationships
Linear Equations
Exponents
Tables/Charts/Graphs
Complex Numbers
Functions
Inequalities
Matrices
Quadratic Inequalities
Quadratic Formula
Systems of Equations

Coordinate Geometry: 30%

Rational Expressions
Solving Radical Equations
Distance and Midpoint
Conic Sections
Equations of Lines
Parallel and Perpendicular Lines
Number Line/Coordinate Plane
Sequences and Series
Right Triangles
Trigonometry

Plane Geometry: 30%

Polygons
Area/Perimeter/Volume

SCIENCE

Analyzing Data

I have said that the entire Mafula community is for many purposes a composite whole. In many matters they act together as a community. This is especially so as regards the big feast, which I shall describe hereafter. It is so also to a large extent in some other ceremonies and in the organisation of hunting and fishing parties and sometimes in fighting. And the community as a whole has its boundaries, within which are the general community rights of hunting, fishing, etc., as above stated.

But the relationship between a group of villages of any one clan within the community is of a much closer and more intimate character than is that of the community as a whole. These villages of one clan have a common amidi or chief, a common emone or clubhouse, and a practice of mutual support and help in fighting for redress of injury to one or more of the individual members; and there is a special social relationship between their members, and in particular clan exogamy prevails with them, marriages between people of the same clan, even though in different villages, being reprobated almost as much as are marriages between people of the same village. Nonetheless, the clans separate in village settings.[5] (Williason, *The Mafula*)

Which of the following diagrams best represents what a Mafula village looks like?

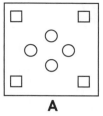

A

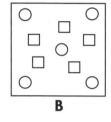

B

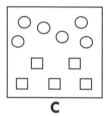

C

VOCABULARY

The Principles of Gothic Ecclesiastical Architecture[6]
Matthew Holbeche Bloxam

Amongst the <u>vestiges</u> of antiquity which abound in this country, are the visible memorials of those nations which have succeeded one another in the occupancy of this island. To the age of our Celtic ancestors, the earliest possessors of its soil, is ascribed the erection of those altars and temples of all but primeval <u>antiquity</u>, the Cromlechs and Stone Circles which lie scattered over the land; and these are conceived to have been derived from the Phoenicians, whose merchants first introduced amongst the aboriginal Britons the arts of incipient civilization. Of these most ancient relics the prototypes appear, as described in Holy Writ, in the pillar raised at Bethel by Jacob, in the altars erected by the <u>Patriarchs</u>, and in the circles of stone set up by Moses at the foot of Mount Sinai, and by Joshua at Gilgal. Many of these structures, perhaps from their very rudeness, have survived the <u>vicissitudes</u> of time, whilst there scarce remains a vestige of the temples erected in this island by the Romans; yet it is from Roman edifices that we derive, and can trace by a gradual <u>transition</u>, the progress of that peculiar kind of architecture called Gothic, which presents in its later stages the most striking contrast that can be imagined to its original <u>precursor</u>.

The Romans having conquered almost the whole of Britain in the first century, retained possession of the southern parts for nearly four hundred years; and during their occupancy they not only instructed the natives in the arts of civilization, but also with their aid, as we learn from Tacitus, began at an early period to erect temples and public <u>edifices</u>, though doubtless much inferior to those at Rome, in their municipal towns and cities. The Christian religion was also early introduced, but for a time its progress was slow; nor was it till the conversion of Constantine, in the fourth century, that it was openly tolerated by the state, and churches were publicly constructed for its worshippers; though even before that event, as we are led to infer from the testimony of Gildas, the most ancient of our native historians, particular structures were appropriated for the performance of its divine mysteries: for that historian <u>alludes</u> to the British Christians as reconstructing the churches which had, in the Dioclesian persecution, been levelled to the ground.[7]

Define the suggested vocabulary words underlined in the above passage.

R EADING

Details

The churches of this country were anciently so constructed as to display, in their internal arrangement, certain appendages designed with architectonic skill, and adapted purposely for the celebration of mass and other religious offices.

At the Reformation, when the ritual was changed and many of the formularies of the church of Rome were discarded, some of such appendages were destroyed; whilst others, though suffered to exist, more or less in a mutilated condition, were no longer appropriated to the particular uses for which they had been originally designed.

On entering a church through the porch on the north or south side, or at the west end, we sometimes perceive on the right hand side of the door, at a convenient height from the ground, often beneath a niche, and partly projecting from the wall, a stone basin: this was the stoup, or receptacle for holy water, called also the aspersorium, into which each individual dipped his finger and crossed himself when passing the threshold of the sacred edifice. The custom of aspersion at the church door appears to have been derived from an ancient usage of the heathens, amongst whom, according to Sozomen, the priest was accustomed to sprinkle such as entered into a temple with moist branches of olive. The stoup is sometimes found inside the church, close by the door; but the stone appendage appears to have been by no means general, and probably in most cases a movable vessel of metal was provided for the purpose; and in an inventory of ancient church goods at St. Dunstan's, Canterbury, taken A.D. 1500, we find mentioned "a stope off lede for the holy watr atte the church dore." We do not often find the stoup of so ancient a date as the twelfth century; one much mutilated, but apparently of that era, may however be met with inside the little Norman church of Beaudesert, Warwickshire, near to the south door.

The porch was often of a considerable size, and had frequently a groined ceiling, with an apartment above; it was anciently used for a variety of religious rites, for before the Reformation considerable portions of the marriage and baptismal services, and also much of that relating to the churching of women, were here performed, being commenced "ante ostium ecclesiae," and concluded in the church; and these are set forth in the rubric of the Manual or service-book, according to the use of Sarum, containing those and other occasional offices.[8] (Bloxam)

■ ■ ■

The porch was very large in early pre-Reformation English churches because:

A. in Roman Catholic liturgy considerable portions of the marriage and baptismal services occur on the porch.

B. the porch reminds the congregant of the Temple of Solomon.

C. the porch offered a more comfortable, generous feeling to the worship participants.

D. the porch was a convention important to early Roman architecture.

Some ACT test takers use their wrist watches as a stop watch, not as a time piece. For example, if they have a 45 minute test they set their watch at 45 minutes. Caution: turn off the alarm!

M ATH

Geometric Word Problems

A stream flows at the rate of a miles an hour, and a man can row in still water b miles an hour. How far can the man row up the stream in an hour? In six hours? How far down the stream in an hour? In three hours?

W RITING

Writing Style

Which part of the sentence below is wrong?

When I say a great man, I not (A) only mean a man intellectually great but also morally, (B) who has no preference for diplomacy at all events which is mean, petty, and underhanded to secure ends which can be secured by an honest policy equally (C) good, who prefers to get at truth by untruthful tricks, and (D) who considers truth a carp which is to be caught by the bait falsehood. We cannot call a petty intriguer great, though we may be forced to call an unscrupulous man by that name.

The Closing of the
AMERICAN MIND

SCRIPTURE

"It has given me great joy to find some of your children walking in the truth, just as the Father commanded us. And now, dear lady, I am not writing you a new command but one we have had from the beginning. I ask that we love one another. And this is love: that we walk in obedience to his commands. As you have heard from the beginning, his command is that you walk in love."

~ 2 John 1:1–6

Yale professor Allan Bloom, in *The Closing of the American Mind*,[1] argues that as it now stands, post-moderns (an expression describing the generation that emerged after 1990 that rejected modernist faith in science and embraced a form of subjectivity) have a powerful image of what a perfect body is and pursue it incessantly. But deprived of guidance, they no longer have any image of a perfect soul and hence do not long to have gain that vision before chaos ensues. The eternal conflict between good and evil has been replaced with "I'm okay, you're okay." Men and women once paid for difficult choices with their reputations, their sanity, and even their lives. But no more. Post-modern America has no-fault automobile accidents, no-fault insurance, no-consequence choices. The Church has struggled in this era.

> O father, father
> Gone from us, lost to us,
> The church lies bereft,
> Alone,
> Desecrated, desolated.
> And the heathen shall build
> On the ruins
> Their world without God.
> I see it.
> I see it.[2]

Our society purports to build their world without God. But the dance is almost over. Before long, post-modern man will lose his bearings. Post-modern sensibility does not lament the loss of narrative coherence any more than the loss of being. But the loss will be acutely felt when the post-modern faces crises, say, death. This crisis is one that drove many old, earlier, romantics back to the faith, too. The romanticism of Ralph Waldo Emerson is fine and good on a warm, spring day. But is a paltry offering to a crying, dying soul.

A sidebar is the computer. This has hastened the stampede to post-modernism. The computer has transformed knowledge into information, that is, coded messages within a system of transmission and communication. Analysis of this knowledge calls for a pragmatic approach to communication insofar as the phrasing of messages, their transmission and reception, must follow rules in order to be accepted by those who judge them. Reality, then, originates and ends in the recipient of the IM or e-mail.

From T.S. Eliot in "The Rock":

Where is the Life we have lost in living?
Where is the wisdom we have lost in knowledge?
Where is the knowledge we have lost in information?[3]

PRAYER POINTS

REVERENTIAL
FEAR OF GOD

"The LORD listened and heard. A scroll of remembrance was written in his presence concerning those who feared the LORD and honored his name."

~ Malachi 3:16

Thus, the individual, and by implications, society, compartmentalizes knowledge. The compartmentalization of knowledge and the dissolution of epistemic coherence is a concern for Christians. If knowledge is subjective then truth will be the next victim. If post-moderns don't believe a tree is a tree, then what will they do with faith? There will no longer be a redemptive narrative for millions of post-modern Americans whose subjectivity has stampeded any semblance of metaphysical objectivity from the barn.

Furthermore, the loss of a continuous, historically true, biblical narrative in American society was/is disastrous. Post-modernism breaks the subject into heterogeneous moments of subjectivity that do not cohere into an identity. Quite literally separating the parts into parts means that there is no whole.

What does this mean? It means that millions of Americans will not know who they are. Really. Their subjective interpretations of who they think they are — roughly based on perceived needs and desires — will not suffice to create a coherent whole. Like Oedipus in Sophocles' *Oedipus Rex*, Americans will rail against the fates while standing squarely in the path of inevitable destruction — and not knowing what is happening.

> What's done was well done. Thou canst never shake
> My firm belief. A truce to argument.
> For, had I sight, I know not with what eyes
> I could have met my father in the shades,
> Or my poor mother, since against the twain
> I sinned, a sin no gallows could atone.
> Aye, but, ye say, the sight of children joys
> A parent's eyes. What, born as mine were born?
>
> Dark, dark! The horror of darkness, like a shroud,
> Wraps me and bears me on through mist and cloud.
> Ah me, ah me! What spasms athwart me shoot,
> What pangs of agonizing memory?[4]

"Only the fool, fixed in his folly, may think he can turn the wheel on which he turns," T.S. Eliot writes.[5] Post-modern Americans, sooner or later, will fall and not know what knocked them down.

I ask that we love one another. And this is love: that we walk in obedience to His commands. As you have heard from the beginning, His command is that you walk in love.

"A book is the only place in which you can examine a fragile thought without breaking it, or explore an explosive idea without fear it will go off in your face. It is one of the few havens remaining where a man's mind can get both provocation and privacy."[6]

— Edward P. Morgan

R E A D I N G

Interpretation

"Slumber and waking" are examples of what type of metaphors?

A. hyperbole
B. ethos, logos, and pathos
C. personification
D. simile

The following are metaphors for "love" in the poem "Love."

A. A red, red rose.
B. A cool day in summer
C. A breach in the walls
D. A cold breeze

W R I T I N G

Writing Style

Which part of the sentence below is wrong?

The rest of the generals were willing to surrender unconditionally, (A) depressed by this unforeseen calamity; (B) only the young colonel, who retained his presence of mind, represented to them that they were increasing the difficulties of a position in itself very difficult (C) by their conduct.

1914 and Other Poems[7]
Rupert Brooke

Never has a war so devastated a generation as World War I cruelly injured England. Author Tim Cross compiled an anthology entitled *The Lost Voices of World War I: An International Anthology of Writers, Poets and Playwrights*, with works by more than 50 authors who died in the four years of fighting in World War I. To read the works of these authors is unsettling, because the reader is constantly aware of how much talent was lost when these men died so young. The appendix to Cross's anthology is even more tragic in its implications, for it is a necrology (i.e., death list) of creative people who were killed from 1914 to 1918. As Cross says, "A complete list of all poets, playwrights, writers, artists, architects, and composers who died as a result of the First World War is an impossible task," but even so, he has compiled a list of about 750 names.

Cross's list includes only people who had already accomplished something of note in their fields. We are left to ponder how many of the nine million young men lost in the war might have gone on to do great things in the arts, sciences, medicine, and politics. Given the official number of military personnel killed between the years 1914 and 1918 — over one million dead soldiers from the British Empire and the United States alone — a handful of artists might seem insignificant. A few survived — J.R.R. Tolkien, for instance.[8]

Rupert Brooke(1887–1915) was a good student and athlete, and — in part because of his strikingly handsome looks — a popular young man who eventually numbered among his friends E.M. Forster and Virginia Woolf. Brooke actually saw little combat during the war; he contracted blood poisoning from a small neglected wound and died in April 1915.[9]

The Dead

These hearts were woven of human joys and cares,
Washed marvellously with sorrow, swift to <u>mirth</u>.
The years had given them kindness. Dawn was theirs,
And sunset, and the colours of the earth.
These had seen movement, and heard music; known
<u>Slumber</u> and waking; loved; gone proudly friended;
Felt the quick stir of wonder; sat alone;
Touched flowers and furs and cheeks. All this is ended.
There are waters blown by changing winds to laughter
And lit by the rich skies, all day. And after,
Frost, with a <u>gesture</u>, stays the waves that dance
And wandering loveliness. He leaves a white
Unbroken glory, a gathered radiance,
A width, a shining peace, under the night.

— Rupert Brooke

Love

Love is a <u>breach</u> in the walls, a broken gate,
Where that comes in that shall not go again;
Love sells the proud heart's <u>citadel</u> to Fate.
They have known shame, who love unloved. Even then,
When two mouths, thirsty each for each, find slaking,
And agony's forgot, and hushed the crying
Of <u>credulous</u> hearts, in heaven — such are but taking
Their own poor dreams within their arms, and lying
Each in his lonely night, each with a ghost.
Some share that night. But they know, love grows colder,
Grows false and dull, that was sweet lies at most.
Astonishment is no more in hand or shoulder,
But darkens, and dies out from kiss to kiss.
All this is love; and all love is but this.

— Rupert Brooke

Define the suggested vocabulary words underlined in the above passage.

The Soldier

If I should die, think only this of me:
That there's some corner of a foreign field
That is for ever England. There shall be
In that rich earth a richer dust concealed;
A dust whom England bore, shaped, made aware,
Gave, once, her flowers to love, her ways to roam,
A body of England's, breathing English air,
Washed by the rivers, blest by suns of home.
And think, this heart, all evil shed away,
A pulse in the eternal mind, no less
Gives somewhere back the thoughts by England given;
Her sights and sounds; dreams happy as her day;
And laughter, learnt of friends; and gentleness,
In hearts at peace, under an English heaven.

— Rupert Brooke

"Now, God be thanked
Who has matched us with
His hour, and caught our
youth, and wakened us from
sleeping."[10]

— Rupert Brooke

Fractions

1. Divide x+ 3x− 2x − 5 by x − 2

2. Divide $2x^5 − x3 + 2x − 1$ by x + 2

3. Divide x3 + $6x^2$ + 10x − 1 by x − 0.09

Percentages

1. A merchant mixes a pounds of tea worth x cents a pound with b pounds worth y cents a pound. How much is the mixture worth per pound?

2. If a man bought a horse for x dollars and sold him so as to gain 5%, what will represent the number of dollars he gained?

3. The difference between two numbers is 6, and if 4 be added to the greater, the result will be three times the smaller. What are the numbers? Of how many terms does the expression $x3 − 4x^2y + y^3$ consist? How many factors has each of the terms? What is the value of a number, one of whose factors is zero?

E N G L I S H

Grammar

Which parts of the sentences below are wrong?

(A) I met the students from (B) Pittsburgh, PA, Columbus, OH, and Kansas City, MO.

(A) I am not sure what to do,(B) however, I think I will go anyway.

(A) My three loves are: (B) reading, writing, and arithmetic.

■ ■ ■

Denotation means "literal meaning." Connotation means "contextual meaning." You will need to discern both on the ACT English exam.

"Isn't it odd how much fatter a book gets when you've read it several times?" Mo had said . . . "As if something were left between the pages every time you read it. Feelings, thoughts, sounds, smells . . . and then, when you look at the book again many years later, you find yourself there, too, a slightly younger self, slightly different, as if the book had preserved you like a pressed flower . . . both strange and familiar."[11]

— Cornelia Funke (*Inkspell*)

Analysis

Race or breed was a moment ago described as a factor in human nature. But to break up human nature into factors is something that we can do, or try to do, in thought only. In practice we can never succeed in doing anything of the kind. A machine such as a watch we can take to bits and then put together again. Even a chemical compound such as water we can resolve into oxygen and hydrogen and then reproduce out of its elements. But to dissect a living thing is to kill it once and for all. Life, as was said in the first chapter, is something unique, with the unique property of being able to evolve. As life evolves, that is to say changes, by being handed on from certain forms to certain other forms, a partial rigidity marks the process together with a partial plasticity. There is a stiffening, so to speak, that keeps the life-force up to a point true to its old direction; though, short of that limit, it is free to take a new line of its own. Race, then, stands for the stiffening in the evolutionary process. Just up to what point it goes in any given case we probably can never quite tell. Yet, if we could think our way anywhere near to that point in regard to man, I doubt not that we should eventually succeed in forging a fresh instrument for controlling the destinies of our species, an instrument perhaps more powerful than education itself — I mean, eugenics, the art of improving the human breed.

To see what race means when considered apart, let us first of all take your individual self, and ask how you would proceed to separate your inherited nature from the nature which you have acquired in the course of living your life. It is not easy. Suppose, however, that you had a twin brother born, if indeed that were possible, as like you as one pea is like another. An accident in childhood, however, has caused him to lose a leg. So he becomes a clerk, living a sedentary life in an office. You, on the other hand, with your two lusty legs to help you, become a postman, always on the run. Well, the two of you are now very different men in looks and habits. He is pale and you are brown. You play football and he sits at home reading. Nevertheless, any friend who knows you both intimately will discover fifty little things that bespeak in you the same underlying nature and bent. You are both, for instance, slightly colour-blind, and both inclined to fly into violent passions on occasion. That is your common inheritance peeping out — if, at least, your friend has really managed to make allowance for your common bringing-up, which might mainly account for the passionateness, though hardly for the colour-blindness.

But now comes the great difficulty. Let us further suppose that you two twins marry wives who are also twins born as like as two peas; and each pair of you has a family. Which of the two batches of children will tend on the whole to have the stronger legs? Your legs are strong by use; your brother's are weak by disuse. But do use and disuse make any difference to the race? That is the theoretical question which, above all others, complicates and hampers our present-day attempts to understand heredity.

In technical language, this is the problem of use-inheritance, otherwise known as the inheritance of acquired characters. It is apt to seem obvious to the plain man that the effects of use and disuse are transmitted to offspring. So, too, thought Lamarck, who half a century before Darwin propounded a theory of the origin of species that was equally evolutionary in its way. Why does the giraffe have so long a neck? Lamarck thought it was because the giraffe had acquired a habit of stretching his neck out. Every time there was a bad season, the giraffes must all stretch up as high as ever they could towards the leafy tops of the trees; and the

one that stretched up farthest survived, and handed on the capacity for a like feat to his fortunate descendants. Now Darwin himself was ready to allow that use and disuse might have some influence on the offspring's inheritance; but he thought that this influence was small as compared with the influence of what, for want of a better term, he called spontaneous variation. Certain of his followers, however, who call themselves Neo-Darwinians, are ready to go one better. Led by the German biologist, Weismann, they would thrust the Lamarckians, with their hypothesis of use-inheritance, clean out of the field. Spontaneous variation, they assert, is all that is needed to prepare the way for the selection of the tall giraffe. It happened to be born that way. In other words, its parents had it in them to breed it so. This is not a theory that tells one anything positive. It is merely a caution to look away from use and disuse to another explanation of variation that is not yet forthcoming.[12] (Robert Marett, *Anthropology*)

■ ■ ■

What is the problem with the use-inheritance theory?

A. This is not a theory that tells one anything positive. It is merely a caution to look away from use and disuse to another explanation of variation that is not yet forthcoming.

B. It conflicts with the theory of natural selection.

C. One cannot lose the use of an object created by God.

D. None of the above

Reading Test: Scaffolding

Again, the key to a high score on all parts of the ACT is determined by your ability to read well. Reading effectiveness is enhanced by something called "scaffolding." Scaffolding is an artificial structure created to repair or build another structure. It is not permanent and will be taken down when the structure is built.

"A set of training wheels on a bicycle is a classic example of scaffolding. It is adjustable and temporary, providing the young rider with the support he or she needs while learning to ride a two-wheeler. Without an aid of this sort, the complex tasks of learning to pedal, balance, and steer all at one time would be extremely difficult, if not impossible, for many youngsters. This scaffold—training wheels—allows the learners to accomplish a goal, riding a bicycle successfully, and then to happily pedal his or her way into the wider world."[13]

The most important part of scaffolding is marking up the text.

Circle the thesis statement.

Check and box the topic sentences of each paragraph.

Star the conclusions.

Circle individual words or facts that catch your eye.

You should predict what conclusion the author will offer. Engage the text. Make it part of you. Try what is called KWL.

All these activities relating to scaffolding — marking up the text, predicting, and KWL — will greatly enhance your reading comprehension and therefore your ACT score.

K	W	L
What I KNOW	What I WANT to know	What I LEARNED

A PARABLE

Once upon a time there was a man, a man who was very happy but also unhappy . . . he was happy because God gave him a very good job and his family had many, many things. He was a good thing-maker. But he was unhappy because he did not spend very much time with his children. To others they were ordinary children. But to the man they were very special. He was happiest when he spent time with them. He, however, was busy making money so they could have things, things, things. And I guess they were happy with things, things, things. He wanted to be with them . . . but he had no time, time, time. Only things, things, things. In time, the man grew happy with things and forgot about time. Being a good thing-maker made him feel important. One day a very bad thing happened to the man. He lost his thing-making-ability. With no money to buy things, he suddenly had more time. More time, time, time. More time than he wanted. And truthfully, he missed all the things, things, things. So did his children. They liked standing in the gap. Now they stood in the army!

One day, when the man was feeling sorry for himself he saw his son draw a butterfly. He had never seen a butterfly that his son drew. The next day he heard his daughter crying because she could not do her math. The man helped her and she stopped crying. The man was amazed. On the third day, his other son asked him what "mauldin" meant. He did not know, but he liked being asked. And on the same day he took a splinter out of his daughter's finger. He had not seen a butterfly, or helped with a math problem, or held his daughter when she cried. He had always answered every question his kids asked him because people who are thing-providers must know everything or pretend to know everything. But people who have time, time, time do not have to pretend anymore. He had never had time for splinters, or paper airplanes, or math problems, or anything else. Because he was too busy doing his thing-making. Suddenly . . . he liked it. He liked having time. He missed the things sometimes. But he liked the time more. Soon he wanted to have more time with more children. And a nice man let him work for him and enjoy time and thing-making! He had time with lots more children. And the man was very, very, happy!

SCRIPTURE

"The kingdom of heaven is like treasure hidden in a field. When a man found it, he hid it again, and then in his joy went and sold all he had and bought that field."

~ Matthew 13:44

PRAYER POINTS

HOLINESS OF GOD

"For you are a people holy to the LORD your God. The LORD your God has chosen you out of all the peoples on the face of the earth to be his people, his treasured possession."

~ Deuteronomy 7:6

WRITING

Writing Style

Which part of the sentence below is wrong?

The universal (A) opinion of all the citizens was that the citadel had been (B) betrayed, (C) having been captured in broad daylight by a very small number of the enemy, and those unprovided with scaling ladders, and admitted by a postern gate, (D) and much wearied by a long march.

VOCABULARY

Lincoln's Second Inaugural Address[1]
March 4, 1865

The American Civil War is almost over. The South has been thoroughly defeated. The Union has been preserved. President Abraham Lincoln has every reason to be vindictive and vengeful. The North has suffered greatly to win this war against the recalcitrant. But Abraham Lincoln, showing great poise and candor, offers an olive branch to his erstwhile fellow Americans.

Suggested Vocabulary Words

Fellow countrymen: At this second appearing to take the oath of the presidential office, there is less occasion for an extended address than there was at the first. Then a statement, somewhat in detail, of a course to be pursued, seemed fitting and proper. Now, at the expiration of four years, during which public declarations have been constantly called forth on every point and phase of the great contest which still absorbs the attention and engrosses the energies of the nation, little that is new could be presented. The progress of our arms, upon which all else chiefly depends, is as well known to the public as to myself; and it is, I trust, reasonably satisfactory and encouraging to all. With high hope for the future, no prediction in regard to it is ventured.

On the occasion corresponding to this four years ago, all thoughts were anxiously directed to an impending civil war. All dreaded it — all sought to avert it. While the inaugural address was being delivered from this place, devoted altogether to saving the Union without war, insurgent agents were in the city seeking to destroy it without war — seeking to dissolve the Union, and divide effects, by negotiation. Both parties deprecated war; but one of them would make war rather than let the nation survive; and the other would accept war rather than let it perish. And the war came.

One-eighth of the whole population were colored slaves, not distributed generally over the Union, but localized in the Southern part of it. These slaves constituted a peculiar and powerful interest. All knew that this interest was, somehow, the cause of the war. To strengthen, perpetuate, and extend this interest was the object for which the insurgents would rend the Union, even by war; while the government claimed no right to do more than to restrict the territorial enlargement of it.

Neither party expected for the war the magnitude or the duration which it has already attained. Neither anticipated that the cause of the conflict might cease with, or even before, the conflict itself should cease. Each looked for an easier triumph, and a result less fundamental and astounding. Both read the same Bible, and pray to the same God; and each invokes his aid against the other. It may seem strange that any men should dare to ask a just God's assistance in wringing their bread from the sweat of other men's faces; but let us judge not, that we be not judged. The prayers of both could not be answered — that of neither has been answered fully.

The Almighty has his own purposes. "Woe unto the world because of offenses! for it must needs be that offenses come; but woe to that man by whom the offense cometh." If we shall suppose that American slavery is one of those offenses which, in the providence of God, must needs come, but which, having

continued through his appointed time, he now wills to remove, and that he gives to both North and South this terrible war, as the woe due to those by whom the offense came, shall we discern therein any departure from those divine attributes which the believers in a living God always ascribe to him? Fondly do we hope — fervently do we pray — that this mighty scourge of war may speedily pass away. Yet, if God wills that it continue until all the wealth piled by the bondsman's two hundred and fifty years of unrequited toil shall be sunk, and until every drop of blood drawn by the lash shall be paid by another drawn with the sword, as was said three thousand years ago, so still it must be said, "The judgments of the Lord are true and righteous altogether."

With malice toward none; with charity for all; with firmness in the right, as God gives us to see the right, let us strive on to finish the work we are in; to bind up the nation's wounds; to care for him who shall have borne the battle, and for his widow, and his orphan — to do all which may achieve and cherish a just and lasting peace among ourselves, and with all nations.

The Causes of the American Civil War

As the Civil War was beginning to unfold, the Southerner Mary Chestnut wrote, "We [the North and the South] are divorced because we have hated each other so!"[2] This hatred lead to a bloody and horrible civil war.

For years the question "What caused the Civil War?" has puzzled historians. They have suggested many reasons, but what is the real cause? Slavery was the chief irritant but did not cause the conflict. Both Rachel and Samuel Cormany, typical Civil War contemporaries, supported their government's efforts to quell the southern rebellion. But neither of them was irritated by slavery. Rachel blamed the war on the "hotheadedness of the South, and the invisibleness of the North."[3] In fact, there were many things that contributed to the Civil War — some more than others. Certainly slavery was a cause but not *the* cause.

The Civil War was caused because Southern and Northern Americans chose not to live together. Again, the operative word is "chose." They chose to fight a war. The North and the South were always two nations, and by 1860 it was difficult to live together in the same house. It was not impossible, though. They chose to live apart. They had solved their problems before — in 1820 and 1850, for instance. But suddenly in 1860, the political system failed.

The Civil War was neither the fault of the North nor the South. Or, rather, it was the fault of both! An expanding economy, a flood of immigrants, the Second Great Awakening, Manifest Destiny, and the failure of the American political system — the combination of these events brought the young republic to the brink of the Civil War. Ultimately, though, the failure of nerve manifested by American political leaders thrust the nation into its bloodiest war in American history.

I agree with a historian's assessment of the causes of the Civil War: When the Union was originally formed, the United States embraced too many degrees of latitude and longitude, and too many varieties of climate and production, to make it practicable to establish and administer justly one common government which should take charge of all the interests of society. To the wise men who were entrusted with the formation of that union and common government, it was obvious enough that each separate society should be entrusted with the management of its own peculiar interests, and that the united government should take charge only of those interests which were common and general.[4]

What is ironic is that, in a way, the North and the South were fighting for the same thing. They both saw themselves preserving what was vitally important to America. The Confederacy was really fighting for the American dream as much as the Union! They saw themselves as the new patriots. The South had some justification. Many of the Founding Fathers owned slaves. George Washington, Thomas Jefferson, and James Madison were all slaveholding presidents.

In summary, the Civil War was a struggle between conflicting worldviews. Each section held to a belief system that increasingly felt alienated from the other. They disagreed over the power of the federal government; they disagreed over tariffs; and they especially disagreed over slavery and its expansion westward. However, these disagreements were nothing new and did not bring a civil war. The War was not inevitable. By the middle of the 19th century, these differing viewpoints — coupled with the almost violent change inflicted on America, and the collapse of compromise as a viable option in the political arena — brought the young Republic into a horrendous civil war. Americans chose to fight because they were unwilling to choose an alternative.

The first American to observe that the Civil War was avoidable, not inevitable, was former President Buchanan. He argued that the cause of the Civil War was to be found in the long, active, and persistent hostility of the Northern abolitionists, both in and out of Congress, against Southern slavery, until the final triumph of President Lincoln; and on the other hand, the corresponding antagonism and violence with which the advocates of slavery resisted efforts, and vindicated its preservation and extension up till the period of secession.

Buchanan's assumption that the war need not have taken place had it not been for Northern fanatics and, to a lesser extent,

Southern extremists, was essentially correct. To put it another way, there was no substantive issue important enough in 1861 to necessitate a resort to arms; the war had been brought on by extremists on both sides. The moderate political center refused to solve the problem and left the solution to extremists. The extremists brought on a civil war.[5] (James Stobaugh, *Rhetoric*)

■ ■ ■

The argument of this essay is:

A. The American Civil War was caused by slavery.
B. The American Civil War was caused by slavery expansion.
C. The American Civil War was caused by economic tension.
D. The American Civil War was caused by a failure of the American political system to create a consensus.

SCIENCE

Analysis of Burial Practices

The Boeothick Native Americans appear to have shown great respect for their dead, and the most remarkable remains of them commonly observed by Europeans at the sea coasts are their burial places. They had several modes of interment — one was when the body of the deceased had been wrapped in birch rind, it was then, with his property, placed on a sort of scaffold about four feet from the ground — the scaffold supported a flooring of small squared beams laid close together, on which the body and property rested.

A second method was when the body, bent together and wrapped in birch rinds, was enclosed in a sort of box on the ground — this box was made of small square posts laid on each other horizontally and notched at the corners to make them meet close. It was about four feet high, three feet broad, and two-feet-and-a-half deep, and well lined with birch rind so as to exclude the weather from the inside. The body was always laid on its right side.

A third, and the most common method of burying among this people, was to wrap the body in birch rind and then cover it over with a heap of stones on the surface of the earth; but occasionally in sandy places, or where the earth was soft and easily removed, the body was sunk lower in the earth and the stones omitted.

Interestingly, no possessions were added to the body.

From these observations the following assumptions can be made:

I. They Boeothick really respected their dead.
II. The dead to the Boeothick had no real significance.
III. The dead body was always placed on its right side.
IV. Because there were no possessions added to the body, it is unlikely that the Boeothick believed in an afterlife, or at least, they did not believe that the deceased could take possessions with them.

A. I
B. II
C. III
D. IV
E. None
F. All
G. I, III, and IV

Troublesome Verbs

Lie and lay in use and meaning

Some sets of verbs are often confused by students, weak forms being substituted for correct, strong forms.

Lie and lay need close attention. These are the forms:

Present Tense	Past Tense	Present Participle	Past Participle
1. Lie	lay	lying	lain
2. Lay	laid	laying	laid

The distinctions to be observed are as follows:

(1) Lie, with its forms, is regularly intransitive as to use. As to meaning, lie means to rest, to recline, to place one's self in a recumbent position; as, "There lies the ruin."

(2) Lay, with its forms, is always transitive as to use. As to meaning, lay means to put, to place a person or thing in position, as, "Slowly and sadly we laid him down." Also lay may be used without any object expressed, but there is still a transitive meaning, as in the expressions, "to lay up for future use," "to lay on with the rod."

Sit and set have principal parts as follows

Present Tense	Past Tense	Present Participle	Past Participle
1. Sit	sat	sitting	sat
2. Set	set	setting	set

Notice these points of difference between the two verbs:

(1) Sit, with its forms, is always intransitive in use. In meaning, sit signifies (a) to place one's self on a seat, to rest; (b) to be adjusted, to fit; (c) to cover and warm eggs for hatching, as, "The hen sits."

(2) Set, with its forms, is always transitive in use when it has the following meanings: (a) to put or place a thing or person in position, as "He set down the book;" (b) to fix or establish, as, "He sets a good example."

Set is intransitive when it means (a) to go down, to decline, as, "The sun has set;" (b) to become fixed or rigid, as, "His eyes set in his head because of the disease;" (c) in certain idiomatic expressions, as, for example, "to set out," "to set up in business," "to set about a thing," "to set to work," "to set forward," "the tide sets in," "a strong wind set in," etc.

Examine the forms of lie, lay, sit, and set in these sentences. Give the meaning of each, and correct those used wrongly.

1. If the phenomena which lie before him will not suit his purpose, all history must be ransacked.

2. He set with his eyes fixed partly on the ghost and partly on Hamlet, and with his mouth open.

3. The days when his favorite volume sat him upon making wheelbarrows and chairs . . . can never again be the realities they were.

4. To make the jacket set yet more closely to the body, it was gathered at the middle by a broad leathern belt.

5. He had set up no unattainable standard of perfection.

You can usually determine the meaning of figurative language (metaphors) by first identifying the main idea determined by the context. For example, Henry David Longfellow's poem "A Psalm of Life" begins "in the world's broad field of battle." Of course Longfellow does not mean a real battle between military forces — he means that life is full of struggles, wins, and losses.

M A T H

Word Problems

1. If a boy can do a piece of work in x minutes, how many hours would it take him to perform 12 times as much work?

2. A man has x dollars, y acres of land worth m dollars an acre, and c houses, each worth b dollars. What is my share if I am one of n heirs?

3. A storekeeper mixed m pounds of coffee worth a cents a pound with p pounds worth b cents a pound. How much is the mixture worth per pound?

4. If John is y years old, how old was he 11 years ago?

FIRES OF LIFE

SCRIPTURE

"Praise be to the Lord, the God of Israel, because he has come and has redeemed his people."

~ Luke 1:68

Elie Wiesel was born in 1928 and lived through one of the most horrible periods in history. During World War II, he, with his family and other Jews from Romania, were sent to Auschwitz concentration camp where his parents and little sister were gassed and cremated. Wiesel and his two older sisters survived. But Wiesel's faith and heart were broken. "My God died," Wiesel said, "in the fires of Auschwitz." Wiesel changed from a devout Jew to a broken, bitter young man who doubted his belief in God. *If there is a God, how could he allow this to happen?* he wonders. Elie Wiesel speaks for a generation of 21st-century people who doubt the existence of God.

Elie Wiesel in the book *Night* laments, "I lost my faith in the shadow of the gas chambers."[1] Wiesel, a survivor of a Nazi concentration camp, was not an agnostic, nor an atheist; he was a believer who decided to stop believing because God seemed to be cruel and unloving. The compassionate God Wiesel had known in youth seemed to have turned into a vindictive, destructive, vengeful creature. Wiesel echoed the words of Aeschylus in his Greek tragedy Agamemnon, "From the gods who sit in grandeur/grace comes somehow violent."

Likewise, in the midst of tragedy, Jeremiah, the author of Lamentations, as his name and family are taken into captive to Babylon, honestly began to question if God really loved Israel, if He would ever show them grace. And worse than that, while Israel floundered, while Jerusalem lay in ruins, sinful, heathen adjacent nations prospered. Jeremiah complained, "All my enemies have heard of my calamity; they are glad that you have done it" (Lamentations 1:21).

I once saw a Peanuts cartoon strip. With his typewriter, Snoopy is writing a novel. The first words are, "It was a dark and stormy night." In Lucy's characteristic forceful manner, she sees what is on the page and gives Snoopy some advice.

"You stupid idiot! That's the dumbest thing I've ever read. Who ever heard of such a silly way to begin a story? Don't you know that all the good stories begin, 'Once upon a time.' '"

Snoopy, taking her advice, began his novel, "Once upon a time, it was a dark and stormy night."

If that were our lives, would it begin the same way? It seems that our lives, that begin so promising, always end in dark and stormy nights. Our fairy godmother never appears and we never wear glass slippers. Other people seem to have it so easy — especially wicked people! A survivor of the Lodz Ghetto, a Jewish internment camp in Poland during World War II, describes how devastating it was to look through barbed wire at laughing, fat, healthy sons and

PRAYER POINTS
STRENGTH TO FOLLOW CHRIST

"When he has brought out all his own, he goes on ahead of them, and his sheep follow him because they know his voice."

~ John 10:4

daughters of his Nazi captors playing on a merry-go-round while the Lodz emaciated children had to work from dawn to dark. The protagonist in *Fiddler on The Roof* shakes a half-cynical fist at God in the wake of another Russian pogrom, "And you call us the chosen people!"[2]

Well, I am no longer very young, I know, but what do I know? I know this: There will be Lodz ghettos and gas chambers. But I know that hope lives yet. That there is no tragedy that cannot be overcome.

S C I E N C E

Comparison/Analysis

Observing these birds, what assumptions can be made?

I. They are birds.
II. Some are nocturnal birds (eyes are on the side of their head).
III. Some are predators (hocked beaks).
IV. They include seashore birds.

A. I
B. II
C. III
D. IV
E. None
F. All
G. I, II, and III

W R I T I N G

Writing Style

Which part of the sentence below is wrong?

He attained a very distinguished position by mere (A) perseverance and common sense, whose (B) qualities are perhaps mostly underrated, (C) though he was deficient in tact and (D) not remarkable for general ability.

" *It is a good rule after reading a new book, never to allow yourself another new one till you have read an old one in between.*"[3]

— C.S. Lewis

VOCABULARY

The Merry Adventures of Robin Hood[4]
Howard Pyle

You who so plod amid serious things that you feel it shame to give yourself up even for a few short moments to mirth and joyousness in the land of Fancy; you who think that life hath nought to do with innocent laughter that can harm no one; these pages are not for you. Clap to the leaves and go no farther than this, for I tell you plainly that if you go farther you will be scandalized by seeing good, sober folks of real history so frisk and caper in gay colors and motley that you would not know them but for the names tagged to them. Here is a stout, lusty fellow with a quick temper, yet none so ill for all that, who goes by the name of Henry II. Here is a fair, gentle lady before whom all the others bow and call her Queen Eleanor. Here is a fat rogue of a fellow, dressed up in rich robes of a clerical kind, that all the good folk call my Lord Bishop of Hereford. Here is a certain fellow with a sour temper and a grim look — the worshipful, the Sheriff of Nottingham. And here, above all, is a great, tall, merry fellow that roams the greenwood and joins in homely sports, and sits beside the Sheriff at merry feast, which same beareth the name of the proudest of the Plantagenets — Richard of the Lion's Heart.

Beside these are a whole host of knights, priests, nobles, burghers, yeomen, pages, ladies, lasses, landlords, beggars, peddlers, and what not, all living the merriest of merry lives, and all bound by nothing but a few odd strands of certain old ballads (snipped and clipped and tied together again in a score of knots) which draw these jocund fellows here and there, singing as they go.

Here you will find a hundred dull, sober, jogging places, all tricked out with flowers and what not, till no one would know them in their fanciful dress. And here is a country bearing a well-known name, wherein no chill mists press upon our spirits, and no rain falls but what rolls off our backs like April showers off the backs of sleek drakes; where flowers bloom forever and birds are always singing; where every fellow hath a merry catch as he travels the roads, and ale and beer and wine (such as muddle no wits) flow like water in a brook.

This country is not Fairyland. What is it? 'Tis the land of Fancy, and is of that pleasant kind that, when you tire of it — whisk! — you clap the leaves of this book together and 'tis gone, and you are ready for everyday life, with no harm done.

And now I lift the curtain that hangs between here and No-man's-land. Will you come with me, sweet Reader? I thank you. Give me your hand.

Suggested Vocabulary Words

A. Up rose Robin Hood one merry morn when all the birds were singing blithely among the leaves, and up rose all his merry men, each fellow washing his head and hands in the cold brown brook that leaped laughing from stone to stone.

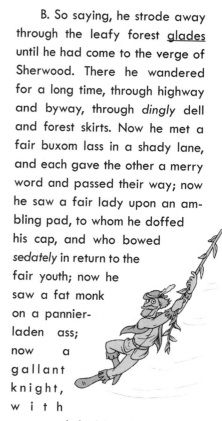

B. So saying, he strode away through the leafy forest glades until he had come to the verge of Sherwood. There he wandered for a long time, through highway and byway, through dingly dell and forest skirts. Now he met a fair buxom lass in a shady lane, and each gave the other a merry word and passed their way; now he saw a fair lady upon an ambling pad, to whom he doffed his cap, and who bowed sedately in return to the fair youth; now he saw a fat monk on a pannier-laden ass; now a gallant knight, with spear and shield and armor that flashed brightly in the sunlight.

ENGLISH

General Review

1. Whom they were I really cannot specify.

2. Truth is mightier than us all.

3. If there ever was a rogue in the world, it is me.

4. They were the very two individuals whom we thought were far away.

5. "Seems to me as if them as writes must hev a kinder gift fur it, now."

You will improve your writing a great deal if you can add details that show, instead of tell, your main point. For example, "My stomach growled and my mouth watered when I looked at the juicy T-Bone steak" is better than "I was so hungry!"

"Rikki-Tikki Tavi" in The Jungle Book (1894)
Rudyard Kipling

This is the story of the great war that Rikki-tikki-tavi fought single-handed, through the bathrooms of the big bungalow in Segowlee cantonment. Darzee, the Tailorbird, helped him, and Chuchundra, the musk-rat, who never comes out into the middle of the floor, but always creeps round by the wall, gave him advice, but Rikki-tikki did the real fighting.

He was a mongoose, rather like a little cat in his fur and his tail, but quite like a weasel in his head and his habits. His eyes and the end of his restless nose were pink. He could scratch himself anywhere he pleased with any leg, front or back, that he chose to use. He could fluff up his tail till it looked like a bottle brush, and his war cry as he scuttled through the long grass was: "Rikk-tikk-tikki-tikki-tchk!"

One day, a high summer flood washed him out of the burrow where he lived with his father and mother, and carried him, kicking and clucking, down a roadside ditch. He found a little wisp of grass floating there, and clung to it till he lost his senses. When he revived, he was lying in the hot sun on the middle of a garden path, very draggled indeed, and a small boy was saying, "Here's a dead mongoose. Let's have a funeral."

"No," said his mother, "let's take him in and dry him. Perhaps he isn't really dead."

They took him into the house, and a big man picked him up between his finger and thumb and said he was not dead but half choked. So they wrapped him in cotton wool, and warmed him over a little fire, and he opened his eyes and sneezed.

"Now," said the big man (he was an Englishman who had just moved into the bungalow), "don't frighten him, and we'll see what he'll do."

It is the hardest thing in the world to frighten a mongoose, because he is eaten up from nose to tail with curiosity. The motto of all the mongoose family is "Run and find out," and Rikki-tikki was a true mongoose. He looked at the cotton wool, decided that it was not good to eat, ran all round the table, sat up and put his fur in order, scratched himself, and jumped on the small boy's shoulder.

"Don't be frightened, Teddy," said his father. "That's his way of making friends."

"Ouch! He's tickling under my chin," said Teddy.

Rikki-tikki looked down between the boy's collar and neck, snuffed at his ear, and climbed down to the floor, where he sat rubbing his nose.

"Good gracious," said Teddy's mother, "and that's a wild creature! I suppose he's so tame because we've been kind to him."

"All mongooses are like that," said her husband. "If Teddy doesn't pick him up by the tail, or try to put him in a cage, he'll run in and out of the house all day long. Let's give him something to eat."

They gave him a little piece of raw meat. Rikki-tikki liked it immensely, and when it was finished he went out into the veranda and sat in the sunshine and fluffed up his fur to make it dry to the roots. Then he felt better.

"There are more things to find out about in this house," he said to himself, "than all my family could find out in all their lives. I shall certainly stay and find out."

He spent all that day roaming over the house. He nearly drowned himself in the bath-tubs, put his nose into the ink on a writing table, and burned it on the end of the big man's cigar, for he climbed up in the big man's lap to see how writing was done. At nightfall he ran into Teddy's nursery to watch how kerosene lamps were lighted, and when Teddy went to bed Rikki-tikki climbed up, too. But he was a restless companion, because he had to get up and attend to every noise all through the night, and find out what made it. Teddy's mother and father came in, the last thing, to look at their boy, and Rikki-tikki was awake on the pillow. "I don't like that," said Teddy's mother.

"He may bite the child." "He'll do no such thing," said the father. "Teddy's safer with that little beast than if he had a bloodhound to watch him. If a snake came into the nursery now —"

But Teddy's mother wouldn't think of anything so awful.

Early in the morning Rikki-tikki came to early breakfast in the veranda riding on Teddy's shoulder, and they gave him banana and some boiled egg. He sat on all their laps one after the other, because every well-brought-up mongoose always hopes to be a house mongoose some day and have rooms to run about in; and Rikki-tikki's mother (she used to live in the general's house at Segowlee) had carefully told Rikki what to do if ever he came across white men.

Then Rikki-tikki went out into the garden to see what was to be seen. It was a large garden, only half cultivated, with bushes, as big as summerhouses, of Marshal Niel roses, lime and orange trees, clumps of bamboos, and thickets of high grass. Rikki-tikki licked his lips. "This is a splendid hunting-ground," he said, and his tail grew bottle-brushy at the thought of it, and he scuttled up and down the garden, snuffing here and there till he heard very sorrowful voices in a thorn-bush.

It was Darzee, the Tailorbird, and his wife. They had made a beautiful nest by pulling two big leaves together and stitching them up the edges with fibers, and had filled the hollow with cotton and downy fluff. The nest swayed to and fro, as they sat on the rim and cried.

"What is the matter?" asked Rikki-tikki.

"We are very miserable," said Darzee. "One of our babies fell out of the nest yesterday and Nag ate him."

"H'm!" said Rikki-tikki, "that is very sad — but I am a stranger here. Who is Nag?"

Darzee and his wife only cowered down in the nest without answering, for from the thick grass at the foot of the bush there came a low hiss — a horrid cold sound that made Rikki-tikki jump back two clear feet. Then inch by inch out of the grass rose up the head and spread hood of Nag, the big black cobra, and he was five feet long from tongue to tail. When he had lifted one-third of himself clear of the ground, he stayed balancing to and fro exactly as a dandelion tuft balances in the wind, and he looked at Rikki-tikki with the wicked snake's eyes that never change their expression, whatever the snake may be thinking of.

"Who is Nag?" said he. "I am Nag. The great God Brahm put his mark upon all our people, when the first cobra spread his hood to keep the sun off Brahm as he slept. Look, and be afraid!"

■ ■ ■

Predict the ending of this short story.

M A T H

Word Problems

1. Divide the number 105 into three parts, such that the second shall be 5 more than the first, and the third three times the second.

2. A man had a certain amount of money; he earned four times as much the next week, and found $30. If he then had seven times as much as at first, how much had he at first?

3. How many fourths are there in $7x$?

4. How long will it take a man to build x yards of wall if he builds z feet a day?

PHILOSOPHY

SCRIPTURE

"To God belong wisdom and power; counsel and understanding are his. What he tears down cannot be rebuilt; the man he imprisons cannot be released."

~ Job 12:13–14

I have always loved reading philosophy. I always have. Philosophy to me is what Plato calls "that dear delight." As Will Durant explains in *The Story of Philosophy*, I am like the character Mitya in *The Brothers Karamazov* — "one of those who don't want millions but an answer to their questions."[1] The English philosopher Francis Bacon says, "Seek ye first the good things of the mind and the rest will either be supplied or its loss will not be felt."[2] Indeed.

So I like reading philosophy these days. In a day where there is so much abstract, opinionated news, it is refreshing to read good old philosophy.

Young Christians, you too need to read philosophy. Every educated person does. As Socrates understood, a society must be governed by its wisest men/women or it will fall. Wise people understand how our world views have emerged. They understand what knowledge is and how views of its acquisition emerged.

Of course, the greatest philosopher was Solomon, who fills Scripture with wise aphorisms (e.g., Proverbs).

It feels like I am being governed by people who are not so wise. Socrates warned his followers, "Woe to him who teaches men faster than they can learn."[3] It feels like the guys running the show are learning on the job. Slowly learning on the job. Socrates continues, "Now when a man has taken away the money of the citizens and made slaves of them, then, instead of swindler and thief he is called happy and blessed by all," Socrates ends, "For injustice is censured because those who censure it are afraid of suffering, and not from any scruple they might have of doing injustice themselves."[4]

My heart is breaking for my country. "They enslave the nobler natures, and they praise justice only because they are cowards"[5] (Plato, *Gorgias*). Every form of government tends to perish by excess of its basic principle. Has the American experiment run its course? Or are the dreams of our forefathers being kindled anew?

Most American political leaders, I fear, do not think deeply and do not find any workable answers. We have lost the art of rhetoric; we cannot discuss weighty things. We act out of praxis; we act out of need. There is no nobility left. "The end comes when we no longer talk with ourselves. It is the end of genuine thinking and the beginning of the final loneliness"[6] (Edward Gibbon).

The good news is that you are graduating in ever-increasing numbers. You, the new generation of spirit-filled, godly young people who honor the inspired, inerrant Word of God but who are not reticent to quote Aristotle. You will be the next governors, senators, CEOs, artists, playwrights. All our prayers are with you! And we stand in awe of what God is doing!

PRAYER POINTS
MISSION HEART

"Declare his glory among the nations, his marvelous deeds among all peoples."

~ Psalm 96:3

VOCABULARY

Up From Slavery[7]
Booker T. Washington

I was born a slave on a plantation in Franklin County, Virginia. I am not quite sure of the exact place or exact date of my birth, but at any rate I suspect I must have been born somewhere and at some time. As nearly as I have been able to learn, I was born near a cross-roads post office called Hale's Ford, and the year was 1858 or 1859. I do not know the month or the day. The earliest impressions I can now recall are of the plantation and the slave quarters — the latter being the part of the plantation where the slaves had their cabins.

My life had its beginning in the midst of the most miserable, desolate, and discouraging surroundings. This was so, however, not because my owners were especially cruel, for they were not, as compared with many others. I was born in a typical log cabin, about fourteen by sixteen feet square. In this cabin I lived with my mother and a brother and sister till after the Civil War, when we were all declared free.[8]

It could not have been expected that a people who had spent generations in slavery, and before that generations in the darkest heathenism, could at first form any proper conception of what an education meant. In every part of the South, during the Reconstruction period, schools, both day and night, were filled to overflowing with people of all ages and conditions, some being as far along in age as sixty and seventy years. The ambition to secure an education was most praiseworthy and encouraging. The idea, however, was too prevalent that, as soon as one secured a little education, in some unexplainable way he would be free from most of the hardships of the world, and, at any rate, could live without manual labour. There was a further feeling that a knowledge, however little, of the Greek and Latin languages would make one a very superior human being, something bordering almost on the supernatural. I remember that the first coloured man whom I saw who knew something about foreign languages impressed me at the time as being a man of all others to be envied.

Naturally, most of our people who received some little education became teachers or preachers. While among those two classes there were many capable, earnest, godly men and women, still a large proportion took up teaching or preaching as an easy way to make a living. Many became teachers who could do little more than write their names. I remember there came into our neighbourhood one of this class, who was in search of a school to teach, and the question arose while he was there as to the shape of the earth and how he could teach the children concerning the subject. He explained his position in the matter by saying that he was prepared to teach that the earth was either flat or round, according to the preference of a majority of his patrons.

The ministry was the profession that suffered most — and still suffers, though there has been great improvement — on account of not only ignorant but in many cases immoral men who claimed that they were "called to preach." In the earlier days of freedom almost every coloured man who learned to read would receive "a call to preach" within a few days after he began reading. At my home in West Virginia the process of being called to the ministry was a very interesting one. Usually the "call" came when the individual was sitting in church. Without warning the one called would fall upon the floor as if struck by a bullet, and would lie there for hours, speechless and motionless. Then the news would spread all through the neighborhood that this individual had received a "call." If he were inclined to resist the summons, he would fall or be made to fall a second or third time. In the end he always yielded to the call. While I wanted an education badly, I confess that in my youth I had a fear that when I had learned to read and write very well I would receive one of these "calls"; but, for some reason, my call never came.[9]

■ ■ ■

Define the suggested vocabulary words.

S C I E N C E

Conclusions

Catalogue of Earthquakes in the Philippines, 1599–1608

No.	Date					Intensity
	Y.	M.	d.	h.	m.	
1.	1599	VI	25	3	20	IX

Manila and neighboring provinces. Damaged many private buildings in Manila; cracked the vault of the Jesuit Church so badly that it had to be demolished and replaced by a ceiling; fissured the walls and ruined the roof of Santo Domingo Church.

No.	Date					Intensity
2.	1601	I	16	0	–	VIII

Manila and adjacent provinces. Did considerable damage to some churches and many private houses in Manila. Its duration was unusually great, it being said that during 7 minutes the shocks were almost continuous. There were several dead and a great number of injured. The repetitions were frequent throughout the year.

No.	Date					Intensity
3.	1608	XII	3	–	–	VI–VII

Leyte Island. Violent chiefly in the country around Dulag and Palo (E coast of northern Leyte). It does not appear to have been destructive. The historians mention it as one of the earthquakes which caused the greatest convulsions in northern Luzon, especially in Ilocos Norte and Cagayan, but above all in the region of the Central Central Cordillera, Lepanto, and Bontoc. The data are somewhat vague. It is said that part of the northern Caraballo Mountains subsided.

The following conclusions are correct:

I. Earthquakes in the Philippines, 1599–1608, are relatively mild.

II. Earthquakes in the Philippines, 1599–1608, occur throughout the year.

    A. I
    B. II
    C. Both
    D. Neither

E N G L I S H

General Review

1. Let you and I look at these, for it says there are none such in the world.

2. "Nonsense!" said Amyas, "we could kill every soul of them in half an hour, and they know that as well as me."

3. They are coming for a visit to she and I.

■ ■ ■

This is really terrific writing. Notice the precise verbs.

Less than a mile from the entrance I saw a bear beside the road, and it ambled out as though to flag me down. Instantly a change came over Charley. He shrieked with rage. His lips flared, showing wicked teeth that have some trouble with a dog biscuit. He screeched insults at the bear, which hearing, the bear reared up and seemed to me to overtop the car. Frantically I rolled the windows shut and, swinging quickly to the left, grazed the animal, then scuttled on while Charley raved and ranted beside me, describing in detail what he would do to that bear if he could get at him. I was never so astonished in my life.[10] (John Steinbeck, *Travels With Charley*)

■ ■ ■

Remember: write with specificity, cogency, and vigor!

M A T H

Word Problems

1. Mr. Ames builds three houses. The first cost $2,000 more than the second, and the third twice as much as the first. If they all together cost $18,000, what was the cost of each house?

2. An artist who had painted three pictures charged $18 more for the second than the first, and three times as much for the third as the second. If he received $322 for the three, what was the price of each picture?

3. Three men, A, B, and C, invest $47,000 in business. B puts in $500 more than twice as much as A, and C puts in three times as much as B. How many dollars does each put into the business?

4. In three lots of land there are 80,750 feet. The second lot contains 250 feet more than three times as much as the first lot, and the third lot contains twice as much as the second. What is the size of each lot?

5. A man leaves by his will $225,000 to be divided as follows: his son to receive $10,000 less than twice as much as the daughter, and the widow four times as much as the son. What was the share of each?

TEST-TAKING INSIGHT

Reading Test Preparation Summary

From the beginning I have told you that reading is the single most important skill that you bring to the ACT. To that end I want to include one last summary of reading test questions and offer some insightful, test-taking strategies. Oh, and by the way, as an added bonus, these type questions will also be on the science test section!

Vocabulary in context questions ask you to determine the meanings of words from their context in the reading passage. I told you during the first week you began this course that learning vocabulary roots (Latin and Greek) are especially helpful in this section.

Literal comprehension questions appraise your understanding of significant information explicitly stated in the passage.

Extended reasoning questions measure your ability to synthesize and analyze information, as well as to evaluate the assumptions made and the techniques used by the author. Most of the reading questions fall into this category. You may be asked to identify cause and effect, make inferences, recognize a main idea or an author's tone, and follow the logic of an analogy or an argument. You will not be asked to draw a picture of your pet! But that is about all the certainty I can offer. Be prepared for anything!

Primary purpose questions ask about the main idea of a passage or about the author's primary purpose.

Rhetorical strategies questions usually focus on a specific part of a passage. They ask why this particular element is present. It is teasing out your reading comprehension.

Implication and evaluation (tone and attitude) questions ask about the author's tone or attitude in a specific part of a passage. It is a mood thing!

Application and analogy questions address a specific idea or relationship in a passage.

W R I T I N G

Writing Style

Which part of the following sentence is wrong?

Even if (A) it were attended with extenuating circumstances, such conduct would deserve severe approbation, (B) and it is the more called for because it would seem that (C) it was the intention of the author of the crime, in perpetrating (D) it, to inflict all the misery that was possible, upon his victim.

R E A D I N G

Details

What is the main reason that the Christian faith has suffered among African-Americans?

A. Syncretism with African religions

B. Apostasy

C. Ignorant men who claimed to be "called to preach"

D. Liberal theology

HONEY BUNNY

SCRIPTURE

"I am convinced that neither death nor life, neither angels nor demons, neither the present nor the future, nor any powers, neither height nor depth, nor anything else in all creation, will be able to separate us from the love of God that is in Christ Jesus our Lord."

~ Romans 8:38–39

My local newspaper featured the following 6 by 4 inch, relatively speaking, huge personal ad: "Happy 42nd Wedding Anniversary Honey Bunny! I Love you More Today Than Yesterday, But Not As Much As Tomorrow. Love Your Hubby, Blue Eyes."

I wonder how Honey Bunny reacted to the sobriquet and gut-wrenching, embarrassing show of emotion that her Blue Eyes so gratuitously shared with 75,000 people. One hopes she did not mind — or Blue Eyes might not have a happy 43rd!

Yet, there is something wholesome, real, and invorgorating about a love that can engender such awkwardness among its hearers, and perhaps its recipient. It is extravagant love, love that doesn't care what others think. Love that goes beyond appearances and etiquette, that forces the recipient to respond. This love is not ordinary, reserved, controlled love. It is love that is excessive, full of risk. Blue Eyes simply did not care how people would react — perhaps even Honey Bunny — because he had to tell the world, in no uncertain terms, that he loves his Honey Bunny. He loves his Honey Bunny more today than yesterday but not as much as tomorrow.

Young people, my prayer for you is that you will experience anew the spontaneous, extravagant love of God Our Father, through His Son our Lord Jesus Christ. A love that loved us yesterday, more today than yesterday, but not as much as tomorrow!

Ephesians 1:15–23: "For this reason, ever since I heard about your faith in the Lord Jesus and your love for all the saints, I have not stopped giving thanks for you, remembering you in my prayers. I keep asking that the God of our Lord Jesus Christ, the glorious Father, may give you the Spirit of wisdom and revelation, so that you may know him better. I pray also that the eyes of your heart may be enlightened in order that you may know the hope to which he has called you, the riches of his glorious inheritance in the saints, and his incomparably great power for us who believe. That power is like the working of the mighty strength, which he exerted in Christ when he raised him from the dead and seated him at his right hand in the heavenly realms, far above all rule and authority, power and dominion, and every title that can be given, not only in the present age but also in the one to come. And God placed all things under his feet and appointed him to be head over everything for the church, which is his body, the fullness of him who fills everything in every way."

PRAYER POINTS
WORSHIPFUL HEART

"Let the heavens rejoice, let the earth be glad; let the sea resound, and all that is in it; let the fields be jubilant, and everything in them."

~ Psalm 96:11–12

VOCABULARY

In *The Screwtape Letters*, C.S. Lewis is using the devil and his nephew Wormwood to tell the Christian community important truths. He wants Christians to laugh at themselves so that they can learn something. In a way, C.S. Lewis is writing what Shakespeare wrote in one of his soliloquies: "O what fools we mortals be" (from Hamlet).

Suggested Vocabulary Words

I [Screwtape] once had a patient, a sound <u>atheist</u>, who used to read in the British Museum. One day, as he sat reading, I saw his mind beginning to go the wrong way. The enemy (God) of course was at his elbow in an instant. . . Before I knew where I was I saw my twenty years' work beginning to totter. If I had lost my head and begun to attempt a defense by argument, I should have been undone. But I was not such a fool. I struck instantly at the part of the man which I had best under my control, and suggested that it was just about time to have some lunch. The Enemy presumably made the <u>counter-suggestion</u> (you know how one cannot quite overhear what He says to them?) that this was more important than lunch. At least I think that this must have been his line, for when I said, "Quite, in fact much too important to tackle at the end of a morning," the patient brightened up quite considerably; and by the time I had added, "much better to come back after lunch and go into with a fresh mind," he was already halfway to the front door.[1]

WRITING

Choosing the Best Title

In England, there was scarcely an amount of order and protection to justify much national boasting. Daring burglaries by armed men, and highway robberies, took place in the capital itself every night; families were publicly cautioned not to go out of town without removing their furniture to upholsterers' warehouses for security; the highwayman in the dark was a City tradesman in the light, and, being recognised and challenged by his fellow-tradesman whom he stopped in his character of "the Captain," gallantly shot him through the head and rode away; the mail was waylaid by seven robbers, and the guard shot three dead, and then got shot dead himself by the other four, "in consequence of the failure of his ammunition:" after which the mail was robbed in peace; that magnificent potentate, the Lord Mayor of London, was made to stand and deliver on Turnham Green, by one highwayman, who despoiled the illustrious creature in sight of all his retinue; prisoners in London gaols fought battles with their turnkeys, and the majesty of the law fired blunderbusses in among them, loaded with rounds of shot and ball; thieves snipped off diamond crosses from the necks of noble lords at Court drawing-rooms; musketeers went into St. Giles's, to search for contraband goods, and the mob fired on the musketeers, and the musketeers fired on the mob, and nobody thought any of these occurrences much out of the common way. In the midst of them, the hangman, ever busy and ever worse than useless, was in constant requisition; now, stringing up long rows of miscellaneous criminals; now, hanging a housebreaker on Saturday who had been taken on Tuesday; now, burning people in the hand at Newgate by the dozen, and now burning pamphlets at the door of Westminster Hall; today, taking the life of an atrocious murderer, and to-morrow of a wretched pilferer who had robbed a farmer's boy of sixpence.[2] (Charles Dickens, *A Tale of Two Cities*)

■ ■ ■

What is the best title?

I.   It Ain't all that Bad
II. English Hypocrisy
III. Wild Times on the Thames
IV. The Best of Times, the Worst of Times

Tone and Mood

Compare and contrast the mood/tone of the previous passage from *The Screwtape Letters* with this passage from "The Fall of the House of Usher" by Edgar Allan Poe.

During the whole of a dull, dark, and soundless day in the autumn of the year, when the clouds hung oppressively low in the heavens, had been passing alone, on horseback, through a singularly dreary tract of country; and at length found myself, as the shades of the evening drew on, within view of the melancholy House of Usher. I know not how it was — but, with the first glimpse of the building, a sense of insufferable gloom pervaded my spirit. I say insufferable; for the feeling was unrelieved by any of that half-pleasurable, because poetic, sentiment, with which the mind usually receives even the sternest natural images of the desolate or terrible. I looked upon the scene before me — upon the mere house, and the simple landscape features of the domain — upon the bleak walls — upon the vacant eye-like windows — upon a few rank sedges — and upon a few white trunks of decayed trees — with an utter depression of soul which I can compare to no earthly sensation more properly than to the after-dream of the reveler upon opium — the bitter lapse into everyday life — the hideous dropping off of the veil. There was an iciness, a sinking, a sickening of the heart — an unredeemed dreariness of thought which no goading of the imagination could torture into aught of the sublime. What was it — I paused to think — what was it that so unnerved me in the contemplation of the House of Usher? It was a mystery all insoluble; nor could I grapple with the shadowy fancies that crowded upon me as I pondered. I was forced to fall back upon the unsatisfactory conclusion, that while, beyond doubt, there are combinations of very simple natural objects which have the power of thus affecting us, still the analysis of this power lies among considerations beyond our depth.

It was possible, I reflected, that a mere different arrangement of the particulars of the scene, of the details of the picture, would be sufficient to modify, or perhaps to annihilate its capacity for sorrowful impression; and, acting upon this idea, I reined my horse to the precipitous brink of a black and lurid tarn that lay in unruffled lustre by the dwelling, and gazed down — but with a shudder even more thrilling than before — upon the remodeled and inverted images of the gray sedge, and the ghastly tree-stems, and the vacant and eye-like windows.[3]

General Review
Writing Style

Which part of the sentence below is wrong?

To contend for advantageous monopolies, which are regarded with a dislike and a suspicion (A) which daily (B) increasing; (C) however natural it may be to be annoyed at the loss of that which one has once possessed, (D) is useless.

???
Are you reading
50 to 100 pages
a day
???

Comparison
The Ruby

Another characteristic which, in the eyes of the expert, invariably isolates a real from an artificial ruby is its curious mild brilliance, which as yet has not been reproduced by any scientific method in paste or any other material, but perhaps the safest test of all is the crystalline structure, which identical structure appears in no other stone, though it is possible, by heating alumina coloured with oxide of iron and perhaps also a trace of oxide of chromium to a very high temperature for a considerable time, and then cooling very slowly, to obtain a ruby which is nearly the same in its structure as the real gem; its specific gravity and hardness may perhaps be to standard, and when properly cut, its brilliance would deceive all but an expert. And as in some real rubies there are found slight hollows corresponding or analogous to the bubbles found in melted glass, it becomes a matter of great difficulty to distinguish the real from the imitation by such tests as hardness, specific gravity, dichroism, and the like, so that in such a case, short of risking the ruin of the stone, ordinary persons are unable to apply any convincing tests.[4]

The Sapphire

The Sapphire is not so easy to imitate, as its hardness exceeds that of the ruby, and imitations containing its known constituents, or of glass, are invariably softer than the natural stone. . . . The blue sapphire is of all shades of blue, from cornflower blue to the very palest tints of this colour, all the gradations from light to dark purple blues, and, in fact, so many shades of tone and colour that they become almost as numerous as the stones. These stones are usually found in similar situations to those which produce the ruby, and often along with them. The lighter colours are usually called females, or feminine stones, whilst the darker ones are called masculine stones. Some of these dark ones are so deep as to be almost black, when they are called "ink" sapphires, and if inclining to blue, "indigo" sapphires, in contradistinction to which the palest of the stones are called "water" sapphires. The colouring matter is not always even, but is often spread over the substance of the stone in scabs or "splotches," which rather favours imitation, and, where this unevenness occurs, it may be necessary to cut or divide the stone, or so to arrange the form of it that the finished stone shall be equally blue throughout.[5]

■ ■ ■

I. The ruby is naturally red; the sapphire is naturally blue.
II. The sapphire is harder to duplicate because it breaks so easily.

    A. I
    B. II
    C. Both
    D. None

M A T H

Word Problems

1. Samuel is 16 years older than James; 4 years ago he was three times as old. How old is each?

2. Martha is 5 years old and her father is 30. In how many years will her father be twice as old as Martha?

3. George is three times as old as Amelia; in 6 years his age will be twice hers. What is the age of each?

4. Esther is three-fourths as old as Edward; 20 years ago she was half as old. What is the age of each?

5. Mary is 4 years old and Flora is 9. In how many years will Mary be two-thirds as old as Flora?

6. Harry is 9 years older than his little brother; in 6 years he will be twice as old. How old is each?

ENDNOTES

Introduction

1. James R. Van Tholen and Susan Dykstra-Poel, *Where All Hope Lies: Sermons for the Liturgical Year* (Grand Rapids, MI: William B. Eerdmans Publishing Co., 2003), p. 16.

Lesson 1

1. http://quotationsbook.com/quote/17756/.
2. Alene H. Harris, *Greek Morphemes Lessons: It's NOT Greek to Me!* 3rd edition (2010), http://www.christianbook.com/greek-morphemes-lessons-alene-harris/9886400109/pd/468109; Alene H. Harris, *Latin Morphemes Lessons: Latin and Loving It!* 2nd edition (2010), http://ready-to-teach.com/greek-purchasenow.php.
3. http://thinkexist.com/quotes/charles_r._swindoll/.
4. http://thinkexist.com/quotation.
5. http://www.brainyquote.com/quotes/quotes/a/adolfhitle125155.html.

Lesson 2

1. Thomas Wood, *Practical Grammar and Composition* (New York: D. Appleton Co.), p. 121.
2. www.quotationspage.com/quote/3040.html.
3. www.quotationspage.com/quote/3039.html.
4. http://www.vajraenterprises.com/quotes.htm.
5. Charles and Mary Bear, *History of the United States* (New York: MacMillan, 1921).
6. www.quotationspage.com/quote/3040.html.
7. Thomas Wood, *Practical Grammar and Composition*, (New York: D. Appleton Co.), p. 121.
8. wikiquote.org/wiki/John_Maynard_Keynes.
9. www.quotationspage.com/quote/3039.html.
10. http://quotationspage.com/quote/32942.html.

Lesson 3

1. http://quotedb.com/quotes/362.
2. http://quotegarden.com/math.html.
3. M.M. Pattison Muir, *The Story of Alchemy and the Beginnings of Chemistry* (New York: D. Appleton and Company, 1903).
4. http://quotationspage.com/quote/24949.html.
5. Agatha Christie, *And Then There Were None* (1939).
6. James Stobaugh, *Companion to 50 Classics* (self-published).
7. http://womensquotes.com/truth/.

Lesson 4

1. http://wikiquote.org/wiki/C.S._Lewis.
2. John Richard Hale, *Famous Sea Fights* (New York: L MacVeagh, The Dial Press, 1931).
3. George Orwell, *Animal Farm*, 1945.
4. http://quotationspage.com/quote/32863.html.
5. http://goodreads.com/quotes/show/129088.
6. Hale, *Famous Sea Fights*.

Lesson 5

1. Sharon Begley, "I Can't Think," *Newsweek* (March 7, 2011), http://www.archangelicbody.org/trans/trans0411.html.
2. George Loewen, unpublished quote.
3. Mary Ann Loughborough, *My Cave Life in Vicksburg*, 1864.
4. Benjamin Franklin, *Autobiography*, 1791.
5. http://brainyquote.com/quotes/authors/k/katherine_anne_porter.html.

Lesson 6

1. Jeff Gordinier, "Masters of Disguise Among Meatless Burgers," *New York Times*, March 22, 2011.
2. Leo Tolstoy, *War and Peace*, 1869.
3. http://quotedb.com/quotes/3474.
4. Aldous Huxley, *Brave New World* (NY: HarperCollins, 1932).
5. *The New York Times Current History: A Monthly Magazine: The European War, Volume I, From the Beginning to March 1915* (New York: The New York Times Company, 1915), p. 222–223, issued by the German government to the Associated Press from General Headquarters, Sept. 2.
6. Neil Postman, *Amusing Ourselves to Death* (New York: Penguin Group, 1985), foreword.
7. Charles, Kuralt, host of "On the Road."
8. http://quotegarden.com/books.html.

Lesson 7

1. http://quotationsbook.com/quote/27240/.
2. http://.superteacherworksheets.com/probability/probability.pdf.
3. http://www.lhup.edu/~dsimanek/eduquote.htm.
4. Fyodor Dostoyevsky, *The Brothers Karamazov* (1880).
5. http://www.amazon.com/Brothers-Karamazov-ebook/dp/B002Z13UAY.
6. Ibid.
7. William Allen, *Ulysses S. Grant* (Boston, MA: Mifflin, 1901), p. 2–3.
8. www.quotationsbook.com/quote/35158/.

Lesson 8

1. http://thinkexist.com/quotes/john_wayne/.
2. Anthony Breznican, " 'Captain America': A Different Superhero," *USA Today*, 3/24/2011, www.usatoday.com/LIFE/.../2011-03-25-captain25_ST_U.htm.
3. http://quotationspage.com/quote/2111.html.
4. http://www.goodreads.com/author/quotes/197092.A_C_Grayling.
5. Stephen Crane, *The Red Badge of Courage*, 1894.
6. Ellen Dallas and Caroline Burgin, *Among the Mushrooms* (New York: Biddle Publishers, 1900), section 30.
7. Chaim Potok, *The Chosen* (New York: Random House, 1969).
8. http://nanoethics.org/good.htm.
9. http://.gbt.org/text/sayers.html.

Lesson 9

1. Shelby Foote, *The Civil War* (New York: Random House, 1986).
2. Ibid., back cover.
3. Based on Louis G. Perez, *The History of Japan* (Westport, CT: Greenwood Press, 1998), http://questia.com.
4. Jack London, *Call of the Wild* (New York: Library of America, 1906).
5. http://dedroidify.com/ignorance.htm.
6. Kurt Vonnegut Jr., *Cat's Cradle* (New York: Rosetta Books, 1963).

Lesson 10

1. Clinton C. Gardner, *Beyond Belief: Discovering Christianity's New Paradigm* (White River Junction, VT: White River Press, 2008), p. 40.
2. Edward O. Wilson, *Consilience: The Unity of Knowledge* (New York: Random House, 1999).
3. http://purplemath.com/modules/perimetr2.htm.
4. Alexandre Dumas, The Count of Monte Cristo (New York: Penguin Classics, 1844).
5. Monica Stanley, *My Diary in Serbia* (London: Simpkin, Marshall, & Co., 1916), p. 38, 77.
6. http://quotationsbook.com/quote/18135/.
7. www.pitt.edu/~super1/lecture/lec10511/009.htm.
8. http://crossroad.to/Persecution/Bonhoffer.html.

Lesson 8 (continued)

9. George Herbert, "The Collar," unpublished essay (the student wishes to remain anonymous).
10. http://.gbt.org/text/sayers.html.
11. Charles Coffin, *Winning His Way* (Boston, MA: Perry Mason & Co., 1888), p. 1.

Lesson 11

1. Reinhold Niebuhr, *Moral Man and Immoral Society* (New York: Charles Scribner, 1934), p. xiv–xv.

2. Ibid., p. xi–xii.

3. http://quotationspage.com/quote/2087.html.

4. Trumbull White , *Our War with Spain for Cuba's Freedom* (New York: Freedom Press, 1898).

5. http://quotationspage.com/quote/9733.html.

6. Adapted from http://owl.english.purdue.edu/owl.

7. Arthur Miller, *The Crucible* (New York: Viking Press, 1953).

Lesson 12

1. Louisa May Alcott, *Little Women*, 1868.

2. Franz Litszt, *Life of Chopin* (1863).

3. http://quotationspage.com/quote/248.html.

4. "Effects of DDT" http://www.chem.duke.edu/~jds/cruise_chem/pest/effects.html.

Lesson 13

1. http://www.purplemath.com/modules/mixture.htm.

2. http://quotegarden.com/math.html.

3. http://actstudent.org/.

4. Miguel de Cervantes, *Don Quixote* (New York: Harper Collins, 2003).

5. http://poemhunter.com/quotations.

6. Joseph Quincy Adams, *Shakespearean Playhouses* (New York: Houghton Mifflin, 1917, 1960).

Lesson 14

1. Walter Brueggemann, *The Prophetic Imagination* (Philadelphia, PA: Fortress Press,1978), p. 13.

2. C.S. Lewis, *The Weight of Glory and Other Addresses* (Grand Rapids, MI: Eerdmans, 1965), p. 1–2. This quote is referenced in John Piper, *Desiring God* (Portland, OR: Multnomah Press, 1986), p. 16.

3. Jane Austen, *Emma* (New York: Penguin Classics, 1815 original).

4. Unknown, *A Diary of a U-Boat Commander*, 1918.

5. Robert Jennings, *Cattle and Their Diseases* (Philadelphia, PA: Potter Co., 1864).

6. http://pemberley.com/janeinfo/beechclf.html.

Lesson 15

1. Clement Clarke Moore, "Twas the Night before Christmas."

2. Walter Brueggemann, *Hopeful Imagination* (Minneapolis, MN: Fortress Press, 1989).

3. http://poemhunter.com/poem/arithmetic.

4. http://goodreads.com/author/quotes.

5. http://quoteworld.org/quotes/1496.

6. Mark Twain, *The Adventures of Huckleberry Finn*, 1884.

7. Edmund Spenser, The Fairie Queen, 1596.

Lesson 16

1. Walter Brueggemann, *Hopeful Imagination* (Minneapolis, MN: Fortress Press, 1989).

2. Ibid.

3. Quotes in this section are from John Bartlett, *Familiar Quotations* (Boston, MA: Little & Brown, 1905).

4. Gerald Lee, *The Lost Art of Reading* (New York: Putnam Co., 1903).

5. William Faulkner, *The Sound and the Fury* (New York: Vintage, 1929).

6. William Faulkner, *Intruder in the Dust* (New York: Vintage, 1948).

Lesson 17

1. http://great-quotes.com/quotes.

2. Ivan Turgenev, *Fathers and Children* (New York: The Macmillan Co., 1906).

3. http://quotegarden.com/math.html.

4. Ivan Sergeevich Turgenev, translated by Constance Garnett, *The House of Gentlefolk*, "Criticisms and Interpretations," by Maurice Baring (New York: P.F. Collier & Son Company, 1917), p. xix.

5. http://quotationsbook.com/quote/32588.

6. http://www.webmd.com/cold-and-flu/cold-guide/common_cold_causes.

7. http://quotationspage.com/quote.

8. Ibid.

9. Charles Kingsley, *Town Geology* (Rockville, MD: Serenity Publishers, 2009 reprint).

Lesson 18

1. http://forums.philosophyforums.com.

2. Gertrude Himmelfarb, *Looking Into the Abyss: Untimely Thoughts on Culture and Society* (New York: Alfred Knopf Co., 1994).

3. Michele Gilman et al., *The ACT for Dummies* (New York: Wiley Publishing Co., 2006).

4. Pearl S. Buck, *The Good Earth* (New York: Enriched Classics Reprint, 2006).

5. http://brainyquote.com/quotes/authors/t/toni_morrison.

6. Janice E. Stockard, *Daughters of the Canton Delta* (Stanford, CA: Stanford University Press, 1989), quoted in "The Role of Women in The Good Earth," http://faculty.randolphcollege.edu/fwebb/buck/mewarley/GoodEarth.html.

7. W. Hornaday, *The Extermination of the American Bison* (Washington DC: Washington Printing Office, 1889).

Lesson 19

1. http://quotationspage.com/quote/492.html.

2. http://actstudent.org/scores/index.html.

3. Charles Dickens, *Great Expectations* (1867).

4. en.wikiquote.org/wiki/Charles_Dickens.

5. http://pinkmonkey.com/booknotes/barrons/grtexpt64.asp.

6. William Faulkner, *As I Lay Dying* (New York: Vintage, 1929).

7. http://brainyquote.com/quotes/quotes/c/calvintril106046.html.

Lesson 20

1. Arthur O. Clarke, *Wildflowers of the Farm* (London: Oxford University Press), http://gutenberg.org.

2. Sinclair Lewis, *Babbitt* (1922).

3. Based on William L. Phelps, *Notes on Russian Literature* (New York: Macmillan Co., 1911), p. 11.

Lesson 21

1. http://www.goodreads.com/quotes/show/56598.

2. E. Abbott, *How to Write Clearly* (London: University Press, 1883), http://Gutenberg.org.

3. Charles Dickens, *Hard Times* (1854), p. 1. http://gutenberg.org.

4. Ibid.

5. http://pinkmonkey.com/booknotes/barrons/hardtimes55.asp.

6. Illustrations in this section are from *Elements of Structural and Systematic Botany*, by Douglas Houghton Campbell (Boston, MA: Ginn & Co., 1890).

Lesson 22

1. http://quotegarden.com/writing.html.

2. Adapted from Douglas H. Campbell, *Elements of Botany* (Boston, MA: Ginn & Co., 1890), p. 1.

3. Ernest Hemingway, "The End of Something."

4. thinkexist.com.

5. Suzee Vlk, et al., *The ACT for Dummies* (Hoboken, NJ: Wiley Publishing, Inc., 2005), p. 16–17.

6. William Shakespeare, *Hamlet*, c 1600.

Lesson 23

1. Karen L. Anglin, *Math Word Problems* (Hoboken, NJ: Wiley, 2004), p. 149.

2. Thornton Wilder, *Our Town* (1937).

3. http://goodreads.com/quotes/show/332822.

Lesson 24

1. http://brainyquote.com/quotes/authors/s/shelby_foote.html.

2. http://http://freefictionbooks.org/books/d/6304-damn-by-h-l-mencken?start=6.

3. http://www.actstudent.org/scores/index.html.

4. http://http://freefictionbooks.org/books/d/6304-damn-by-h-l-mencken?start=6.

5. John Steinbeck, *The Grapes of Wrath* (1939).

6. Karen L. Anglin, *Math Word Problems* (Hoboken, NJ: Wiley, 2004), p. 162.

Lesson 25

1. H.L. Mencken, *Damn! A Book of Calumny* (New York: Philip Goodman Co., 1918), section XIII, "History," p. 34.

2. http://breakoutofthebox.com/goodog.htm.

3. http://quotationspage.com/quote/713.html.

4. Thomas Wood, *Practical Grammar and Composition*, 1914.

5. Ernest Hemingway, *The Old Man and the Sea* (New York: Scribner, 1952).

6. http://scribd.com/doc.

7. Quotes in this section are from W.M. Baskervill and J.W. Sewell, *English Grammar* (1895), sections 411–412.

Lesson 26

1. http://quotesoncards.com/topic/thing/index_14.shtml.

2. Oscar Wilde, *The Picture of Dorian Gray* (1890). http://gutenberg.org.

3. Albert Gardner Robinson, *Cuba, Old and New* (New York: Longmans, Green, and Co.1915), p. 253–256; http://http://google.com/search?tbm=bks&tbo=1&q=The+development+of+Cuba%27s+commerce+since+the+withdrawal+of+Spain%2C+and+the+substitution+of+a+modern+fiscal+policy+for+an+antiquated+and+indefensible+system%2C+has+been+notable&btnG=.

4. Quote in this section are from W.M. Baskervill and J.W. Sewell, *English Grammar* (1895).

Lesson 27

1. www.brainyquote.com/quotes/authors/p/paul_tillich.html quoted in James Stobaugh, *A Gathered Inheritance* (Hollsopple, PA: Stobaugh Publishing, 2006), preface.

2. Walter Brueggemann, *The Land* (Philadelphia, PA: Fortress Press, 1977), p. 1.

3. H.G. Wells, *The War of the Worlds* (1898).

4. www.archive.org/.../intelligencetest00natirich/intelligencetest.

5. Sentences in this section are from W.M. Baskervill & J.W. Sewell, *An English Grammar* (1896).

6. www.goodreads.com/author/quotes/10427.James_Baldwin.

Lesson 28

1. Bernard Bailyn, *Ideological Origins of the American Revolution* (Cambridge, MA: Harvard University Press, 1967).

2. Oscar Handlin, *Race and Nationality in American Life* (Boston, MA: Little, Brown, 1957).

3. Sydney Ahlstrom, *The Religious History of the American People* (New Haven, CT: Yale University Press, 1973).

4. George Billias, et al., *Interpretations of American History* (New York: Maxwell Macmillan International, 1991), preface.

5. W.M. Baskervill & J.W. Sewell, *An English Grammar* (1896).

6. Jules Verne, *Around the World in 80 Days* (1889).

7. Ibid.

Lesson 29

1. http://bible.org/netbible.

2. James Stobaugh, *Companion to 50 Classics* (Green Forest, AR: New Leaf Press, 2012).

3. David Nash Ford, http://earlybritishkingdoms.com.

4. https://http://forsuchatimeasthis.com/blog/?p=677.; James P. Stobaugh, *British History* (Green Forest, AR: New Leaf Press, 1912).

5. http://flickr.com/photos/katerha/5592478529.

6. http://http://actstudent.org.

7. Mark Twain, *The Connecticut Yankee in King Arthur's Court* (1889).

8. Quotes in this section are from Baskervill & Sewell, *An English Grammar*, rule 411.

Lesson 30

1. Ellen Churchill Semple, *Influences of Geographic Environment* (1904); www.gutenberg.org/ebooks/15293.

2. www.stumbleupon.com.

3. H. Rider Haggard, *King Solomon's Mines* (1885).

4. James Stobaugh, *British History* (Green Forest, AR: New Leaf Press, 2012).

Lesson 31

1. http://gutenberg.ca/ebooks/sayers-greatest/sayers-greatest-00-h.html.

2. Neil Postman, *Amusing Ourselves To Death* (New York: Viking, 1985).

3. Alexis de Tocqueville, *Democracy in America* (New York: George Dearborn & Co., 1838).

4. Ibid.

5. www.dnaalchemy.com/Inspriational_Quotes.html.

6. Quotes in this section are from W.M. Baskervill and J.W. Sewell, *English Grammar* (1895), exercise 451.

7. Ellen Churchill Semple, *Influences of Geographic Environment* (1904); www.gutenberg.org/ebooks/15293.

Lesson 32

1. Baskervill & Sewell, *An English Grammar* (1895) Exercise 452

2. Quotes in this section are from W.M. Baskervill & J.W. Sewell, *An English Grammar* (1896).

3. Mark Twain, *Life on the Mississippi* (Boston, MA: James R. Osgood & Co., 1883).

Lesson 33

1. www.goodreads.com/quotes/show/6493.

2. Baroness Emmuska Orczy, *The Scarlet Pimpernel* (1903).

3. Ibid., p. 1.

Lesson 34

1. T.S. Eliot, *Murder in the Cathedral* (1935).

2. Ibid.

3. Ibid.

4. Ibid.

5. G.K. Chesterton, *Orthodoxy*, The Romance of Faith (1908), Section III, "The Suicide of Thought."

6. G.K. Chesterton, *Orthodoxy*, The Romance of Faith (1908) Section II, "The Maniac."

7. http://brainyquote.com.

Lesson 35

1. There are 15,000 cool phrases at this web address: http://http://.gutenberg.org/cache/epub/18362/pg18362.html.

2. Quotes in this section are from W.M. Baskervill and J.W. Sewell, *English Grammar* (1895), Section 283.

3. Rudyard Kipling, Kim (1900).

4. James Stobaugh, *British History* (New Leaf Press, 2012).

Lesson 36

1. Alvin Toffler, *The Futurists*, "The Nature of Future," by Bertrand de Jouvenel (New York: Random House, 1972), p. 277–283.

2. Thomas Sowell, *The Vision of the Anointed*, referenced in rightwingnews.com/quotes/anointed.php.

3. Thomas Sowell, *The Vision of the Anointed*, in a book review by Richard M. Ebeling, December 1995, http://www.fff.org/freedom/1295h.asp.

4. A.J. Devereaux, *Secrets to Empowered English* (Ebooks-Empire), p. 7.

5. Seymour I. Schwartz, *French and Indian War, 1754–1763: The Imperial Struggle for North America* (New York: Simon & Schuster, 1994), foreword.

6. http://centuryinter.net/tjs11/hist/fiwar.htm.

7. James Stobaugh, *American History* (Green Forest, AR: New Leaf Press, 2012).

8. James Fenimore Cooper, *The Last of the Mohicans* (1826).

Lesson 37

1. Homer, *Odyssey*, 8th century B.C., translated by Samuel Bulter.

2. Rafael Sabatini, *Captain Blood* (1922).

3. Quotes in this section are from W.M. Baskervill & J.W. Sewell, *An English Grammar* (1896), exercise 457.

4. Edward Jenner, *An Inquiry into the Causes and Effects of the Variolae Vaccinae*; http://www.bartleby.com/38/4/1.html.

5. Edwin Abbott, *How to Write Clearly* (1883).

Lesson 38

1. Joseph Devlin, *How to Speak and Write Correctly* (New York: Christian Herald, 1910), chapter 7.

2. www.healthguidance.org.

3. A.W. Tozer, *The Pursuit of God*, www.gutenberg.org/ebooks/25141, chapter 1.

4. Ibid.

5. Ibid.

Lesson 39

1. www.flickr.com/photos/lighthearted/1517641570.

2. Joseph Devlin, *How to Speak and Write Correctly* (New York: Christian Herald, 1910), chapter 2.

3. Jack London, *The Sea Wolf* (1904)

4. A.N. Whitehead, *Process and Reality* (1929).

5. www.brainyquote.com/quotes/quotes/a/alfrednort146957.html.

Lesson 40

1. http://www.dawn.com/2011/05/14/german-grandchildren-of-nazis-delve-into-past.html.

2. http://www.jewishvirtuallibrary.org/jsource/Holocaust/Izieu.html.

3. Rev. Edwin A. Abbott, *How to Write Clearly* (Boston, MA: Roberts Brothers, 1883), p. 48; www.scribd.com/doc/2336508/5.

4. Mary F. Porter, *Applied Psychology for Nurses* (Philadelphia, PA and London: W.B. Saunders Co., 1921).

5. James Stobaugh, *World History* (Green Forest, AR: New Leaf Press, 2012).

Lesson 41

1. Diogenes Allen, *Christian Belief in a Post-modern World* (Louisville, KY: Westminster/ John Knox Press, 1989),

2. Kenneth J. Gergen, *The Saturated Self: Dilemmas of Identity in Contemporary Life* (New York: Basic Books, 1991).

3. www.tumblr.com/tagged/charles+w+eliot.

4. http://.gutenberg.org/files/13309/13309-pdf.pdf ex. 29, p. 54–55.

5. Sigmund Freud, *Dream Psychology* (1920), p. 1–2.

6. G.A. Henty, *At Agincourt*; www.inspiring-shortstories.finecrypt.net/index.php?b=At_Agincourt.

7. James Stobaugh, *British History* (Green Forest, AR: New Leaf Press, 2012).

Lesson 42

1. Emily Dickinson, "Because I Could Not Stop for Death."

2. Emily Dickinson, "If I Should Die."

3. quote.robertgenn.com/auth_search.php?authid=1176Cached - Similar.

4. James Stobaugh, *American History* (Green Forest, AR: New Leaf Press, 2012).

5. Edward Hale, *A Man Without a Country*, preface (www.bartleby.com).

6. Edwin Abbott, *How to Write Clearly* (1883) p. 62.

7. Wallace Boyden, *First Book of Algebra* (1895), p. 56, http://gutenberg.org/files/13309.

8. www.goodreads.com/author/quotes/10427.James_Baldwin.

9. Abbott, *How to Write Clearly* (1883), p. 62.

10. quote.robertgenn.com/auth_search.php?authid=1176.

Lesson 43

1. Albert Camus, *The Stranger* (New York: Alfred A. Knopf, Inc., 1988), p. 116.

2. Ibid., p. 122–123.

3. Washington Irving, *The Legend of Sleepy Hollow* (1917).

4. Garrett P. Serviss, *Curiosities of the Sky* (New York: Harper & Brothers Publishing, 1909), p. 39–43.

Lesson 44

1. Emily Dickinson, "My Life Closed Twice Before Its Close."

2. Edward Taylor, "I Go to Prepare a Place for You."

3. Joseph Conrad, *Heart of Darkness* (Edinburgh; London: W. Blackwood and Sons, 1902).

4. Emile Cammaerts, *Through the Iron Bars* (New York: John Lane Company, 1917).

5. Ibid., p. 9–10.

6. academic.brooklyn.cuny.edu/english/melani/cs6/hope.html.

7. W.M. Baskervill & J.W. Sewell, *An English Grammar* (1896).

8. www.1-love-quotes.com/quote/7156.

9. Cammaerts, *Through the Iron Bars*, p. 56–57.

Lesson 45

1. Joseph Conrad, *Heart of Darkness* (Edinburgh; London: W. Blackwood and Sons, 1902), p. 47.

2. Ibid., p. 191–192.

3. Ibid., p. 202–204.

4. www.grammarmudge.cityslide.com.

5. Robert W. Williamson, *The Mafulum Mountain People of British New Guinea* (London: MacMillan Co., 1912), p. 84.

6. Matthew Holbeche Bloxam, *The Principles of Gothic Ecclesiastical Architecture* (London: D. Bogue, 1846).

7. Ibid.

8. Ibid.

Lesson 46

1. Allan Bloom, *The Closing of the American Mind* (1987).

2. T.S. Eliot, *Murder in the Cathedral* (1935).

3. T.S. Eliot, "The Rock."

4. Sophocles, *Oedipus Rex*.

5. Eliot, *Murder in the Cathedral*.

6. www.goodreads.com/author/quotes/494055.Edward_P_Morgan.

7. Rupert Brooke, *1914 and Other Poems* (1915).

8. James Stobaugh, *British Literature* (Green Forest, AR: New Leaf Press, 2012).

9. Ibid.

10. Rupert Brooke, "Now God Be Thanked Who Has Matched Us with His Hour."

11. Cornelia Funke, *Inkspell* (New York: Chicken House/Scholastic, 2005), p. 61.

12. Robert Ranulph Marett, *Anthropology* (New York: H. Holt and Company, 1911), p. 62–65.

13. Michael F. Graves, Bonnie Graves, and Sheldon Braaten, "Scaffolded Reading Experiences for Inclusive Classes"; www.iscaffold.com.cn/news/news_1085.html.

Lesson 47

1. http://www.bartleby.com/124/pres32.html.

2. Mary Boykin Chesnut, *A Diary from Dixie* (New York: D. Appleton and Co., 1905), p. 20.

3. James C. Mohr, editor, *The Cormany Diaries* (Pittsburgh, PA: University of Pittsburgh Press, 1982), p. 132.

4. R.M.T. Hunter, *Southern Historical Society Papers* (Richmond, VA: Southern Historical Society, 1876), Vol. 1, p. 1.

5. James Stobaugh, *Rhetoric* (Green Forest, AR: New Leaf Press, 2012).

Lesson 48

1. Elie Wiesel, *Night* (New York: Hill and Wang, 1960).

2. Joseph Stein, Fiddler on the Roof, 1964.

3. http://goodreads.com/author/quotes/1069006.

4. Howard Pyle, *The Merry Adventures of Robin Hood*, 1933.

Lesson 49

1. Will Durant, *The Story of Philosophy* (1926), introduction.

2. http://www.brainyquote.com/quotes/quotes/f/francisbac133503.html.

3. Will Durant, *The History of Philosophy* (New York: Simon and Shuster, 1926), ch. 1, Plato, quotationsbook.com/quote/38348.

4. Ibid.

5. Plato, *Gorgias*, translated by Benjamin Jowett, http://www.gutenberg.org/files/1672.

6. http://quotationsbook.com/quote/1546.

7. Booker T. Washington, *Up from Slavery* (New York: Doubleday, Page & Co., 1907).

8. Ibid., p. 1–2.

9. Ibid., p. 80–82.

10. John Steinbeck, *Travels with Charley; in Search of America* (New York: Viking Press, 1962), p. 124.

Lesson 50

1. C.S. Lewis, *The Screwtape Letters* (London: G. Bles, 1942), p. 12–13.

2. Charles Dickens, *A Tale of Two Cities*, 1859.

3. Edgar Allan Poe, "The Fall of the House of Usher," 1839.

4. http://www.crystalandstones.com/about-precious-stones/ruby.html.

5. http://popearrings.com/sapphire-earrings.html.

ANSWERS

LESSON 1

Reading
E

English
The sentence should read "Everyone should work hard in his/her studies." Everyone is a singular indefinite pronoun that requires a singular possessive pronoun in subsequent constructions.

Martin Luther King is the earliest leader in the Civil Rights' movement.

Writing
First person; the narrator is sarcastically describing his pejorative views toward modern technology.

Science
All

LESSON 2

Math
x = -5

Vocabulary
anthropophobiac means "afraid of people"
philanthropy means "love of mankind"
misanthrope means "someone who hates people"

Reading
B

English
C

Writing
I. Introduction: A year-long school would enable students to progress in their learning without any regression and as a result will help them compete in the world market.

II. Body

A. American students are behind foreign students in almost every academic area.

1. Students forget things in the summer.

2. Students need more time to learn difficult subjects.

B. Americans are not competitive in the job market.

1. Most engineers are from overseas.

2. Many students cannot read and write when they graduate.

III. Conclusion: Because of the crisis looming in American education students should stay in school all year.

Science
A

LESSON 3

Math
D

Vocabulary
A. There was a silence — a comfortable replete (complete, full) silence. Into that silence came The Voice. Without warning, inhuman, penetrating (strong; intrusive) . . . "Ladies and gentlemen! Silence, please! . . . You are charged with the following indictments (criminal charges)."

B. But — incongruous (paradoxically out of order) as it may seem to some — I was restrained (hindered) and hampered (restricted) by my innate (internal) sense of justice. The innocent must not suffer.

Reading
A and C are true.

A. I English
B

Writing
Pascal D. Forgione Jr., PhD, U.S. Commissioner of Education Statistic, argues that American education is in trouble. By the time our students are ready to leave high school — ready to enter higher education and the labor force — they are doing so badly with science they are significantly weaker than their peers in other countries. Our idea of "advanced" is clearly below international standards. One reason this is the case is that American students enjoy a summer break. What if that was removed? Clearly education would improve and scores would increase.

Science
A

LESSON 4

Math
C and D

Vocabulary
A. The pigs had an even harder struggle to counteract (replace) the lies put about by Moses, the tame raven. . . . The animals hated Moses because he told tales and did no work, but some of them believed in Sugarcandy Mountain, and the pigs had to argue very hard to persuade (convince) them that there was no such place.

B. The animals were not badly off throughout that summer. . . . The advantage (benefit) of only having to feed themselves, and not having to support five extravagant (generous to excess) human beings as well, was so great that it would have taken a lot of failures to outweigh it. And in many ways the animal method of doing things was more efficient (productive) and saved labour. Such jobs as weeding, for instance, could be done with a thoroughness impossible to human beings. And again, since no animal now stole, it was unnecessary to fence off pasture from arable (dry and fit for growing crops) land.

C. As yet no animal had actually retired on pension, but of late the subject had been discussed more and more. Now that the small field beyond the orchard had been set aside for barley, it was rumoured that a corner of the large pasture was to be fenced off and turned into a grazing-ground for superannuated (disqualified for active duty by advanced age) animals.

D. There was the same hearty cheering as before, and the mugs were emptied to the dregs. But as the animals outside gazed at the scene, it seemed to them that some strange thing was happening. What was it that had altered (changed) in the faces of the pigs?

Reading

D and A

English

B — parallel structure is necessary.

B — Turkish fleet requires a singular, third person possessive pronoun — its.

Writing

Write the body of an essay where you extend your argument introduced in lesson 3.

American education would benefit from full-year school, and American education needs help

(Argument 1). By grade 4, American students only score in the middle of 26 countries reported. By grade 8 they are in the bottom third, and at the finish line, where it really counts, we're near dead last. It's even worse when you notice that some of the superior countries in grade 8 (especially the Asians) were not included in published 12th grade results. They do not need 12 grades (Evidence 1). Part if not most of the problem is that American students forget most of their information in the summer and have to relearn it in the fall. Many studies have shown that in some subjects — especially math — students never really relearn what they have forgotten and therefore never really progress. The net result is that American education is in big trouble. A full-year school would remove a lot of these troubles.

Science

C. Both

LESSON 5

Math

The sum of two numbers is 60, and the greater is four times the less. What are the numbers?

Let x = the less number; then $4x$ = the greater number, and $4x + x = 60$, or $5x = 60$; therefore $x = 12$, and $4x = 48$. The numbers are 12 and 48.
Answer: 12 and 48.

If the difference between two numbers is 48, and one number is five times the other, what are the numbers?

Let x = the less number; then $5x$ = the greater number, and $5x ; x = 48$, or $4x = 48$; therefore $x = 12$, and $5x = 60$.

The num[...]

There ar[...]
sum is 96[...]
times the[...]
four times[...]
numbers?

X = first n[...]
$3x$ = second number,
$4x$ = third number.
$x + 3x + 4x = 96$
$8x = 90$
$x = 12$
$3x = 36$
$4x = 48$
The numbers are 12, 36, and 48.

Divide the number 126 into two parts such that one part is 8 more than the other.
X = less part,
$x + 8$ = greater part.
$x + x + 8 = 126$
$2x + 8 = 126$
$2x = 1181$
$x = 59$
$x + 8 = 67$
The parts are 59 and 67.

Vocabulary

A. Having emerged from the poverty and obscurity (anonymity) in which I was born and bred, to a state of affluence (prosperity) and some degree of reputation in the world, and having gone so far through life with a considerable share of felicity (great happiness), the conducing (contributing) means I made use of, which with the blessing of God so well succeeded, my posterity (descendants) may like to know, as they may find some of them suitable to their own situations, and therefore fit to be imitated.

B. It was written in 1675, in the home-spun verse of that time and people, and addressed to those then concerned in the government there. It was in favor of liberty of conscience, and in behalf of the Baptists, Quakers, and other sectaries that had been under

bing the In-
... other distresses
...efallen the country,
...persecution, as so many
...gments of God to punish so
...einous (terrible) an offense,
and exhorting (strongly urging)
a repeal of those uncharitable
(unjust; ungenerous) laws.

C. At his table he liked to have,
as often as he could, some sensible friend or neighbor to converse with, and always took care
to start some ingenious (original)
or useful topic for discourse (conversation), which might tend to
improve the minds of his children.

D. I continu'd this method some
few years, but gradually left
it, retaining only the habit of
expressing myself in terms of
modest diffidence (shyness).

E. In his house I lay that night,
and the next morning reach'd
Burlington, but had the mortifica-
tion (humiliation; shame) to find
that the regular boats were gone
a little before my coming. . . .

F. My ideas at that time were,
that the sect should be begun
and spread at first among young
and single men only; that each
person to be initiated should not
only declare his assent to such
creed, but should have exercised
himself with the thirteen weeks'
examination and practice of the
virtues as in the before-mention'd
model; that the existence of such
a society should he kept a secret,
till it was become considerable,
to prevent solicitations (entreat-
ies, allurements) for the admission
of improper persons, but that the
members should each of them
search among his acquaintance
for ingenuous (natural; genuine),
well-disposed youths, to whom,
with prudent (wise) caution, the
scheme should be gradually communicated these proverbs, which
contained the wisdom of many

ages and nations, I assembled
and form'd into a connected discourse prefix'd to the Almanack
of 1757, as the harangue (angry
diatribe) of a wise old man to
the people attending an auction.

G. In 1751, Dr. Thomas Bond, a
particular friend of mine, conceived the idea of establishing a
hospital in Philadelphia, a very
beneficent (beneficial; advantageous) design, which has been
ascrib'd to me, but was originally
his, for the reception and cure
of poor sick persons, whether
inhabitants of the province or
strangers. He was zealous (enthusiastic) and active in endeavoring
to procure subscriptions for it,
but the proposal being a novelty
(new thing) in America, and at
first not well understood, he met
with but small success.

Reading

A and D

English

I effected the outcome by my
choices.

I affected the outcome of my
choices.

It was alright for me to borrow
my mother's car.

It was all right for me to borrow
my mother's car.

Please lay next to the water
fountain.

Please lie next to the water
fountain.

I cannot choose between the
three food dishes.

I cannot choose among the three
food dishes.

Writing

As we move into the 21st century it
is imperative that America's leadership look again at its education.
It is failing. One easily implemented and highly effective way to

improve education is to institute
a full-year program. No doubt,
with this intervention America will
again be competitive in the world
arena.

Science

D and E

LESSON 6

Math

Divide the number 126 into two
parts such that one part is 8
more than the other.

x = less part,
$x + 8$ = greater part.
$x + x + 8 = 126$
$2x + 8 = 126$
$2x = 1181$
$x = 59$
$x + 8 = 67$
The parts are 59 and 67.

The sum of two numbers is 25,
and the larger is 3 less than three
times the smaller. What are the
numbers?

Let x = smaller number,
$3x \text{ } ¡ \text{ } 3$ = larger number.
$x + 3x \text{ } ¡ \text{ } 3 = 25$
$4x \text{ } ¡ \text{ } 3 = 25$
$4x = 282$
$x = 7$
$3x \text{ } ¡ \text{ } 3 = 18$
The numbers are 7 and 18.

Mr. Y gave $6 to his three boys.
To the second he gave 25 cents
more than to the third, and to
the first three times as much as to
the second. How much did each
receive?

X = number of cents third boy
received,
$x + 25$ = number of cents second
boy received,
$3x + 75$ = number of cents first
boy received.
$x + x + 25 + 3x + 75 = 600$
$5x + 100 = 600$
$5x = 500$
$x = 100$
$x + 25 = 125$

$3x + 75 = 375$
1st boy received $3.75,
2d boy received $1.25,
3d boy received $1.00.

Arthur bought some apples and twice as many oranges for 78 cents. The apples cost 3 cents apiece, and the oranges 5 cents apiece. How many of each did he buy?

Let x = number of apples,
$2x$ = number of oranges,
$3x$ = cost of apples,
$10x$ = cost of oranges.
$3x + 10x = 78$
$13x = 78$
$x = 6$
$2x = 12$

Vocabulary

A. The Director opened a door. They were in a large bare room, very bright and sunny; for the whole of the southern wall was a single window. Half a dozen nurses, trousered (wearing pants) and jacketed in the regulation white viscose-linen (clear; like rayon) uniform, their hair aseptically (extremely clean) hidden under white caps, were engaged in setting out bowls of roses in a long row across the floor. Big bowls, packed tight with blossom. Thousands of petals, ripe-blown and silkily smooth, like the cheeks of innumerable (a large number) little cherubs (angels), but of cherubs, in that bright light, not exclusively pink and Aryan, but also luminously (light) Chinese, also Mexican, also apoplectic (debilitative) with too much blowing of celestial (heavenly) trumpets, also pale as death, pale with the posthumous (after-death) whiteness of marble. (ch. 2)

B. An almost naked Indian was very slowly climbing down the ladder from the first-floor terrace of a neighboring house — rung after rung, with the tremulous (extreme) caution of extreme old age. His face was profoundly (deeply; throughly) wrinkled and black, like a mask of obsidian (black). The toothless mouth had fallen in. At the corners of the lips, and on each side of the chin, a few long bristles gleamed almost white against the dark skin. The long unbraided hair hung down in grey wisps (small strands) round his face. His body was bent and emaciated (thin to the extreme) to the bone, almost fleshless. Very slowly he came down, pausing at each rung before he ventured another step.

C. Lenina alone said nothing. Pale, her blue eyes clouded with an unwonted (unusual) melancholy (sadness), she sat in a corner, cut off from those who surrounded her by an emotion which they did not share. She had come to the party filled with a strange feeling of anxious exultation (celebration).

D. But who was he to be pampered (spoiled) with the daily and hourly sight of loveliness? Who was he to be living in the visible presence of God? . . . Seeing them, the Savage made a grimace (frown); but he was to become reconciled (at peace) to them in course of time; for at night they twinkled gaily with geometrical constellations, or else, flood-lighted, pointed their luminous (full of light) fingers (with a gesture whose significance nobody in England but the Savage now understood) solemnly towards the plumbless mysteries of heaven.

Reading

C and A

English

D, A, and B

Writing

Problem Sentence

Problem Number

Correct Sentence

(3) Nazi Germany started World War II.

(10) Hitler attacked Stalin in 1941; furthermore, he destroyed most of Russia's military.

(4) The Germany army attacked on July 22, 1941, but the Russian army was not ready.

(5) The German soldier with a black SS uniform attacked the railroad station.

(8) The surprise attack completely affected the outcome of the first year of fighting.

(7) The German army loved fighting and overwhelming its enemies.

(2) Germany almost captured Moscow in 1941.

(1) Every soldier finished his tour of duty.

(6) Hitler and his generals enjoyed their victories.

(9) Ultimately the German army won the Kiev campaign because they tried.

Science

C and A

Another way to phrase the problem would be, "The length of the waves varies inversely as the number of times the current is closed per second."

length of waves = x
frequency of closure = y

This leads to the equation, "$x = k/y$." Plugging in the values given, we find the constant k.

$1 = k/186{,}000$
$186{,}000 = k$

So the constant k is 186,000. Our equation now becomes $x = 186{,}000/y$.

Now we can solve the problem.

$x = 186{,}000/10$

$x = 18{,}600$ (answer A)

LESSON 7

Math

If you roll a die, what are the chances of rolling a two? 1 out of 6

If you roll a die, what is the probability that you will roll an even number? 1 out of 2

A bag contains 3 red marbles, 3 blue marbles, and 1 green marble. 3 out of

A bag contains 6 numbered tiles . . . 5 out of 6

Mr. Jones has a hot air balloon . . . 1 out of 3

What is the probability that he will select a girl? 2 out of 3

Vocabulary

A. At the time of Yefim Petrovitch's death, Alyosha had two more years to complete at the provincial (country; unsophisticated) gymnasium. The inconsolable (unable to be comforted) widow went almost immediately after his death for a long visit to Italy with her whole family, which consisted only of women and girls.

B. As he hastened out of the hermitage precincts (districts) to reach the monastery in time to serve at the Father Superior's dinner, he felt a sudden pang (pain) at his heart, and stopped short. He seemed to hear again Father Zossima's words, foretelling his approaching end. What he had foretold so exactly must infallibly (without fail) come to pass. Alyosha believed that implicitly (with no evidence). But how could he go?

C. "Quite so, quite so," cried Ivan, with peculiar (unique) eagerness, obviously annoyed (irritated) at being interrupted, "in anyone else this moment would be only due to yesterday's impression and would be only a moment. But with Katerina Ivanovna's character, that moment will last all her life. What for anyone else would be only a promise is for her an everlasting burdensome, grim perhaps, but unflagging (untiring) duty. And she will be sustained (supported; nourished) by the feeling of this duty being fulfilled. Your life, Katerina Ivanovna, will henceforth be spent in painful brooding (contemplating) over your own feelings, your own heroism, and your own suffering; but in the end that suffering will be softened and will pass into sweet contemplation (deep thought) of the fulfillment of a bold and proud design.

D. "After a month of hopeless love and moral degradation (humiliation), during which he betrayed his betrothed (fiancée) and appropriated (took) money entrusted to his honour, the prisoner was driven almost to frenzy, almost to madness by continual jealousy — and of whom? His father! And the worst of it was that the crazy old man was alluring and enticing (tempting; attracting) the object of his affection.

Reading

D, B, and D

English

Not that General Rosecran shouldn't be in the mix. He was a pretty good general.

George Washington, of course, lived in Virginia anyway.

And you should think about World War II — now that was a great war.

Writing

The struggle is daily. There are choices we make, people we talk to, and sights that we see. This all is unavoidable, and goes on outside of us but mostly inside. This struggle forces us to choose between the hard way of the cross, or the easy broad path leading to destruction. For example, George Herbert (1593–1633), one of the 17th century poets, wrote a beautiful poem titled, "The Collar." This poem is written in the first person about himself, and not only identifies the struggle between good and evil, but in it he also faces the struggle, and in the end, he wins. The poem begins with the words, "I struck the board, and cried, "No more! I will abroad." Here Herbert is fearfully running away from God and telling Him "no more," and to leave him alone. He knows that he has been given free will, "My lines and life are free; free as the road, loose as the wind, as large as store." But he is not sure he wants to use it, "Shall I still be in suit?" Next, he begins to struggle with what he has lost, "Have I no harvest but a thorn to let me blood, and not restore what I have lost with cordial fruit? Is the year only lost to me? Have I no bays to crown it? No flowers no garlands gay? All blasted? All wasted?" But telling himself that, that cannot be all, "Not so, my heart; but there is fruit, and thou hast hands," he begins to calm down, and see what he has really been given. Then the struggle changes, from being a struggle between running away or staying and becoming having to let go. "Leave thy cold dispute of what is fit and not; forsake thy cage, thy rope of sands, which petty thoughts have made." Here Herbert writes beautiful examples of how we are often tied up in things that we think are important. But in reality if we shake them off, we find that they are of no use to us at all.

He goes on to say, "Tie up thy fears," which is another example of leaving behind something that we do not need and cannot enter the Kingdom with. The poem ends very simply in submission, "Me thoughts I heard one calling, 'Child'; and I replied, 'My Lord.'" At that point there is no struggle, he is at complete peace.

Leaving behind the struggle to immerse oneself in complete submission is an idea at which some people would laugh. But not George Herbert. When he wrote this poem, he knew that it was a beautiful action. And so it has been captured onto paper, for all of us (Anna).

Topic Sentence
That I, whose experience of teaching is extremely limited, should presume to discuss education is a matter, surely, that calls for no apology. It is a kind of behavior to which the present climate of opinion is wholly favorable. Bishops air their opinions about economics; biologists, about metaphysics; inorganic chemists, about theology; the most irrelevant people are appointed to highly technical ministries; and plain, blunt men write to the papers to say that Epstein and Picasso do not know how to draw. Up to a certain point, and provided that the criticisms are made with a reasonable modesty, these activities are commendable. Too much specialization is not a good thing. There is also one excellent reason why the veriest amateur may feel entitled to have an opinion about education. For if we are not all professional teachers, we have all, at some time or another, been taught. Even if we learnt nothing — perhaps in particular if we learnt nothing — our contribution to the discussion may have a potential value.

However, it is in the highest degree improbable that the reforms I propose will ever be carried into effect. Neither the parents, nor the training colleges, nor the examination boards, nor the boards of governors, nor the ministries of education, would countenance them for a moment. For they amount to this: that if we are to produce a society of educated people, fitted to preserve their intellectual freedom amid the complex pressures of our modern society, we must turn back the wheel of progress some four or five hundred years, to the point at which education began to lose sight of its true object, towards the end of the Middle Ages. . . .

When we think about the remarkably early age at which the young men went up to university in, let us say, Tudor times, and thereafter were held fit to assume responsibility for the conduct of their own affairs, are we altogether comfortable about that artificial prolongation of intellectual childhood and adolescence into the years of physical maturity which is so marked in our own day? To postpone the acceptance of responsibility to a late date brings with it a number of psychological complications which, while they may interest the psychiatrist, are scarcely beneficial either to the individual or to society. The stock argument in favor of postponing the school-leaving age and prolonging the period of education generally is there is now so much more to learn than there was in the Middle Ages. This is partly true, but not wholly. The modern boy and girl are certainly taught more subjects — but does that always mean that they actually know more?

Science
A

LESSON 8

Math
What number added to twice itself and 40 more will make a sum equal to eight times the number?

x = the number.
$x + 2x + 40 = 8x$
$3x + 40 = 8x$
$40 = 5x$
$8 = x$
The number is 8.

Divide the number 72 into two parts such that one part shall be one-eighth of the other.

x = greater part,
$\frac{1}{8}x$ = lesser part.
$x + \frac{1}{8}x = 72$
$\frac{9}{8}x = 72$
$\frac{1}{8}x = 8$
$x = 64$
The parts are 64 and 8.

Vocabulary
A. I had spent five days in a hospital and the world around seemed sharpened (to become sharp) now and pulsing (moving with purpose) with life.

B. A span of life is nothing. But the man who lives that span (determined length), he is something.

C. It makes us aware of how frail (weak) and tiny we are and of how much we must depend upon the Master of the Universe.

D. We shook hands and I watched him walk quickly away, tall, lean, bent forward (pushing ahead) with eagerness and hungry for the future, his metal capped shoes tapping against the sidewalk.

Reading

D, A, C, C, and A

English

Indian history begins 4,000 years ago. India is a success story. India's population recently exceeded one billion people, yet a noted Indian historian said that "although it is difficult to accept, the Indians totally lacked the historical sense." The ancient Indians made great inroads into astronomy, physics, mathematics, all kinds of literature and arts, but never seriously took to documenting their history — and their indifference has cost their posterity very dearly. Civilization, when an agricultural economy, gave rise to extensive urbanization and trade. The second stage occurred around 1000 B.C., when the Ganga-yamuna river basin and several southern river deltas experienced extensive agricultural expansion and population growth.

Writing

Main Idea: When we think about the remarkably early age at which the young men went up to university in, let us say, Tudor times, and thereafter were held fit to assume responsibility for the conduct of their own affairs, are we altogether comfortable about that artificial prolongation of intellectual childhood and adolescence into the years of physical maturity which is so marked in our own day?

Detail: To postpone the acceptance of responsibility to a late date brings with it a number of psychological complications which, while they may interest the psychiatrist, are scarcely beneficial either to the individual or to society.

Detail: The stock argument in favor of postponing the school-leaving age and prolonging the period of education generally is there is now so much more to learn than there was in the Middle Ages.

Detail: This is partly true, but not wholly. The modern boy and girl are certainly taught more subjects — but does that always mean that they actually know more?

Science

E

LESSON 9

Math

The half and fourth of a certain number are together equal to 75. What is the number?

x = the number.

$\frac{1}{2}x + \frac{1}{4}x = 75.$

$\frac{3}{4}x = 75$

$\frac{1}{4}x = 25$

x = 100

The number is 100.

What number is that which being increased by one-third and one-half of itself equals 22?

x = the number.

$x + \frac{1}{3}x + \frac{1}{2}x = 22.$

$\frac{15}{6}x = 22$

$\frac{11}{6}x = 22$

$\frac{1}{6}x = 2$

x = 12

The number is 12

Vocabulary

A. Perhaps by now McClellan had learned to abide the tantrums (fits of bad temper) and exasperations (irritations) of his former friend and sympathizer.
B. McClellan was quite aware of the danger of straddling (going on both sides of) what he called "the confounded (frustrating) Chickahominy."
C. In addition to retaining the services of Seward and Chase, both excellent men at their respective (particular) posts, he had managed to turn aside the wrath (intense anger) of the Jacobins (extreme political radicals) without increasing their bitterness toward himself or incurring (bringing upon himself) their open hatred. . . . Paradoxically (the opposite of expected), because of the way he had done it.
D. Stuart had accepted the gambit (sacrifices to gain advantage; maneuver).
E. Poor as the plan was in the first place, mainly because of its necessary surrender of the initiative (making the first move) to the enemy, it was rendered even poorer — in fact, inoperative (dysfunctional; not working) — by the speed in which Sherman moved through the supposedly impenetrable (impassable) swamps.

Reading

Setting is a critical component of this book. What is the setting in chapter 1? The setting begins in Southern California but moves to Alaska.

Which setting is most friendly? Southern California. This is important because Buck (the dog) changes from the soft, domesticated pet in the beginning of the novel to the wild, assertive animal in Alaska. Buck, in effect, answers the "call of the wild."

English

B, E, A, D, C, and F

Writing

B does not belong.

Science

B

LESSON 10

Math

The surface area is 272(pi) square feet.

The rectangle is 7 centimeters long and 14 centimeters wide.

Vocabulary

A. Now, in spite of the mobility (changeability) of his countenance (face), the command of which, like a finished actor, he had carefully studied before the glass, it was by no means easy for him to assume an air of judicial (legal) severity (seriousness). Except the recollection of the line of politics his father had adopted, and which might interfere (impede), unless he acted with the greatest prudence (cautious wisdom), with his own career, Gerard de Villefort was as happy as a man could be.

B. "Then," answered the elder prisoner, "the will of God be done!" and as the old man slowly pronounced (declared) those words, an air of profound (deep) resignation (surrender; acceptance) spread itself over his care-worn (grieving; anguished) countenance. Dantès gazed on the man who could thus philosophically (thoughtfully and theoretically) resign hopes so long and ardently (fervently) nourished (maintained) with an astonishment (extreme excitement) mingled (mixed) with admiration (astonished approbation).

C. He had a very clear idea of the men with whom his lot had been cast. . . . It spared him interpreters (people who explain), persons always troublesome (causing problems) and frequently indiscreet (imprudent), gave him great facilities (aptitudes) of communication, either with the vessels he met at sea, with the small boats sailing along the coast, or with the people without name, country, or occupation, who are always seen on the quays (landing places; docks) of seaports, and who live by hidden and mysterious means which we must suppose to be a direct gift of providence, as they have no visible means of support. It is fair to assume that Dantès was on board a smuggler.

D. It would be difficult to describe the state of stupor (a state of supreme, debilitative disbelief) in which Villefort left the Palais. Every pulse (heartbeat) beat with feverish (extreme) excitement, every nerve was strained (under stress), every vein swollen, and every part of his body seemed to suffer distinctly from the rest, thus multiplying his agony a thousand-fold. He made his way along the corridors (passageways) through force of habit; he threw aside (away) his magisterial (official; ceremonial) robe, not out of deference (respect) to etiquette (polite custom), but because it was an unbearable (too much to carry) burden, a veritable (genuine; true) garb of Nessus, insatiate (unable to be satisfied) in torture. Having staggered (walked in uncoordinated style) as far as the Rue Dauphine, he perceived his carriage, awoke his sleeping coachman by opening the door himself, threw himself on the cushions, and pointed towards the Faubourg Saint-Honoré; the carriage drove on. The weight of his fallen fortunes seemed suddenly to crush him; he could not foresee the consequences (outcome; results); he could not contemplate the future with the indifference (without regard) of the hardened criminal who merely faces a contingency (unforeseen result) already familiar. God was still in his heart. "God," he murmured (spoke in complaint), not knowing what he said — "God — God!" Behind the event that had overwhelmed (deeply upset) him he saw the hand of God. The carriage rolled rapidly onward. Villefort, while turning restlessly on the cushions, felt something press against him. He put out his hand to remove the object; it was a fan which Madame de Villefort had left in the carriage; this fan awakened a recollection (remembrance) which darted through his mind like lightning. He thought of his wife.

Reading

E, A

English

1. The president recently finished reading the Bible.

2. Our company is called For Such A Time As This.

3. "Open the door now!" exclaimed the soldier.

4. I visited the Washington Monument.

5. The North defeated the South in the American Civil War.

Writing

Answers will vary.

Science

E, B

LESSON 11

Math

$X + X + 10 = 180$
$2X = 170$
$X = 85$
$Y = 95$

Vocabulary

A. I look for John Proctor that took me from my sleep and put knowledge in my heart! I never knew what pretense (falsity; fraud) Salem was, I never knew the lying lessons I was taught by all these Christian women and their covenanted (contracted) men! And now you bid me tear the light out of my eyes? I will not, I cannot! You loved me, John Proctor, and whatever sin it is, you love me yet!

B. This is a sharp time, now, a precise (exact) time — we live no longer in the dusky afternoon when evil mixed itself with good and befuddled (confused) the world.

Reading

The world has never seen a contest like it (hyperbole). Nations have fought for territory and for gold, but they have not fought for the happiness of others (generalization).

Men have gone on crusades to fight for holy tombs and symbols, but armies have not been put in motion to overthrow vicious (inflammatory diction) political systems and regenerate iniquitous (inflammatory diction) governments for other peoples.

For more than four centuries Spain has held the island of Cuba as her chattel, and there she has revelled in corruption, and wantoned in luxury wrung from slaves with the cruel hand of unchecked power (inflammatory diction).

But the end has come at last. The woe, the grief, the humiliation, the agony, the despair that Spain has heaped upon the helpless, and multiplied in the world until the world is sickened with it, will be piled in one avalanche on her own head (hyperbole and inflammatory diction).

Liberty has grown slowly. Civilization has been on the defensive. Now liberty fights for liberty, and civilization takes the aggressive in the holiest (emotional language) war the world has even known

English

1. Mark is ready, but Mary is not.

2. I know who is listening when I speak.

3. Nothing matters more to a mom because she loves to see her daughters safe.

4. When I step up to the plate, I hit a ball.

5. I love eating berries but they do not love me!

Writing

Remove these two paragraphs:

In the 1870s Japanese leadership sent a group on a diplomatic mission around the world. Under the leadership of Iwakura Tomomi, they were to learn about technologically advanced countries of the West. The Iwakura mission's direct observation of the West left them feeling challenged but hopeful and it seemed possible that Japan could catch up with the Western nations.

Japan lost World War II but emerged as one of the premier economic powers of the post-World War II world.

Science

C

LESSON 12

Math

B

Vocabulary

A. Amy rebelled outright, (overtly with vigor) and passionately (with emotion and enthusiasm) declared that she had rather have the fever than go to Aunt March. Meg reasoned, pleaded, and commanded, all in vain. Amy protested that she would not go, and Meg left her in despair to ask Hannah what should be done. Before she came back, Laurie walked into the parlor to find Amy sobbing, with her head in the sofa cushions. She told her story, expecting to be consoled (comforted), but Laurie only put his hands in his pockets and walked about the room, whistling softly, as he knit his brows in deep thought. Presently he sat down beside her, and said, in his most wheedlesome (patient, bordering on patronizing) tone, "Now be a sensible little woman, and do as they say. No, don't cry, but hear what a jolly plan I've got. You go to Aunt March's, and I'll come and take you out every day, driving or walking, and we'll have capital times. Won't that be better than moping (sulking) here?"

B. Jo's face was a study next day, for the secret rather weighed upon her, and she found it hard not to look mysterious and important. Meg observed it, but did not trouble herself to make inquiries, for she had learned that the best way to manage Jo was by the law of contraries (opposites), so she felt sure of being told everything if she did not ask. She was rather surprised, therefore, when the silence remained unbroken, and Jo assumed a patronizing (superior, pejorative) air, which decidedly aggravated Meg, who in turn assumed an air of dignified reserve and devoted herself to her mother. . . . Amy being gone, Laurie was her only refuge(safe and private), and much as she enjoyed his society, she rather dreaded him just then, for he was an incorrigible (adamant, stubborn) tease, and she feared he would coax the secret from her.

C. There were to be no ceremonious performances, everything was to be as natural and home-like as possible, so when Aunt March arrived, she was scandalized (to have the appearance of a scandal) to see the bride come running to welcome and lead her in, to find the bridegroom fastening up a garland that had fallen down, and to catch a glimpse of the paternal (fatherly) minister marching upstairs with a grave countenance (facial expression) and a wine bottle under each arm.

D. "You look like the effigy (image, usually of a dead person on his tomb) of a young knight asleep on his tomb," she said, carefully tracing the well-cut profile defined against the dark stone.

E. Yes, Jo was a very happy woman there, in spite of hard work, much anxiety, and a perpetual (continual) racket. She enjoyed it heartily and found the applause of her boys more satisfying than any praise of the world, for now she told no stories except to her flock of enthusiastic believers and admirers. As the years went on, two little lads of her own came to increase her happiness — Rob, named for Grandpa, and Teddy, a happy-go-lucky baby, who seemed to have inherited his papa's sunshiny temper as well as his mother's lively spirit. How they ever grew up alive in that whirlpool of boys was a mystery to their grandma and aunts, but they flourished like dandelions in spring, and their rough nurses loved and served them well.

Reading
B

English
1. The mayor is not a mean man, but he has limits. (Join with but)

2. He was sure there would be an end to the war when the enemy surrendered. (Join with when)

3. I really want to go to Dallas, Texas, and I want to watch the Steelers beat the Cowboys. (Join with and)

Writing
1. The Germans caused World War II.

2. Mary published her first novel at age 12.

3. Although, I never visited Hong Kong, my wife tells me it is beautiful.

Science
11.8 grams of DDT (11.8g + delta)

LESSON 13

Math
Since we expect about 13,000 people, this works out to about 10,343 adult tickets. The remaining 2657 tickets will be child tickets. Then the expected total ticket revenue totals to $58,357.50, of which ($5.00)(10,343) = $51,715 will come from adult tickets, and ($2.50)(2,657) = $6,642.50 will come from child tickets.

Vocabulary
A. You must know, then, that the above-named gentleman whenever he was at leisure (which was mostly all the year round) gave himself up to reading books of chivalry (with courtesy and decorum) with such ardor and avidity (affinity) that he almost entirely neglected the pursuit of his field-sports, and even the management of his property; and to such a pitch did his eagerness and infatuation (foolish and extravagant love) go that he sold many an acre of land to buy books of chivalry to read, and brought home as many of them as he could get.

B. He approved highly of the giant Morgante, because, although of the giant breed which is always arrogant (harsh and haughty) and ill-conditioned, he alone was affable (friendly) and well-bred.

C. Thus setting out, our new-fledged adventurer paced along, talking to himself and saying, "Who knows but that in time to come, when the veracious history of my famous deeds is made known, the sage who writes it, when he has to set forth my first sally in the early morning, will do it after this fashion? 'Scarce had the rubicund (red) Apollo spread o'er the face of the broad spacious earth the golden threads of his bright hair, scarce had the little birds of painted plumage attuned their notes to hail with dulcet (agreeable) and mellifluous (richly flowing and generous) harmony the coming of the rosy Dawn. . . . And thou, O sage (wise) magician, whoever thou art, to whom it shall fall to be the chronicler of this wondrous history, forget not, I entreat (beg) thee, my good Rocinante, the constant companion of my ways and wanderings." Presently he broke out again, as if he were love-stricken in earnest, "O Princess Dulcinea, lady of this captive heart, a grievous wrong hast thou done me to drive me forth with scorn, and with inexorable(relentless) obduracy (stubbornness) banish me from the presence of thy beauty. O lady, deign to hold in remembrance this heart, thy vassal, that thus in anguish pines for love of thee."

D. Seeing what was going on, Don Quixote said in an angry voice, "Discourteous (impolite) knight, it ill becomes you to assail (accost; attack) one who cannot defend himself; mount your steed and take your lance" (for there was a lance leaning against the oak to which the mare was tied), "and I will make you know that you are behaving as a coward." The farmer, seeing before him this figure in full armor brandishing a lance over his head, gave himself up for dead, and made answer meekly, "Sir Knight, this youth that I am chastising (scolding) is my servant, employed by me to watch a flock of sheep that I have hard by, and he is so careless that I lose one every day, and when I punish him for his carelessness and knavery (mischievously evil) he says I do it out of niggardliness, to escape paying him the wages I owe him, and before God, and on my soul, he lies."

E. Such was the end of the Gentleman of La Mancha, whose village Cide Hamete would not indicate precisely, in order to leave all the towns and villages of La Mancha to contend among themselves for the right to adopt him and claim him as a son, as the seven cities of Greece contended for Homer. The lamentations (expressions of grief) of Sancho and the niece and housekeeper are omitted here, as well as the new epitaphs (brief, pithy statements) upon his tomb.

Reading
D and A

English
Active: The car hit the deer.

Active: The workers built the football stadium in five months.

Passive: His homework was finished by Rosco.

Passive: His tricks were practiced by my dog.

Writing
False. Robert Frost likes to play in the snow.

True. Someone must have hurt Frost.

True. Frost seems to be unhappy as he writes this poem.

False. Frost is writing a poem about fire and ice.

True. Frost is writing a poem about love and hatred.

Science
Many chimneys offer affordable heat; close auxilliary buildings can be reached in the winter; high, pitched roofs provide quick snow removal. High ceilings offer cool summer comfort.

Leaks will occur where adjacent buildings are joined, where adjacent rooms are joined on corners, and places where standing water and snow will settle.

LESSON 14

Math
1,662 square feet

Vocabulary
A. Harriet Smith's intimacy at Hartfield was soon a settled thing. Quick and decided in her ways, Emma lost no time in inviting, encouraging, and telling her to come very often. . . . Her father never went beyond the shrubbery, where two divisions of the ground sufficed (archaic use of the word "sufficient" meaning adequate) him for his long walk, or his short, as the year varied; and since Mrs. Weston's marriage her exercise had been too much confined.

B. In short, she sat, during the first visit, looking at Jane Fairfax with twofold complacency (peaceful composure). . . that case, nothing could be more pitiable or more honourable than the sacrifices she had resolved on. Emma was very willing now to acquit (to absolve, to remove all guilt) her of having seduced Mr. Dixon's actions from his wife, or of any thing mischievous which her imagination had suggested at first . . . and from the best, the purest of motives, might now be denying herself this visit to Ireland, and resolving to divide herself effectually (successfully accomplish) from him and his connections by soon beginning her career of laborious duty.

C. As long as Mr. Knightley remained with them, Emma's fever continued; but when he was gone, she began to be a little tranquilized and subdued — and in the course of the sleepless night . . . but she flattered herself, that if divested (to remove forcefully) of the danger of drawing her away, it might become an increase of comfort to him. . . . At any rate, it would be a proof of attention and kindness in herself, from whom every thing was due; a separation for the present; an averting of the evil day, when they must all be together again.

Reading
The main character, a German U-boat captain, is developed through dialogue and narrative. We never know what the captain is really thinking.

English
Answers will vary

Writing
Problem: Again, this was awfully good news to a community that faced the awful King Sennacherib. King Hezekiah, Uzziah's successor, was sorely tempted to trust in Egypt, but frankly, Isaiah in chapter 35 is making an offer that Hezekiah cannot refuse.

Solution: The really good news of Isaiah 35, and of the gospel, is that as we — the chosen community, today the Church — rejoice, grow healthy, and find ourselves living in Zion, so also will the land and those who live in it find hope, health, and wholeness. Health to the Jew, as it was to the Greek, means far more than physical health. It means healing, wholeness. Indeed, the Greek word salvation has at its root the word health. We are the light of the world, and we can change our world as we share the good news. The Christ whom we represent is the only real hope the world has for wholeness. And we should be outspoken and unequivocal with this message. As we sing, with our words and our lives, the land will be saved, made whole. "Say to those with fearful hearts: 'Be strong; do not fear! Then the eyes of the blind will be opened and the ears of the deaf unstopped' " (Is. 35:4–5).

End Result: Likewise, today, when we live a holy life, when we trust in God with faith and hope, the land in which we work and live becomes holy. In this God, of whom we bear witness with our words and lives, we, like the faithful Israelites, find wholeness, health, and life. This news is good news!

Science

1. What is disease? Disease is the general term for any deviation from the normal or healthy condition of the body.

2. What is a predisposing cause? The predisposing causes are such factors as tend to render the body more susceptible to disease or favor the presence of the exciting cause. Exciting cause? The exciting causes are the immediate causes of the particular disease. Exciting causes usually operate through the environment.

LESSON 15

Math
8/15 of the cistern

Vocabulary
A. Scarsely (barely; infrequently) had Phoebus in the glooming (dawning) East / Yet harnessed (attached) his firie-footed teeme

B. For all so soone, as Guyon thence was gon / Vpon his voyage with his trustie guide, / That

wicked band of villeins fresh begon / That castle to assaile on euery side, / And lay strong siege about it far and wide. / So huge and infinite their numbers were, / That all the land they vnder them did hide; / So fowle and vgly, that exceeding (excessive) feare / Their visages imprest, when they approched neare.

C. Who backe returning, told as he had seene, / That they were doughtie knights of dreaded (fearful) name; / And those two Ladies, their two loues vnseene; / And therefore wisht them without blot or blame, / To let them passe at will, for dread of shame. / But Blandamour full of vainglorious (prideful) spright, / And rather stird by his discordfull Dame, / Vpon them gladly would haue prov'd his might, / But that he yet was sore of his late lucklesse fight.

Reading
Two descriptions:

I got into my old rags and my sugar-hogshead again, and was free and satisfied. But Tom Sawyer he hunted me up and said he was going to start a band of robbers, and I might join if I would go back to the widow and be respectable. So I went back.

The widow she cried over me, and called me a poor lost lamb, and she called me a lot of other names, too, but she never meant no harm by it.

Twain creates humor mostly through exaggeration.

English
D and D

Writing
Answers will vary.

Science
A and B

LESSON 16

Math
$2a2 + 7a - 4 = 0$
First we factor: $(2a - 1)(a + 4) = 0$
This brings us to our first solution:
$a = -$

For our second solution, we bring the first set of parentheses out and solve for zero:
$2a - 1 = 0$
$2a = 1$
$a = 1/2 = 0.5$
Our two solutions are -4 and 0.5 (answer B)

Vocabulary
A. You can be oblivious (unable to discern or to respond) to the sound for a long while, then in a second of ticking it can create in the mind unbroken the long diminishing parade of time you didn't hear.

B. From then on until he had you completely subjugated he was always in or out of your room, ubiquitous (everywhere present) and garrulous (talkative), though his manner gradually moved northward as his raiment improved, until at last when he had bled you until you began to learn better he was calling you Quentin or whatever. . . .

C. . . . and I suppose that with all his petty chicanery (mischievious behavior) and hypocrisy (insincere behavior) he stank no higher in heaven's nostrils than any other.

D. Suddenly I held out my hand and we shook, he gravely, from the pompous (indigenous hubris) height of his municipal and military dream.

E. . . . where only he and the gull, the one terrifically motionless, the other in a steady and measured pull and recover that partook of inertia (tendency to remain in its original position) itself. . . .

F. . . . all I had felt suffered without visible form antic and perverse mocking without relevance inherent (internal) themselves with the denial of the significance they should have affirmed. . . .

G. The air brightened, the running shadow patches were not the obverse (main side), and it seemed to him that the fact the day was cleaning was another cunning stoke on the part of the foe.

H. . . . and suddenly with an old premonition (prediction; prophecy) he clapped the brakes and stopped and sat perfectly still. . . . For a moment Benjy sat in an utter hiatus (cessation).

Reading

D and D

English

1. England in the eleventh century was conquered by the Normans.

2. Amid the angry yells of the spectators, he died.

3. For the sake of emphasis, a word or a phrase may be placed out of its natural order.

4. In *The Pickwick Papers*, the conversation of Sam Weller is spiced with wit.

5. New York, on the contrary, abounds in men of wealth.

6. It has come down by uninterrupted tradition from the earliest times to the present day. (No Punctuation)

Writing

Answers will vary.

Science

E

LESSON 17

Math

12 yards

Vocabulary

A. The servant, from a feeling of propriety (conventional standards), and perhaps, too, not anxious to remain under the master's eye, had gone to the gate, and was smoking a pipe. Nikolai Petrovitch bent his head, and began staring at the crumbling steps; a big mottled (spotted or streaked) fowl walked sedately (quietly, confidently) towards him, treading firmly with its great yellow legs; a muddy cat gave him an unfriendly look, twisting herself coyly (reticent) round the railing.

B. She used suddenly to go abroad, and suddenly return to Russia, and led an eccentric life in general. She had the reputation of being a frivolous (superficial, humorous) coquette (superficial), abandoned herself eagerly to every sort of pleasure, danced to exhaustion, laughed and jested with young men, whom she received in the dim light of her drawing-room before dinner; while at night she wept and prayed, found no peace in anything, and often paced her room till morning, wringing (grasping and moving) her hands in anguish, or sat, pale and chill, over a psalter.

C. Nikolai Petrovitch had made Fenitchka's acquaintance in the following manner. He had once happened three years before to stay a night at an inn in a remote district town. He was agreeably struck by the cleanness of the room assigned to him, the freshness of the bed-linen. Surely the woman of the house must be a German? was the idea that occurred to him; but she proved to be a Russian, a woman of about fifty, neatly dressed, of a good-looking, sensible countenance (face) and discreet (measured, careful, confidential) speech.

Reading

D and B

English

1 A, 2 B, 3 A

Writing

The author uses a series of rhetorical questions that he then answers himself. For example, "Freedom: what do we want freedom for? For this, at least; that we may be each and all able to think what we choose; and to say what we choose also, provided we do not say it rudely or violently, so as to provoke a breach of the peace."

Science

A, D, C

LESSON 18

Math

We know that it is a parallelogram because the question states that we have two pairs of equal sides. One pair is twice as long as the other pair.

We will let the long side be y and the short side be x.

The question stated that the long side is exactly twice the length of the short side. Mathematically, this can be expressed as:

$$y = 2x$$

It also stated that the total perimeter of the rectangle was 250 feet. This can be expressed as:

$$2y + 2x = 250$$
$$(2y/2) + (2x/2) = (250/2)$$
$$y + x = 125$$

Our two equations are therefore:

1. $y = 2x$
2. $2y + 2x = 250$

We can solve this rather easily by substitution. Substituting equation one into equation 2:

$$2x + x = 125$$
$$3x = 125$$

$(3x/3) = (125/3)$
$x = 41.6667$ or 41 and 2/3

Substituting back into the original equation:

$y = 2(x)$
$y = 2(41.6667)$
$y = 83.3333$ or 83 and 1/3

The solution for the equation is (41.6667,83.3333).

The north and south gutters measure 83"4' and the east and west gutters measure 41"8'

If we double the solutions of the equation and add them, we get 250, which shows us that our solution was correct. Vocabulary
A. There was only this perfect sympathy (relationship; affinity) of movement, of turning this earth of theirs over and over to the sun, this earth which formed their home and fed their bodies and made their gods.

B. But Wang Lung thought of his land and pondered (considered) this way and that, with the sickened heart of deferred (postponed) hope, how he could get back to it. He belonged, not to this scum which clung to the walls of a rich man's house; nor did he belong to the rich man's house. He belonged to the land and he could not live with any fullness until he felt the land under his feet and followed a plow in the springtime and bore a scythe (cutting blade) in his hand at harvest.

Reading
D

English
1. This (direct object), and other measures (direct object) of precaution, I (subject) took.

2. The pursuing the inquiry under the light of an end or final cause (subject clause), gives wonderful animation (direct object), a

sort of personality to the whole writing.

3. Why does the horizon (subject) hold me (direct object) fast, with my joy and grief, in this center?

4. His books (subject) have no melody (direct object), no emotion (direct object), no humor (direct object), no relief (direct object) to the dead prosaic level.

5. On the voyage to Egypt, he (subject) liked, after dinner, to fix on three or four persons to support a proposition, and as many to oppose it.

Writing
1. Her "baby" son is 67 The author is writing this passage as if this, her youngest son, was a mid-twenty marriage ceremony.

2. The notion that New Yorkers are mowing their lawns at Christmas is an anomaly!

Science
G and F

LESSON 19

Math
10

Vocabulary
A. I could faintly make out the only two black things in all the prospect that seemed to be standing upright; one of these was the beacon by which the sailors steered — like an unhooped cask upon a pole — an ugly thing when you were near it; the other, a gibbet (historical), with some chains hanging to it which had once held a pirate.

B. She concluded by throwing me — I often served as a connubial (matrimonial) missile — at Joe, who, glad to get hold of me on any terms, passed me on into the chimney and quietly fenced me up there with his great leg.

C. My sister had a trenchant (strident; combative) way of cutting our bread and butter for us. . . . Then she took some butter (not too much) on a knife and spread it on the loaf, in an apothecary kind of way, as if she were making a plaster — using both sides of the knife with a slapping dexterity . . . before separating from the loaf, hewed (cut) into two halves, of which Joe got one, and I the other.

D. My sister, having so much to do, was going to church vicariously (done as if one were someone else); that is to say, Joe and I were going.

Reading
C and F

English
D, C, A

Writing
B

Science
B, C, H

LESSON 20

Math
$27,205.20 (remember: 1% of his commission, not 1% of his sale), 7500 books

Vocabulary
A. Myra Babbitt — Mrs. George F. Babbitt — was definitely mature. She had creases from the corners of her mouth to the bottom of her chin, and her plump neck bagged. But the thing that marked her as having passed the line was that she no longer had reticences (shyness) before her husband, and no longer worried about not having reticences. She was in a petticoat now, and corsets which bulged, and unaware of being seen in bulgy corsets. She had become so dully habituated (to be accustomed to) to married life that in her full

matronliness (characteristics of a mother) she was as sexless as an anemic (pale) nun. She was a good woman, a kind woman, a diligent (conscientious; hard working) woman, but no one, save perhaps Tinka her ten-year-old, was at all interested in her or entirely aware that she was alive.

B. After a rather thorough discussion of all the domestic and social aspects of towels she apologized to Babbitt for his having an alcoholic headache; and he recovered enough to endure the search for a B.V.D. undershirt which had, he pointed out, malevolently (with malfeasance or evil) been concealed among his clean pajamas.

C. He was fairly amiable (friendly) in the conference on the brown suit.

Reading

The Babbitt family was a typical, upper middle class, late 19th century nouveau rich family. The represented the worst of the Gilded Age, a time when unprecedented wealth was accompanied by no particular increase in morality or perspicacity.

English

1. I felt that I breathed an atmosphere of sorrow (functions as a direct object).

2. But the fact is, I was napping (functions as a predicate nominative).

3. Shaking off from my spirit what must have been a dream (functions in apposition to the subject I), I scanned more narrowly the aspect of the building.

4. Except by what he could see for himself (functions in apposition to the direct object nothing), he could know nothing.

5. Whatever he looks upon (function as a subject) discloses a second sense.

Writing

C

Science

E

That is because the plants sowed their own seed. The flowers faded; then the seed-cases shed their seed upon the ground. Next spring the seeds produced fresh plants. Most annual wild flowers sow their own seed in this way, but we must not mistake them for perennials because year after year they grow in the same place.

LESSON 21

Math

1 hour 12 minutes (1 1/5 hours)

Vocabulary

A. The square finger, moving here and there, lighted suddenly on Bitzer, perhaps because he chanced to sit in the same ray of sunlight which, darting in at one of the bare windows of the intensely white-washed room, irradiated (shined on) Sissy.

B. Whether I was to do it or not, ma'am, I did it. I pulled through it, though nobody threw me out a rope. Vagabond, errand-boy, vagabond, labourer, porter, clerk, chief manager, small partner, Josiah Bounderby of Coketown. Those are the antecedents (precedents), and the culmination (the highest point)

C. In truth, Mrs. Gradgrind's stock of facts in general was woefully (sadly) defective; but Mr. Gradgrind in raising her to her high matrimonial (concerning marriage) position, had been influenced by two reasons.

D. "Whether," said Gradgrind, pondering with his hands in his pockets, and his cavernous (immense) eyes on the fire.

Reading

C and B

English

1. There were passages that reminded me perhaps too much of Massillon. (modifies the noun passages)

2. I walked home with Calhoun, who said that the principles which I had avowed were just and noble. (modifies the proper noun Calhoun)

3. Other men are lenses through which we read our own minds. (modifies the noun lenses)

Writing

THE INDUSTRY OF LAWYER

Oddly enough, hardly any notice is taken of an industry in which the United States towers in unapproachable supremacy above all other nations of the earth. The census does not say a word about it, nor does there exist more than the merest word about it in all the literature of American self-praise.

The author is calling attention to his point, "industry in the United States," by stating that it is hardly noticed when comparisons are made to other nations. This is an effective way to pique the interests of readers.

MY CHILDHOOD FEAR OF GHOSTS

Nothing stands out more keenly in the recollection of my childhood, than the feelings of terror which I experienced when forced to go to bed without the protecting light of a lamp. Then it was that dread, indefinite ghosts lurked behind every door, hid in every clothes-press, or lay in wait beneath every bed.

Using a personal anecdote, the author is drawing the reader into his narrative. Clearly, he will be discussing electricity. By evoking a personal story, the author is hoping that the reader will be stimulated to identify with him and, therefore, join the author in the spirit of the occasion. In other words, the author is saying "this is important to you so you should read it."

THE USES OF IRON

No other metal is put to so many uses and is so indispensable as iron.

This author is employing my personal favorite: a direct, cogent, straightforward introduction that clearly states his purpose in one sentence. This reader would enjoy a small quote or two, but overall, this is an effective way to begin an essay. Especially an ACT essay that must be informative from the beginning!

Science
Figure 2 is a single-cell animal without any connection to other organisms.

A

LESSON 22

Math
17 inches

Vocabulary
A. A mote (particle) it is to trouble the mind's eye.

In the most high and palmy (alive) state of Rome,

A little ere the mightiest Julius fell,

The graves stood tenantless, and the sheeted dead

Did squeak and gibber in the Roman streets;

As, stars with trains of fire and dews of blood,

Disasters in the sun; and the moist star,

Upon whose influence Neptune's empire stands,

Was sick almost to doomsday (end times) with eclipse (declining):

And even the like precurse of fierce events —

As harbingers preceding still the fates,

And prologue to the omen (foreboding prophecy) coming on —

B. Think it no more:
For nature, crescent (curved shape like a half moon), does not grow alone

C. Then weigh what loss your honour may sustain (keep healthy)
If with too credent (credible) ear you list his songs,
Or lose your heart, or your chaste treasure open
To his unmaster'd importunity (opportunity)

D. Out of the shot and danger of desire.
The chariest maid is prodigal (recalcitrant, wayward) enough

E. And in the morn and liquid dew of youth
Contagious blastments (set backs, obstacles) are most imminent (inevitable)
Be wary then; best safety lies in fear:
Youth to itself rebels, though none else near

Reading
While they once were very close, sustaining friends, they now struggle to be close. Their relationship is strained.

English
See underline:
As I was clearing away the weeds from this epitaph, the little sexton

drew me on one side with a mysterious air, and informed me in a low voice that once upon a time, on a dark wintry night, when the wind was unruly, howling and whistling, banging about doors and windows, and twirling weathercocks, so that the living were frightened out of their beds, and even the dead could not sleep quietly in their graves, the ghost of honest Preston was attracted by the well-known call of "waiter," and made its sudden appearance just as the parish clerk was singing a stave from the "mirrie garland of Captain Death."

Writing
1. They can go everywheres.
They can go anywhere they wish.

2. He spends all his time grinding.
He spends all his time grinding corn.

3. There ain't a sightlier town in the state.
There is no prettier town in the state.

4. He ate the whole hunk of cake.
He ate the entire cake.

5. Smith's new house is very showy.
Smith's new house if very ostentatious.

Science
E and E

LESSON 23

Math
The train traveling east is traveling at a speed of 65 mph.
The westbound train is traveling 90mph.

The swimming portion of the race was 4 miles, the running part was 9 miles, and the bicycling part was 55 miles.

Vocabulary
A. That's what it was like to be alive. To move about in a cloud

of ignorance; to go up and down trampling (stomping) on the feelings of those . . . of those about you. To spend and waste time as though you had a million years. To be always at the mercy of one self-centered passion, or another.

B. Never support two weaknesses at the same time. It's your combination sinners — your lecherous (immoral) liars and your miserly (parsimonious) drunkards — who dishonor the vices and bring them into bad repute (reputation; character).

C. He regarded love as a sort of cruel malady (sickness) through which the elect are required to pass in their late youth and from which they emerge, pale and wrung (disheveled; diminished), but ready for the business of living.

Reading

B

English

1. The horse with the rider holding a young girl went into the barn.

2. Mary drove the automobile with its tank full of gas.

3. The dancer dazzled the audience full of loyal patrons.

Writing

C. The pronoun *myself* requires a singular form of the verb *speaks*.

Science

All the answers are plausible answers except IV. So the answer is F.

LESSON 24

Math

$3,700 was invested in the technology fund that yielded 9% simple interest; $3,900 was invested in the fixed account that yielded 6% simple interest. A total of $7,600 was invested.

Vocabulary

A. Is a tractor bad? Is the power that turns the long furrows (plowed rows) wrong? If this tractor were ours, it would be good — not mine, but ours. . . . The people were driven, intimidated (frightened), hurt by both. We must think about this.

B. And the great owners, who must lose their land in an upheaval (disruption) the great owners with access to history, with eyes to read history and to know the great fact: when property accumulates (collects) in too few hands it is taken away.

C. How can you frighten a man whose hunger is not only in his own cramped (constricted) stomach but in the wretched (awful) bellies of his children? You can't scare him — he has known a fear beyond every other.

Reading

D

English

1. Who they were I really cannot specify.

2. Truth is mightier than we all.

3. If there ever was a rogue in the world, it is I.

4. They were the very two individuals who we thought were far away.

5. Seems to me as if they who write must have a gift for it.

Writing

Mock/Serious. This adds to the irony and humor of the passage.

Science

G and H

LESSON 25

Math

10 green apples

Vocabulary

A. The old man was thin and gaunt (emaciated) with deep wrinkles in the back of his neck. The brown blotches (discolored) of the benevolent skin cancer the sun brings from its reflection on the tropic sea were on his cheeks. . . . They were as old as erosions (deteriorated) in a fishless desert.

B. . . . he looked ahead and saw a flight of wild ducks etching (marking) themselves against the sky over the water, then blurring, (causing to be unclear) then etching again and he knew no man was ever alone on the sea.

Reading

As Madame Defarge knits a covering for a corpse, suspense increases (diction clues). This is developed even more with repetition. Next, there is the drumbeat. Syntax, violent words, builds suspense.

English

Neither of the two sisters were very much deceived. — Thackeray.

Every one must judge of his own feelings. — Byron.

Had the doctor been contented to take my dining tables, as anybody in his senses would have done. — Austen.

If the part deserve any comment, every considering Christian will make it himself as he goes. — Defoe.

Every person's happiness depends in part upon the respect he meets in the world. — Paley.

Every nation has its refinements. — Sterne.

Neither gave vent to his feelings in words. — Scott.

Each of the nations acted according to his national custom. — Palgrave.

Writing

Sad and pensive

This tone is created by heart-wrenching scenes of a poor, defenseless, suffering dog.

Science

B

LESSON 26

Math

$3x^2 - 5xy - 2y^2$

Vocabulary

A. No, you don't feel it now. Some day, when you are old and wrinkled and ugly, when thought has seared (burned) your forehead with its lines, and passion branded your lips with its hideous (awful, terrible) fires, you will feel it, you will feel it terribly.

B. It cannot be questioned. It has its divine right of sovereignty (ownership). It makes princes of those who have it.

C. Every month as it wanes brings you nearer to something dreadful (terrifying).

D. Don't squander the gold of your days, listening to the tedious (predictable, boring), trying to improve the hopeless failure, or giving away your life to the ignorant, the common, and the vulgar.

E. We degenerate (break down) into hideous puppets, haunted by the memory of the passions of which we were too much afraid, and the exquisite temptations that we had not the courage to yield to. Youth! Youth! There is absolutely nothing in the world but youth!

F. A few wild weeks of happiness cut short by a hideous, treacherous (pejorative, dangerous) crime. Months of voiceless agony, and then a child born in pain.

G. Behind every exquisite (wonderful) thing that existed, there was something tragic. There was something terribly enthralling (engrossing) in the exercise of influence.

Reading

Argument: Has American intervention in post-Spanish American Cuba been a good thing? Yes! The development of Cuba's commerce since the withdrawal of Spain, and the substitution of a modern fiscal policy for an antiquated and indefensible system, has been notable.

Detail: Imports are higher than ever. Cuba is prospering and so is the USA.

Detail. Exports to Cuba are higher, too.

Detail: Political stability in the region is higher than ever.

English

1. And sharp Adversity will teach at last Man — and, as we would hope — perhaps the devil, That neither of its intellects are vast. — Byron.

2. Both death and I are found eternal. — Milton.

3. How each of these professions is crowded. — Addison.

4. Neither of his counselors were to be present. — Id.

5. Either of them are equally good to the person to whom he is significant. — Emerson.

Writing

B, E, D, A, C

Science

F

LESSON 27

Math

Answer is C. The slope of the line perpendicular to Z has a negative value. The only answer choices with negative slopes are C and D. You can back solve from there.

Vocabulary

A. The growing crowd, he said, was becoming a serious impediment (obstacle) to their excavations, especially the boys. . . . The case appeared to be enormously thick, and it was possible that the faint sounds we heard represented a noisy tumult (uproar) in the interior.

B. I was very glad to do as he asked, and so become one of the privileged spectators within the contemplated (analyzed; well considered) enclosure (compound; stockade). I failed to find Lord Hilton at his house, but I was told he was expected from London by the six o'clock train from Waterloo; and as it was then about a quarter past five, I went home, had some tea, and walked up to the station to waylay (stop; cause impediment) him.

C. Two large dark-coloured eyes were regarding me steadfastly (firmly). . . . The whole creature heaved (moved up substantially) and pulsated (throbbing, bumping) convulsively. A lank tentacular appendage (extension) gripped the edge of the cylinder, another swayed in the air.

D. Those who have never seen a living Martian can scarcely imagine the strange horror of its appearance. The peculiar V-shaped mouth with its pointed upper lip, the absence of brow ridges, the absence of a chin beneath the wedgelike lower lip, the incessant (without ceasing) quivering (spasmodic moving) of this mouth, the Gorgon (fierce, frightening) groups of tentacles. . . .

Reading

Suspenseful. Wells uses the narration (first person by a participant) and diction ("A sudden chill came over me. There was a loud shriek from a woman behind.")

English

1. They crowned him long ago; But whom they got to put it on nobody seems to know.

2. I experienced little difficulty in distinguishing among the pedestrians who had business with St. Bartholomew.

3. The great difference lies between the laborer who moves to Yorkshire and him who moves to Canada.

4. It can't be worth much to them that hasn't larning.

5. To send me away for a whole year — me who had never crept from under the parental wing — was a startling idea.

Science

D

LESSON 28

Math

Let AM and AH in all the figures denote the positions of the minute and hour hands at 1 o'clock, and AX the position of both hands when together.

Let x = number of minute spaces in arc M X.

M X = M H + H X

x = 5 + x 12

Solution gives x = 5-5/11

Hence, the time is 5-5/11 minutes past 1 o'clock.

Vocabulary

A. It would be rash (precipitous) to predict how Passepartout's lively nature would agree with Mr. Fogg. Passepartout had been a sort of vagrant in his early years, and now yearned (to seek fervently) for repose (to rest); but so far he

had failed to find it, though he had already served in ten English houses. But he could not take root in any of these; with chagrin (embarrassment) he found his masters invariably (inevitably) whimsical (playful) and irregular, constantly running about the country, or on the look-out for adventure.

B. Fix had . . . to take his seat in the car, an irresistible (inexorable) influence held him back.

C. The engineer whistled, the train started, and soon disappeared, mingling its white smoke with the eddies (patterns) of the densely falling snow.

D. The weather was dismal (dreary), and it was very cold. Aouda, despite the storm, kept coming out of the waiting-room, going to the end of the platform, and peering (looking intently) through the tempest of snow. . . . She heard and saw nothing. Then she would return, chilled through, to issue out again after the lapse (cessation) of a few moments, but always in vain.

E. The commander of the fort was anxious, though he tried to conceal his apprehensions (concerns). As night approached, the snow fell less plentifully, but it became intensely cold. Absolute silence rested on the plains. Neither flight of bird nor passing of beast troubled the perfect calm.

F. Throughout the night Aouda, full of sad forebodings (foreshadowing; hints), her heart stifled with anguish (worry; discomfiture), wandered about on the verge (edge) of the plains.

Reading

A

English

1. Let you and me look at these, for they say there are none such in the world.

2. "Nonsense!" said Amyas, "we could kill every soul of them in half an hour, and they know that as well as I."

3. Markland, whom, with Jortin and Thirlby, Johnson calls three contemporaries of great eminence.

5. They are coming for a visit to her and me.

Science

B

LESSON 29

Math

Let x = number of hours the second is traveling.

x + 5 = number of hours the first is traveling.

8 1/2 x = distance the second travels.

6(x + 5) = distance the first travels.

8 1/2 x = 6(x + 5). Solution gives x = 12.

He will overtake the first in 12 hours.

Vocabulary

A. Camelot — Camelot," said I to myself. "I don't seem to remember hearing of it before. Name of the asylum (abode of mentally challenged people), likely."

B. It was a soft, reposeful (restful) summer landscape, as lovely as a dream, and as lonesome as Sunday.

C. She walked indolently (lazily) along, with a mind at rest, its peace reflected in her innocent face.

D. She was going by as indifferently (uninterested) as she might have gone by a couple of cows; but when she happened to notice me, then there was a change!

Up went her hands, and she was turned to stone; her mouth dropped open, her eyes stared wide and timorously, she was the picture of astonished curiosity touched with fear. And there she stood gazing, in a sort of stupefied (mesmerizing) fascination.

E. I couldn't make head or tail of it. And that she should seem to consider me a spectacle, and totally overlook her own merits in that respect, was another puzzling thing, and a display of magnanimity (forgiveness), too, that was surprising in one so young.

"F. As we approached the town, signs of life began to appear. At intervals we passed a wretched (awful) cabin, with a thatched roof, and about it small fields and garden patches in an indifferent state of cultivation.

G. Presently there was a distant blare of military music; it came nearer, still nearer, and soon a noble cavalcade (procession) wound into view, glorious with plumed helmets and flashing mail and flaunting banner. . . .

Reading

A and C

English

1. Neither of the sisters was very much deceived. — Thackeray.

2. Every one must judge of his own feelings. — Byron.

3. Had the doctor been contented to take my dining tables, as anybody in his senses would have done. — Austen.

4. If the part deserve any comment, every considering Christian will make it himself as he goes. — Defoe.

Writing

This essay is a 4 or 5. Essays within this score range demonstrate adequate skill in responding to the task. However, I would like to see more examples (he only offers two).

Science

E

LESSON 30

Math

$y = 5$, $x = 2$

Vocabulary

A. With the first light we were up and making ready for the fray (altercation).

B. With great difficulty, and by the promise of a present of a good hunting-knife each, I succeeded in persuading three wretched (poor) natives from the village to come with us for the. . . . They jabbered (nonsensical sound) and shrugged their shoulders, saying that we were mad and should perish of thirst, which I must say seemed probable; but being desirous (desiring) of obtaining the knives, which were almost unknown treasures up there, they consented to come, having probably reflected (contemplated) that, after all, our subsequent (following) extinction (wiping out) would be no affair of theirs.

C. . . . by a precipitous (steep, dangerous) cliff of rock, and towering in awful white solemnity (quiet; peaceful) straight into the sky.

D. These mountains placed thus, like the pillars of a gigantic gateway, are shaped after the fashion of a woman's breasts, and at times the mists and shadows beneath them take the form of a recumbent (lying prostrate) woman, veiled mysteriously in sleep. The stretch of cliff that connects them appears to be some thousands of feet in height, and perfectly precipitous (dangerous), and on each flank of them, so far as the eye can reach, extent similar lines of cliff. . . .

Reading

B and A

English

1. Mary plays the guitar beautifully, and so we will ask her to play for church. (who)

We asked Mary, who plays the guitar beautifully, to play for church.

2. My homework needs some attention, so I asked my mother to help me. (because)

I asked my mother to help me because my homework needs some attention.

3. I gathered as much coal as I could, and the winter storm struck. (before)

Before the winter storm struck, I gathered as much coal as I could.

4. We slowed down, and we saw the roadblock. (when)

When we saw the roadblock we slowed down.

My friends could hear the enemy growing closer because the enemy was talking. Finally we could see the enemy emerge around the bend. The captain was motioning with his hand to be quiet because the soldiers were laughing. One blew his noise and coughed as he stumbled. All my friends were staring and waiting as the enemy soldiers came forward.

Writing

In fact, this is very close to being perfect. It would be a 6 except there are no counter arguments. Counter-arguments are critical. There are several good examples, fairly well developed. The author repeats his thesis fairly often in an inspiring way. There is a conclusion that stays on point.

Science

E.

LESSON 31

Math

1. $x = \pm 3$.

2. $x = \pm 2$.

3. $x = \pm 5$.

4. $x = \pm 2$.

5. $x = \pm 1/2$.

Vocabulary

Through their means man acquires a kind of preternatural (beyond what is natural) power over the future lot of his fellow-creatures. When the legislator has regulated the law of inheritance, he may rest from his labor. The machine once put in motion will go on for ages, and advance, as if self-guided, towards a given point. When framed in a particular manner, this law unites, draws together, and vests property and power in a few hands: its tendency is clearly aristocratic (high class) On opposite principles its action is still more rapid; it divides, distributes, and disperses both property and power. Alarmed by the rapidity of its progress, those who despair of arresting (stopping) its motion endeavor to obstruct it by difficulties and impediments (obstacles); they vainly seek to counteract its effect by contrary efforts. . . . When the law of inheritance permits, still more when it decrees, the equal division of a father's property amongst all his children, its effects are of two kinds: it is important to distinguish (separate) them from each other, although they tend to the same end.

In virtue of the law of partible (partial) inheritance, the death of every proprietor (owner) brings about a kind of revolution in property; not only do his possessions change hands, but their very nature is altered, since they are parcelled into shares, which become smaller and smaller at each division. This is the direct and, as it were, the physical effect of the law. It follows, then, that in countries where equality of inheritance is established by law, property, and especially landed property, must have a tendency to perpetual (unceasing) diminution (declination).

Reading

C

English

1. There are, then, many things to be considered carefully, if a strike is to succeed. — Laughlin.

2. That the mind may not have to go backwards and forwards in order rightly to connect them. — Herbert Spencer.

3. It may be easier to bear along all the qualifications of an idea . . . than first to imperfectly conceive such idea. — Id.

4. In works of art, this kind of grandeur, which consists in multitude, is to be admitted very cautiously. — Burke.

5. That virtue which requires ever to be guarded is scarcely worth the sentinel. — Goldsmith.

Writing

This would be a 4. There needs to be more than two examples. While it is organized fairly well, the argument/thesis must be repeated several times.

Science

F

LESSON 32

Math

1. M, 390; H, 130.

2. 39; 41; 32; 27.

3. 3205; 2591; 1309.

4. 20 miles; 4 miles; 48 miles.

Vocabulary

Now and then Mr. Bixby called my attention to certain things. Said he, "This is Six-Mile Point." I assented (agreed). It was pleasant enough information, but I could not see the bearing of it. . . . they all looked about alike to me; they were monotonously (boring; in the same tone) unpicturesque (uniform; immemorial; out of date). . . . The "off-watch" was just turning in, and I heard some brutal (cruelly harsh) laughter from them. . . . It seemed to me that I had put my life in the keeping of a peculiarly (strange) reckless outcast. . . . This manner jolted (shook) me. I was down at the foot again, in a moment. But I had to say just what I had said before. . . . Oh, but his wrath (vehemence) was up!

Reading

D

English

1. Only the name of one obscure epigrammatist in the verses of his rival has been embalmed for us. — Palgrave.

2. Do you remember pea shooters? I think we only had them when we went home for holidays. — Thackeray.

3. Affording one horse, Irving could only live very modestly. — Id.

4. By supposing the motive power to have been steam, the arrangement of this machinery could only be accounted for. — Wendell Phillips.

5. No change.

Writing

This essay would be scored a 4. It is neat and well-written.

However, it lacks robust writing. It has too few examples. No counter argument.

Science

D

LESSON 33

Math

1. Dictionary, $7.20; thesaurus, $.90.

2. 112; 4144.

3. Aleck, 56; Arthur, 8.

4. Mother, 28; daughter, 4.

5. John, 15 yrs.; Mary, 5 yrs.

Vocabulary

A. A surging (increasing), seething (penetrating), murmuring (garrulous) crowd of beings that are human only in name, for to the eye and ear they seem naught but savage creatures, animated (made alive) by vile (repulsive) passions and by the lust of vengeance and of hate.

B. During the greater part of the day the guillotine (device to execute criminals) had been kept busy at its ghastly work: all that France had boasted of in the past centuries, of ancient names, and blue blood, had paid toll to her desire for liberty and for fraternity (brotherhood). The carnage had only ceased at this late hour of the day because there were other more interesting sights for the people to witness, a little while before the final closing of the barricades (portable walls) for the night.

C. . . . but a more effectual (successful in producing a desired result) weight, the knife of the guillotine.

Reading

F

English

A. Run-on sentence

B. Parallelism problem

C. Run-on Sentence

Writing

4. This is a solid essay. It borders on a 5. It has sufficient examples (although not terrific ones), some transitions, an introduction, and a conclusion. It has no counter argument. It does not have a robust style. It does not state the argument multiple times.

Science

E

LESSON 34

Math

1. A, 35; B, 15; C, 5.

2. 12; 48.

3. 8 men; 40 women.

4. Henry, $200; John, $400; James, $800.

5. 4500 ft.; 13,500 ft.; 27,000 ft.

Vocabulary

I mean hope, courage, poetry, initiative (to start), all that is human. For instance, when materialism leads men to complete fatalism (pessimism) (as it generally does), it is quite idle to pretend that it is in any sense a liberating force. . . . The determinists (those who believe outside, impersonal forces control fate) come to bind, not to loose. . . . It is the worst chain that ever fettered (bound) a human being. You may use the language of liberty, if you like, about materialistic teaching, but it is obvious that this is just as inapplicable (not applicable) to it as a whole as the same language when applied to a man locked up in a mad-house. . . . In passing from this subject I may note that there is a queer fallacy to the effect that materialistic (of material; palatable) fatalism is in some way favourable to mercy, to the abolition (removal; destruction) of

cruel punishments or punishments of any kind. . . . It is quite tenable (defensible) that the doctrine of necessity makes no difference at all; that it leaves the flogger flogging and the kind friend exhorting (urging) as before.

Reading

E

English

1. fish, animal, creature, goldfish. creature, animal, fish, goldfish

2. foreigner, woman, person, German
person, woman, foreigner, German

3. chicken, main dish, food, meat
food, meat, main dish, chicken

Writing

This would be a 2 or 3. There is no introduction. No conclusion. The author makes no attempt to really develop his argument and there are only two weak examples.

Science

F

LESSON 35

Math

1. 51; 28; 16 sheep.

2. A, 253; B, 350; C, 470 votes.

3. 17; 12; 24 A.

4. 36; 20; 55.

5. $50,000; $44,000; $24,000.

Vocabulary

A. . . . whose caravans penetrated (move into). . . . It concerned all manner of out-of-the-way mountain principalities, (states ruled by a prince) But, recently, five confederated (ruling with sub-kingdoms) Kings . . . accounted for three strange ruffians (outlaws) who might, or might not, have been hired for the job. Therefore Mahbub had avoided halting at the insalubrious (formal) city of Peshawur, and had come through without stop to Lahore, where, knowing his country-people, he anticipated curious developments.

B. . . . the Border hung unfinished on his hands, and when these scores were cleared he intended to settle down as a more or less virtuous (morally good) citizen. He had never passed the serai gate since his arrival two days ago, but had been ostentatious in sending telegrams to Bombay, where he banked some of his money; to Delhi, where a sub-partner of his own clan was selling horses to the agent of a Rajputana state; and to Umballa, where an Englishman was excitedly demanding the pedigree (lineage) of a white stallion.

Reading

D

English

1. The red men were not so infrequent visitors of the English settlements. — Hawthorne. Okay

2. "Huldy was so up to everything about the house, that the doctor didn't miss anything in a temporal way." — Mrs. Stowe.

3. Her younger sister was a wide-awake girl, who hadn't been to school for anything. — Holmes.

4. You will find no battle which will not exhibit the most cautious circumspection. — Bayne.

5. No man can acquire such information, nor should he labor after it. — Grote.

6. Every thoughtful man in America who would consider a war with England the greatest of calamities. — Lowell.

7. In the execution of this task, every man would find it an arduous effort. — Hamilton.

8. "A weapon," said the King, "well worthy to confer honor, and it has been laid on an undeserving shoulder."—Scott.

Writing

1. The poor shipwrecked sailor abandoned all hope of being saved.

2. Good health requires ceaseless vigilance.

3. That Super Bowl win was a dazzling triumph.

Science

H

LESSON 36

Math

1. b − e dollars

2. l + 4 + m − x dollars

3. c − a − b.

4. 429; 636 votes.

5. m + x − y + b − z dollars

Vocabulary

A. The officer proceeded, without affecting to hear the words which escaped the sentinel (guard) in his surprise; nor did he again pause until he had reached the low strand, and in a somewhat dangerous vicinity to the western water bastion (ramparts; wall) of the fort. The light of an obscure (fading) moon was just sufficient to render objects, though dim, perceptible (to be seen) in their outlines. He, therefore, took the precaution to place himself against the trunk of a tree, where he leaned for many minutes, and seemed to contemplate the dark and silent mounds of the English works in profound attention. His gaze at the ramparts (wall of the fort) was not that of a curious or idle spectator; but his looks wandered from point to point, denoting (actual meaning of a word) his knowledge of military

usages, and betraying that his search was not unaccompanied by distrust.

B. Just then a figure was seen to approach the edge of the rampart, where it stood, apparently contemplating (reflecting upon) in its turn the distant tents of the French encampment. . . . left no doubt as to his person in the mind of the observant spectator. Delicacy, no less than prudence (wisdom), now urged him to retire; and he had moved cautiously round the body of the tree for that purpose, when another sound drew his attention, and once more arrested (impeded; hindered) his footsteps. It was a low and almost inaudible (silent; unheard) movement of the water, and was succeeded by a grating of pebbles one against the other.

Reading

D and A

English

1. B. This needs to be closer to "I," its modifier.

2. A. He should have. . . . Never replace a verb with a preposition in a verbal construction.

3. B. Even though there is a linking verb, use "well" instead of "good" when you are speaking of health.

4. C. Use "fewer" eggs. "Fewer" tells how many; "less" tells "how much."

5. A. "Beside" means "by the side of something;" it is a preposition. "Besides" as a preposition means "in addition to." As an adverb, "besides" means "moreover."

Writing

1. I am no sure why you'all folks ain't paying attention to "moi."

I am not sure why you are not paying attention to me.

2, Well, yeah — I guess so — what else could that mean?!?

That may be true.

3. You really mean that? Whatever!

I find it to be incredible that you believe this.

Science

H

LESSON 37

Math

$+ 108ab5$

$- 90a\,2\,b4$

$-80a3\,b3$

$+ 60a4\,b2$

$+ 48a5\,b$

$+ 3a6 - 27b\,6$

Vocabulary

A. There were dark stains of suffering or sleeplessness under the low-lidded eyes, heightening their brilliance and their gentle melancholy (depression). The face was very pale, save for the vivid colour of the full lips and the hectic flush on the rather high but inconspicuous (ordinary) cheek-bones. It was something in those lips that marred (marked; scarred) the perfection of that countenance; a fault, elusive (difficult to retrieve) but undeniable, lurked there to belie the fine sensitiveness of those nostrils, the tenderness of those dark, liquid eyes and the noble calm of that pale brow.

B. The physician in Mr. Blood regarded the man with peculiar interest knowing as he did the agonizing malady from which his lordship suffered, and the amazingly irregular, debauched (wasted; wicked) life that he led in spite of it — perhaps because of it. "Peter Blood, hold up your hand!"

C. Abruptly he was recalled to his position by the harsh voice of the clerk of arraigns. His obedience was mechanical, and the clerk droned (stated in a monotonous, perfunctory tone) out the wordy indictment. . . .

Reading

E

English

1. The doctor used to say 'twas her young heart, and I don't know but that he was right. — S.O. Jewett

2. At the first stroke of the pickax it is ten to one that you are taken up for a trespass. — Bulwer

3. There are few persons of distinction who can hold conversation in both languages. — Swift

4. Who knows but there might be English among those sun-browned half-naked masses of panting wretches? — Kingsley

5. No little wound of the kind ever came to him but that he disclosed it at once. — Trollope

6. They are not so distant from the camp of Saladin but that they might be in a moment surprised. — Scott

Science

G

LESSON 38

Math

1. $5(x + y)$; $4(x - y)$

2. 12/35 of the field

3. $1/a + 1/b$

Vocabulary

A. Before the Lord God made man upon the earth He first prepared for him by creating a world of useful and pleasant things for his sustenance (nourishment) and delight. In the Genesis account of the creation these are called simply "things." They were made for man's uses, but they were meant always to be external to the man and subservient (a servant) to him. In the deep heart of the man was a shrine where none but God was worthy to come.

B. . . . but there in the moral dusk stubborn and aggressive usurpers (rebels) fight among themselves for first place on the throne.

C. This is not a mere metaphor, but an accurate analysis of our real spiritual trouble. There is within the human heart a tough fibrous (characterized by fiber) root of fallen life whose nature is to possess, always to possess.

Reading

D, A, B, C

English

1. Can you imagine Indians or a semi-civilized people engaged on a work such as the canal connecting the Mediterranean and the Red seas?

2. In the friction among an employer and workmen, it is commonly said that the employer's profits are high.

3. None of them is in any wise willing to give his life for the life of his chief.

4. Art is neither to be achieved by effort of thinking, nor to be (parallelism problem) explained by accuracy of speaking.

Writing

1. Fill the glass.

2. They appeared to be talking on private affairs.

3. I saw the boy and his sister in the garden.

4. He went into the country last week and returned yesterday.

5. The subject of his discourse was excellent.

6. You need not wonder that the matter of his discourse was excellent; it was taken from the Bible.

7. They followed him, but could not overtake him.

8. The same sentiments may be found throughout the book.

9. I was very ill every day last week.

10. That was the substance of his discourse.

Science

H

LESSON 39

Math

1. $(5 - x)(3 - x)$.

2. $(6 - x)(7 + x)$.

3. $(11 - x)(3 + x)$.

4. $(x - 3)(x + 3)$.

5. $(y + 5)(y - 5)$.

Vocabulary

I seemed swinging in a mighty rhythm through orbit (curved path) vastness. (large emptiness) Sparkling points of light spluttered (soft explosive sounds)and shot past me. They were stars, I knew, and flaring comets, that peopled my flight among the suns. As I reached the limit of my swing and prepared to rush back on the counter swing, a great gong struck and thundered. For an immeasurable period, lapped in the rippling of placid (tranquil, peaceful) centuries, I enjoyed and pondered my tremendous (vast, huge) flight.

But a change came over the face of the dream, for a dream I told myself it must be. My rhythm grew shorter and shorter. I was jerked from swing to counter swing with irritating haste. I could scarcely catch my breath, so fiercely was I impelled (driven)

through the heavens. The gong thundered more frequently and more furiously. I grew to await it with a nameless dread. Then it seemed as though I were being dragged over rasping (grating) sands, white and hot in the sun. This gave place to a sense of intolerable (unbearable) anguish. My skin was scorching in the torment of fire. The gong clanged and knelled (sound of a bell). The sparkling points of light flashed past me in an interminable stream, as though the whole sidereal (distant stars) system were dropping into the void. I gasped, caught my breath painfully, and opened my eyes. Two men were kneeling beside me, working over me. My mighty rhythm was the lift and forward plunge of a ship on the sea. The terrific gong was a frying-pan, hanging on the wall, that rattled and clattered with each leap of the ship. The rasping, scorching sands were a man's hard hands chafing (irritating) my naked chest. I squirmed under the pain of it, and half lifted my head. My chest was raw and red, and I could see tiny blood globules starting through the torn and inflamed cuticle (skin pore).

Reading

C

English

1. He clobbered the ball over the fence.

2. He consumed all the cake that was left.

3. She screamed for help.

Writing

1. He took wine and water and mixed them together.

2. He descended the steps to the cellar.

3. He fell from the top of the house.

4. I hope you will return soon.

5. The things he took away he restored.

Science

D and B

LESSON 40

Math

1. xy men.

2. 60x/a minutes.

3. 100b/x apples.

Vocabulary

In spite of the fact that Germany had one of the best democracies in world history, the Weimar republic, Germans enthusiastically embraced totalitarianism (autocratic government) during the period between the two world wars. Both the fear of communism and the hope of economic prosperity drove Germans into the Nazi Party.

The Nazi Party was one of the many right-wing parties formed by the monarchist (government by a king or monarch) reactionaries (radicals) who supported the Kaiser's rule and conversely hated the Weimar Republic. Many of these right-wing parties disappeared in the 1920s, but the Nazi Party was an exception. Under the brilliant leadership of Adolf Hitler, it grew as an important political party. It appealed to the unemployed masses and the nationalistic (patriotic) industrialists.

Ironically (unexpectedly; coincidentally), the leader of Nazi Germany was an Austrian. Adolf Hitler, born in 1899, was the son of an Austrian minor customs official. Hitler was an undistinguished boy. . . . The party adopted an emblem, a salute, and a greeting as its distinctives (special characteristics). It had a newspaper through which Hitler fiercely denounced (abrogated) the Treaty of Versailles and the Jews. He also organized the Stormtroopers (S.A. or the Brown Shirts) to disrupt the meetings of opposition parties. . . . To the middle classes, he promised to abolish the Treaty of Versailles and relieve them of the burden of reparations (payments for war damage) payment. To the army, he promised military victory. Hitler was also a gifted orator. His speeches, though they contained little truth, always made successful appeals to the masses. Moreover, the Nazi Party, with its huge parades, attracted the younger generation. Most Germans followed Hitler with religious fervor (excitement). By 1933, Hitler was firmly in control.

Reading

H

English

B, C, and C

Writing

B

Science

B

LESSON 41

Math

1. 3x – y

2. 5x2 – 1

3. 3b2 + 4a

4. x2 – 2y2

5. 1 + 3x

Vocabulary

A. . . . placed the entire government in the hands of the latter (the one next; the last one), who at once began to abuse it to such an extent, by imposing enormous taxes upon the clergy and the people, that he paved the way for the return of his uncle of Burgundy to power.

B. The change was disastrous (terrible) for France. John was violent and utterly unscrupulous

(immoral), and capable of any deed to gratify either his passions, jealousies, or hatreds.

C. When he recovered, the two princes went to mass together, dined at their uncle's, the Duke of Berri, and together entered Paris; and the Parisians fondly hoped that there was an end of the rivalry (contest) that had done so much harm.

D. The Duke of Burgundy at first affected grief and indignation (annoyance) but at the council the next day he boldly avowed that Orleans had been killed by his orders. He at once took a horse and rode to the frontier of Flanders, which he reached safely, though hotly chased by a party of the Duke of Orleans' knights.

E. The duke's widow, who was in the country at the time, hastened up to Paris with her children, and appealed (pleaded) for justice to the king, who declared that he regarded the deed done to his brother as done to himself. . . . no attempt was made at resistance, and the murderer was received with acclamations (affirmations) by the fickle (changeable) populace (community).

Reading

A and C

English

(A) I use to want a pet monkey (B) who could do tricks.
A. I used. . .

(A) About a year ago, (B) I sat in the park and (C) sulked.
C. Parallelism . . .

The trouble (A) started when I went into the house (B) to lay down.
B. To lie down . .

Writing

After reading the assignment, I began making notes on cards, so that I could memorize the main

points in the lesson. Since I was not through when the bell rang, I had to carry my heavy book home.

Science

D

LESSON 42

Math

1. 33 pieces.

2. 74 men.

3. 104.9+ in.

4. 92 trees.

Vocabulary

A. That story shows about the time when Nolan's braggadocio (bragging) must have broken down. At first, they said, he took a very high tone, considered his imprisonment a mere farce (sham), affected to enjoy the voyage. . . .

B. But after several days the Warren came to the same rendezvous (meeting).

C. But this was a distinct (unique) evidence of something he had not thought of, perhaps — that there was no going home for him, even to a prison.

Reading

A

English

A

Writing

C. To mourn

Science

A

LESSON 43

Math

1. 5.46%.

2. 5.57%.

3. 9.70%.

Vocabulary

In this by-place of nature there abode, in a remote (long ago) period of American history, that is to say, some thirty years since, a worthy wight of the name of Ichabod Crane, who sojourned, or, as he expressed it, "tarried," in Sleepy Hollow, for the purpose of instructing the children of the vicinity (location). He was a native of Connecticut, a State which supplies the Union with pioneers for the mind as well as for the forest, and sends forth yearly its legions of frontier woodmen and country schoolmasters. The cognomen of Crane was not inapplicable to his person. He was tall, but exceedingly lank (tall, skinny), with narrow shoulders, long arms and legs, hands that dangled a mile out of his sleeves, feet that might have served for shovels, and his whole frame most loosely hung together. His head was small, and flat at top, with huge ears, large green glassy eyes, and a long snipe nose, so that it looked like a weather-cock perched upon his spindle (long and thin) neck to tell which way the wind blew. To see him striding along the profile of a hill on a windy day, with his clothes bagging and fluttering about him, one might have mistaken him for the genius of famine descending upon the earth, or some scarecrow eloped (escaped) from a cornfield.

His schoolhouse was a low building of one large room, rudely constructed of logs; the windows partly glazed, and partly patched with leaves of old copybooks. It was most ingeniously (dishonestly) secured at vacant hours, by a withe twisted in the handle of the door, and stakes set against the window shutters; so that though a thief might get in with perfect ease, he would find some embarrassment in getting out — an idea most probably borrowed by the architect, Yost Van Houten, from the mystery of an eelpot.

The schoolhouse stood in a rather lonely but pleasant situation, just at the foot of a woody hill, with a brook running close by, and a formidable (substantial) birch-tree growing at one end of it. From hence the low murmur of his pupils' voices, conning over their lessons, might be heard in a drowsy summer's day, like the hum of a beehive; interrupted now and then by the authoritative voice of the master, in the tone of menace or command, or, peradventure, by the appalling (cacophonic) sound of the birch, as he urged some tardy loiterer along the flowery path of knowledge. Truth to say, he was a conscientious man, and ever bore in mind the golden maxim, "Spare the rod and spoil the child." Ichabod Crane's scholars certainly were not spoiled.

I would not have it imagined, however, that he was one of those cruel potentates (officials) of the school who joy in the smart of their subjects; on the contrary, he administered justice with discrimination (prejudicial treatment) rather than severity; taking the burden off the backs of the weak, and laying it on those of the strong. Your mere puny stripling, that winced at the least flourish of the rod, was passed by with indulgence (tolerance); but the claims of justice were satisfied by inflicting a double portion on some little tough wrong-headed, broad-skirted Dutch urchin, who sulked and swelled and grew dogged and sullen beneath the birch. All this he called "doing his duty by their parents"; and he never inflicted a chastisement (scolding) without following it by the assurance, so consolatory (comforting) to the smarting urchin (a mischievous child) that "he would remember it and thank him for it the longest day he had to live."

Reading

H

English

(A) On one occasion, I heard someone say "he is bigger than(B) him."

B. He (is)

(A) Sometimes it is hard to recognize (B) who is having the better time, (C) him or me.

B. He or I (am)

(A) I could hear (B) them speaking (C) to he and to she.

C. To him and to her

Writing

A. Place closer to its modifier.

Science

C

LESSON 44

Math

1. 1, 4

2. −1, −4

3. 0.7, −5.7

4. −0.7, 5.7

5. 2, 2

Vocabulary

A. The German occupation of Belgium may be roughly divided into two periods: Before the fall of Antwerp, when the hope of prompt deliverance was still vivid (clear) in every heart, and when the German policy, in spite of its frightfulness, had not yet assumed its most ruthless (no pity) and systematic (according to a fixed plan) character; and, after the fall of the great fortress, when the yoke of the conqueror weighed more heavily on the vanquished (conquered) shoulders, and when the Belgian population, grim and resolute, (determined) began to struggle to preserve its honour and loyalty and to resist the ever-increasing pressure of the enemy to bring it into complete submission and to use it as a tool against its own army and its own King.

B. I am only concerned here with the second period. The story of the German atrocities (cruel actions) committed in some parts of the country at the beginning of the occupation is too well known to require any further comment. Every honest man, in Allied and neutral countries, has made up his mind on the subject. No unprejudiced person can hesitate between the evidence brought forward by the Belgian Commission of Enquiry and the vague denials, paltry excuses and insolent (disrespectful) calumnies (tragedies) opposed to it by the German Government and the Pro-German Press.

C. Besides, in a way, the atrocities committed during the last days of August 1914 ought not to be considered as the culminating point of Belgium's martyrdom (sacrifice for a cause). They have, of course, appealed to the imagination of the masses, they have filled the world with horror and indignation (offense; affront), but they did not extend all over the country, as the present oppression does; they only affected a few thousand men and women, instead of involving hundreds of thousands.

Reading
F and H

English
C

Writing
1. In the large room some forty or fifty students walked through the party preparation area.

2. A great thick leather garment reaching the knees bound the coat and vest.

3. We joined the crowd, and used our lungs as well as any.

Science
A

LESSON 45

Math
$b - a$; $6(b - a)$; $b + a$; $3(b + a)$ miles

Vocabulary
Amongst the vestiges (remnants) of antiquity which abound in this country are the visible memorials of those nations which have succeeded one another in the occupancy of this island. To the age of our Celtic ancestors, the earliest possessors of its soil, is ascribed the erection of those altars and temples of all but primeval antiquity (ancient times). . . . in the altars erected by the Patriarchs (Church Fathers), and in the circles of stone set up by Moses at the foot of Mount Sinai, and by Joshua at Gilgal. Many of these structures, perhaps from their very rudeness, have survived the vicissitudes (unwelcome change) of time . . . yet it is from Roman edifices that we derive, and can trace by a gradual transition (time of change), the progress of that peculiar kind of architecture called Gothic, which presents in its later stages the most striking contrast that can be imagined to its original precursor (preceding in time).

The Romans . . . as we learn from Tacitus, began at an early period to erect temples and public edifices (structures), though doubtless much inferior to those at Rome, in their municipal towns and cities. The Christian religion was also early introduced, but for a time its progress was slow . . . for that

historian alludes (refers) to the British Christians as reconstructing the churches which had, in the Dioclesian persecution, been leveled to the ground.

Reading
A

English
1. Thou art what I shall be, yet only seem.

2. We shall be greatly mistaken if we thought so.

3. Thou shalt have a suit, and that of the newest cut; the wardrobe keeper shall have orders to supply you. Correct

4. "I will not run," answered Herbert stubbornly.

Writing
C

Science
C

LESSON 46

Math
1. Rem. 11, quot. $x^2 + 5x + 8$

2. -61, $2x^4 - 4x^3 + 7x^2 - 14x + 30$

3. -0.050671, $x^2 + 6.09x + 10.5481$

1. $ax + by/a + b$ cts

2. $5/100 x$ dols

3. 5; 11

Vocabulary
"The Dead"

These hearts were woven of human joys and cares,

Washed marvellously with sorrow, swift to mirth (joy).

The years had given them kindness. Dawn was theirs,

And sunset, and the colours of the earth.

These had seen movement, and heard music; known

Slumber (sleeping) and waking; loved; gone proudly friended;

Felt the quick stir of wonder; sat alone;

Touched flowers and furs and cheeks. All this is ended.

There are waters blown by changing winds to laughter

And lit by the rich skies, all day. And after,

Frost, with a gesture (motion), stays the waves that dance

And wandering loveliness. He leaves a white

Unbroken glory, a gathered radiance,

A width, a shining peace, under the night

"Love"

Love is a breach (break) in the walls, a broken gate,

Where that comes in that shall not go again;

Love sells the proud heart's citadel (fort) to Fate.

They have known shame, who love unloved. Even then,

When two mouths, thirsty each for each, find slaking,

And agony's forgot, and hushed the crying

Of credulous (trembling) hearts, in heaven — such are but taking

Their own poor dreams within their arms, and lying

Each in his lonely night, each with a ghost.

Some share that night. But they know, love grows colder,

Grows false and dull, that was sweet lies at most.

Astonishment is no more in hand or shoulder,

But darkens, and dies out from kiss to kiss.

All this is love; and all love is but this.

Reading
C and C

English
B, B, B

Writing
A

Science
A

LESSON 47

Math
1. x/5 hrs.

2. x + my + bc/ n dols

3. am + bp / m + p cts

4. y − 11 yrs.

Vocabulary

. . . Now, at the expiration (end) of four years, during which public declarations have been constantly called forth on every point and phase of the great contest which still absorbs the attention and engrosses (absorbs) the energies of the nation, little that is new could be presented. . . .

On the occasion corresponding to this four years ago, all thoughts were anxiously directed to an impending civil war. All dreaded it — all sought to avert it. While the inaugural (beginning) address was being delivered from this place, devoted altogether to saving the Union without war, insurgent (active in a revolt) agents were in the city seeking to destroy it without war — seeking to dissolve the Union, and divide effects, by negotiation. Both parties deprecated (unpopular) war; but one of them would make war rather than let the nation survive; and the other would accept war rather than let it perish. And the war came.

One-eighth of the whole population were colored slaves, not distributed generally over the Union, but localized in the Southern part of it. These slaves constituted a peculiar and powerful interest. All knew that this interest was, somehow, the cause of the war. To strengthen, perpetuate (continue indefinitely), and extend this interest was the object for which the insurgents would rend the Union, even by war; while the government claimed no right to do more than to restrict the territorial enlargement of it.

Neither party expected for the war the magnitude or the duration (the length) which it has already attained. . . . It may seem strange that any men should dare to ask a just God's assistance in wringing (squeezing and twisting) their bread from the sweat of other men's faces; but let us judge not, that we be not judged. The prayers of both could not be answered — that of neither has been answered fully. . . . Fondly do we hope — fervently (with sincere enthusiasm) do we pray — that this mighty scourge of war may speedily pass away. Yet, if God wills that it continue until all the wealth piled by the bondsman's two hundred and fifty years of unrequited toil shall be sunk, and until every drop of blood drawn by the lash shall be paid by another drawn with the sword, as was said three thousand years ago, so still it must be said, "The judgments of the Lord are true and righteous altogether."

With malice (ill will) toward none; with charity for all; with firmness in the right, as God gives us to see the right. . . .

Reading

D

English

1. If the phenomena which lay before him will not suit his purpose, all history must be ransacked.

2. He sat with his eyes fixed partly on the ghost and partly on Hamlet, and with his mouth open.

3. The days when his favorite volume set him upon making wheelbarrows and chairs . . . can never again be the realities they were.

4. To make the jacket sit yet more closely to the body, it was gathered at the middle by a broad leathern belt.

5. He had sat up no unattainable standard of perfection.

Writing

C

Science

G

LESSON 48

Math

1. 17; 22; 66.

2. $ 5.

3. 28x fourths.

4. 3x/z days.

Vocabulary

A. Up rose Robin Hood one merry morn when all the birds were singing blithely (happily) among the leaves, and up rose all his merry men, each fellow washing his head and hands in the cold brown brook that leaped laughing from stone to stone.

B. So saying, he strode away through the leafy forest glades (open areas) until he had come to the verge of Sherwood. There he wandered for a long time, through highway and byway, through dingly (deeply wooded) dell and forest skirts. Now he met a fair buxom lass in a shady lane, and each gave the other a merry word and passed their way; now he saw a fair lady upon an ambling pad, to whom he doffed his cap, and who bowed sedately (calmly) in return to the fair youth; now he saw a fat monk on a pannier-laden ass; now a gallant knight, with spear and shield and armor that flashed brightly in the sunlight.

Reading

Given this conversation between Majorie and Nick, what can you infer about their relationship? It is no doubt strained.

Predict the ending of this short story? Answers will vary.

English

1. Who they were I really cannot specify.

2. Truth is mightier than we all.

3. If there ever was a rogue in the world, it is I.

4. They were the very two individuals who we thought were far away.

5. "Seems to me as if they as writes must hev a kinder gift fur it, now."

Writing

B

Science

G

LESSON 49

Math

1. $5000; $3000; $10,000

2. $50; $68; $204

3. A, $5000; B, $10,500; C, $31,500.

4. 8000; 24,250; 48,500

5. Daughter, $25,000; son, $40,000; widow, $160,000.

Vocabulary

The ambition to secure an education was most praiseworthy (laudable) and encouraging. The idea, however, was too prevalent (present) that . . . something bordering almost on the supernatural (metaphysical; beyond the natural).

The ministry was the profession that suffered most — and still suffers, though there has been great improvement — on account of not only ignorant (uneducated) but in many cases immoral men who claimed that they were "called to preach."

Reading

C

English

1. Let you and I look at these, for they say there are none such in the world.

2. "Nonsense!" said Amyas, "we could kill every soul of them in half an hour, and they know that as well as I."

3. They are coming for a visit to she and me.

Writing

A

Science

B

LESSON 50

Math

1. James, 12 years; Samuel, 28 years

2. 20 years

3. Amelia, 6 years; George, 18 years

4. Edward, 40 yrs.; Esther, 30 yrs.

5. 6 yrs.

6. 3; 12 yrs.

Vocabulary

I (Screwtape) once had a patient, a sound atheist (one who does not believe in God), who used to read in the British Museum. . . . The Enemy presumably made the counter suggestion (alternative answer). . . .

Reading

Screwtape is humorous; Usher is very serious. Lewis is poking fun at the Church in a familiar, appropriate way. Poe is exploring the collapse of a family by using a collapsing mansion as his central metaphor.

English

B

Writing

D

Science

C

VOCABULARY HELPS

Because the ACT is essentially a vocabulary and reasoning test you should work at developing your vocabulary. One way to do this is to keep vocabulary cards. When you encounter a new word, try to determine its definition from its use in the sentence. Then look up the word in the dictionary to see if you were correct. Using 3 x 5-inch cards, write the new word on one side and the dictionary definition with the sentence showing its context on the back. These cards will be a quick way to help you increase your vocabulary for the SAT and will be useful throughout your college career.

At first you will find this exercise to be very cumbersome. As time goes on and your 3 x 5-inch card stack grows taller, you will see that your vocabulary will grow, too, and it will not be necessary to look up as many words. At the same time, you must use these words in your spoken vocabulary twice a day for several days or you will forget them. Every Friday your parent or guardian or a friend can quiz you on the words you listed during the week.

A typical vocabulary card might look like the following:

Remember: The primary purpose of this exercise is not to enhance achievement scores or increase knowledge of literature. The purpose is to help you increase your reading speed, improve your comprehension level, and to increase your vocabulary.

pejorative	having negative connotations; tending to disparage or belittle "The man did not appreciate the pejorative comment."

Another important tool is a resource written by Alene Harris — a list of important Greek and Latin morphemes that are on the following pages.

BOOK LIST

The following list represents a fairly comprehensive cross-section of good literature — books, poems, and plays. There are hundreds of other pieces of literature that might be as good. Ask your parents and teachers for suggestions. These particular selections from the *SAT & College Preparation Course for the Christian Student* were chosen because a) their vocabulary is challenging, b) they will help you in college, and c) they are interesting to read. Some of them are relatively easy to read, e.g., *The Adventures of Huckleberry Finn*, by Mark Twain. Others are easier than you think, like *War and Peace*, by Leo Tolstoy. And others are really difficult but good for you, such as *Of Human Bondage*, by Somerset Maugham. So . . . start reading and increase your vocabulary!

FRESHMEN AND SOPHOMORES

Austen, Jane

Emma

Emma Woodhouse is one of Austen's most memorable heroines: "Handsome, clever, and rich" as well as self-assured, she believes herself immune to romance, and wreaks amusing havoc in the lives of those around her. A humorous coming-of-age story about a woman seeking her true nature and finding true love in the process.

Sense and Sensibility

Sense and Sensibility tells the story of the impoverished Dashwood sisters who share the pangs of tragic love. Elinor, practical and conventional, is the perfection of sense. Marianne, emotional and sentimental, is the embodiment of sensibility. Their mutual suffering brings a closer understanding between the two sisters — and true love finally triumphs when sense gives way to sensibility and sensibility gives way to sense. Austen's first novel is a lively tale that deftly explores the tensions that exist in society that force people to be at once very private and very sociable.

Bolt, Robert

A Man for All Seasons

Bolt's classic play is a dramatization of the life of Sir Thomas More, the Catholic saint beheaded by Henry VIII at the birth of the Church of England. More refused to acknowledge the supremacy of England's king over all foreign sovereigns; he was imprisoned then executed in 1535. This is a compelling portrait of a courageous man who died for his convictions.

Bonhoeffer, Dietrich

The Cost of Discipleship

Bonhoeffer pulls no punches as he relates the Scriptures to real life and expounds upon the teachings of Jesus. He plainly teaches that there is a cost to following in the footsteps of Christ, just as Christ Himself taught that Christ must be first and there is no compromise. This work is so intense that even Dietrich himself, later in life, wondered if he had been too blunt.

Bronte, Charlotte

Jane Eyre

Jane Eyre tells the story of a proud young woman and her journey from an orphanage to her role as governess in the Rochester household. A heartbreaking love story that is also full of mystery and drama: fires, storms, attempted murder, and a mad wife conveniently stashed away in the attic.

Buck, Pearl

The Good Earth

The Good Earth depicts peasant life in China in the 1920s — a time before the vast political and social upheavals transformed an essentially agrarian country into a world power. Buck traces the whole cycle of life — its terrors, its passions, its ambitions, and rewards — by combining descriptions of marriage, parenthood, and complex human emotions with depictions of Chinese reverence for the land and for a specific way of life.

Bulfinch, Thomas

The Age of Fable

Love, jealousy, hatred, passion — the full range of human emotions were experienced by the gods and goddesses of ancient Greece. This is a brilliant reconstruction of the traditional myths which form the backbone of Western culture, including those of ancient Greece and Rome that form a great and timeless literature of the past.

Bunyan, John

Pilgrim's Progress

The pilgrim Christian undertakes the dangerous journey to the Celestial City, experiencing physical and spiritual obstacles along the way. The Pilgrim's Progress captures all of the treacherous dangers and triumphant victories we encounter as we live the Christian life.

Carson, Rachel

Silent Spring

Silent Spring offered the first shattering look at widespread ecological degradation and touched off an environmental awareness that still exists. Carson's book focused on the poisons from insecticides, weed killers, and other common products as well as the use of sprays in agriculture, a practice that led to dangerous chemicals in the food source. Presented with thorough documentation, the book opened more than a few eyes about the dangers of the modern world and stands today as a landmark work.

Burdick, Eugene

Fail-Safe

Fail-Safe is a classic novel of the cold war and the limits we face. Although rather faint and shallow by today's techno-thriller standards, Fail-Safe was for its day the story of the world on the edge of nuclear war. This is a good example of a best seller from the cold war crazy early sixties.

Christie, Agatha

And Then There Were None

Christie's mystery novel is the story of ten strangers, each lured to Indian Island by a mysterious host. Once his guests have arrived, the host accuses each person of murder. Unable to leave the island, the guests begin to share their darkest secrets of their past, and then, one by one, they begin to die.

Coleridge, Samuel

The Rime of the Ancient Mariner

One of the 19th century's most enduring narrative poems, The Rime of the Ancient Mariner has also been deemed one of the greatest of all English literary ballads. It is a strange and gripping tale of the ancient mariner who killed the friendly albatross and thereby committed an offense against nature — a ghostly adventure, of terror, retribution, and penance.

Conrad, Joseph

Heart of Darkness

This story reflects the physical and psychological shock Conrad himself experienced in 1890, when he worked briefly in the Belgian Congo. Compelling, exotic, suspenseful, and far more than just an adventure story, this vivid picture of the moral deterioration and reversion to savagery resulting from prolonged isolation explores deep into the dark heart of its characters' souls.

Lord Jim

Conrad explores in great depth the perplexing, ambiguous problem of lost honor and guilt, expiation, and heroism. The title character is a man haunted by guilt over an act of cowardice. He becomes an agent at an isolated East Indian trading post, where his feelings of inadequacy and responsibility are played out to their logical and inevitable end.

Cooper, James F.

The Last of the Mohicans

Hawkeye (Natty Bumpo) and his Mohican Indian friend, Chingachgook, share the solitude and sublimity of the wilderness until the savageries of the French and Indian War force them out of exile. They agree to guide two sisters in search of their father through hostile Indian country. Cooper incorporates massacres and raids, innocent settlers, hardened soldiers, and renegade Indians into his classic tale of romance and adventure.

The Deerslayer

A fine combination of romance, adventure, and morality, *The Deerslayer* follows the adventures of the brave and bold frontiersman Natty Bumpo. The deadly crack of a long rifle and the piercing cries of Indians on the warpath shatter the serenity of beautiful lake Glimmerglass. Danger has invaded the vast forests of upper New York State as Deerslayer and his loyal Mohican friend Chingachgook attempt the daring rescue of an Indian maiden imprisoned in a Huron camp.

Crane, Stephen

The Red Badge of Courage

Crane vividly conveys the terror of battle and the slow-motion torrent of emotions pouring through soldiers under fire through the struggles of a raw recruit, Henry Fleming. Fleming simultaneously lusts for a glorious battle, and worries endlessly about the possibility of his own cowardice. When he finally comes face to face with slaughter, his romantic notions are stripped away as he witnesses brutal deaths and senseless maneuvers.

Day, Clarence

Life with Father

For everyone who has ever had a father. . . . This is a hilarious book about family life that will make everyone laugh out loud. It was first published by chapters in periodicals, and later produced as a Broadway play and a movie.

Defoe, Daniel

Robinson Crusoe

The first and greatest shipwreck/desert island story ever told, *Robinson Crusoe* is a unique fictional blending of the traditions of Puritan spiritual autobiography with an insistent scrutiny of the nature of men and women as social creatures, and it reveals an extraordinary ability to invent a sustaining modern myth. The title character leaves his comfortable middle-class home in England to go to sea. Surviving shipwreck, he lives on an island for twenty-eight years, alone for most of the time until he saves the life of a savage — an outcast Polynesian man whom he names Friday.

Dickens, Charles

Great Expectations

Pip, an orphan growing up in Victorian England, is a blacksmith's apprentice who dreams of a better life. Given the means to become a gentleman by an unknown benefactor, he learns from a dangerous escaped convict, a wealthy old woman, and a secret guardian that outward appearances can be deceiving. A mysterious tale of dreams and heartbreak, *Great Expectations* is widely regarded as one of Dickens' greatest novels.

Oliver Twist

This story of a street boy on the run is an archetypal adventure. Written shortly after adoption of the Poor Law of 1834, which halted government payments to the poor unless they entered workhouses, *Oliver Twist* used the tale of a friendless child as a vehicle for social criticism. While the novel is Victorian in its emotional appeal, it is decidedly unsentimental in its depiction of poverty and the criminal underworld, especially in its portrayal of the cruel Bill Sikes.

Nicholas Nickleby

This melodramatic novel tells the story of young Nickleby's adventures as he struggles to seek his fortune in Victorian England. Dependent on the so-called benevolence of his Uncle Ralph, Nicholas is thrust into the world to care for his mother and sister. Circumstances force Nicholas to enter the nightmarish world of Dotheboys Hall, a school run by the malevolent Wackford Squeers. Comic events are interspersed with Dickens' moving indictment of society's ill treatment of children and the cruelty of the educational system; Yet, with his extraordinary gift for social satire, Dickens gives us a light-hearted tale in which goodness and joy easily defeat the forces of evil.

A Tale of Two Cities

Set in the late 18th century against the violent upheaval of the French Revolution, this complex story involves one man's sacrifice of his own life on behalf of his friends. While political events drive the story, Dickens takes a decidedly antipolitical tone, lambasting both aristocratic tyranny and revolutionary excess — the latter memorably caricatured in Madame Defarge, who knits beside the guillotine. *A Tale of Two Cities* underscores many of Dickens' enduring themes — imprisonment, injustice, and social anarchy, resurrection and the renunciation that fosters renewal.

Doyle, Arthur C.

The Adventures of Sherlock Holmes

Sherlock Holmes, master of deductive reasoning, and his sidekick, Dr. Watson, solve four classic cases. "A Scandal in Bohemia" finds the sleuth committing a crime of his own to protect a royal reputation. Then, in "A Case of Identity," Holmes must unmask a devious disguise to trace a missing person. "The Red-Headed League" and "The Boscombe Valley Mystery" round out a quartet of diabolical deceptions sure to enthrall readers.

Dumas, Alexandre

The Three Musketeers

A historical romance, *The Three Musketeers* relates the adventures of four fictional swashbuckling heroes who lived during the reigns of the French kings Louis XIII and Louis XIV. The young and headstrong d'Artagnan, having proven his bravery by dueling with each, becomes a friend of Athos, Porthos, and Aramis, members of the King's Musketeers. He is in love with Constance Bonancieux and, at her urging, he and his friends head for England to reclaim two diamond studs that the queen has imprudently given to her lover, the Duke of Buckingham.

Eliot, George

Silas Marner

Silas Marner is a friendless weaver who cares only for his cache of gold. After being wrongly accused of a heinous theft and secluding himself, he is ultimately redeemed through his love for Eppie, an abandoned golden-haired baby girl who mysteriously appears at his cottage.

Eliot, T.S.

Murder in the Cathedral

Eliot's dramatization in verse of the murder of Thomas Beckett at Canterbury was written for the Canterbury Festival of 1935. Like Greek drama, its theme and form are rooted in religion and ritual, purgation and renewal. It is a return to the earliest sources of drama.

Fitzgerald, F. Scott

The Great Gatsby

The Great Gatsby offers a very human story about a man torn between the various pressures of life: conformity and individualism, facade and substance. Nick is a silent narrator, but he is also a participant as he wades through an insane and typical world, an outsider and a member. Fitzgerald makes no judgment of morality, grace, or sin, nor does he favor idealism or cynicism.

Tender Is the Night

Fitzgerald's classic story of psychological disintegration is a powerful and moving depiction of the human frailties that affect privileged and ordinary people alike. The world has recently fallen to pieces in what has become known as the Great War. Consequently, most of the characters are falling to pieces, too. Hints about this are to be found everywhere in the book, although Fitzgerald, with his knack for writing about the complicated nature of humans, often hides them in subtle ways.

This Side of Paradise

This Side of Paradise tells the story of Amory Blaine in his adolescence and undergraduate days at Princeton. Largely autobiographical, this classic novel of youth and alienation was written with a grace that captures the essence of an American generation struggling to define itself in the aftermath of World War I and the destruction of "the old order."

Foxe, John

Foxe's Book of Martyrs

Foxe recounts the lives, suffering, and triumphant deaths of Christian martyrs throughout history with a sense of immediacy and insight into suffering that few church historians can match. Beginning with the first martyr, Jesus Christ, the book also focuses on such men as John Wyclyffe, William Tyndale, and Martin Luther, and it is an exceptional historical record tracing the roots of religious persecution.

Frank, Anne

The Diary of a Young Girl

In 1942, with Nazis occupying Holland, a 13-year-old Jewish girl and her family fled their home in Amsterdam and went into hiding. Cut off from the outside world for two years, they faced hunger, boredom, the constant cruelties of living in confined quarters, and the ever-present threat of discovery and death. In her diary, Anne Frank recorded vivid impressions of her experiences during this period. It is a powerful reminder of the horrors of war and an eloquent testament to the human spirit. By turns thoughtful, moving, and amusing, her account offers a fascinating commentary on human courage and frailty and a compelling self-portrait of a sensitive and spirited young woman whose promise was tragically cut short.

Franklin, Benjamin

Autobiography

One of our most inspiring Americans comes to life in this autobiography. Written as a letter to his son, Franklin's account of his life from his childhood in Boston to his years in Philadelphia ends in 1757 with his first mission to England.

Gibson, William

The Miracle Worker

This is the inspiring story of Helen Keller and her teacher, Anne Sullivan—The Miracle Worker. Deaf, blind, and mute twelve-year-old Helen was like a wild animal. Scared out of her wits but still murderously strong, she clawed and struggled against all who tried to help her. Half-blind herself but blessed with fanatical dedication, Annie began a titanic struggle to release the young girl from the terrifying prison of eternal darkness and silence.

Goldsmith, Oliver

The Vicar of Wakefield

This story, a portrait of village life, is narrated by Dr. Primrose, the title character, whose family endures many trials — including the loss of most of their money, the seduction of one daughter, the destruction of their home by fire, and the vicar's incarceration — before all is put right in the end. The novel's idealization of rural life, sentimental moralizing, and melodramatic incidents are countered by a sharp but good-natured irony.

Hawthorne, Nathaniel

The Scarlet Letter

The Scarlet Letter is set in a village in Puritan New England. Hester Prynne, a young woman who has borne an illegitimate child, believes herself a widow, but her husband, Roger Chillingworth, returns to New England very much alive and conceals his identity. He finds his wife forced to wear the scarlet letter A on her dress as punishment for her adultery, and becomes obsessed with finding the identity of his wife's former lover. Hawthorne's greatest novel is a philosophical exploration that delves into guilt and touches upon notions of redemption.

The House of Seven Gables

Set in mid-19th-century Salem, Massachusetts, Hawthorne's gothic masterpiece is a somber study in hereditary sin. It is based on the legend of a curse pronounced on Hawthorne's own family by a woman condemned to death during the infamous Salem witchcraft trials. The greed and arrogant pride of the novel's Pyncheon family through the generations is mirrored in the gloomy decay of their seven-gabled mansion, in which the family's enfeebled and impoverished relations live.

Hemingway, Ernest

A Farewell to Arms

While serving with the Italian ambulance service during World War I, an American lieutenant falls in love with an English nurse who tends him after he is wounded on the Italian front. He deserts during the Italians' retreat after the Battle of Caporetto, and the reunited couple flee into Switzerland. By turns romantic and harshly realistic, Hemingway's story of romance set against the brutality and confusion of World War I is full of disillusionment and heartbreak.

For Whom the Bell Tolls

For Whom the Bell Tolls tells the story of an American in the Spanish War. Robert Jord has drawn the assignment of blowing up a bridge, but as he flees, a shell explodes, top his horse and breaking the soldier's legs. Thus, Jordan not only faces the loss of his lif loss of his love for Maria, a woman he met and fell for during his mountain tour of

The Old Man and the Sea

The Old Man and the Sea tells a triumphant yet tragic story of an old Cuban fisherman and his relentless, agonizing battle with a giant marlin far out in the Gulf Stream. In this short novel, Hemingway combines the simplicity of a fable, the significance of a parable, and the drama of an epic.

The Sun Also Rises

Set in the 1920s, Hemingway's novel deals with a group of aimless expatriates in the cafes of Paris and the bullrings of Spain. They are members of the cynical and disillusioned post-World War I Lost Generation, many of whom suffer psychological and physical wounds as a result of the war. Friendship, stoicism, and natural grace under pressure are offered as the values that matter in an otherwise amoral and often senseless world.

Heyerdahl, Thor

Kon-Tiki

Heyerdahl had heard of a mythical Polynesian hero, Kon-Tiki, who had migrated to the islands from the east. Further investigation led the scientist to believe that the story of the migration of a people across thousands of miles of the Pacific was fact, not a myth, and he decided to duplicate the legendary voyage to prove its accuracy. Limiting himself to a balsa log raft, *Kon-Tiki* is the record of his outrageous and daring expedition.

Hilton, James

Lost Horizon

Hilton's haunting novel takes place in Shangri-La, the valley of enchantment. Amid the towering peaks of the Himalayas, Conway could think only of his crashed plane and the home he might never see again. He couldn't fully realize that he was soon to enter a world of love and peace as no Westerner had ever known.

Goodbye, Mr. Chips

Full of enthusiasm, young English schoolmaster Mr. Chipping came to teach at Brookfield in 1870. It was a time when dignity and a generosity of spirit still existed, and the dedicated new schoolmaster expressed these beliefs to his rowdy students. Nicknamed Mr. Chips, this gentle and caring man helped shape the lives of generation after generation of boys.

Homer

The Odyssey

Odysseus wants to go home. But Poseidon, god of oceans, doesn't want him to make it back across the wine-dark sea to his wife Penelope, son Telemachus, and their high-roofed home at Ithaca. This is the story in Homer's epic poem written 2,700 years ago. *The Odyssey* is a gripping read.

The Iliad

Although typically described as one of the greatest war stories of all time, to say the Iliad is a war story does not begin to describe the emotional sweep of its action and characters: Achilles, Helen, Hector, and other heroes of Greek myth. The Iliad is one of the two great epics of Homer and reveals the history of the tenth and final year of the Greek siege of Troy.

Hudson, W.H.

Green Mansions

An exotic romance set in the jungles of South America, the story is narrated by a man named Abel who as a young man had lived among the Indians. Abel falls in love with Rima, a girl of a magnificent and mystical race, and is led to discover the greatest joy — as well as the darkest despair.

Hugo, Victor

Les Misérables

Set largely in Paris during the politically explosive 1820s and 1830s, this epic follows the life of the former criminal Jean Valjean — an outcast of society — and his unjust imprisonment. Valjean has repented his crimes, but is nevertheless hounded by his nemesis, the police detective Javert. *Les Misérables* is at once a tense thriller, an epic portrayal of the 19th-century French citizenry, and a vital drama of the redemption of one human being. Hugo achieved the rare imaginative resonance that allows a work of art to transcend its genre.

The Hunchback of Notre Dame

Hugo's haunting and tumultuous tale of the horribly deformed bell-ringer, Quasimodo, unfolds in the shadow of Notre Dame cathedral. The hunchback falls hopelessly in love with the beautiful gypsy girl, Esmerelda, and after rescuing her both from hanging and the evil archdeacon Dom Frollo, he reunites her with her mother.

Irving, Washington

The Sketch Book

The Sketch Book is a collection of short stories, most of them based on folklore. Of these, the tales *The Legend of Sleepy Hollow* and *Rip Van Winkle* are the most famous, both of which are Americanized versions of German folktales. In addition to the stories based on folklore, the collection contains travel sketches and literary essays.

Johnson, Paul

Modern Times: The World from the Twenties to the Nineties

This history explores the events, ideas, and personalities of the seven decades since the First World War. It is a superb discussion of the most relevant aspects of the 20th century — including good discussions on the beginnings of the Soviet Union and its close cousin Nazism, Peronism in Argentina and how it destroyed that prosperous country, and the devastation of the third world by the collectivist ideologues.

Kipling, Rudyard

Captains Courageous

This novel of maritime adventure takes place on the *We're Here*, a small fishing boat whose crew members rescue the son of a multi-millionaire, Harvey Cheyne, when he is washed overboard from an ocean liner. The captain refuses to take him back to port and instead makes Harvey a member of the crew, where he quickly learns respect, toughness, and gratitude — and inspires the audience to do the same.

Kim

Kim is an orphan, living from hand to mouth in the teeming streets of Lahore. One day he meets a man quite unlike anything in his wide experience, a Tibetan lama on a quest. Kim's life suddenly acquires meaning and purpose as he becomes the lama's guide and protector — his chela. Other forces are at work as Kim is sucked into the intrigue of the Great Game and travels the Grand Trunk Road with his lama. How Kim and the lama meet their respective destinies on the road and in the mountains of India forms a compelling adventure tale.

Knowles, John

A Separate Peace

Knowles' beloved classic is a story of friendship, treachery, and the confusions of adolescence. Looking back to his youth, Gene Forrester reflects on his life as a student at Devon School in New Hampshire in 1942. Although he is an excellent student, he envies the athleticism and vitality of his friend Finny. Unable to cope with this insecurity, Forrester causes Finny to break his leg, sabotaging his athletic career. *A Separate Peace* looks at this tragic accident involving the two young men and how it forever tarnishes their innocence.

Lewis, C.S.

The Chronicles of Narnia

Lewis's mystical tale of adventure takes the reader on an extraordinary journey to far-off lands. *The Chronicles of Narnia* consists of seven books: *The Magician's Nephew*; *The Lion, the Witch, and the Wardrobe*; *The Horse and His Boy*; *Prince Caspian*; *The Voyage of the "Dawn Treader"*; *The Silver Chair*; and *The Last Battle*. An allegorical saga great for all ages.

The Screwtape Letters

Written in defense of Christian faith, this popular satire consists of a series of thirty-one letters in which Screwtape, an experienced devil, instructs his young charge, Wormwood, in the art of temptation. Confounded by church doctrines and a faithful Christian woman, their efforts are defeated when their subject — a World War II pilot — dies in a bombing raid with his soul at peace. *The Screwtape Letters* is a classic treatise on a human nature that is as old as the world. Through his satiric use of the demonic narrative persona, Lewis examines the opposing sides in the battle between good and evil.

Mere Christianity

In 1943 Great Britain, when hope and the moral fabric of society were threatened by the relentless inhumanity of global war, an Oxford don was invited to give a series of radio lectures addressing the central issues of Christianity. *Mere Christianity* never flinches as it sets out a rational basis for Christianity and builds an edifice of compassionate morality atop this foundation. As Lewis clearly demonstrates, Christianity is not a religion of flitting angels and blind faith, but of free will, an innate sense of justice and the grace of God. Lewis's lucid apologetics will challenge the faithful and convince those who have not previously heard the gospel.

Llewellyn, Richard

How Green Was My Valley

In this nostalgic tale of a young man's coming-of-age, the Morgan family experiences the simple, vital pleasures of life in the coal fields of south Wales in the late 1800s. However, industrial capitalism takes its toll on the family and community. The Morgan boys are driven from their family home because of the stresses and wild cycles of early industrialism, and the town, once a community of friends, gradually becomes a mean, brutal place. Llewellyn looks critically at industrial capitalism from a conservative point of view.

London, Jack

The Call of the Wild

In his classic survival story of Buck, a courageous dog fighting for survival in the Alaskan wilderness, London vividly evokes the harsh and frozen Yukon during the Gold Rush. As Buck is ripped from his pampered, domestic surroundings and shipped to Alaska to be a sled dog, his primitive, wolflike nature begins to emerge. Savage struggles and timeless bonds between man, dog, and wilderness are played to their heartrending extremes, as Buck undertakes a journey that transforms him into the legendary "Ghost Dog" of the Klondike.

White Fang

White Fang is a wolf dog, the offspring of an Indian dog and a wolf, alone in the savage world of the desolate, frozen wilds of the Yukon territory. Weedon Scott rescues the fiercely independent dog from a cruel, ignorant master, training him to be a loving companion. When an escaped convict threatens violence, a savage beast transformed by human kindness must confront a man brutalized by society.

MacDonald, George

The Curate's Awakening

Originally published as *Thomas Wingfold, Curate* in 1876, MacDonald's tale is retold for today's readers in *The Curate's Awakening*. MacDonald masterfully weaves together an old abandoned house, a frightened young fugitive, a tragic murder, and a sister's love, as the Curate's confidence and faith are shaken.

Malory, Sir Thomas

Le Morte D'Arthur

The legendary deeds of King Arthur and his Knights of the Round Table follows Arthur's magical birth and accession to the throne as well as the stories of knights Sir Lancelot, Sir Tristram, and Sir Galahad. Malory's unique and splendid version of the Arthurian legend tells an immortal story of love, adventure, chivalry, treachery, and death.

de Maupassant, Guy

Short Stories

De Maupassant was indeed a great influence. His short stories are considered little masterpieces and have been followed as a model for short story writers since his time.

Melville, Herman

Billy Budd

It is a time of war between nations, but on one ship, a smaller battle is being fought between two men. Jealous of Billy Budd, known as the "Handsome Sailor," the envious Master-At-Arms Claggart torments the young man until his false accusations lead to a charge of treason against Billy.

Moby Dick

Melville tells this story through the eyes of Ishmael. A giant white whale took Captain Ahab's leg on a previous voyage, and now, driven on by the Captain's obsessive revenge, the crew and the outcast Ishmael find themselves caught up in a maniacal pursuit which leads inexorably to an apocalyptic climax.

Monsarrat, Nicholas

The Cruel Sea

The Cruel Sea presents the lives of Allied sailors who must protect the cargo ships and destroy the German submarines. Monsarrat vividly describes the savage submarine battles of the North Atlantic during World War II.

Nordhoff, Charles; Hall, James Norman

Mutiny on the Bounty

In this stirring sea adventure, Nordhoff and Hall tell the story of the historic voyage of the H.M.S. *Bounty* — a journey that culminated in Fletcher Christian's mutiny against Captain Bligh. This unforgettable, fictional tale of the high seas is so realistic it reads like truth.

Poe, Edgar A.

Poems

Poe revolutionized the horror tale, giving it psychological insight and a consistent tone and atmosphere. He invented the modern detective story, penned some of the world's best-known lyric poetry, and wrote a major novella of the fantastic. Some of his more famous works include: "The Raven"; "The Pit and the Pendulum"; "Annabel Lee"; "The Fall of the House of Usher"; and "The Murders in the Rue Morgue."

Remarque, Erich M.

All Quiet on the Western Front

Paul Bäumer and his classmates enlist in the German army of World War II, and they become soldiers with youthful enthusiasm. Through years of vivid horror, Paul holds fast to a single vow: to fight against the principle of hate that meaninglessly pits young men of the same generation but different uniforms against each other.

Potok, Chaim

The Promise

The Promise follows the story of Reuven Malter in his choices between traditionalism and his feelings. As Potok explores the themes of adolescence, morality, and our collective nature, he captures the essence of the Jewish customs and conflicts and puts them in laymen's term. This is an uplifting story realistically and dramatically told.

Sandburg, Carl

Abraham Lincoln: The Prairie Years, and The War Years

The definitive biography of one of America's greatest presidents recounts the fascinating log-cabin-to-the-White House success story. Sandburg aptly describes the complex individual who rose to become an outstanding leader.

Saroyan, William

The Human Comedy

Saroyan's autobiographical story centers around a family whose struggles and dreams reflect those of America's second-generation immigrants. Set in California during World War II, it shows us a boy caught between reality and illusion as delivering telegraphs of wartime death, love, and money brings him face-to-face with human emotion at its most raw.

Scott, Sir Walter

Ivanhoe

Set in 12th-century England, Ivanhoe captures the noble idealism of chivalry along with its often cruel and impractical consequences. It follows the heroic adventures of Sir Wilfred of Ivanhoe as he and his fellow captives are rescued from Knight Templar's castle by Robin Hood; the wounded Ivanhoe's trial by combat with the powerful Knight to save the beautiful Jewess Rebecca from the stake; and King Richard the Lionhearted's aid in Ivanhoe's triumph at evil King John's tournament.

Sebestyen, Ouida

Words by Heart

Hoping to make her adored Papa proud of her and make her white classmates notice her "Magic Mind" and not her black skin, Lena vows to win the Bible-quoting contest. Winning does not bring Lena what she expected. Instead of honor, violence and death erupt and strike the one she loves most dearly. Lena, who has believed in vengeance, must now learn how to forgive.

Shaara, Michael

The Killer Angels

This novel reveals more about the Battle of Gettysburg — in which 50,000 people died — than any piece of learned nonfiction on the same subject. Shaara's account of the three most important days of the Civil War features deft characterizations of all of the main actors, including Lee, Longstreet, Pickett, Buford, and Hancock. In the three most bloody and courageous days of our nation's history, two armies fought for two dreams — one dreamed of freedom, the other of a way of life.

Shakespeare, William

Hamlet

This powerful tale of ghosts, murder, and revenge takes on new meaning with each reading. The play begins as a ghost story, full of mystery and suspense. Then in Acts II and III, it becomes a detective story with Prince Hamlet seeking to find the murderer of his father. Finally, in Acts IV and V, it becomes a revenge story, as Hamlet seeks the ultimate revenge.

Macbeth

Shakespeare's tragedy revolves around destiny, ambition, and murder. It is prophesied that a Scottish lord "shall never vanquished be until great Birnam Wood to high Dunsinane Hill shall come against him." Macbeth luxuriates in his invincibility, knowing that woods don't climb hills. Or do they? As he and Lady Macbeth move from one heinous crime to another, a day of reckoning awaits them.

Julius Caesar

A crafty and ambitious Cassius, envious of Caesar's political and military triumphs, forms a conspiracy against him. After Caesar's assassination, Antony, seeking retribution against the murderers, drives them out of Rome. *Julius Caesar* is one of Shakespeare's greatest works.

Shaw, George Bernard

Pygmalion

The inspiration behind the popular musical and movie *My Fair Lady*, Pygmalion is a perceptive comedy of wit and grit about the unique relationship that develops between spunky cockney flower girl, Eliza Doolittle, and her irascible speech professor, Henry Higgins. The flower girl teaches the egotistical phonetics professor that to be a lady means more than just learning to speak like one.

Shelley, Mary

Frankenstein

After being rescued from an iceberg, Dr. Frankenstein relates his autobiography to the ship's captain. Dr. Frankenstein has been consumed by his desire to create a fully-grown living creature. When he reaches his goal, he perceives his creation as a monster, immediately regrets his work, and promptly abandons it. A story within a story, *Frankenstein* is a subtle and ironic prophecy that raises the question of who exactly is the real monster in this story.

Sinclair, Upton

The Jungle

In Sinclair's book we enter the world of Jurgis Rudkus, a young Lithuanian immigrant who arrives in America fired with dreams of wealth, freedom, and opportunity. And we discover, with him, the astonishing truth about "packingtown," the busy, flourishing, filthy Chicago stockyards, where new world visions perish in a jungle of human suffering. Sinclair explores the workingman's lot at the turn of the century: the backbreaking labor; the injustices of "wage-slavery"; and the bewildering chaos of urban life.

Steinbeck, John

Of Mice and Men

This tragic story, given poignancy by its objective narrative, is about the complex bond between two migrant laborers. The plot centers on George Milton and Lennie Small, itinerant ranch hands who dream of one day owning a small farm. George acts as a father figure to Lennie, who is large and simpleminded, calming him and helping to rein in his immense physical strength.

East of Eden

This sprawling and often brutal novel, set in the rich farmlands of California's Salinas Valley, follows the intertwined destinies of two families — the Trasks and the Hamiltons — whose generations helplessly reenact the fall of Adam and Eve and the poisonous rivalry of Cain and Abel.

The Grapes of Wrath

The Grapes of Wrath is the epic chronicle of man's struggle against injustice and inhumanity. It tells the story of the Joads and their journey to "the golden land." It is not so much just the story of one family and one time, but the story of the courage and passion of all men throughout history.

Stevenson, Robert Louis

Dr. Jekyll and Mr. Hyde

Stevenson's supernatural story of good versus evil centers around the well-intentioned, wealthy physician Dr. Jekyll. As he drinks the potion that is the culmination of his research, he unleashes the dark side of his nature, turning into the hideous Mr. Hyde. This book is one of the most horrific depictions of the human potential for evil ever written.

Treasure Island

When young Jim Hawkins finds a treasure map in Captain Flint's chest, he must outwit the dead Captain's collaborators if he is to keep it for himself. Only his two companions, Squire Trelawney and Dr. Livesey, share Jim's secret, and the three decide to set off on a seafaring adventure in this classic tale of exploits on the high seas.

Kidnapped

In this spirited saga, a young heir is seized by his villainous uncle and sold into slavery. Saved ironically in a shipwreck, he travels with a Scot expatriate until they become suspects in a murder. More than just a "boy's story," this is the tale of a brave young man and the amazing odyssey that takes him halfway around the world.

Stone, Irving

Lust for Life

Vincent Van Gogh was a tragic figure in his time, beseiged by uncertainty, disappointment, and a tortured mind. The heroic devotion of his brother was the most important sustaining influence on his life. In *Lust for Life*, Stone uses the techniques of a fiction writer and the approach of a biographer in recreating the storm and stress of this artist's life.

Stowe, Harriet Beecher

Uncle Tom's Cabin

This is a book that changed history. Stowe was appalled by slavery, and she took one of the few options open to 19th century women who wanted to affect public opinion: She wrote a novel — a huge, enthralling narrative that claimed the heart, soul, and politics of pre-Civil War Americans. It is unabashed propaganda and overtly moralistic, an attempt to make whites — North and South — see slaves as mothers, fathers, and people with (Christian) souls. In a time when many whites claimed slavery had "good effects" on blacks, *Uncle Tom's Cabin* paints pictures of three plantations, each worse than the other, where even the best plantation leaves a slave at the mercy of fate or debt.

Swift, Jonathan

Gulliver's Travels

This four-part, satirical novel is the story of Lemuel Gulliver, a surgeon and sea captain who visits remote regions of the world. Gulliver is shipwrecked on Lilliput, where people are six inches tall. His second voyage takes him to Brobdingnag, where lives a race of giants of great practicality who do not understand abstractions. Gulliver's third voyage takes him to the flying island of Laputa and the nearby continent and capital of Lagado, where he finds pedants obsessed with their own specialized areas of speculation and utterly ignorant of the rest of life. At Glubdubdrib, the Island of Sorcerers, he speaks with great men of the past and learns from them the lies of history. He also meets the Struldbrugs, who are immortal and, as a result, utterly miserable. In the extremely bitter fourth part, Gulliver visits the land of the Houyhnhnms, a race of intelligent, virtuous horses served by brutal, filthy, and degenerate creatures called Yahoos.

Tolkien, J.R.R.

The Lord of the Rings Trilogy

Tolkien's trilogy of fantasy novels, drawn from his extensive knowledge of philology and folklore, consists of *The Fellowship of the Ring*, *The Two Towers*, and *The Return of the King*. The novels, set in the Third Age of Middle Earth, formed a sequel to Tolkien's *The Hobbit*. The trilogy is the saga of a group of sometimes reluctant heroes who set forth to save their world from consummate evil. At 33, the age of adulthood among hobbits, Frodo Baggins receives a magic Ring of Invisibility from his uncle Bilbo. A Christlike figure, Frodo learns that the ring has the power to control the entire world and, he discovers, to corrupt its owner. A fellowship of hobbits, elves, dwarves, and men is formed to destroy the Ring; they are opposed on their harrowing mission by the evil Sauron and his Black Riders.

Tolstoy, Leo

War and Peace

This epic, historical novel is a panoramic study of early 19th-century Russian society. *War and Peace* is primarily concerned with the histories of five aristocratic families, the members of which are portrayed against a vivid background of Russian social life during the war against Napoleon (1805–14). The theme of war, however, is subordinate to the story of family existence, which involves Tolstoy's optimistic belief in the life-asserting pattern of human existence. The novel also sets forth a theory of history, concluding that there is a minimum of free choice; all is ruled by an inexorable historical determinism.

Twain, Mark

The Adventures of Huckleberry Finn

Twain's book tells the story of a teenaged misfit who finds himself floating on a raft down the Mississippi River with an escaping slave, Jim. In the course of their perilous journey, Huck and Jim meet adventure, danger, and a cast of characters who are sometimes menacing and often hilarious. This book's humor is found mostly in Huck's unique worldview and his way of expressing himself. Underlying Twain's good humor, however, is a dark subcurrent of cruelty and injustice that makes this a frequently funny book with a serious message.

The Adventures of Tom Sawyer

Twain's story of a mischievous Missouri schoolboy combines humor, terror, and astute social criticism in a delightful tale of life on the Mississippi. Written in 1876, Tom Sawyer became the model for an ideal of American boyhood in the 19th century, and many story elements — such as the fence-painting episode — are now woven into the fabric of our culture.

Verne, Jules

Master of the World

"It was seen first in North Carolina, or something was, smoking up from a mountain crater. With blinding speed, it roared past cars on a Pennsylvania road. It skimmed the Atlantic, then at the flick of its captain's will dove beneath the waves. . . . It was the 'Terror' . . . ship, sub, plane, and land vehicle in one and a letter from its inventor claimed that with it, he would rule the world." Long recognized as a truly prophetic science fiction classic, this adventure was also Verne's last novel.

Twenty Thousand Leagues Under the Sea

Professor Pierre Aronnax, the narrator, boards an American frigate commissioned to investigate a rash of attacks on international shipping by what is thought to be an amphibious monster. The supposed sea creature, which is actually the submarine Nautilus, sinks Aronnax's vessel and imprisons him along with his devoted servant Conseil and Ned Land, a temperamental harpooner. The survivors meet Captain Nemo, an enigmatic misanthrope who leads them on a worldwide, yearlong underwater adventure. The novel is noted for its exotic situations and the technological innovations it describes.

Wallace, Lewis

Ben-Hur

This historical novel depicts the oppressive Roman occupation of ancient Palestine and the origins of Christianity. The Jew Judah Ben-Hur is wrongly accused by his former friend, the Roman Messala, of attempting to kill a Roman official. He is sent to be a slave and his mother and sister are imprisoned. Years later he returns, wins a chariot race against Messala, and is reunited with his now leprous mother and sister.

Washington, Booker T.

Up From Slavery

Illustrating the human quest for freedom and dignity, Washington's American classic recounts his triumph over the legacy of slavery, his founding of Tuskegee Institute, and his emergence as a national spokesman for his race.

Wells, H.G.

Collected Works of H.G. Wells

Wells is the founder of modern science-fiction. His stories include "The Crystal Egg," "The Strange Orched," and "The Invisible Man" — a serious study of egotism.

Wouk, Herman

The Caine Mutiny: A Novel of World War II

Generally, books about war fit their stereotype quite well — the hero is the commanding officer who leads his men courageously into battle. However, Wouk showed that even our most heralded commanders are human and make mistakes like the rest of us. Captain Queeg was unbalanced, but was he so unbalanced as to warrant a mutiny? That is one of the central themes of *The Caine Mutiny*, along with Willie Keith's change from an immature mama's boy into a man capable of commanding an entire ship in the United States Navy. Wouk shows how most men are vulnerable, and military men are no exception.

JUNIORS

Bellamy, Edward

Looking Backward

Bellamy's story, first published in 1888, is a passionate attack on the social ills of 19th century industrialism, Bellamy makes a plea for social reform and moral renewal; however, the action takes place in the year 2000. Julian West awakens after more than a century of sleep to find himself in twentieth century America — a land full of employment, material abundance, and social harmony.

Benet, Stephen

John Brown's Body

This is not the history of John Brown, nor a verse history of the civil war, but a narrative of the great and complex struggles between civilization, where nearly everyone is right and wrong. Benet's saga is an epic poem of the civil war.

Bronte, Emily

Wuthering Heights

The tempestuous and mythic story of Catherine Earnshaw, the precocious daughter of the house, and the ruggedly handsome, uncultured foundling her father brings home and names Heathcliff. Brought together as children, Catherine and Heathcliff quickly become attached to each other. As they grow older, their companionship turns into obsession. Family, class, and fate work cruelly against them, as do their own jealous and volatile natures, and much of their lives is spent in revenge and frustration. Wuthering Heights is a classic tale of possessive and thwarted passion, and it embodies Bronte's philosophy and spiritual quality.

Buechner, Frederick

Peculiar Treasures

In these short, pithy portraits of 125 Bible characters, Buechner has put together a humorous and entertaining bunch of folks who in most ways are just like ourselves. Buechner writes with a light touch, and his witty yet solidly instructive characterizations of these Biblical figures underscore lessons for Christians today.

Cather, Willa

My Antonia

Cather's novel honors the immigrant settlers of the American plains. Narrated by the protagonist's lifelong friend, Jim Burden, the novel recounts the history of Antonia Shimerda, the daughter of Bohemian immigrants who settled on the Nebraska frontier. The book contains a number of poetic passages about the disappearing frontier and the spirit and courage of frontier people.

Death Comes for the Archbishop

Death Comes for the Archbishop traces the friendship and adventures of Bishop Jean Latour and vicar Father Joseph Vaillant as they organize the new Roman Catholic diocese of New Mexico. Latour is patrician, intellectual, introverted; Vaillant, practical, outgoing, sanguine. Friends since their childhood in France, the clerics triumph over corrupt Spanish priests, natural adversity, and the indifference of the Hopi and Navajo to establish their church and build a cathedral in the wilderness. The novel, essentially a study of character, is considered emblematic of the author's moral and spiritual concerns.

de Cervantes, Miguel

Don Quixote

Humor, insight, compassion, and knowledge of the world underlie the antic adventures of the lanky knight clad in rusty armor and his earthy squire, Sancho Panza. The unforgettable characters they encounter on their famous pilgrimage form a brilliant panorama of society and human behavior.

Dostoyevsky, Fyodor

Crime and Punishment

Dostoyevsky's first masterpiece, the novel is a psychological analysis of the poor student Raskolnikov, whose theory that humanitarian ends justify evil means leads him to murder a St. Petersburg pawnbroker. The act produces nightmarish guilt in Raskolnikov. The narrative's feverish, compelling tone follows the twists and turns of Raskolnikov's emotions and elaborates his struggle with his conscience and his mounting sense of horror as he wanders the city's hot, crowded streets. In prison, Raskolnikov comes to the realization that happiness cannot be achieved by a reasoned plan of existence but must be earned by suffering.

Faulkner, William

The Hamlet, The Town, and The Mansion

The trilogy follows the origin, rise, and dominance of the Snopes family. The Snopes took root in Yoknapatawpha County and proliferated through and beyond it until they outmaneuvered and overpowered a society that had little defense against their invincible rapacity.

Go Down, Moses

Go Down, Moses consists of seven interrelated stories, all of them set in Faulkner's Yoknapatawpha County. From a variety of perspectives, Faulkner examines the complex, changing relationships between blacks and whites and between man and nature.

The Bear

The Bear is the story of a boy's coming to terms with the adult world. By learning how to hunt, he is taught the real meaning of pride, humility, and courage — virtues that Faulkner feared would be almost impossible to learn with the destruction of the wilderness.

Galsworthy, James

The Forsythe Saga

Galsworthy's saga chronicles the lives of three generations of a monied, middle-class English family at the turn of the century. Soames Forsythe, a solicitor and "the man of property," is married to the beautiful, penniless Irene, who falls in love with Philip Bosinney, the French architect whom Soames had hired to build a country house. The rest of the saga concerns itself with Soames, Irene, and Philip, and the generations that follow.

Justice

Justice is Galsworthy's tragic play about the irony of punishing by rule rather than helping or training the individual. It is full of irony, justice, and injustice.

Loyalties

Loyalties treats incidentally the clash of classes and social groups. Its main purpose is to throw up into relief the incessant clash of differing loyalties, which makes the path of right action so difficult.

Hansberry, Lorraine

Raisin in the Sun

When it was first produced in 1959, A Raisin in the Sun was awarded the New York Drama Critics Circle Award for that season and hailed as a watershed in American drama. A pioneering work by an African-American playwright, the play was a radically new representation of black life.

Hardy, Thomas

The Return of the Native

This novel sets in opposition two of Hardy's most unforgettable characters: his heroine, the sensuous, free-spirited Eustacia Vye, and the solemn, majestic stretch of upland in Dorsetshire he called Egdon Heath. The famous opening reveals the haunting power of that dark, forbidding moon where proud Eustacia fervently awaits a clandestine meeting with her lover, Damon Wildeve. But Eustacia's dreams of escape are not to be realized — neither Wildeve nor the returning native Clym Yeobright can bring her salvation. Injured by forces beyond their control, Hardy's characters struggle vainly in the net of destiny.

Mayor of Casterbridge

This is a classic tale of a successful man who cannot escape his past nor his own evil nature. Michael Henchard is the respected mayor of Casterbridge, a thriving industrial town — but years ago, under the influence of alcohol, he sold his wife Susan to a sailor at a country fair. Although repentant and sober for 21 years, Henchard cannot escape his destiny when Susan and her daughter return to Casterbridge.

Hersey, John

Hiroshima

When the atomic bomb was dropped on Hiroshima, few could have anticipated its potential for devastation. Hersey recorded the stories of Hiroshima residents shortly after the explosion, giving the world firsthand accounts from people who had survived it. The words of Miss Sasaki, Dr. Fujii, Mrs. Nakamara, Father Kleinsorg, Dr. Sasaki, and the Reverend Tanimoto gave a face to the statistics that saturated the media and solicited an overwhelming public response.

James, Henry

The Turn of the Screw

One of the most famous ghost stories, the tale is told mostly through the journal of a governess and depicts her struggle to save her two young charges from the demonic influence of the eerie apparitions of two former servants in the household. The story inspired critical debate over the question of the "reality" of the ghosts and of James's intentions. Whether accepted as a simple ghost story or an exercise in the literary convention of the unreliable narrator, this story is classically, relentlessly horrifying.

Lee, Harper

To Kill a Mockingbird

Through the eyes of young Scout Finch, one of the most endearing and enduring characters of Southern literature, Lee explores with rich humor and unswerving honesty the irrationality of adult attitudes toward race and class in the Deep South of the 1930s. The conscience of a town steeped in prejudice, violence, and hypocrisy is pricked by the stamina and quiet heroism of one man's struggle for justice.

Lamb, Charles

The Essays of Elia

Lamb's personality is projected in all his literary work, but in *The Essays of Elia* it shines through. This collection of essays contains a vast deal of autobiographical material, and it is candidly personal in atmosphere and structure.

Lewis, Sinclair

Babbitt

Babbitt, a conniving, prosperous real-estate man, is one of the ugliest figures in American fiction. A total conformist, he can only receive self-esteem from others, and is loyal to whoever serves his need of the moment. Babbitt gives consummate expression to the glibness and irresponsibility of the hardened, professional social climber.

Arrowsmith

Lewis' book follows the life of Martin Arrowsmith, a rather ordinary fellow who gets his first taste of medicine at 14 as an assistant to the drunken physician in his home town. He is forced to give up his trade for reasons ranging from public ignorance to the publicity-mindedness of a great foundation, and becomes an isolated seeker of scientific truth.

Marquand, John P.

The Late George Apley

The Late George Apley is a wicked, brilliantly etched satire. A portrait of a Bostonian and of the tradition-bound, gilded society in which he lived, it is the story of three generations of Apley men, the maturing America, and the golden era of American security from 1866 to 1933.

Masters, Edgar Lee

A Spoon River Anthology

Masters introduces the reader to a selection of souls who describe their lives and their relationships (or lack thereof) through simplistic, poetic epitaphs. The collection of dramatic monologues by over 200 former inhabitants of the fictional town of Spoon River topples the myth of moral superiority in small-town America, as the dead give testimony to their shocking scandals and secret tragedies. Masters seems to place the reader in St. Peter's wings, inviting — almost daring — that reader to decide eternal placement for his characters.

Maugham, Somerset

Of Human Bondage

Maugham uses the tale of Phillip Carey, an innocent, sensitive crippled man in Victorian-era Europe as a front for his own autobiography. Phillip was left an orphan at a young age and was continually taunted for his club-foot and the limp that resulted. His early rejection from society gives him time to seek out his purpose in life and travel across Europe. This book is truly great for the in-depth examination of love and the human animal.

O'Neill, Eugene

The Emperor Jones

This play, as well as Anna Christie and The Hairy Ape, deals with the misery of man — not immediate, physical, or social, but metaphysical. The central character, a Negro, is insulted and injured. The "emperor" Brutus Jones, typifies all men with their raw ignorance and hysterical fear under the layers of intellect.

Orwell, George

Animal Farm

A farm is taken over by its overworked, mistreated animals. With flaming idealism and stirring slogans, they set out to create a paradise of progress, justice, and equality. Thus the stage is set for a telling anti-utopian satires — a razor-edged fable that records the evolution from revolution against tyranny to a totalitarianism dictatorship even more oppressive and heartless than that of their former human masters.

Paine, Thomas

The Rights of Man

The Rights of Man is unquestionably one of the great classics on the subject of democracy. Paine's vast influence on our system of government is due less to his eloquence and literary style, than to his steadfast bravery and determination to promote justice and equality.

Paton, Alan

Cry, the Beloved Country

Set in the troubled South Africa of the 1940s amid a people riven by racial inequality and injustice, Cry, the Beloved Country is a beautiful and profoundly compassionate story of the Zulu pastor Stephen Kumalo and his son Absalom. Everyone can relate to the pathos of Rev. Kumalo in his journey to reunite the tribe and his gradual awakening to the fact that there are changes that are occurring that his compassion and tears can do nothing for.

Plato

The Republic

In Plato's *Republic* exists a guide to life and living for every person alive. By trying to describe the ideal state, Plato creates the first "Utopia" and in the meantime questions our perceptions of reality. Through Plato's thought we can see the only way to judge fairness and equality is through the ideal state and what man could be, not what man is. Plato's look on justice and reality is unmatched despite hundreds of attempts to replicate his thought and style in the past few millennia.

Rolvaag, O.E.

Giants in the Earth: A Saga of the Prairie

This refreshingly stark view of pioneer life reflects the hardships, fear, and depression that one woman experiences when her husband takes her from her Norwegian homeland and moves her steadily westward across the northern plains. This novel is gothic in dimensions — the physical landscape becomes the characters' mental landscape — the vast expanse of snow in winter and grass in summer become a metaphor for boredom and isolation. Rolvaag writes of a lifestyle and of motivations unimaginable to the modern American, and yet, he writes of a time that was shockingly recent in the history of the Midwest.

Rostand, Edmund

Cyrano de Bergerac

Set in 17th-century Paris, the action revolves around the emotional problems of the noble, swashbuckling Cyrano, who, despite his many gifts, feels that no woman can ever love him because he has an enormous nose. Secretly in love with the lovely Roxane, Cyrano agrees to help his inarticulate rival, Christian, win her heart by allowing him to present Cyrano's love poems, speeches, and letters as his own work, and Cyrano remains silent about his own part in Roxane's courtship.

Sophocles

The Three Theban Plays
Oedipus Rex
Oedipus at Colonus
Antigone

This trilogy is Greek tragedy and compelling drama. It is the eloquent story of a noble family moving toward catastrophe, and dragged down by pride from wealth and power. *Oedipus Rex* raises basic questions about human behavior. *Antigone* examines the conflicting obligations of civic duties versus personal loyalties and religious mores.

Swarthout, Glendon

Bless the Beasts and the Children

Swarthout gives readers an opportunity to view six adolescents whom society has already labeled misfits from the inside out. As the book progresses, you gradually learn the history of each member of the group from past incidents, namely unintentional mental abuse by parents. The teenagers set out on a quest to free a herd of buffaloes from a senseless slaughter. Ironically, the freedom and fate of these animals parallel that of the young men. Their freeing the buffaloes symbolizes their own self-discovery, initiation into manhood, and entry into a realm of humanity that transcends the violent, "dog-eat-dog" society that has excluded them.

Turgenev, Ivan

Fathers and Sons

Fathers and Sons concerns the inevitable conflict between generations and between the values of traditionalists and intellectuals. The physician Bazarov, the novel's protagonist, is a nihilist, denying the validity of all laws save those of the natural sciences. He scorns traditional Russian values, shocks respectable society and, for the young, represents the spirit of rebellion. Uncouth and forthright in his opinions, Bazarov is nonetheless susceptible to love and by that fact doomed to unhappiness.

Thackeray, William Makepeace

Vanity Fair

Vanity Fair is a story of two heroines — one humble, the other scheming and social-climbing — who meet in boarding school and embark on markedly different lives. Amid the swirl of London's posh ballrooms and affairs of love and war, their fortunes rise and fall. Through it all, Thackeray lampoons the shallow values of his society, reserving the most pointed barbs for the upper crust. What results is a prescient look at the dogged pursuit of wealth and status — and the need for humility.

Vonnegut, Kurt

Cat's Cradle

Cat's Cradle is Vonnegut's satirical commentary on modern man and his madness. An apocalyptic tale of this planet's ultimate fate, it features a midget as the protagonist; a complete, original theology created by a calypso singer; and a vision of the future that is at once blackly fatalistic and hilariously funny. These assorted characters chase each other around in search of the world's most important and dangerous substance, a new form of ice that freezes at room temperature.

Wharton, Edith

Ethan Frome

Although Ethan Frome, a gaunt, patient New Englander, seems ambitious and intelligent, his wife, Zeena, holds him back. When her young cousin Mattie comes to stay on their New England farm, Ethan falls in love with her. But the social conventions of the day doom their love and their hopes. Ethan is tormented by a passionate love for Mattie, and his desperate quest for happiness leads to pain and despair.

READING JOURNAL

Reading great books — Students should read a novel, play, or a collection of short stories or poems every five lessons. Ideally, students will complete ten reading journal entries like the one below.

Date:

Name of book: *Watership Down*   Name of author: *Richard Adams*

Publisher: *Scribners*   Copyright date: *1972*

I. Briefly describe:

   Protagonist — *Hazel — Hazel is a charismatic leader who recognizes and employs the skills of his fellow bucks to great success.*

   Antagonist — *General Woundwort — He is a mean, vicious, cunning foe.*

   Other characters used to develop protagonist: *Fiver, Bigwig, et al.*

   Do any of the characters remind me of a Bible character? Who? Why? — *Hazel is a Christ-like character.*

II. Setting: *English rabbit warrens*

III. Point of view: Circle one

   First person,   Third person,   (Third Person Omniscient)

IV. Brief summary of the plot: *It is a heroic fantasy novel about a small group of rabbits. These are special rabbits — they possess their own culture, language, and mythology. Evoking epic themes, the novel recounts the rabbits' odyssey as they escape the destruction of their warren to seek a place in which to establish a new home, encountering innumerable perils along the way.*

V. Theme (the quintessential meaning or purpose of the book in one or two sentences): *This novel celebrates loyalty and perseverance as these rabbits preserve tradition and move forward into new homes. There is a strong journey motif.*

VI. Author's worldview: *Clearly the author celebrates Judeo-Christian morality, including justice, forgiveness, and loyalty.*

   How do you know this? What behaviors does the character manifest that lead you to this conclusion? *The protagonist is essentially a Christ-like character.*

VII. Why did you like or dislike this book? *I really liked Watership Down. Not only was it entertaining, but it also offered a well-developed plot and a life-sustaining message.*

VIII. List at least five new vocabulary words from this book. Define and use in a sentence.

   Buoyant: (adj.) — light, floating; shrewd: (adj.) — clever. There was a shrewd, buoyant air about him as he sat up, looked around and rubbed both front paws over his nose.

   Wearily: (adv.) — with fatigue and carefulness; troublesome: (adj.) — problematic; perplexity: (n.) — consternation, confusion. Hazel realized wearily that Bigwig was probably going to be troublesome. . . . To him, perplexity was worse than danger. . . . He thought of the Threarah and his wily courtesy.

   IX. Name of next book I will read:

   Signature of parent(s)

DEVOTIONAL JOURNAL

A Thirty-Minute Prayer Devotional Time

Date:

Passage: Esther 4

1. Focusing time (a list of those things that I must do later) (three minutes): *Feed the dog and perform other chores.*

2. Discipline of silence (remain absolutely still and quiet) (two minutes):

3. Reading Scripture passage (with notes on text — this is not a time to do Bible study) (five minutes):

4. Meditating in Scripture (ten minutes):

   A. How does the passage affect the person mentioned in the passage? How does he or she feel? *Esther's cousin Mordecai comes to warn Esther than she must give up her anonymity and take a stand or they will all perish. All Esther wants to do is slip back into the safety of her role. Who can blame her? But for the sake of the nation, Esther will risk everything to do what is necessary. Though her knees must be shaking, she determines to stare death in the face and stand up for her people. Which is what she does. Unless summoned by her husband, Esther faces certain death by approaching him, for one never approaches an Oriental monarch unsummoned. Especially if one is a lowly woman — even a wife. Why should she help her relatives and countrymen? What had they done for her lately? No doubt they had scorned her for her fraternization with the enemy. Esther would have known much condemnation and rejection. I doubt that she had any love loss with the Jews. Why should she put herself and her children in jeopardy for people who had no doubt rejected and derided her?*

   B. How does the passage affect my life? What is the Lord saying to me through this passage? *Esther had no status, very little influence really, and she had no obligations to anyone but herself. But she obeyed God and saved a nation. In chapter 4 when she turns the corner and faces her husband unsummoned, she is facing death . . . or eternal victory. In the courts, in the business world, in higher education, our children are doing the same. Will I prepare them to do this? We stand with those facing death. We stand against systems that tyrannize, abuse, demean, and destroy. We stand for life — all life, everywhere. We stand because we know that we are loved. That He died for our sins so that we might live, and love others, too. We daily dare to search our hearts, minds, and behavior and risk new ways of thinking, speaking, and living for the sake of our suffering neighbors, sisters, brothers, mother, fathers, sons, and daughters. We will not necessarily succeed . . . but we will try. The German theologian Karl Barth urges every church to ask constantly this question, —Is it time? — Could we be God's instrument? Is this our time? Could we be called for just such a time as this?*

   C. How has God spoken to me in the last 24 hours?

5. Prayers of adoration and thanksgiving, intercession, and future prayer targets (eight minutes):

6. Discipline of silence (two minutes):

GREEK MORPHEMES INDEX

PREFIXES

MORPHEME	MEANING	MORPHEME	MEANING
a-; an-	not; without	hyper-	over; too much
allo-	other	ideo-	idea
ana-	up	idio-	one's own
anti-	against	iso-	equal
auto-	self	kilo-	thousand
bi-	two; twice	macro -	large
caco-	bad; ill	mega-; megalo -	large
cata-	down; completely; against	micro-	small
deca-	ten	mono	one
deutero-	second	neo-	new
di-	two; twice	olig-	few
dia-	through; across	ortho-	right; correct
dys-	difficult; bad	pachy-	thick
ec-	home	paleo-	ancient
ec-; ex-	out	pan-; pant-; panto-	all
en-	in	penta-	five
epi-	upon	peri-	around
eu —	good	poly-	many
hemi-	half	pro-	before
hetero-	unlike; various	proto-	first
hier-	sacred	pseudo-	false
holo-	whole	sym- ; syn-	with; together
homo-	same	tauto-	same
hypo-	under	tel-; tele-	far; distant

This Greek morphemes section is from: Alene H. Harris, PhD, *Greek Morphemes Lessons: It's NOT Greek to Me!* (3rd edition, 2010). Her website is http://readytoteach.com.

ROOTS

MORPHEME	MEANING	MORPHEME	MEANING
acro	tip; top; end	dem	people
aer	lower air	dendr	tree
aesth	feeling; perception	derm; dermat	skin
agog	lead	dox	belief; opinion
anth	flower	drom	a running; course
anthrop	man; mankind	dyn; dynam	power; force
arch	govern	entom	insect
archae	ancient	ep	word
arthr	joint	erg; urg	work
astr	star	esth	feeling; perception
athl	prize	eth	moral; habit
ball	throw	ether	upper air
bar	weight; pressure	ethn	nation
bat	step; go	etym	word
batho	depth	gam	marriage
bibl; biblio	book	gen	kind; race; origin
bio	life	geo	earth
caust	burn	glot	tongue; language
centr; center	center	glyph	carving
cephal	head	gno; gnos	know
chir	hand	gon	angle
chlor	light green	graph; gram	write; draw; record
chrom	color	gyn	woman
chron	time	haem; hem ; aem; em	blood
clin	lie; lean; recline	helio	sun
cosm	world; order	hipp	horse
crat	mix	hydr	water
crit	judge; discern	hygr	moisture
crypt	hidden	ichthy	fish
cycle	circle	icon	image; idol
cyt; cyte; cyto	cell	kine	movement
dactyl	finger; toe	lith	stone

ROOTS CONTINUED

MORPHEME	MEANING	MORPHEME	MEANING
log	idea; word; speech; study	pod	foot
meter; metr	measure	polis; polit	city
mim	imitate	psych	mind; soul; spirit
miso	hate	pyr	fire
mne; mnes	memory	rrh; rhea; rheo	gush; flow
morph	form	schism	split; cleave
nau	ship	scop; skept	look at; examine
necro	dead	sept	poison by decay
neur	nerve	somat	body
nom	law; arrangement	soph	wise
od	way; path	spor	seed; sowing
onym; onoma	name	stas; stat	stop; stand
op; ops; opt	eye; view; sight	tact; tax	arrangement; order
opthalm	eye	taph	tomb
ornith	bird	techn	art; skill
osteo	bone	thalass	sea
path	feeling; disease	thana	death
ped	child; instruction	thaumat	wonder
petr	rock	the	put; place
phag	eat	theo	god
phan	shine; show; appear	therap	cure
phil	love	therm	heat
phon	sound	tom	cut
phos; phot	light	top	tune; stretch
phyll; phyllo	leaf	top	put; place
phys	nature; growth	tox	poison
phyt	plant	trop	turn
plasm; plast	substance; form; shape	troph	feed; nourish
plut	wealth	type	model
pneu	air	zo	animal

SUFFIXES

MORPHEME	MEANING	MORPHEME	MEANING
-algia	pain	-mancy	prophecy; prediction
-clast	one who shatters or destroys	-mania	a madness for
-cracy	rule	-maniac	one who has a madness for
-crat	one who rules	-ologist	one who studies
-ia	makes abstract noun	-ology	study of
-iatry; -iatrics	a healing	-orama	view
-ic	makes a noun or adjective	-ous	full of
-ics	makes a noun	-phobia	a fear of
-ism	makes an abstract noun	-phobiac	one who has a fear of
-ist	one who	-phor; -phoria	a bearing; carrying; production
-itis	inflammation	-poly	sale
-latry	worship	-sis	makes abstract noun
-lysis	loosening; solution	-y	makes abstract noun
-machia; -machy	war; fight		

LATIN MORPHEMES INDEX

PREFIXES

MORPHEME	MEANING	MORPHEME	MEANING
ad-; af-; ag-; ap-; as-	to; toward; near	mill-	thousand
ante-	before	multi-	many
ben-	good	ne-	not
bi-	two; twice; double	novem-	nine
cent-	hundred	oct-	eight
co-	together	omni-	all
com-; con-	with; together	op-	against
de-	down; from; away; very	pre-; pro-	before
dec-; decem-	ten	prim-	first
deci-	tenth	quadr-	four
di-; dis-	not; apart	quasi-	seemingly; as if
du-	two	quatr-	fourth
ex-; e-	out	re-	again; anew
extra-	outside	semi-	half
il-	in; not	sept-	seven
in-; im-; en-	in; not	sex-	six
inter-	between	sub-	under; less than
intra-	within	super-	above; over; more than
intro-	within	tert-	third
mal-	bad; ill	trans-	across; through; into another state
medi-	middle	un-	not
		uni-	one

This Latin morphemes section is from: Alene H. Harris, PhD, *Latin Morphemes Lessons: Latin and Loving It!* (2nd edition, 2010). Her website is http://readytoteach.com.

ROOTS

MORPHEME	MEANING	MORPHEME	MEANING
ali	feed; nourish; support	crim	crime; judgment; accusation
alt	tall; high	cumb	lie; recline
ambul	walk	cur	care
anim	life; spirit; soul; mind	curs	run
angul	angle	dent	tooth
annu; enni	year	dict; dicat	say; speak; proclaim; set apart
aqua	water	digit	finger; toe
arbitr	consider; judge	divis	separate
arg	silver	doc	teach
aud; aur	hear	dorm	sleep
aug; auct	increase; grow	dub	doubt
aur	gold	duc	lead
belli; bellum	war	equ	equal; fair
brev	short	err	stray; wander
cad; casc	fall	esse	be; exist
capit	head	fa	speak
card; cord	heart	fact	do; make; cause
cardin	essential; chief	far	divine law
carn	flesh	fatu	foolish
ced	move; withdraw	ferr	iron (mineral)
cept; cip	take	fict	imagine
cern	sift; separate; distinguish; decide	fid	faith
clin	lean; incline	fili	son; daughter
cogn	recognize	fisc	purse
corpor	body	fix	fasten; pierce
crea	create; make	flex	bend
cred; credit	believe; trust	fort	strong
cresc	grow		

ROOTS CONTINUED

MORPHEME	MEANING	MORPHEME	MEANING
fortu	chance	lin	line; thread
frag ; frang	break	lingu	language; tongue
frater ; fratr	brother	liter	letter
fugit	flee	litig	dispute
garrul	chatter; talk	locat	place
gen ; gener	origin; kind (type)	long	long
gest	bear; carry	loqu	speak
gress	step	lucr	gain; profit
gust	taste	magn	great; large
habil	able; fit	mand	to put into the hands of; entrust; order
habit	dwell	mani; manu	hand
her; hes	stick; cling	mani ; manu	hand
ig; ag	do; drive; act	mater; matr	mother
ign	fire	merc	trade
inhib	hold in	migrat	move; travel
Integer; integr	whole; untouched	mir	wonder
jace	lie	misc	mix
ject	throw	miss	send; let go
judic	judge; decide	mob	move
jur	right; justice; law	mod	manner; measure
juven	young	mor	custom
langu	faint; weary	morb	illness
lat	wide	mord	bite; sting
late	hide	mort	death
later	side	mur	wall
leg	read	nasc ; nat	be born
leg	law	negat	deny
lig	bind; gather; choose	mir	wonder

ROOTS CONTINUED

MORPHEME	MEANING	MORPHEME	MEANING
neutr	neither	preci	price; value
nom; nomin	name	prehen	grasp
norm	rule; pattern	press	press
nov	new	prob	test; prove
numer	number	prol	offspring
nutr	nourish	propr	one's own; individual
ocul	eye	pug; pugn	fight; fist
ora	mouth; speech; prayer	punct; pung	point; prick
ordin	order; rank; series	put	think; suppose
oscill	swing	quadr	four
oss	bone	quart	fourth
palp	touch	queru	complain
pans; pand	spread	quis	seek; ask
par; peer	equal	ratio	relationship; reason
part	separate; divide	roga	ask
pass	suffer; feel	rota	wheel
pater; patr	father	rupt	burst
patri	fatherland	sag	wise; shrewd
pauci	few	sanguin	blood
pecu	one's own	sanct	holy; sacred
ped	foot	sci	know
pell	Drive; push	script	write
pend	hang	sed	settle
pens	pay	semble	together
pet	seek; attack	sen	old
plic	fold; twist; weave	sens	feel; be aware
pon ; pos	put; place	sequ	follow
pond	weigh	serve	save; protect
preca	pray	sesqu	one and one-half

ROOTS CONTINUED

MORPHEME	MEANING	MORPHEME	MEANING
serve	serve	ten; tend; tens	stretch
sesqu	one and one-half	terr	land
simul	likeness; pretense	torp	stupor; numbness
sinu	bend; wind	tort	twist
sip	taste; discern; be wise	tot	whole; entire
sist	stand	tract	draw; pull
soli	alone; only	trud	thrust
solut	loose; set free	vacill	waver
somn	sleep	vag	wander
son	sound	ven	come
soror	sister	ver	truth
spect	look at; examine	verb	word
spir	breathe; coil	verge	tend towards; bend
stat	stand	verse	turn
stimul	goad; rouse	veter	experienced; old
stinct	prick out	vir	man
strict; string	bind	virtu	strength; virtue; skill; artistry
sui	oneself	vis	see
tac	silent	vit ; viv	live
tain; ten; tent; tenu	hold	voc	voice; call
tang	touch	vol	wish; will
tect	cover	vola	fly
tempor	time	volu	roll
		vor	eat

SUFFIXES

MORPHEME	MEANING	MORPHEME	MEANING
-able; -ible; -ble	able to be (adj.)	-ic; -ile; -ive	relating to (adj.)
-acious	having the quality of (adj.)	-id	relating to (adj.)
-age	thing which (n.)	-ify	do; make; cause
-al	relating to; like (adj.)	-ion	condition; quality; act (n.)
-ant; -ent	relating to (adj.); thing which (n)	-ist	one who
-ary	person who; relating too	-ity	condition; quality; act (n.)
-ate	do; make; cause (v.)	-ium	place in which
-ate	having the quality of (adj.)	-ize	do; make; cause
-cide	kill	-late; -lation; -lative	carry; bear
-ence	condition; quality; act (n.)	-ory	thing which; relating to
-escent	growing	-ous; -ose	full of (n.)
-ferous	bearing; carrying (adj.)	-parous	bearing; producing
-fic	causing	-ude; -ure	act; state (n.)
-ian	person who		

Prepare

Study Rhetoric, Writing, Literature & History

Master Books® and Dr. James Stobaugh are working together to provide curriculum to help junior and senior high school students excel as adult Christian leaders.

Written by Dr. Stobaugh, a Harvard, Vanderbilt, Princeton & Gordon-Conwell graduate, these studies offer the highest quality of education with a focus on devotion to God, our Creator. Since 1975, Master Books® has provided creation-based material for all ages; including apologetics, home-school resources, reference titles, and quality children's literature.

Connect with Master Books® online for updates on new releases by Dr. James Stobaugh.

masterbooks.net　f　facebook.com/**masterbooks**

o Lead

Master Books®